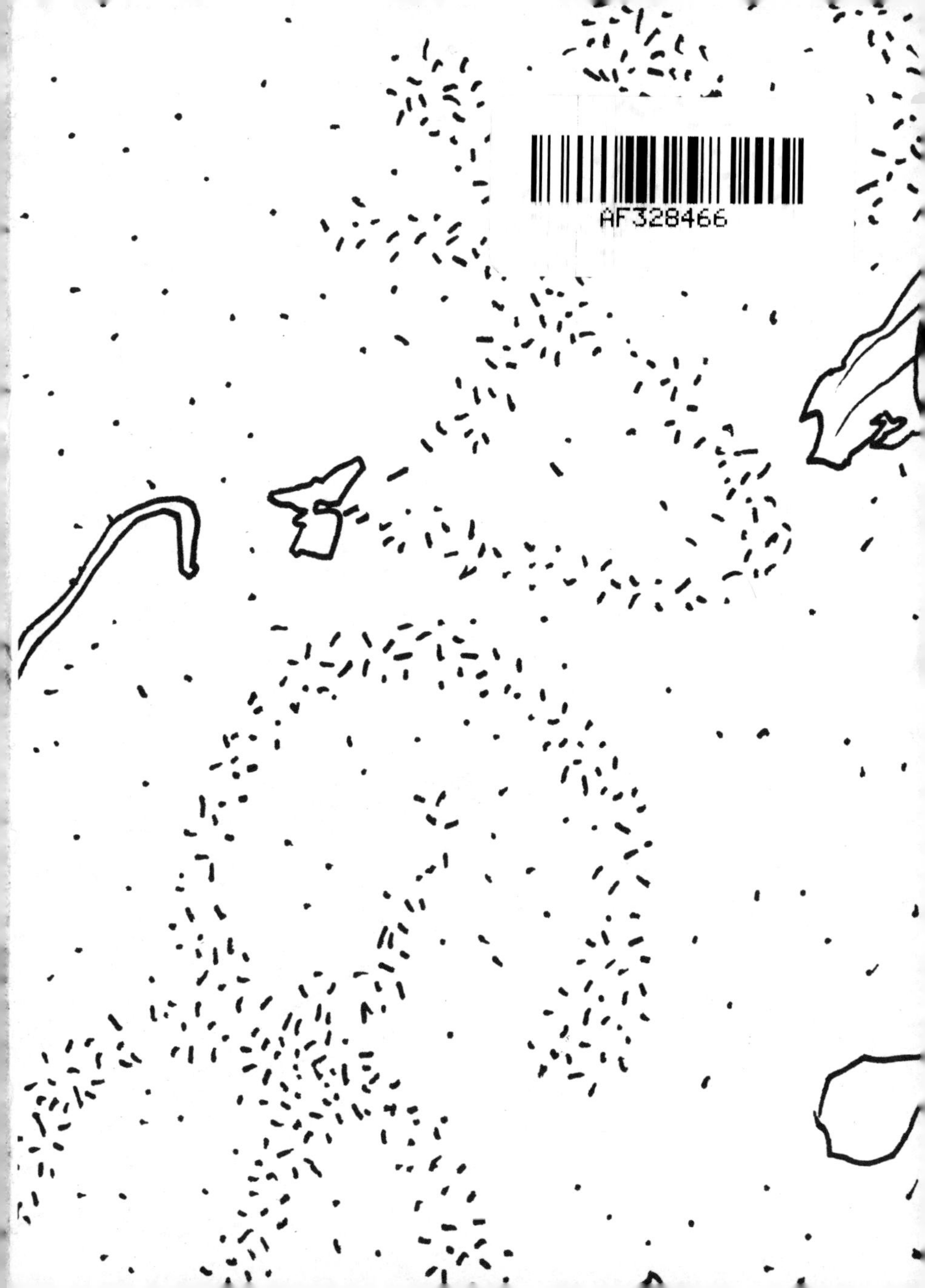

AF328466

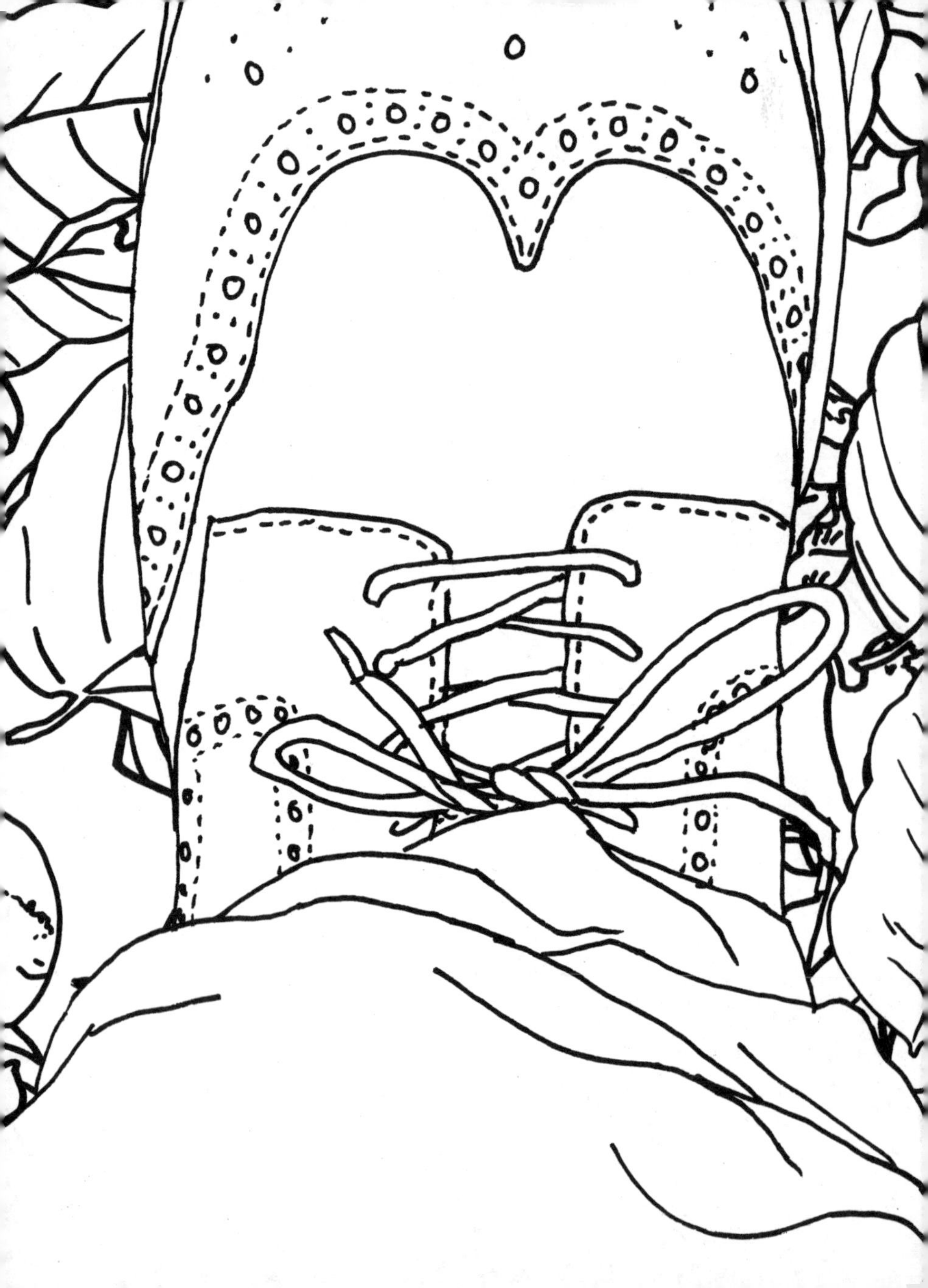

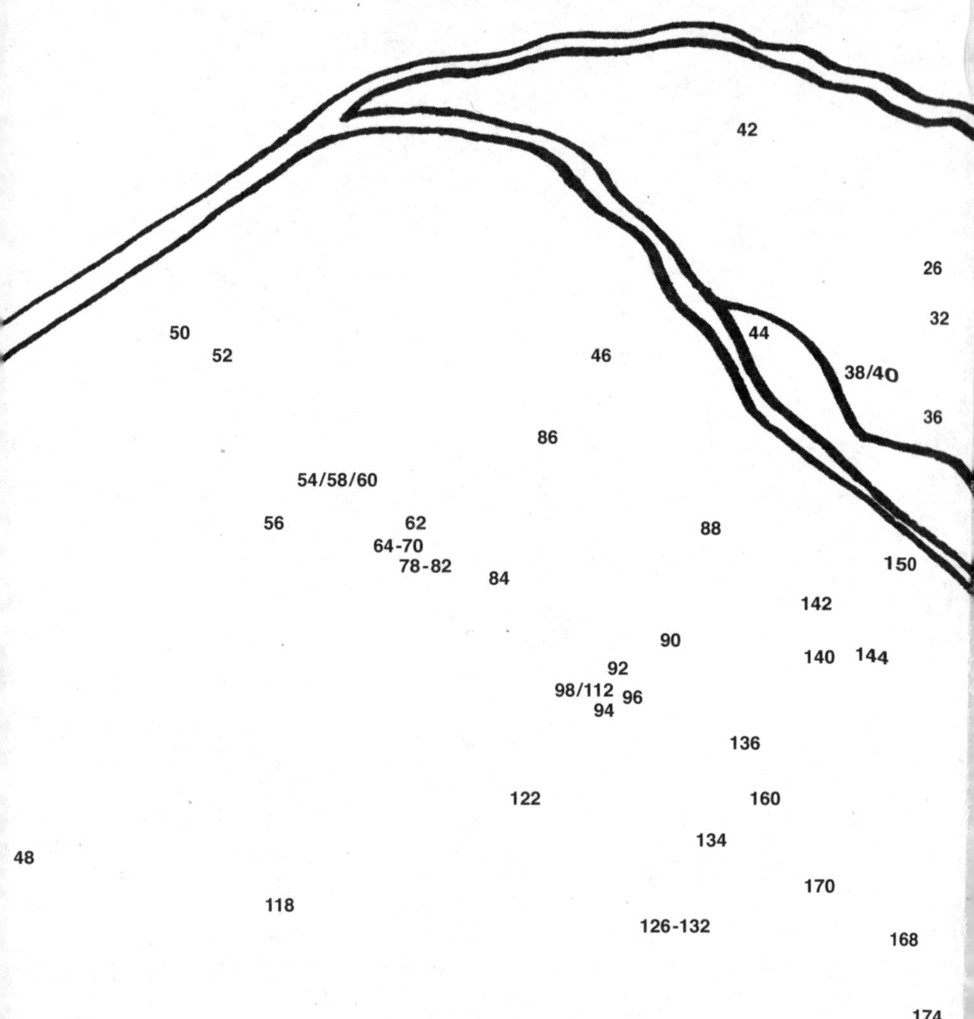

42
26
32
50
52
46
44
38/40
36
86
54/58/60
56
62
88
64-70
78-82
84
150
142
90
140
144
92
98/112
96
94
136
122
160
134
48
170
118
126-132
168
114/116
124
174

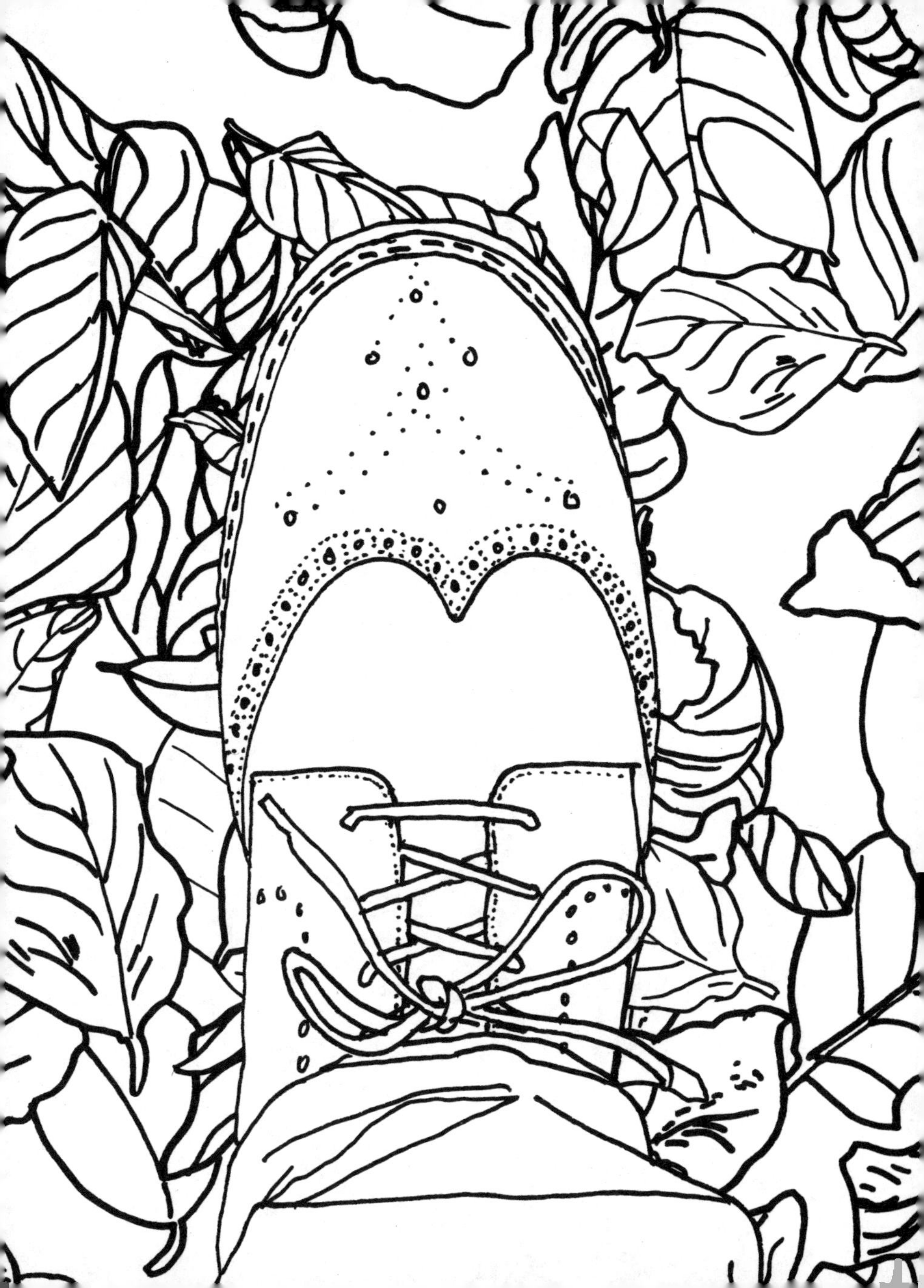

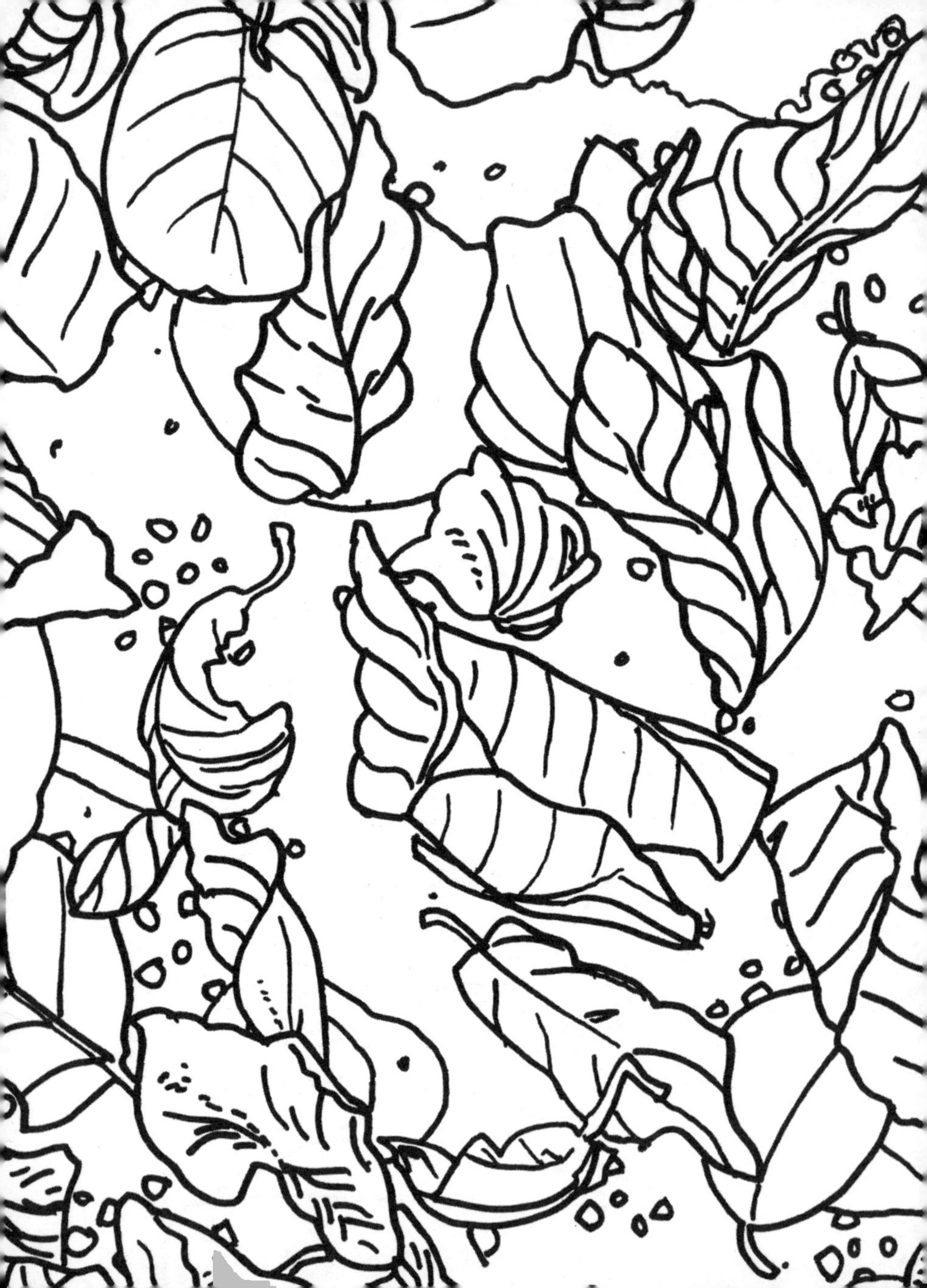

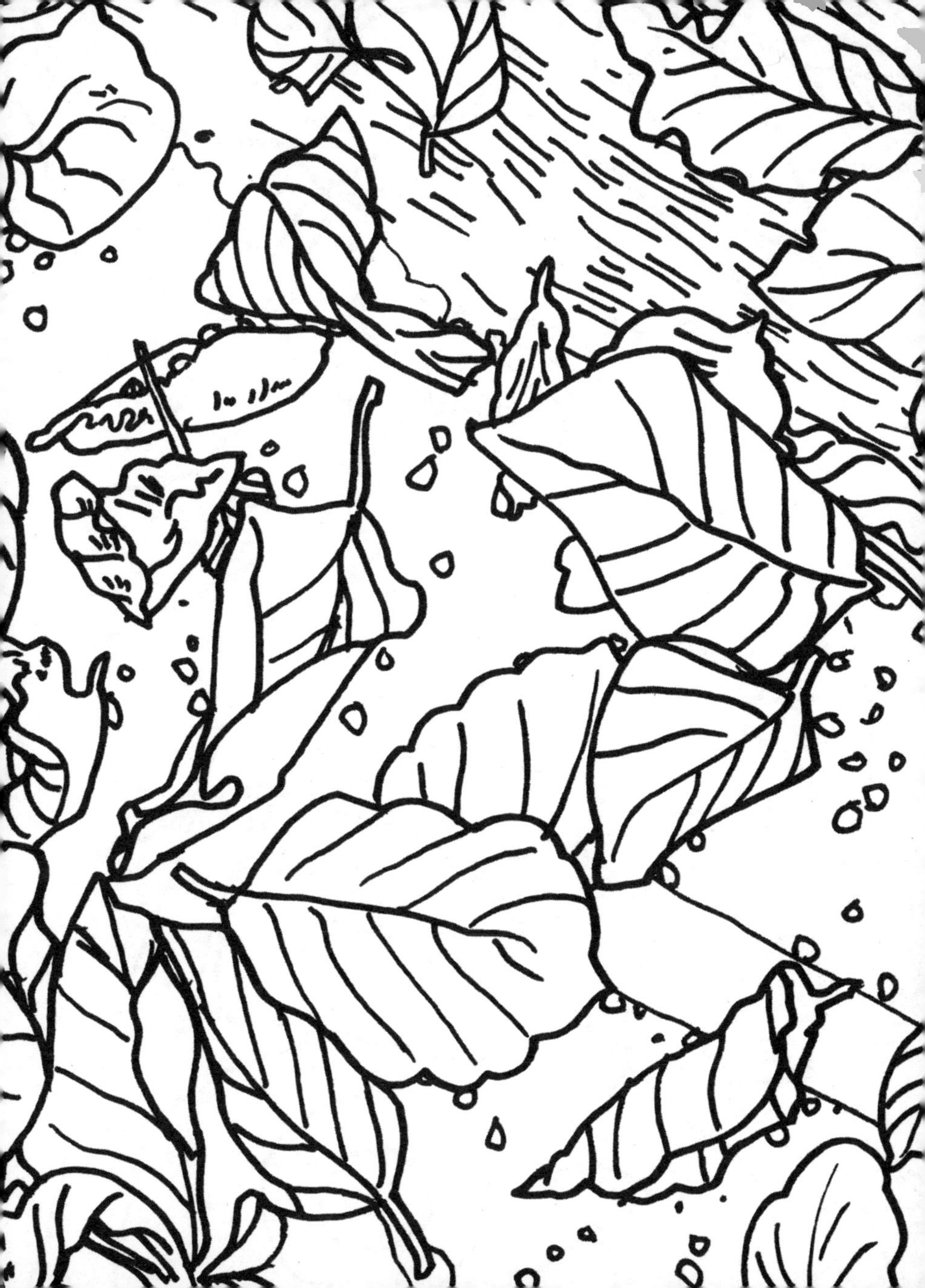

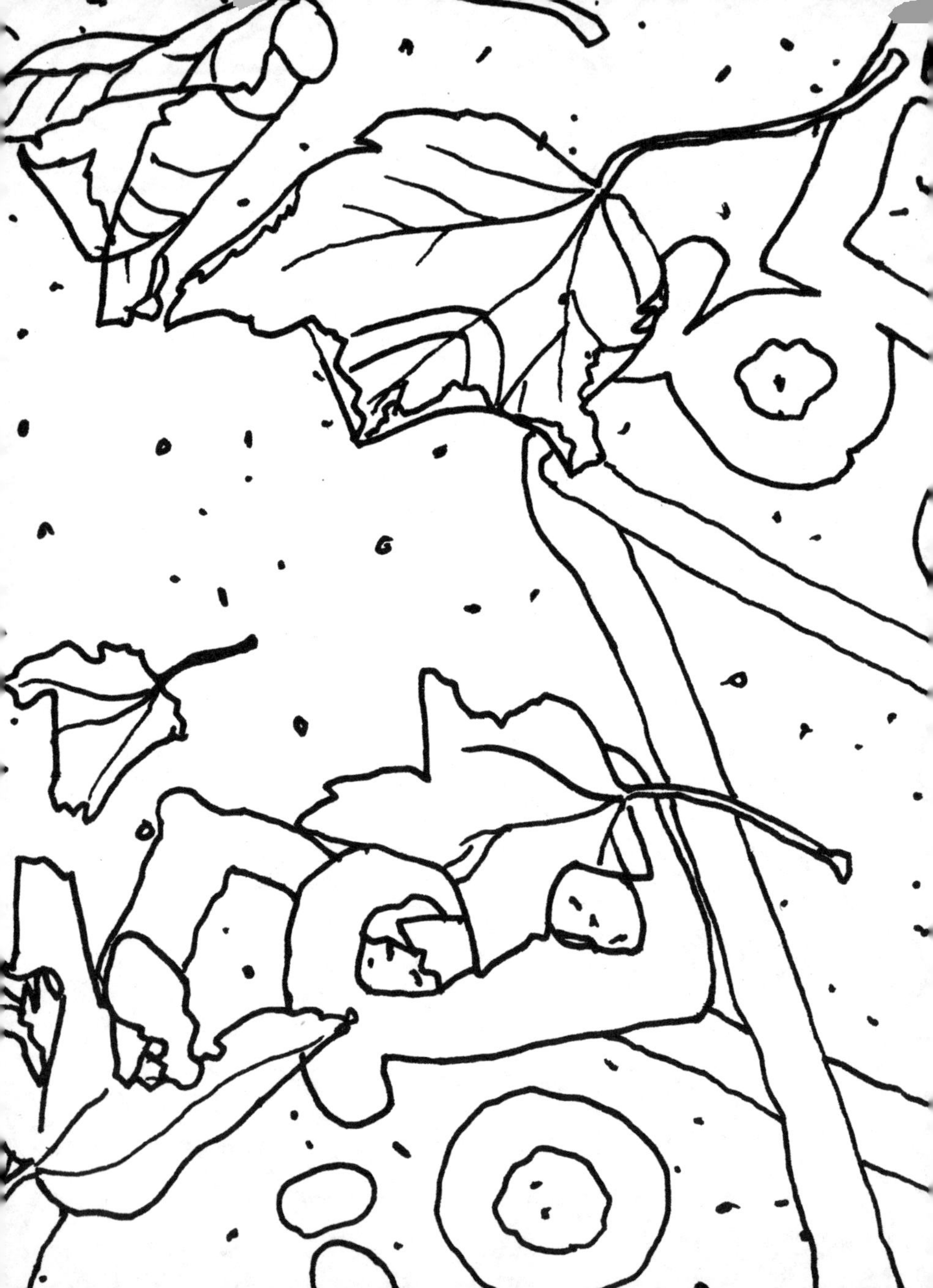

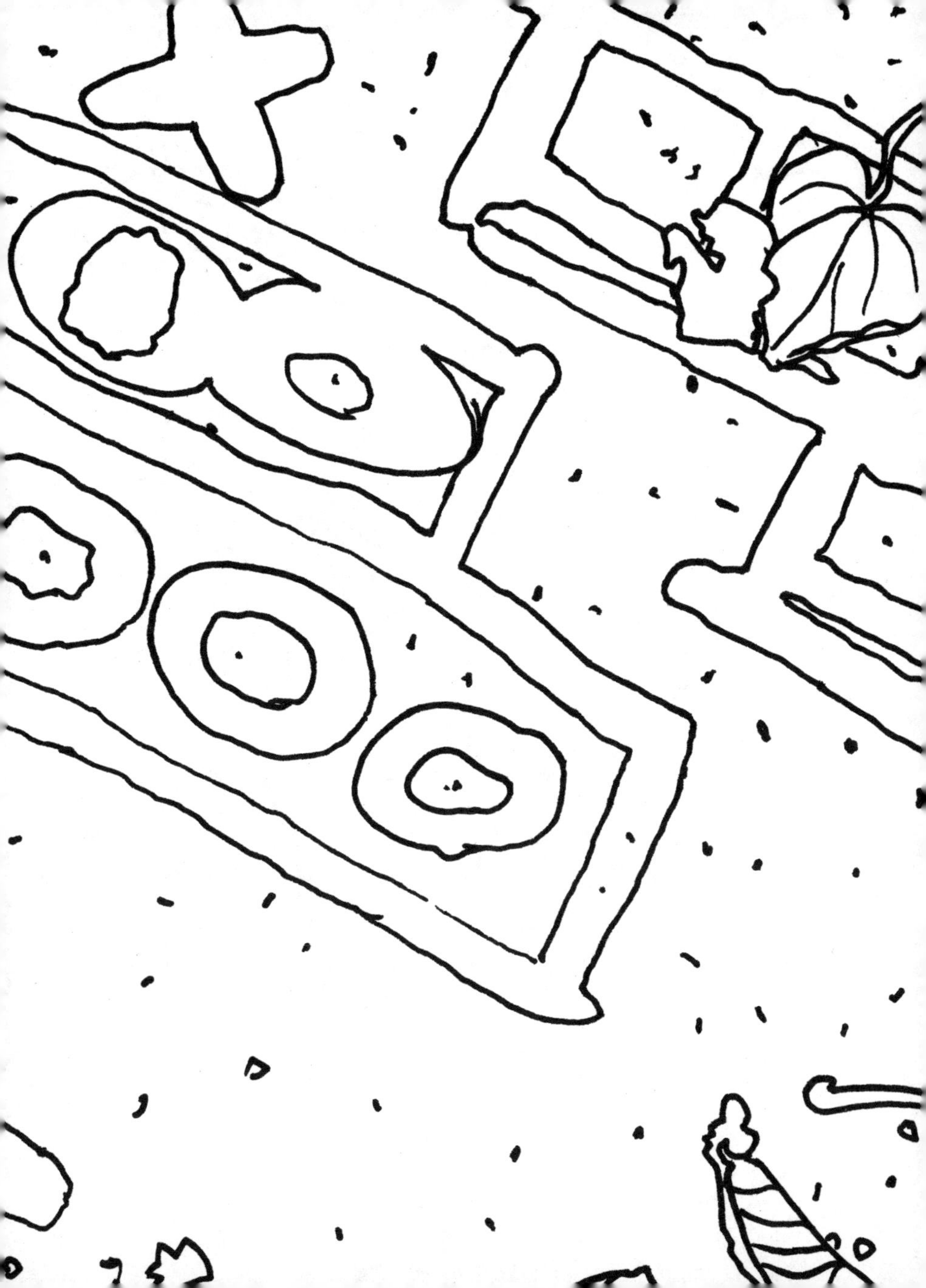

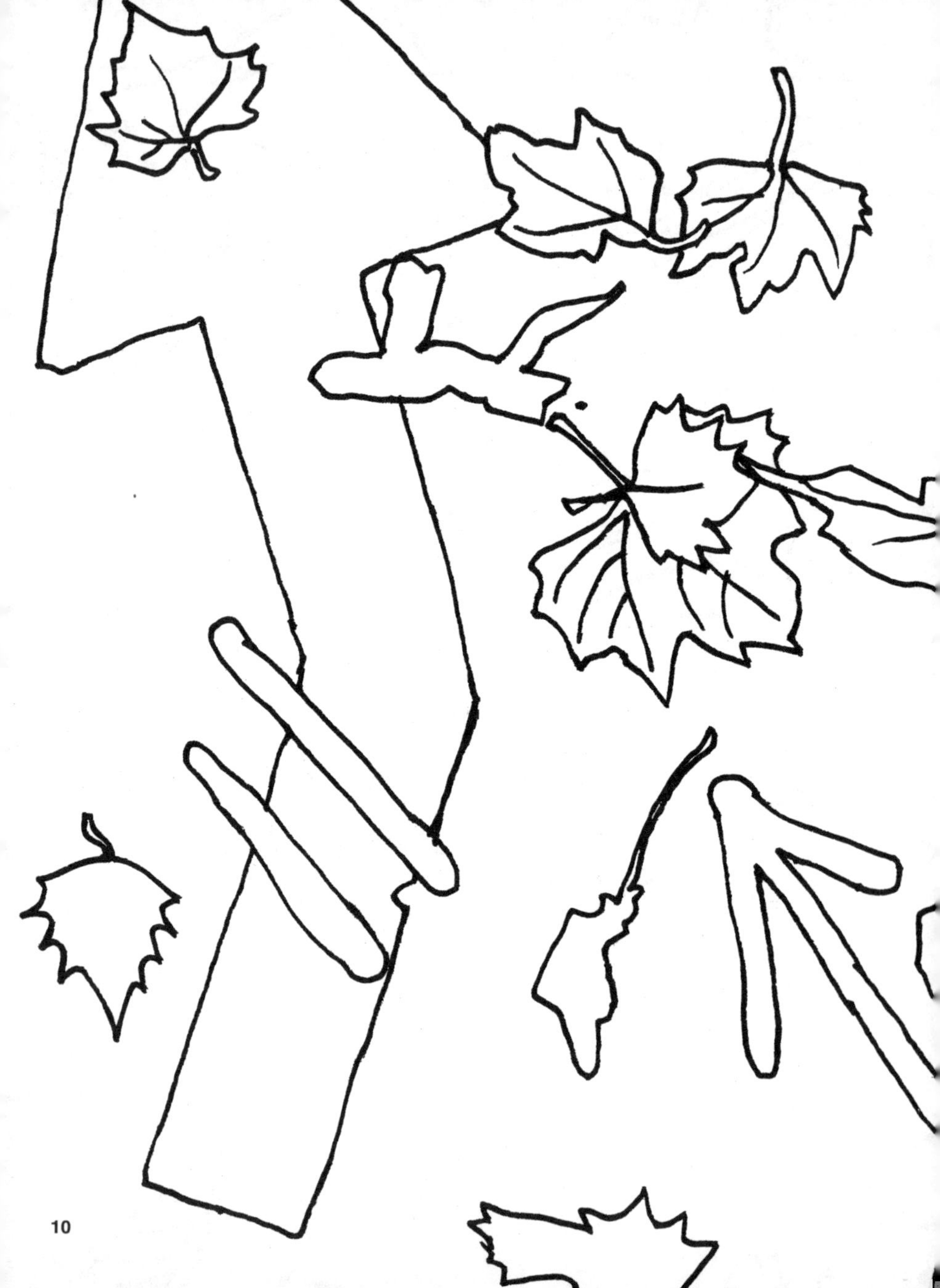

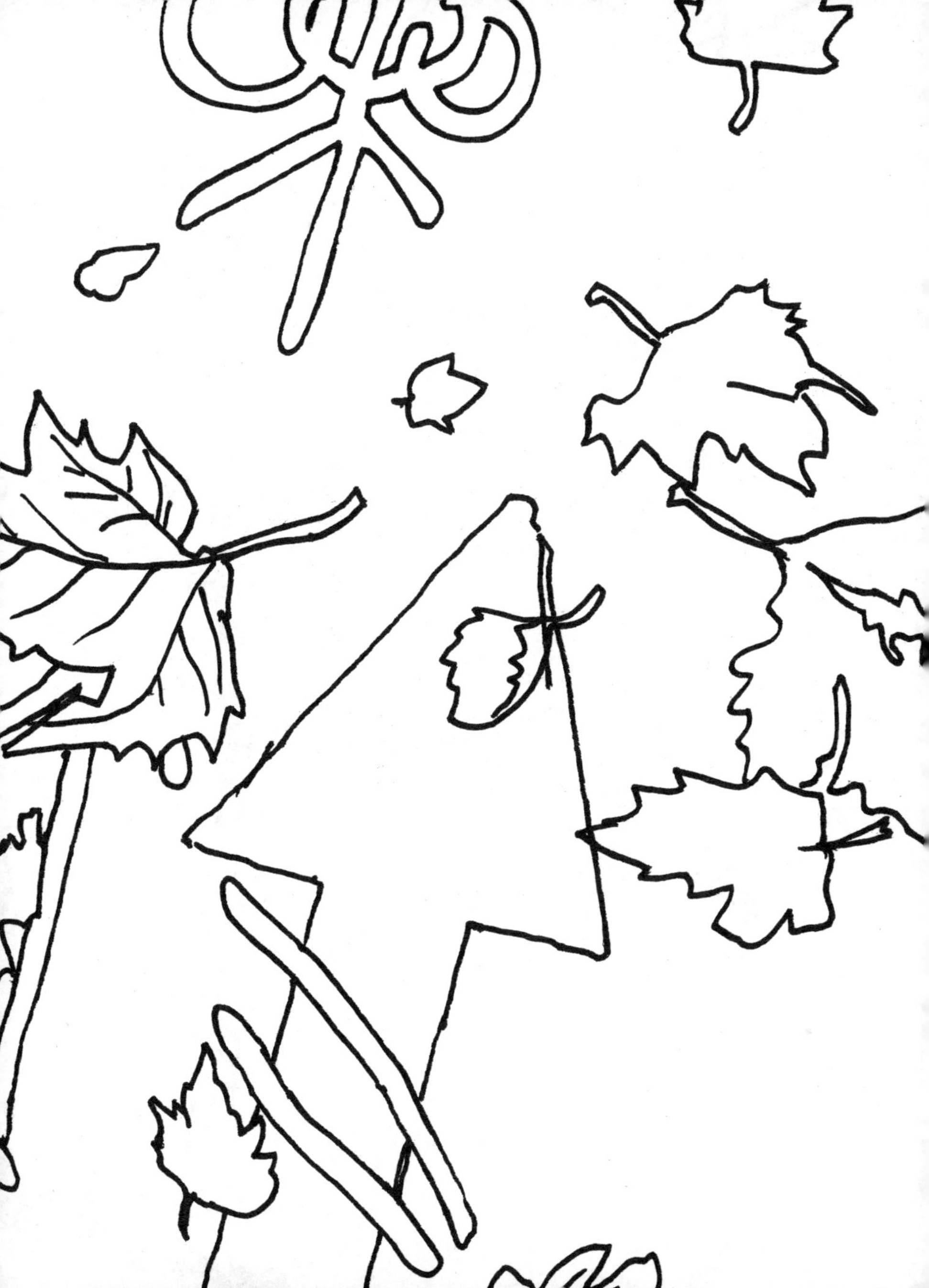

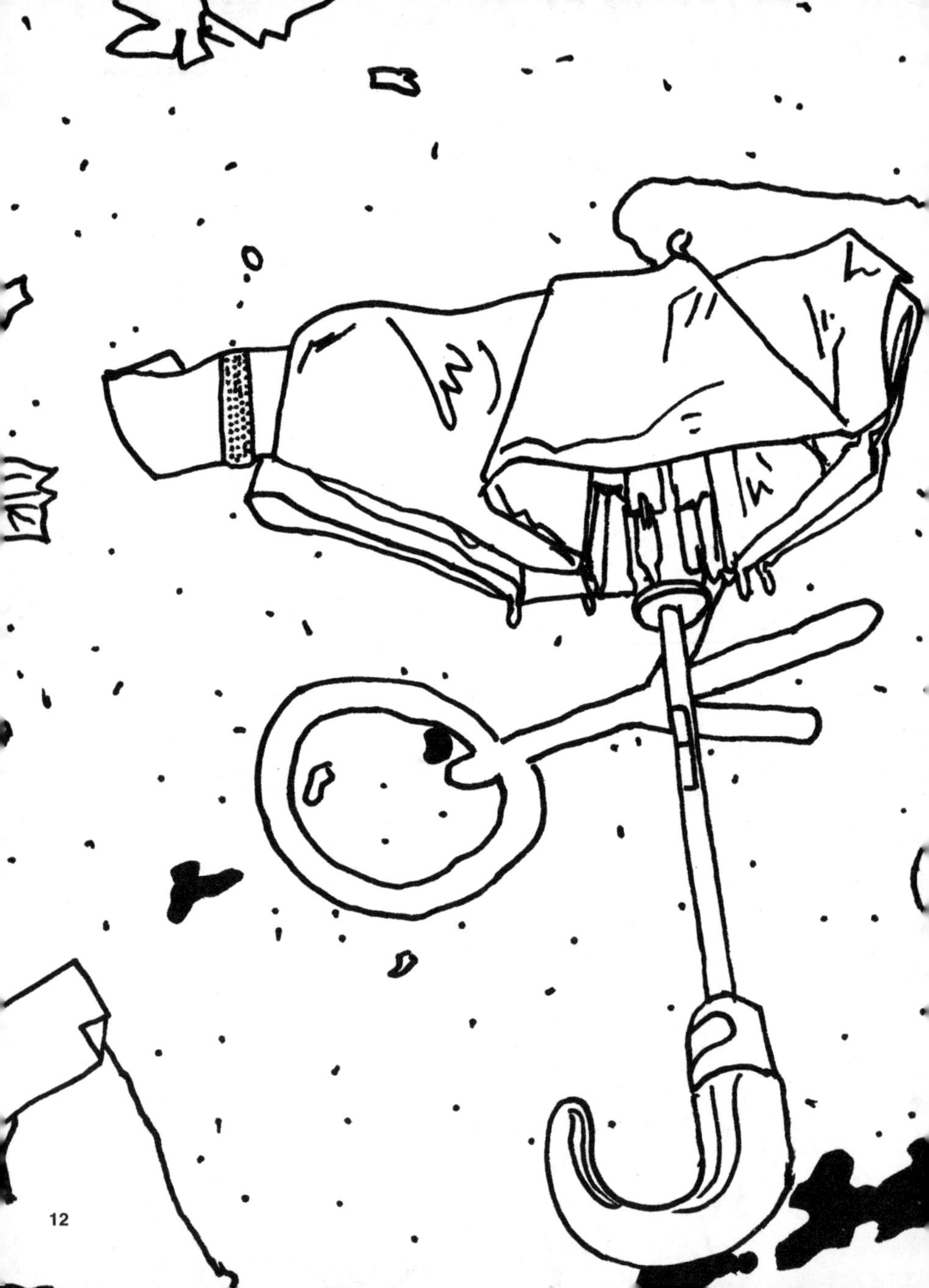

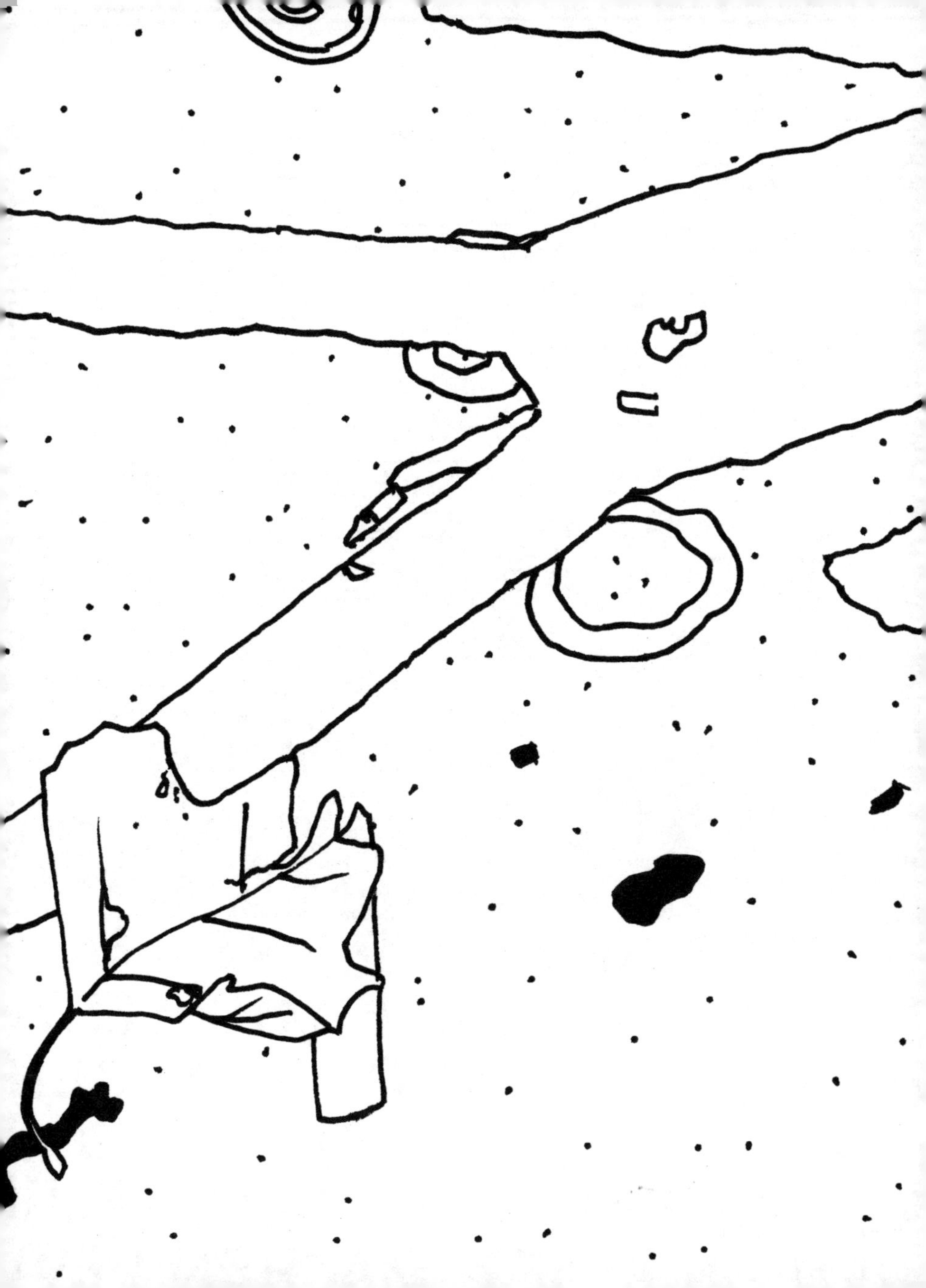

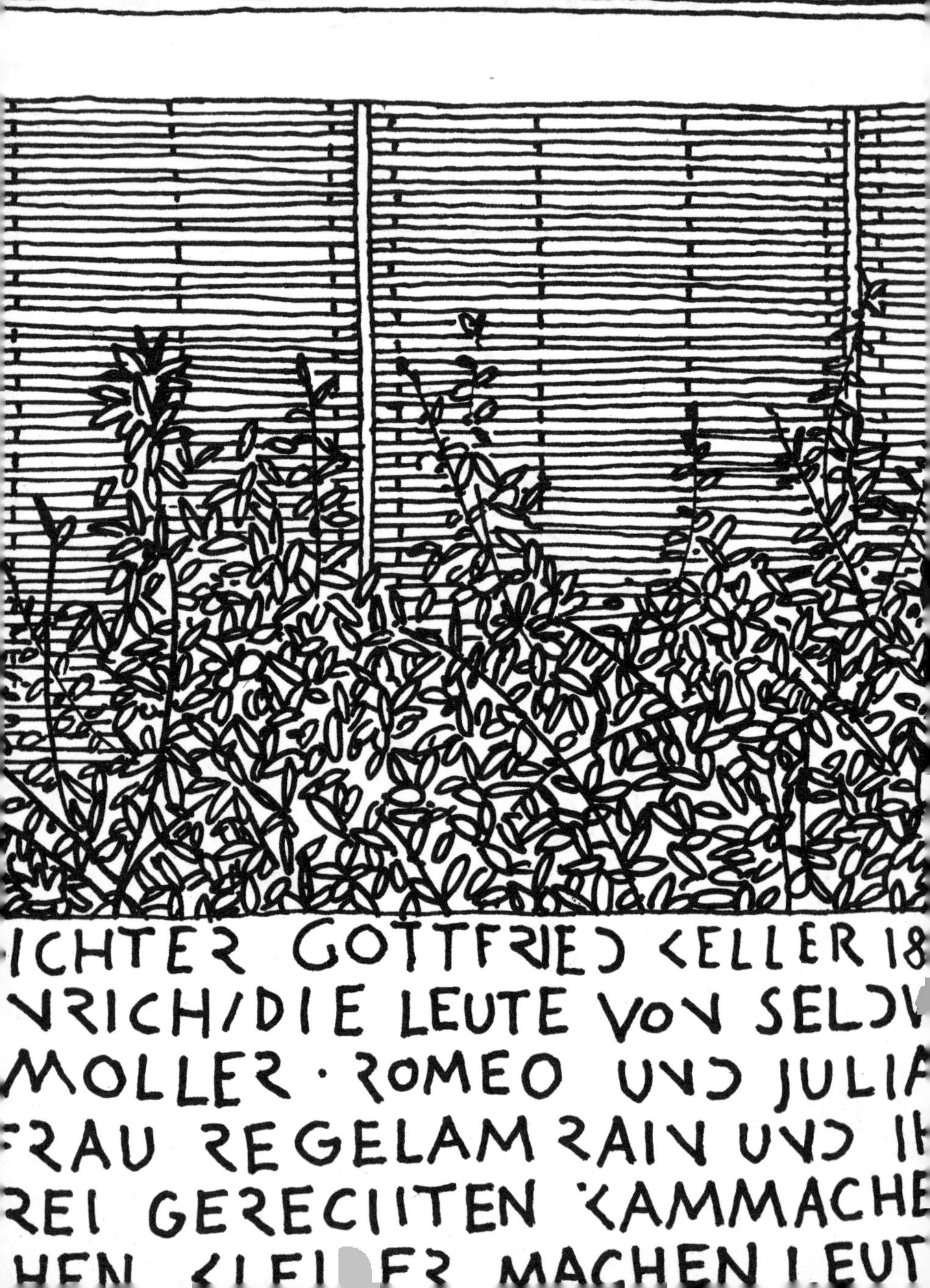
ICHTER GOTTFRIED (ELLER 18
VRICH/DIE LEUTE VON SELDW
MOLLER · ROMEO UND JULIA
FRAU REGELAM RAIN UND I
REI GERECHTEN KAMMACHE
HEN KLEIDER MACHEN LEUT

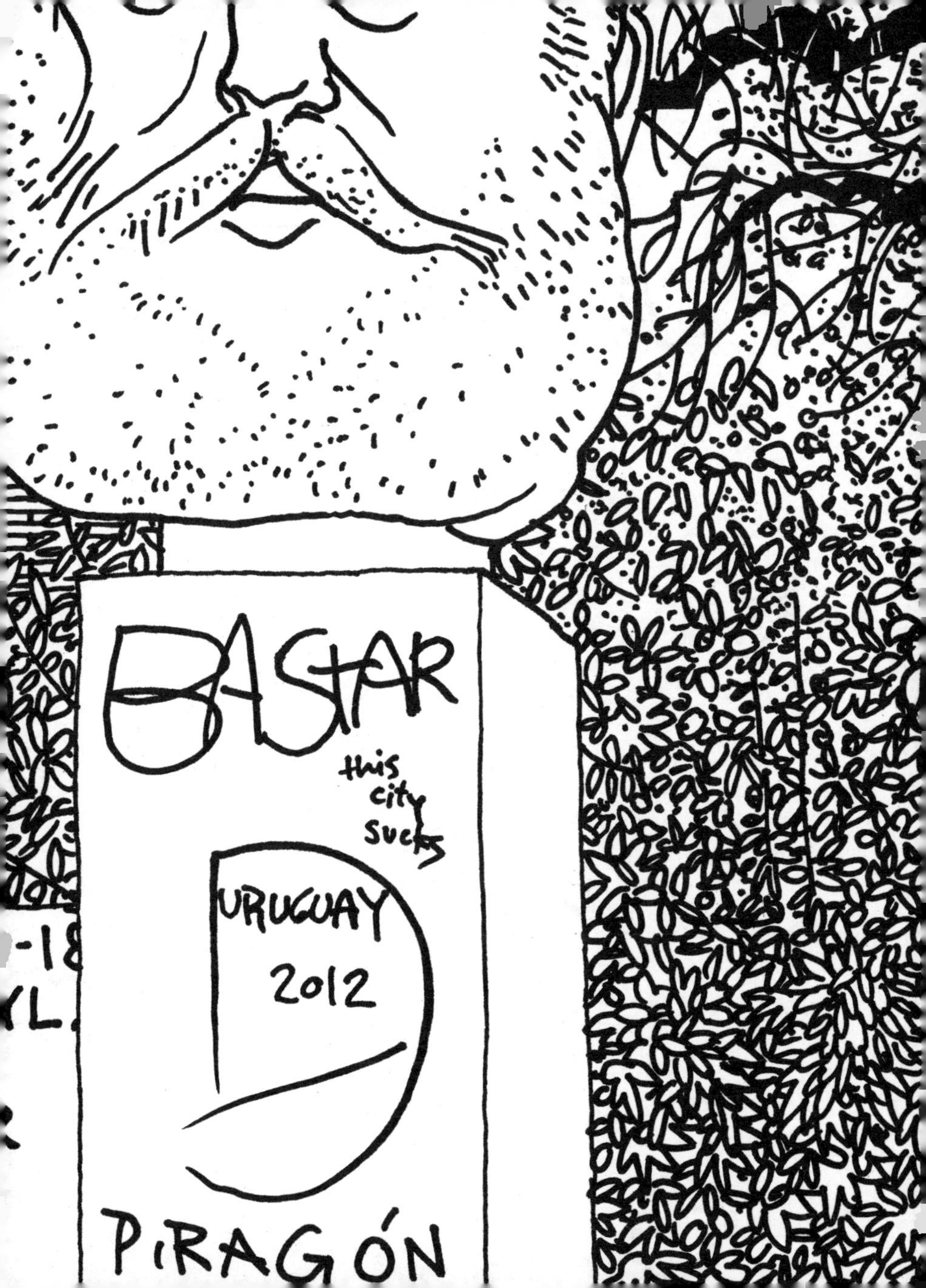
BASTAR
this city sucks
URUGUAY 2012
PiRAGÓN

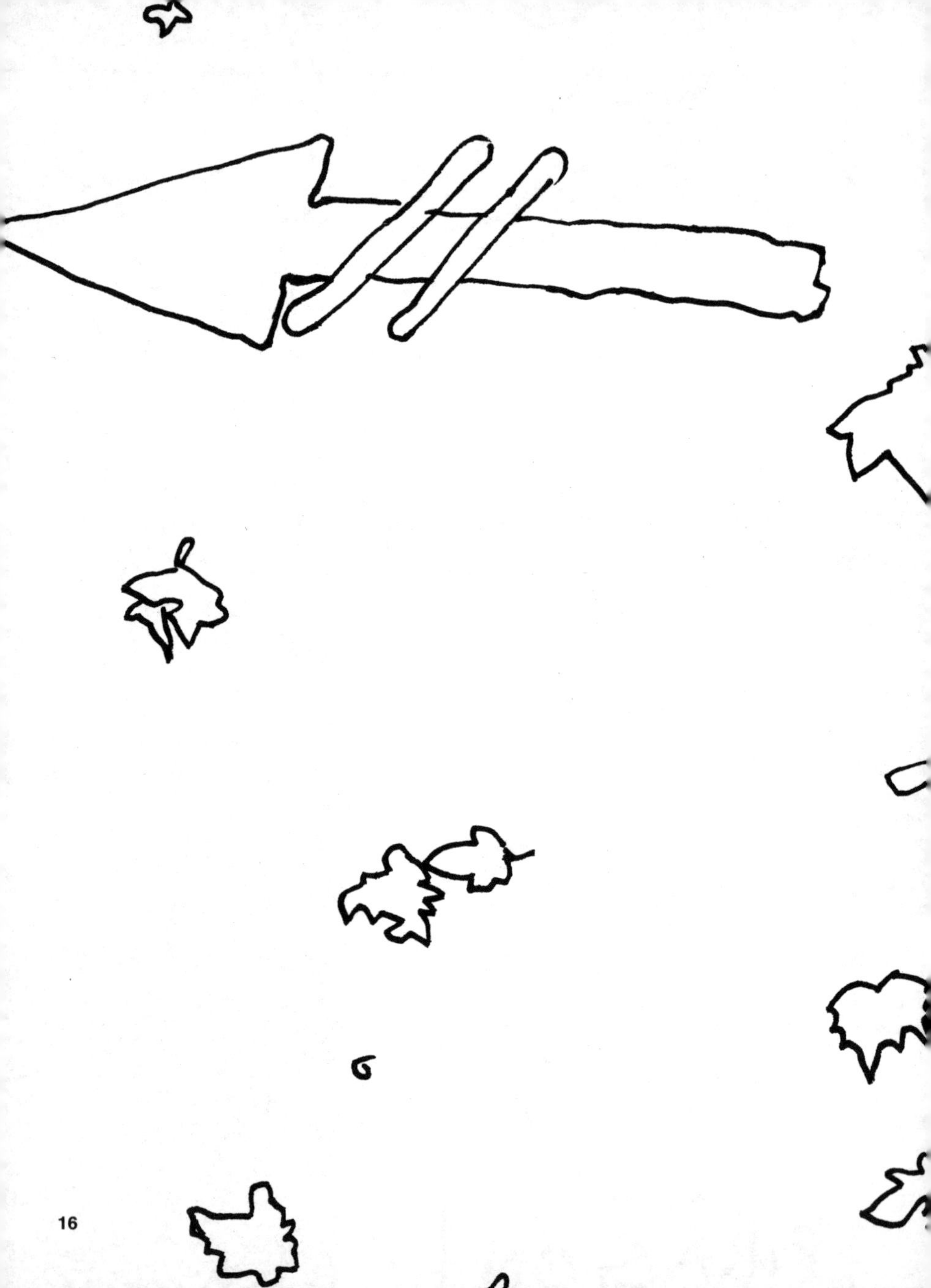

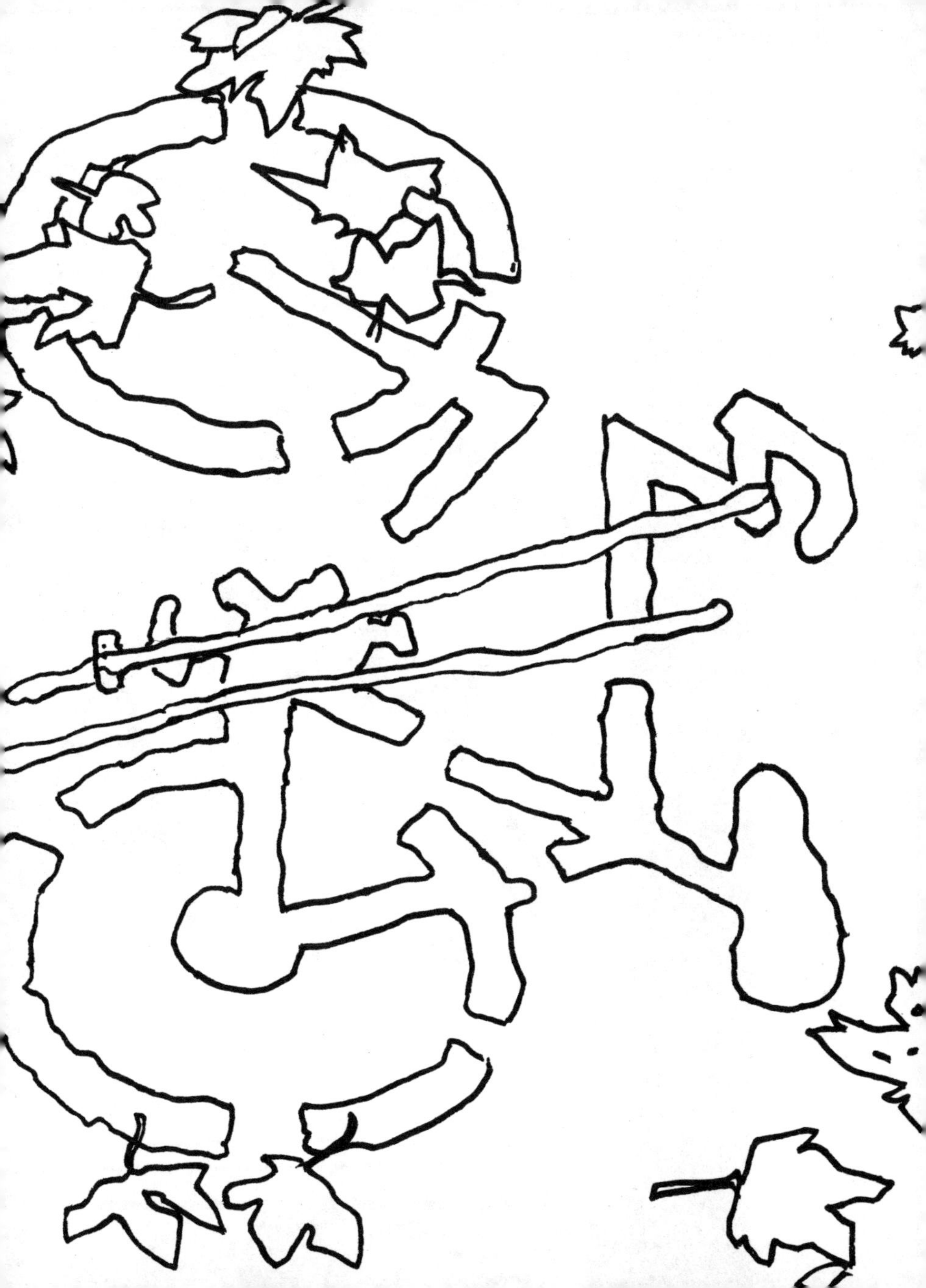

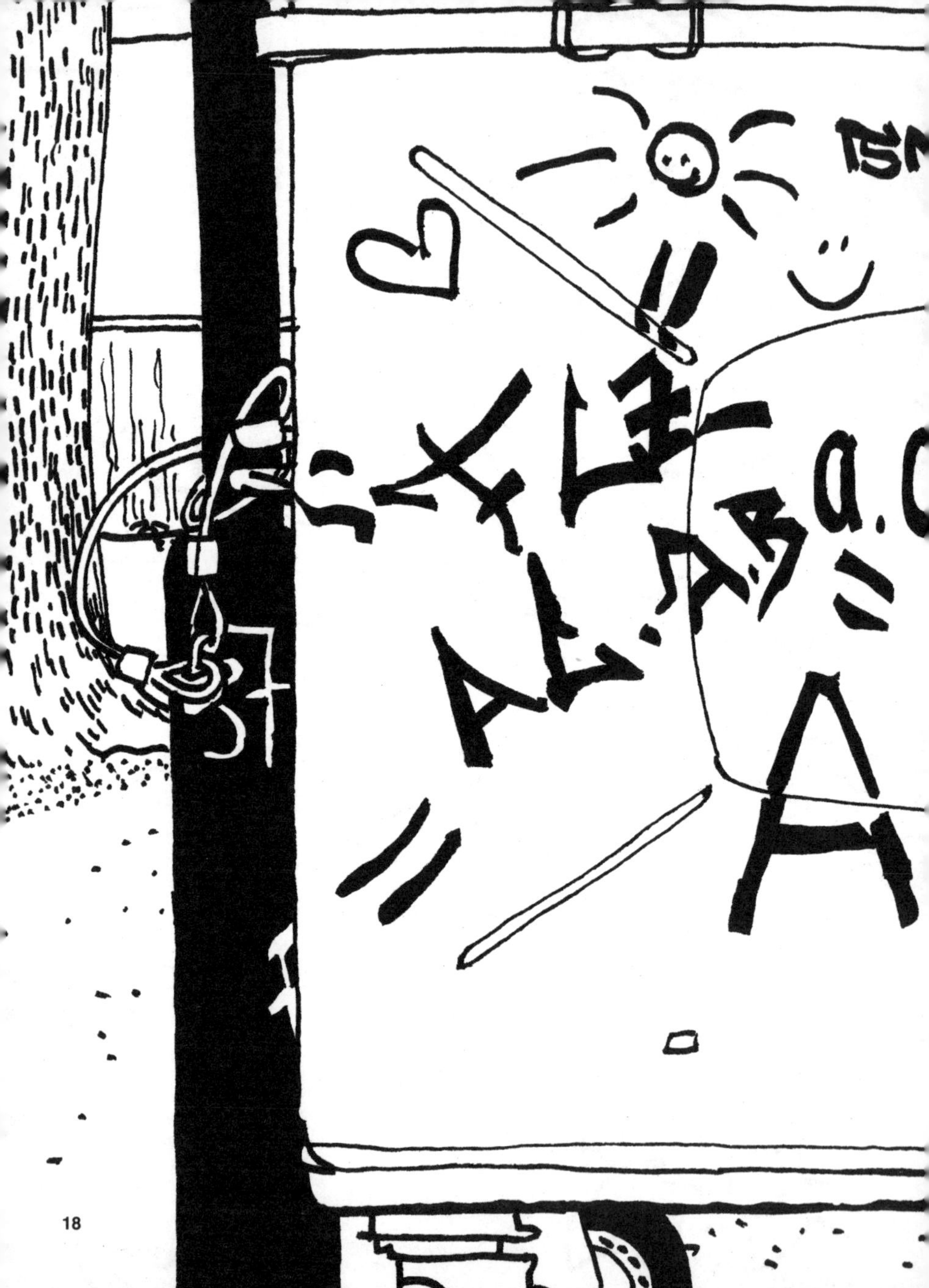

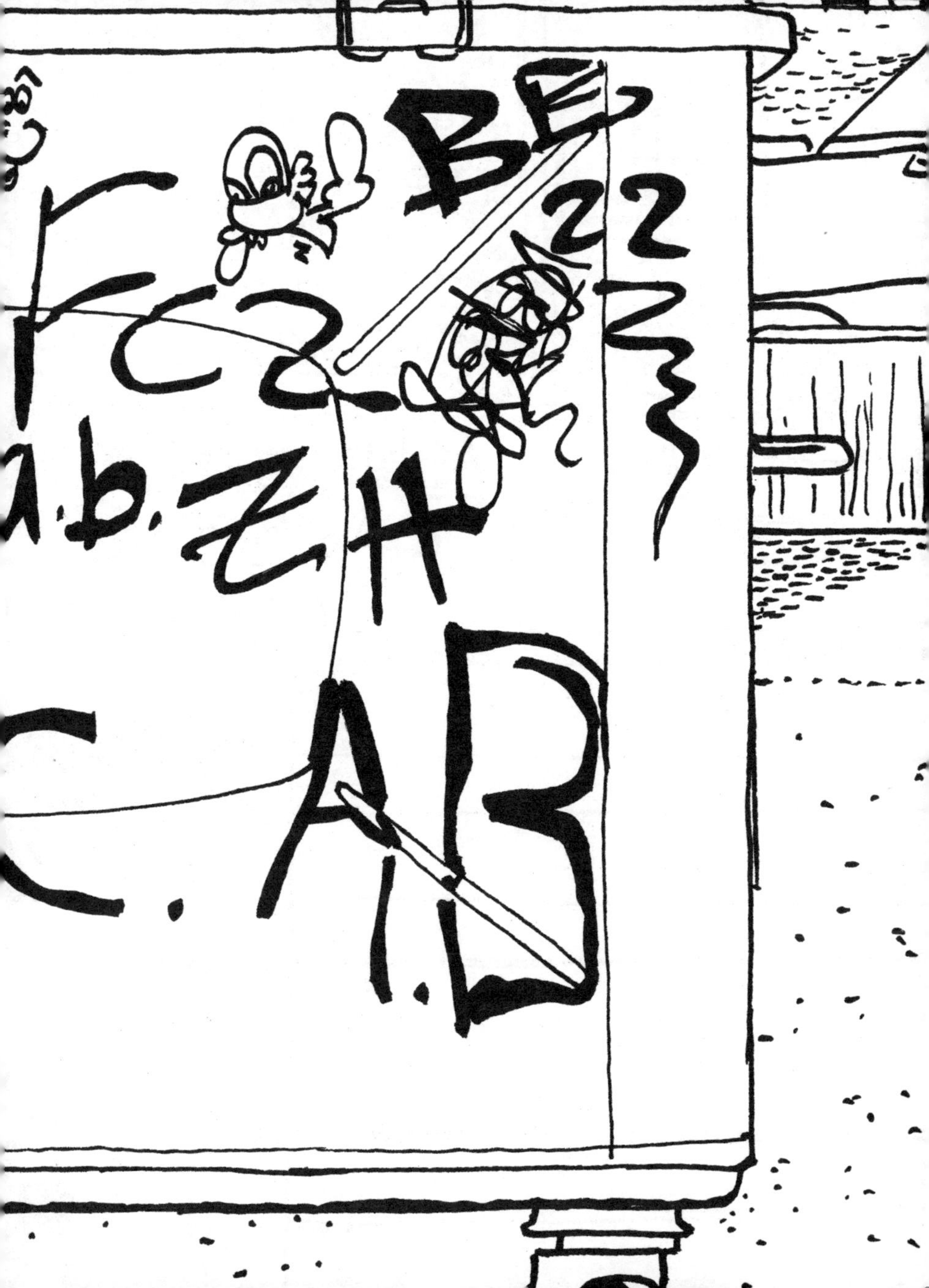

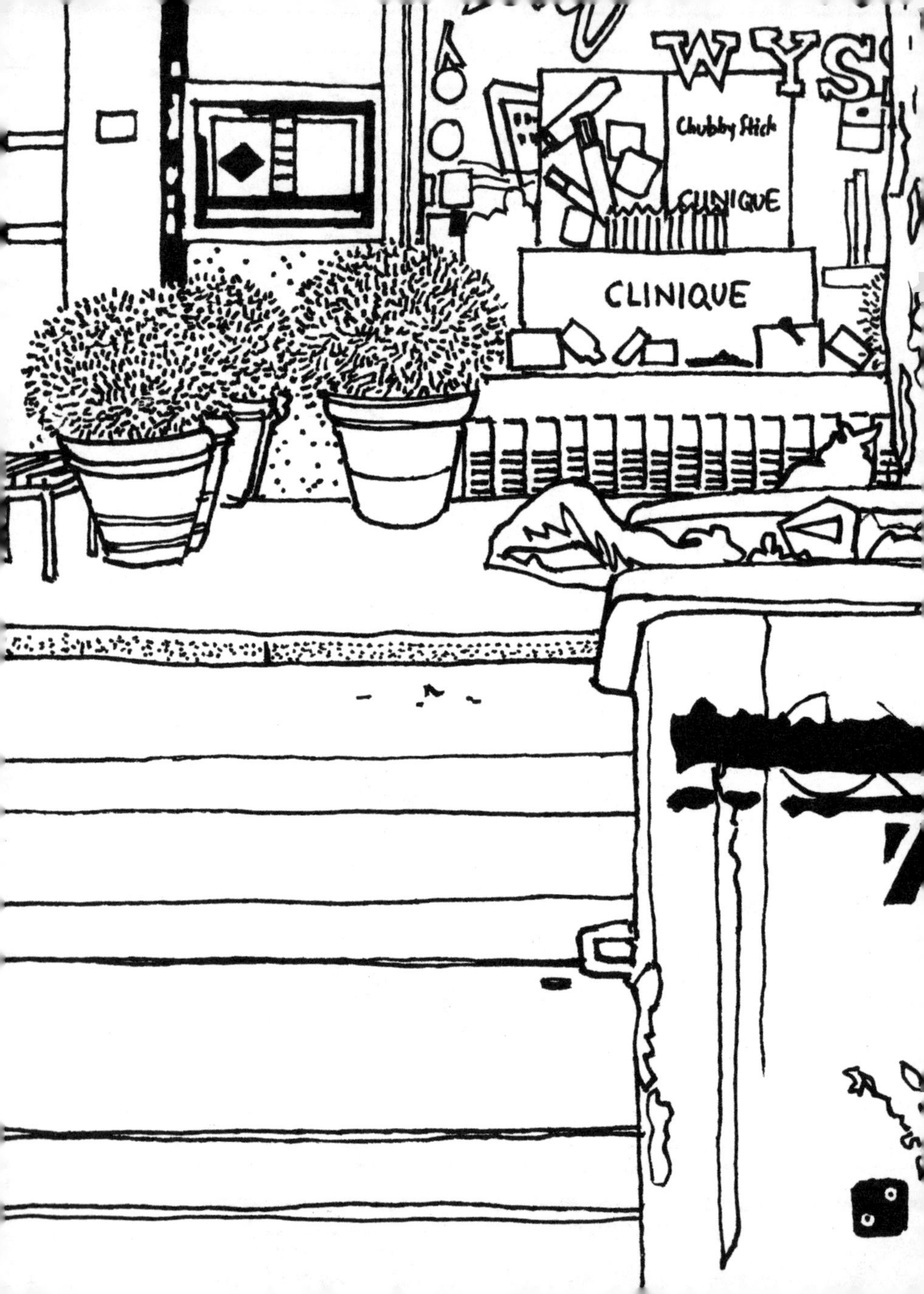

WYS
Chubby Stick
CLINIQUE
CLINIQUE

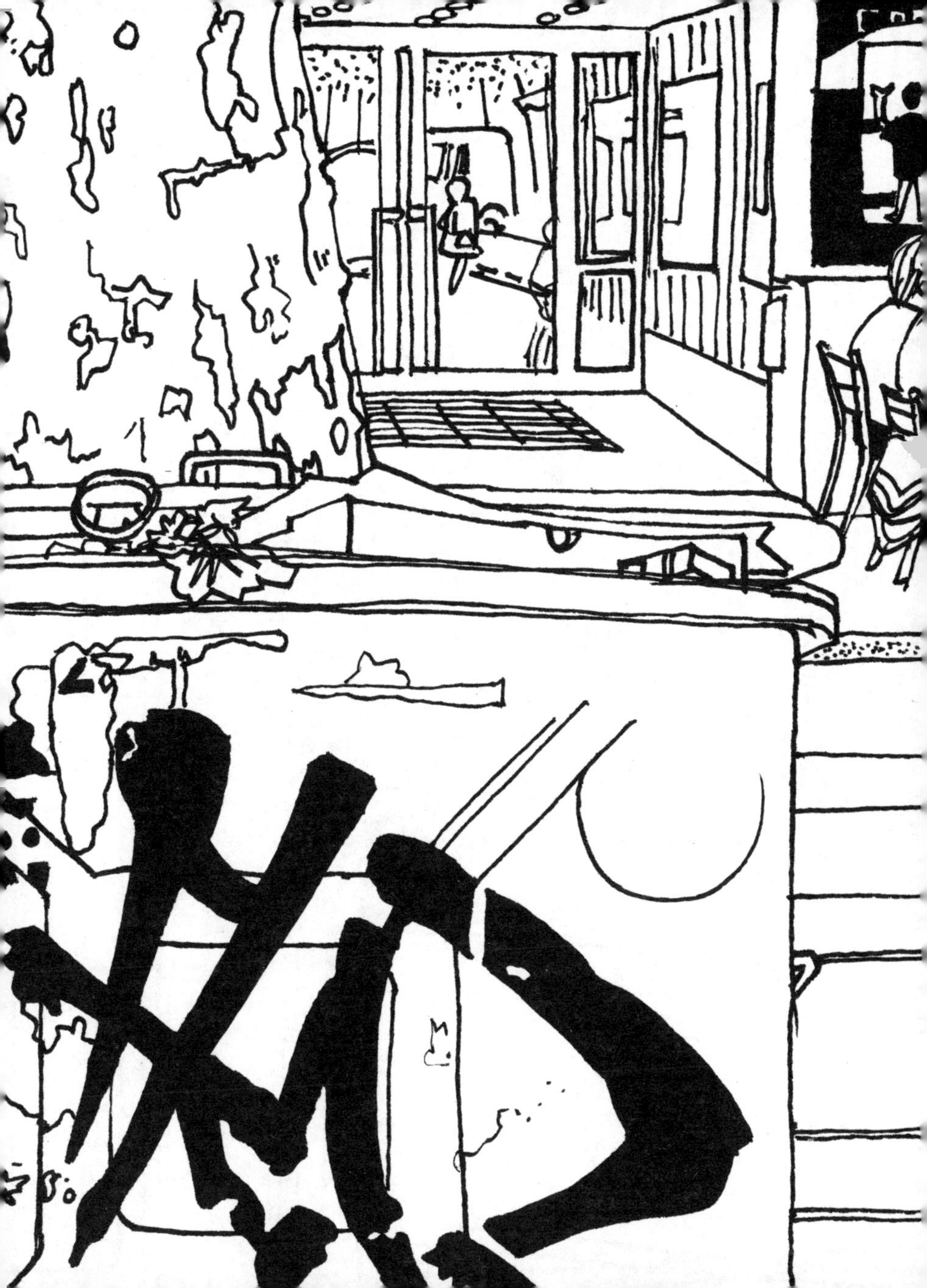

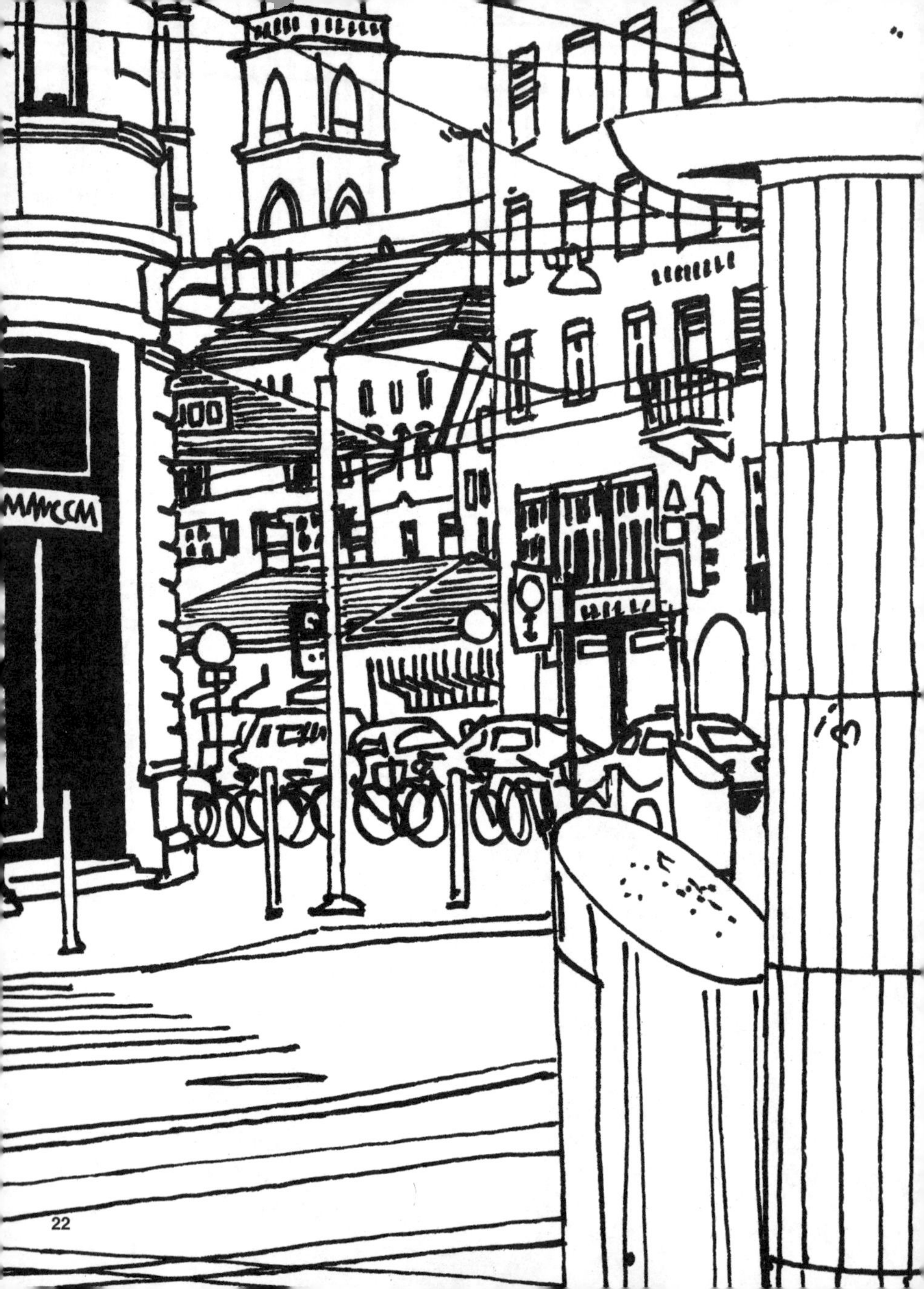

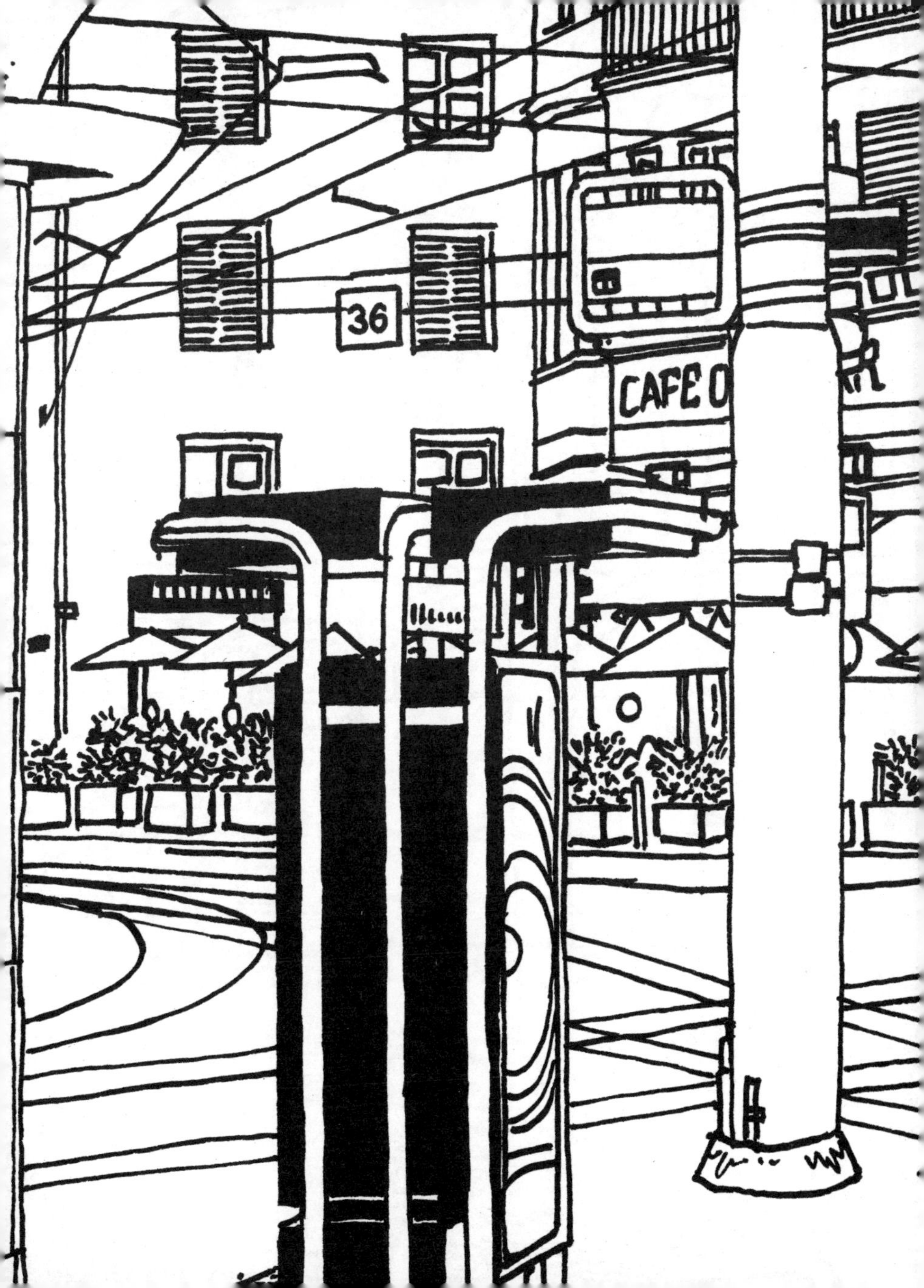

36
CAFE O

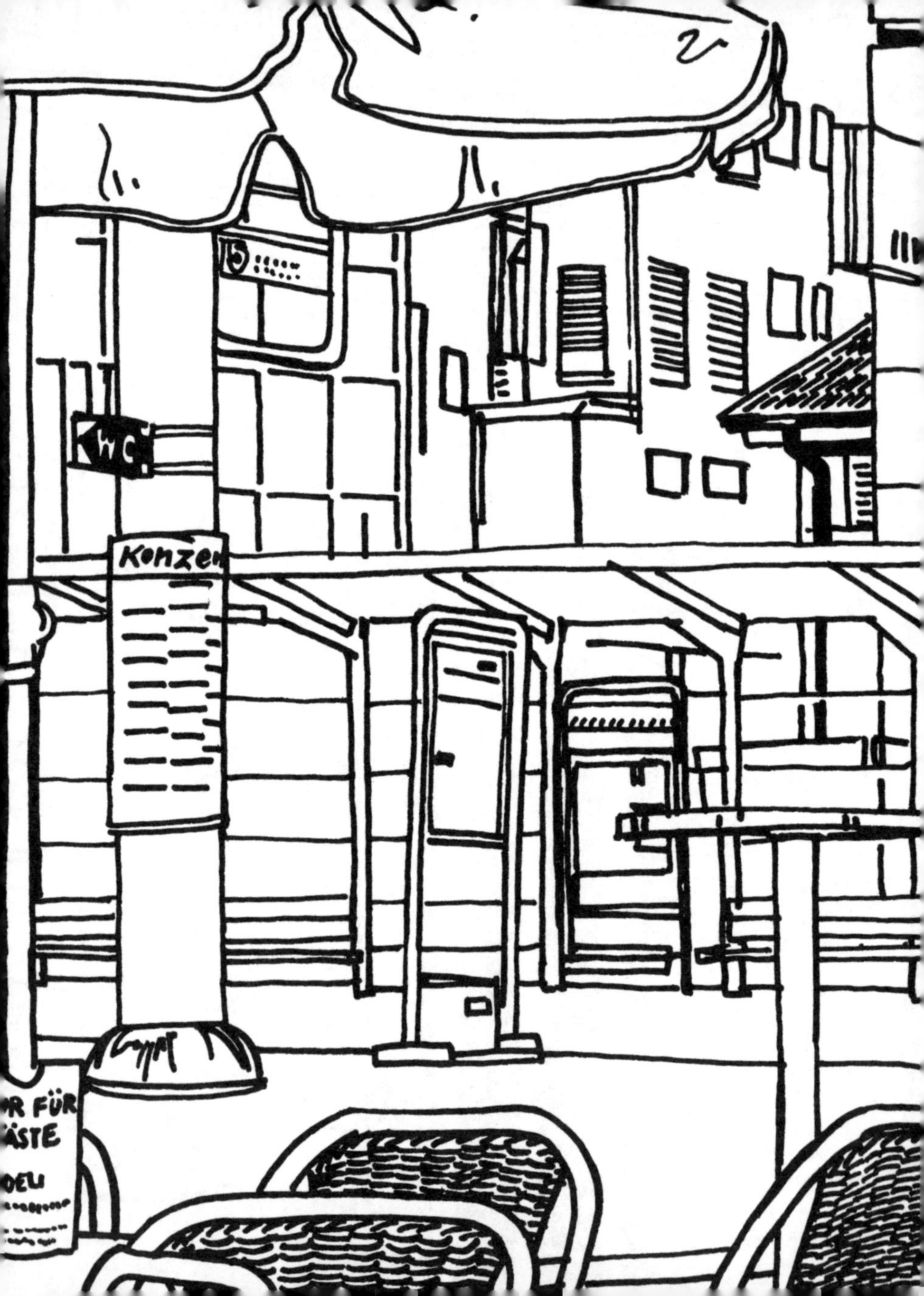

WC
Konzen
R FÜR
ÄSTE
DELI

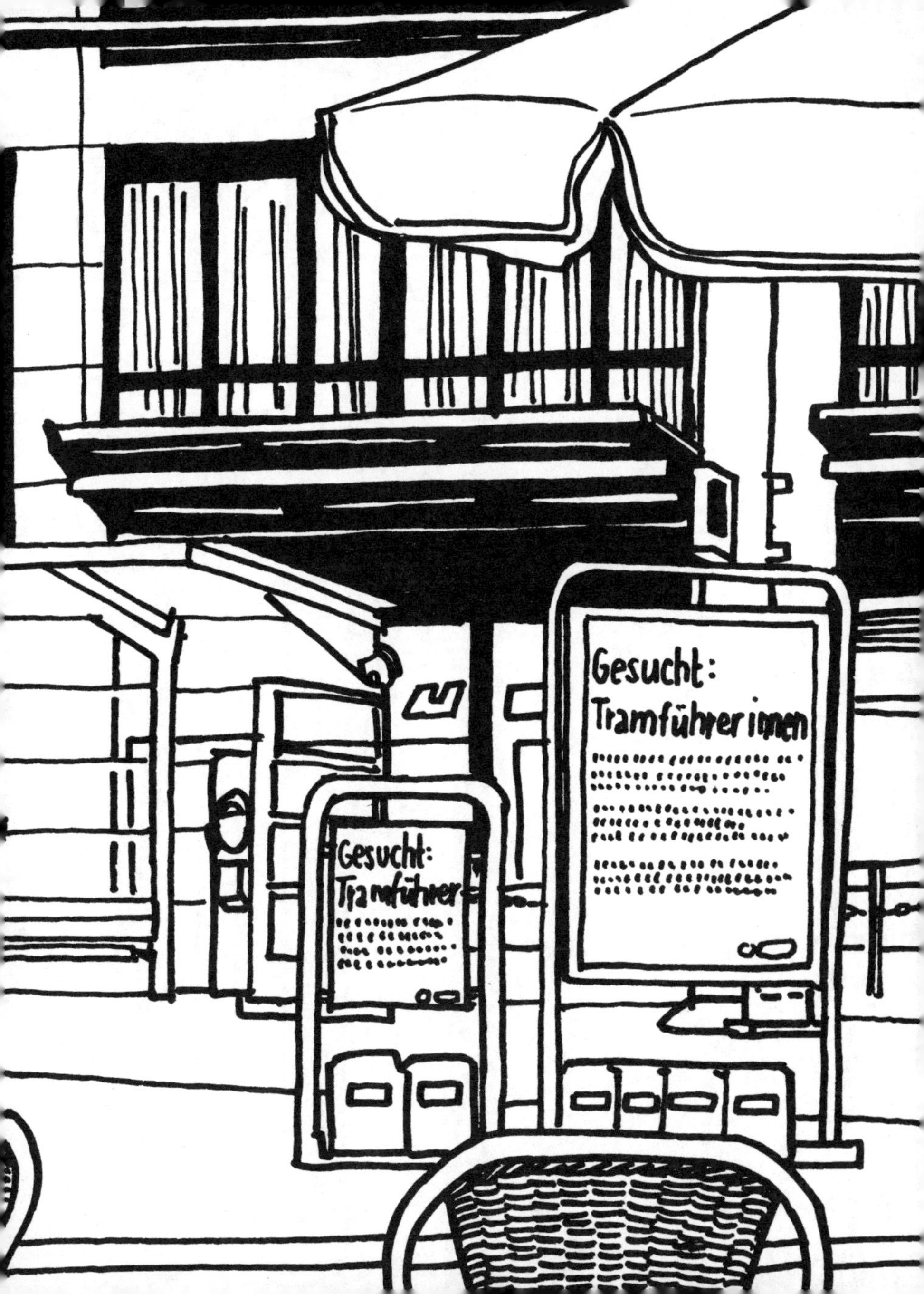

Gesucht:
Tramführer innen
Gesucht:
Tramführer

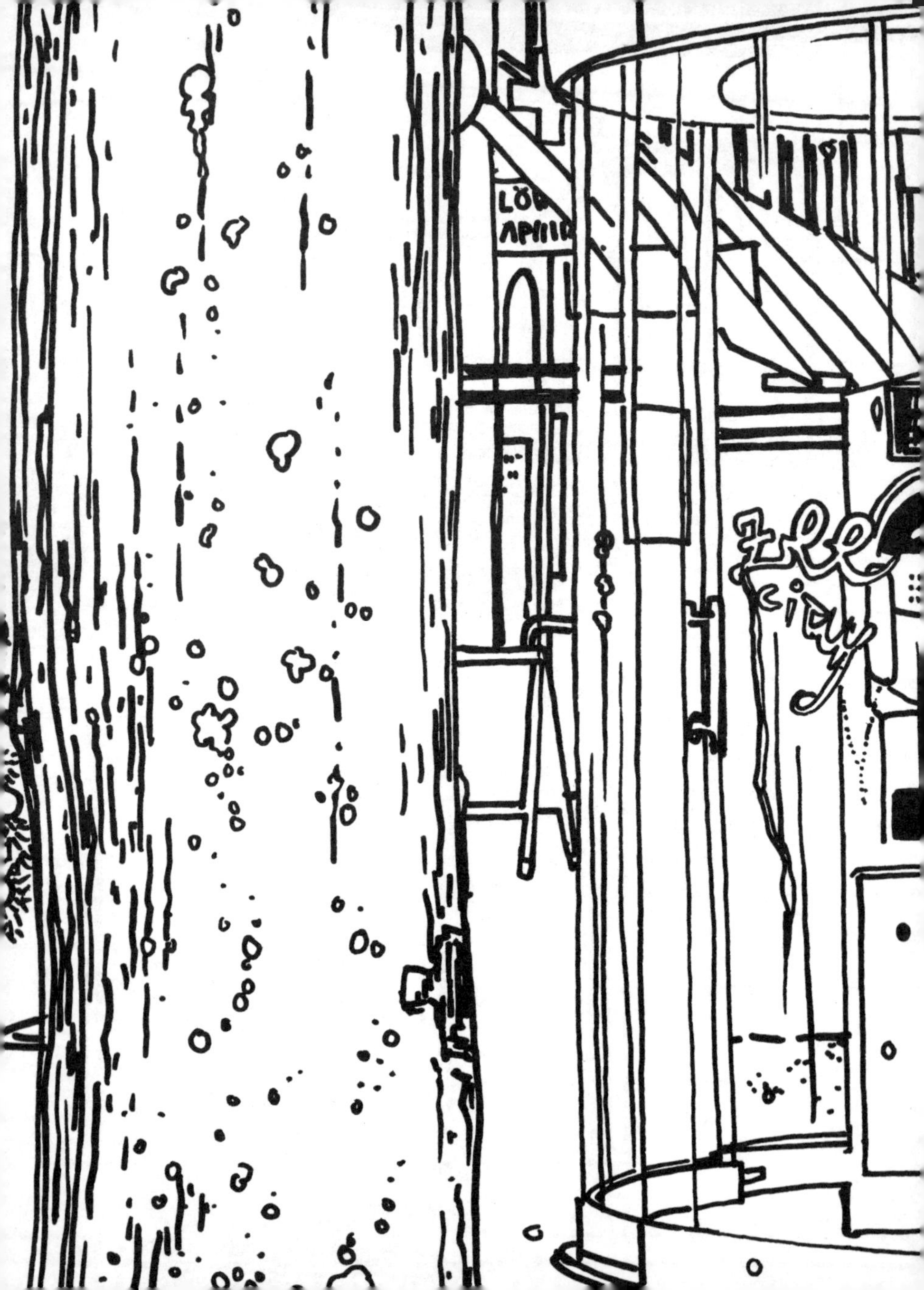

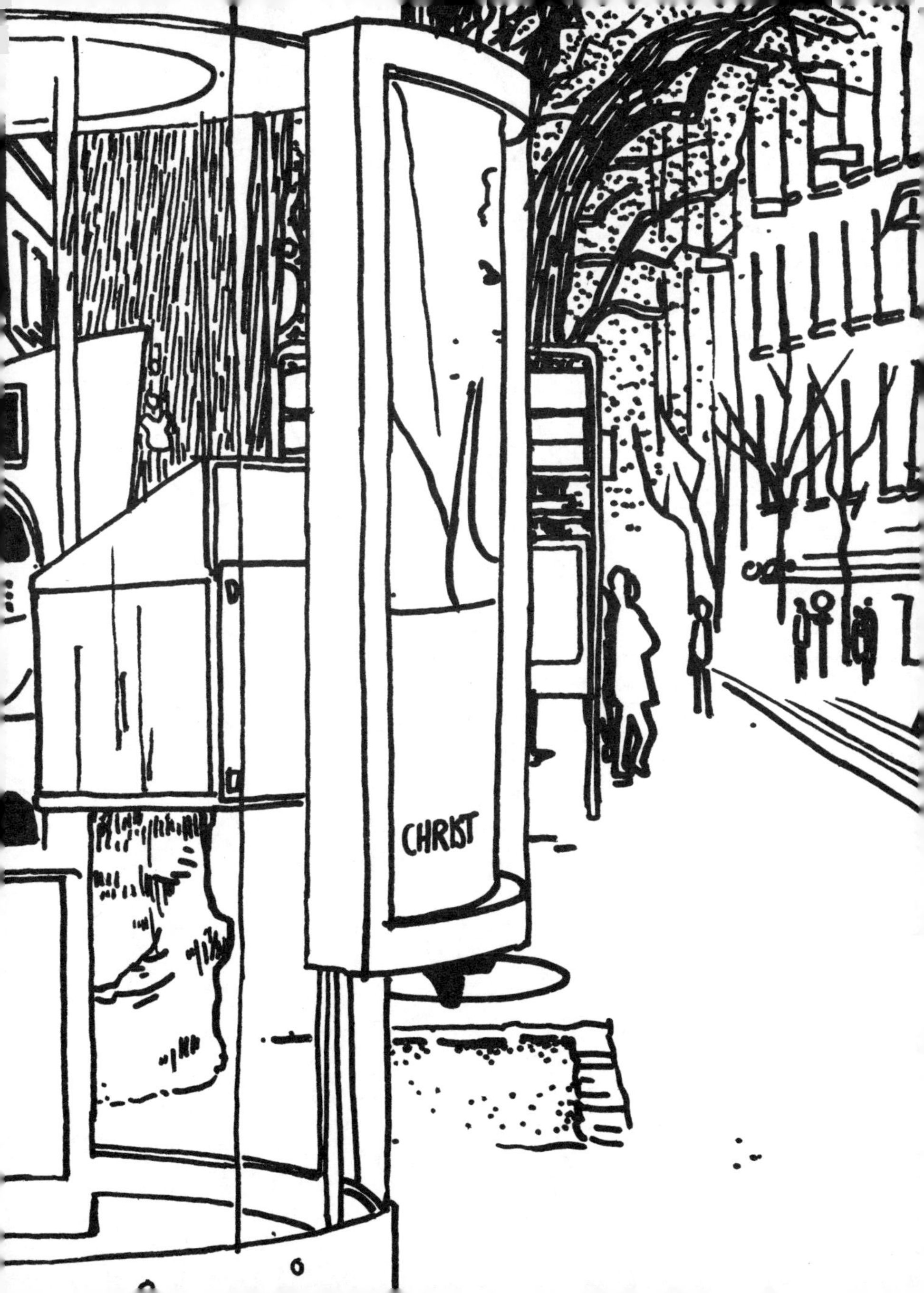

CHRIST

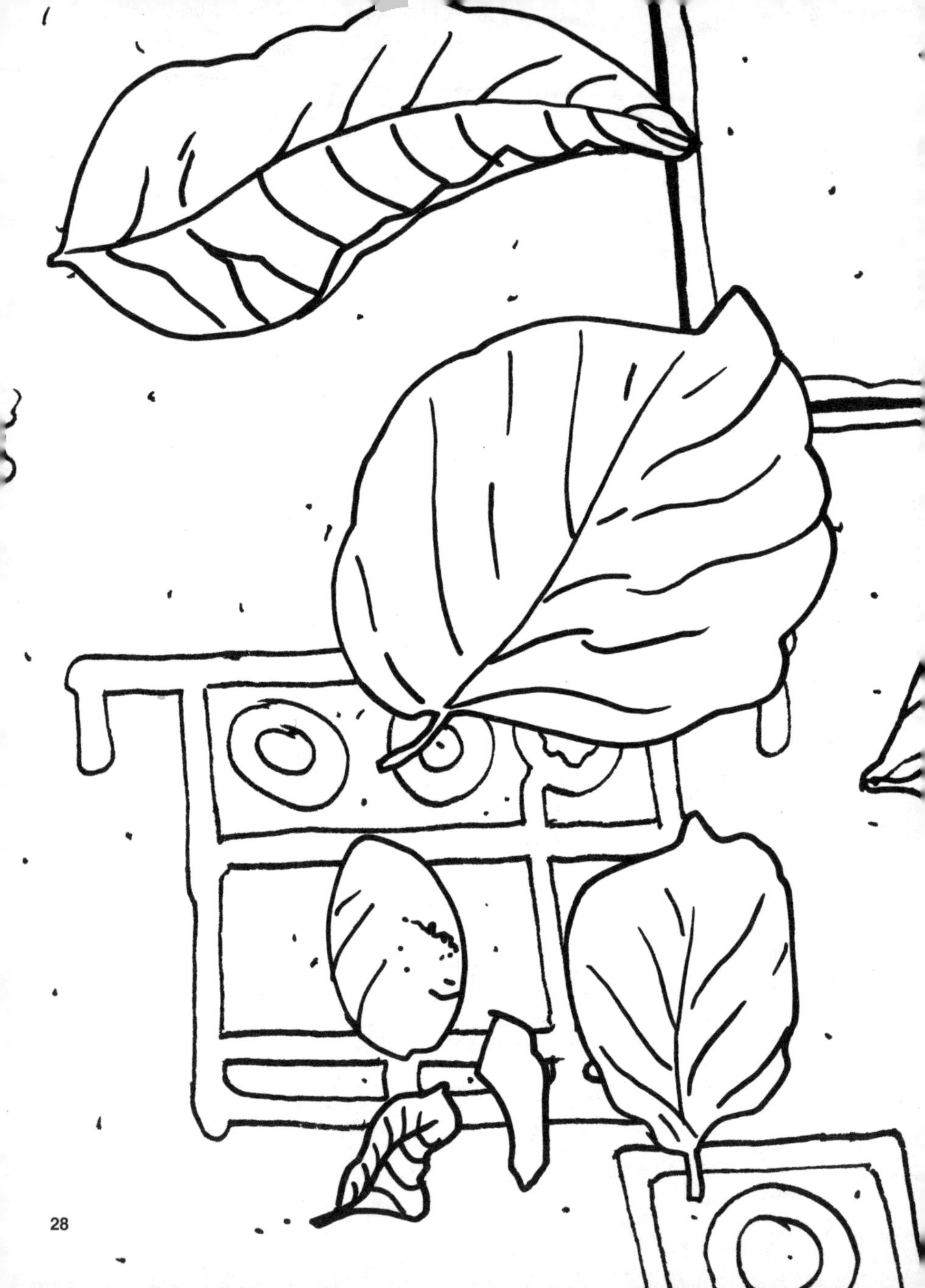

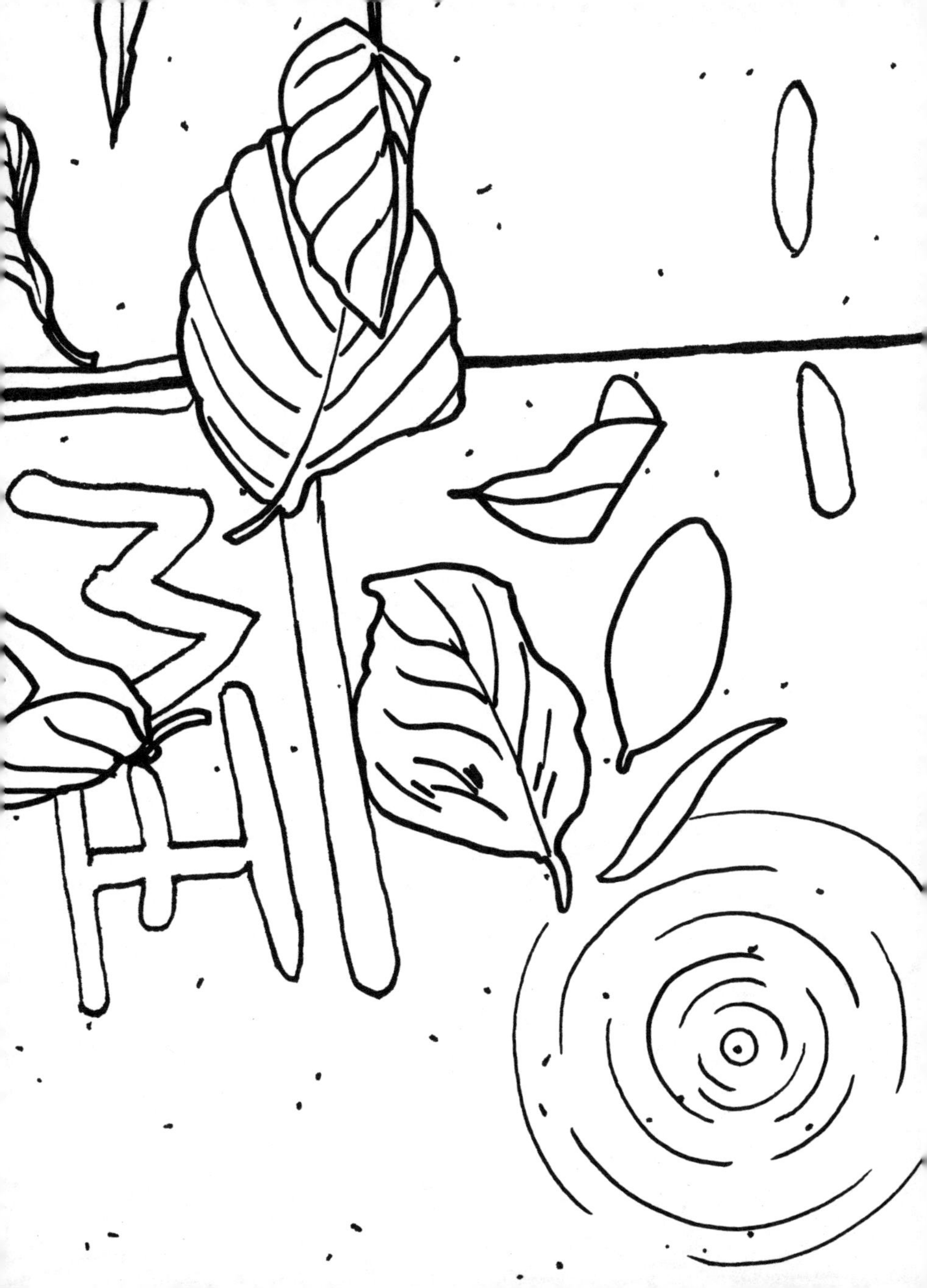

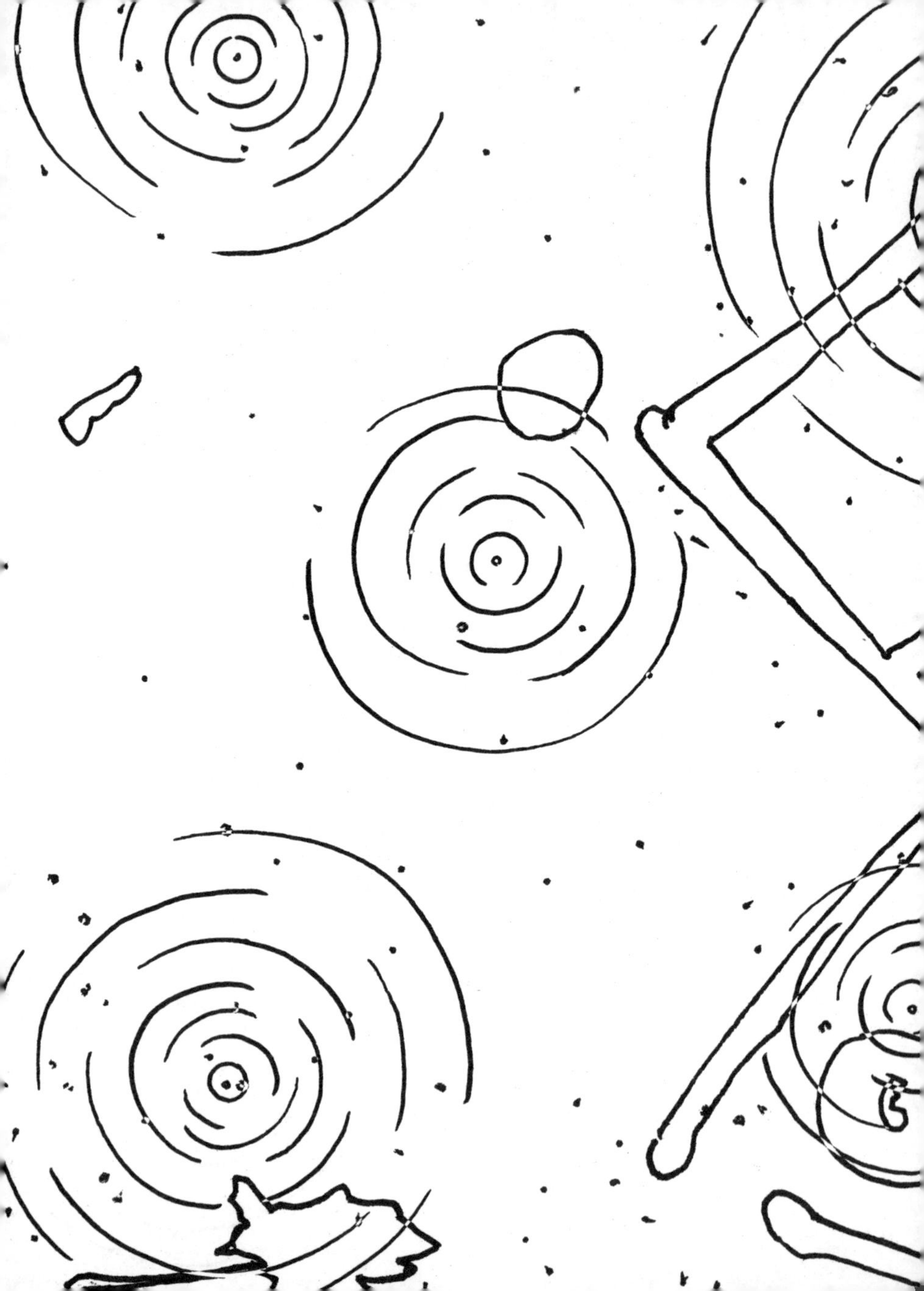

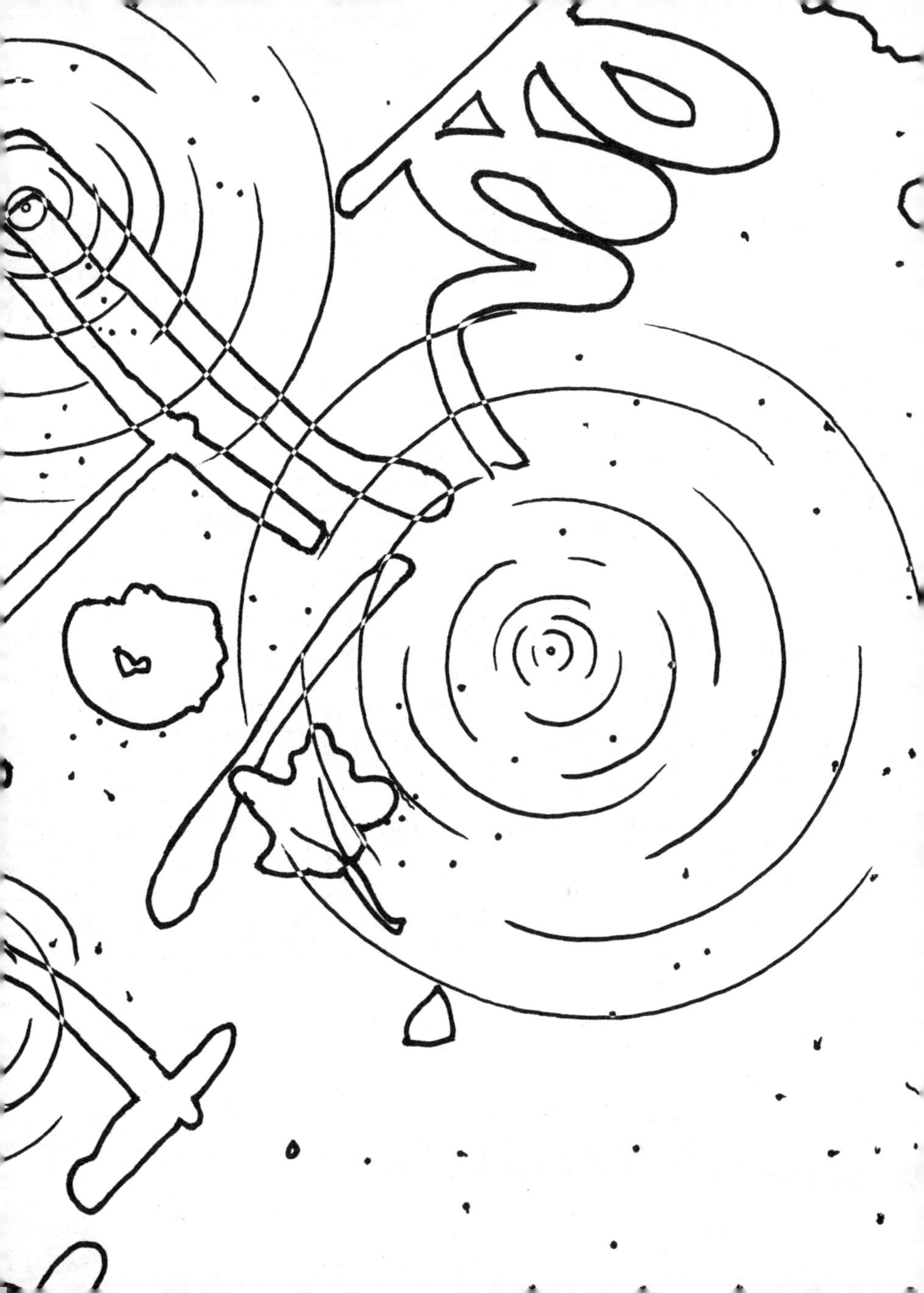

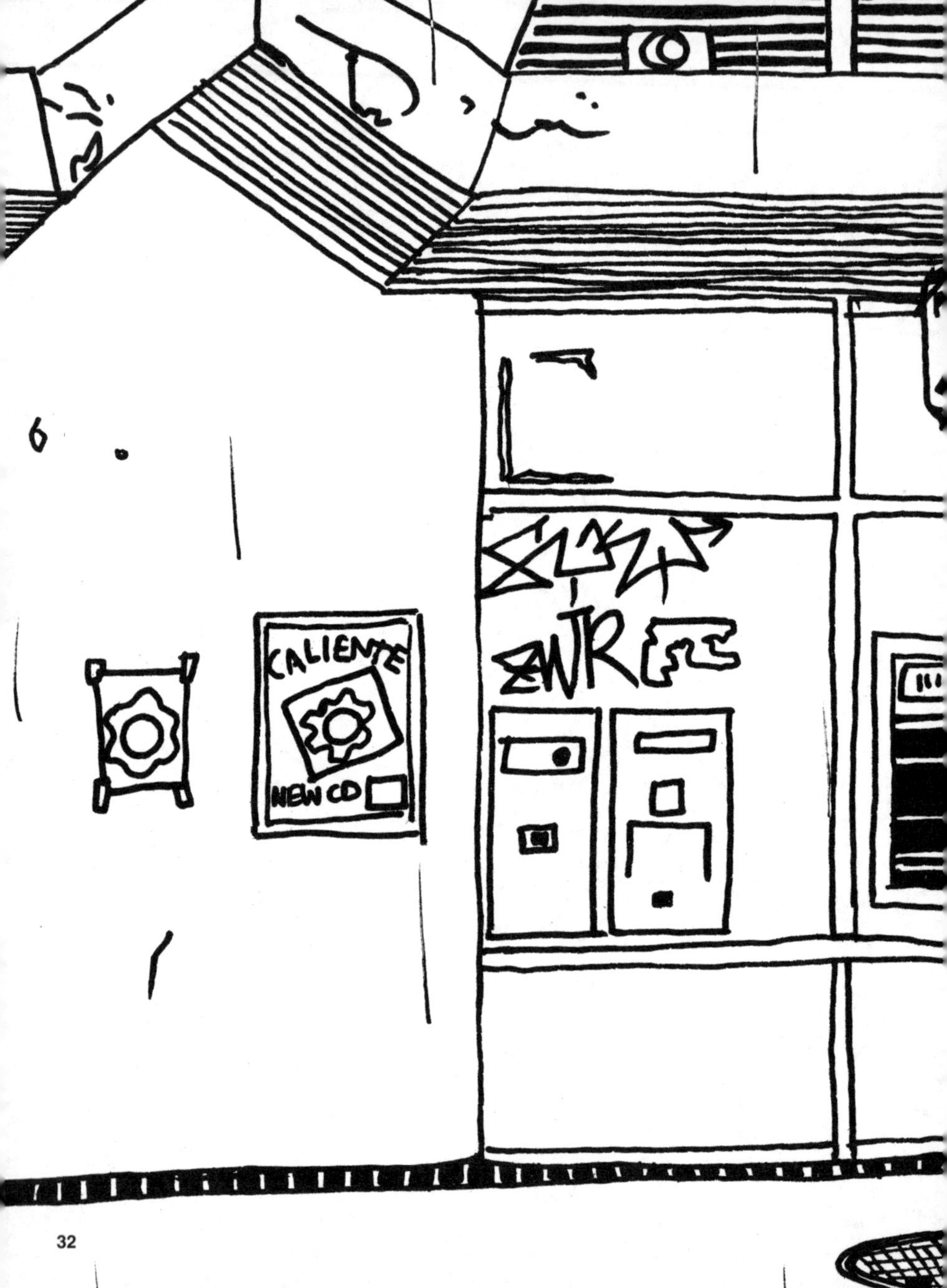
CALIENTE
NEW CD
ENTR

6
ROB
MORE
BAN

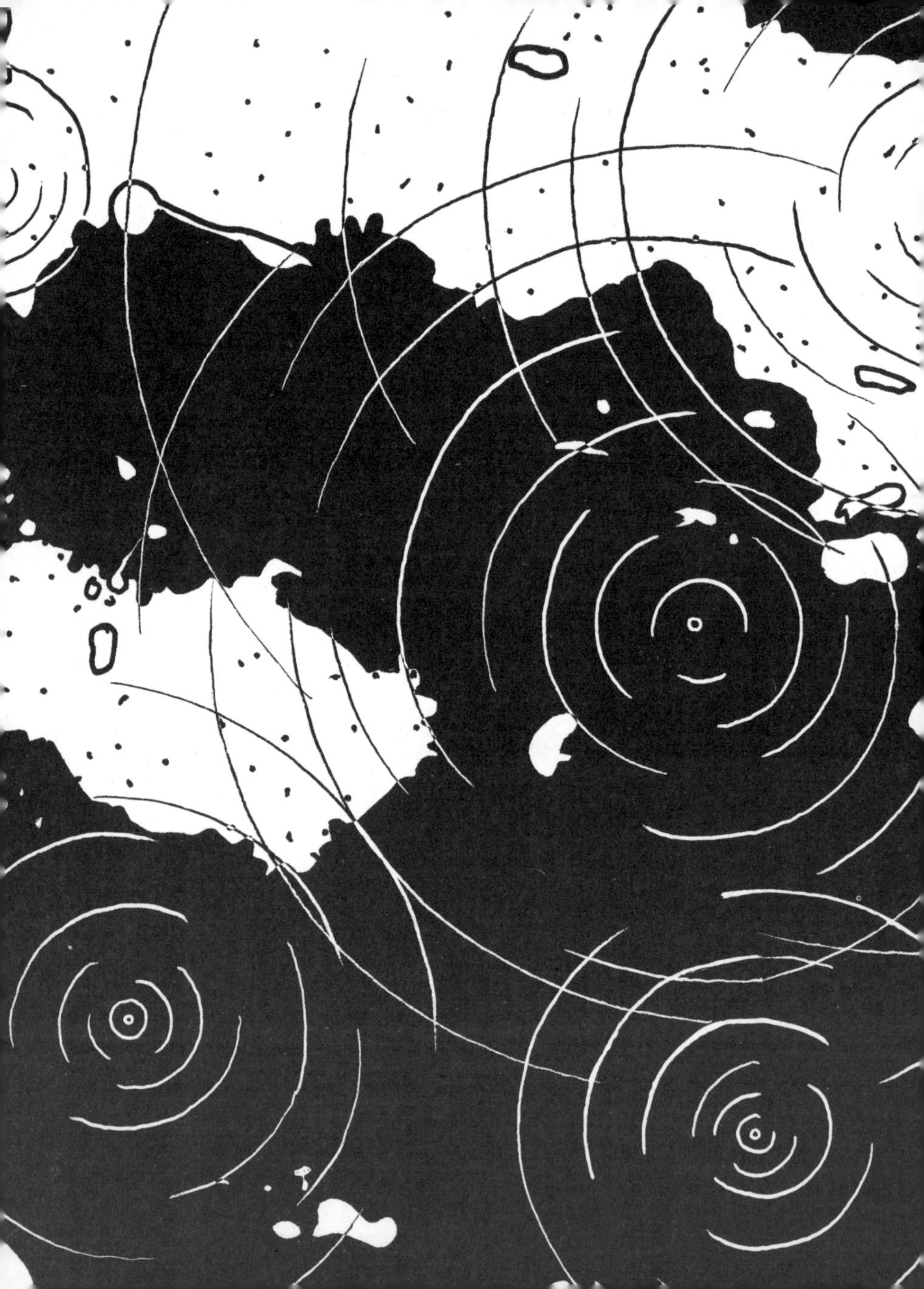

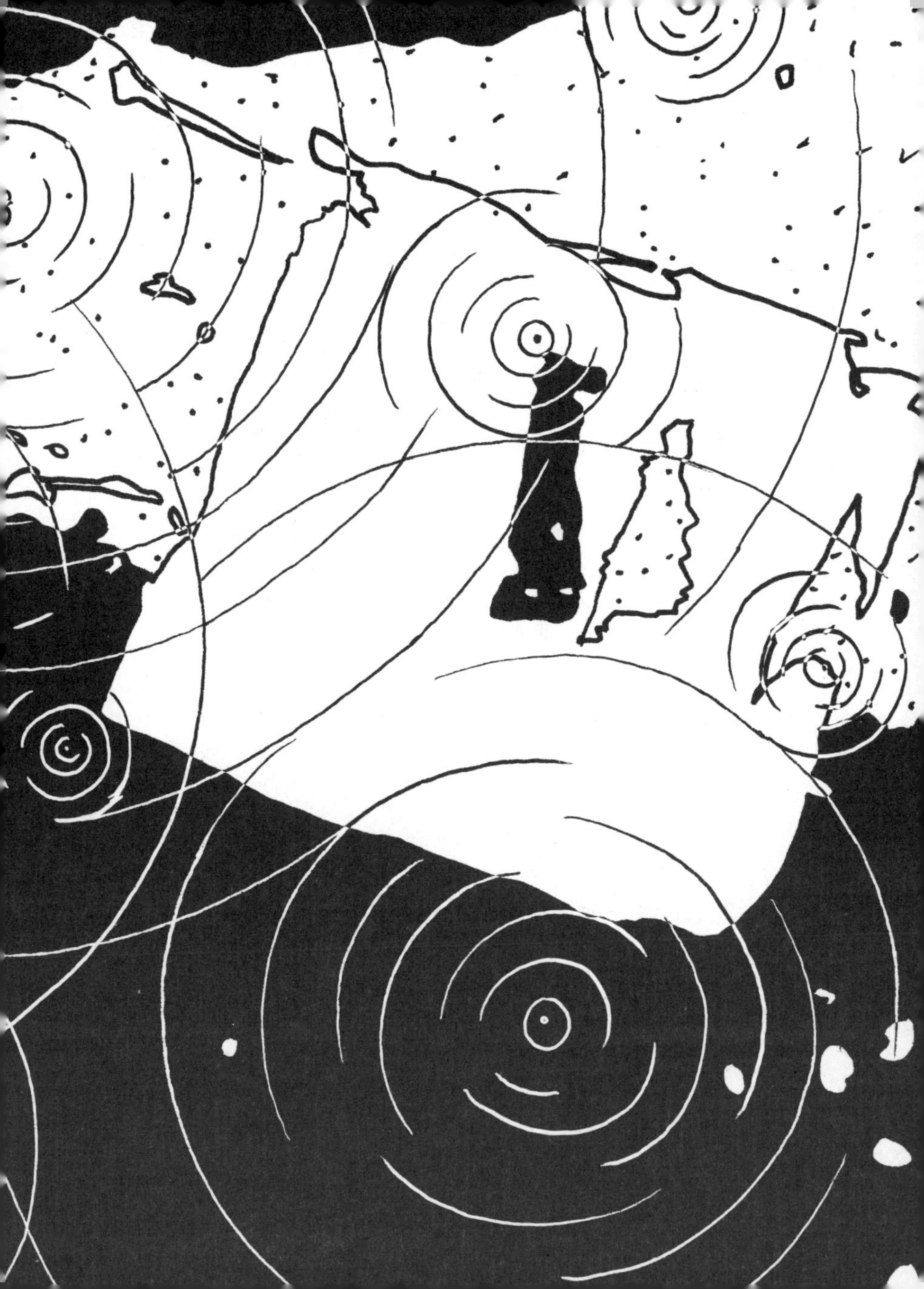

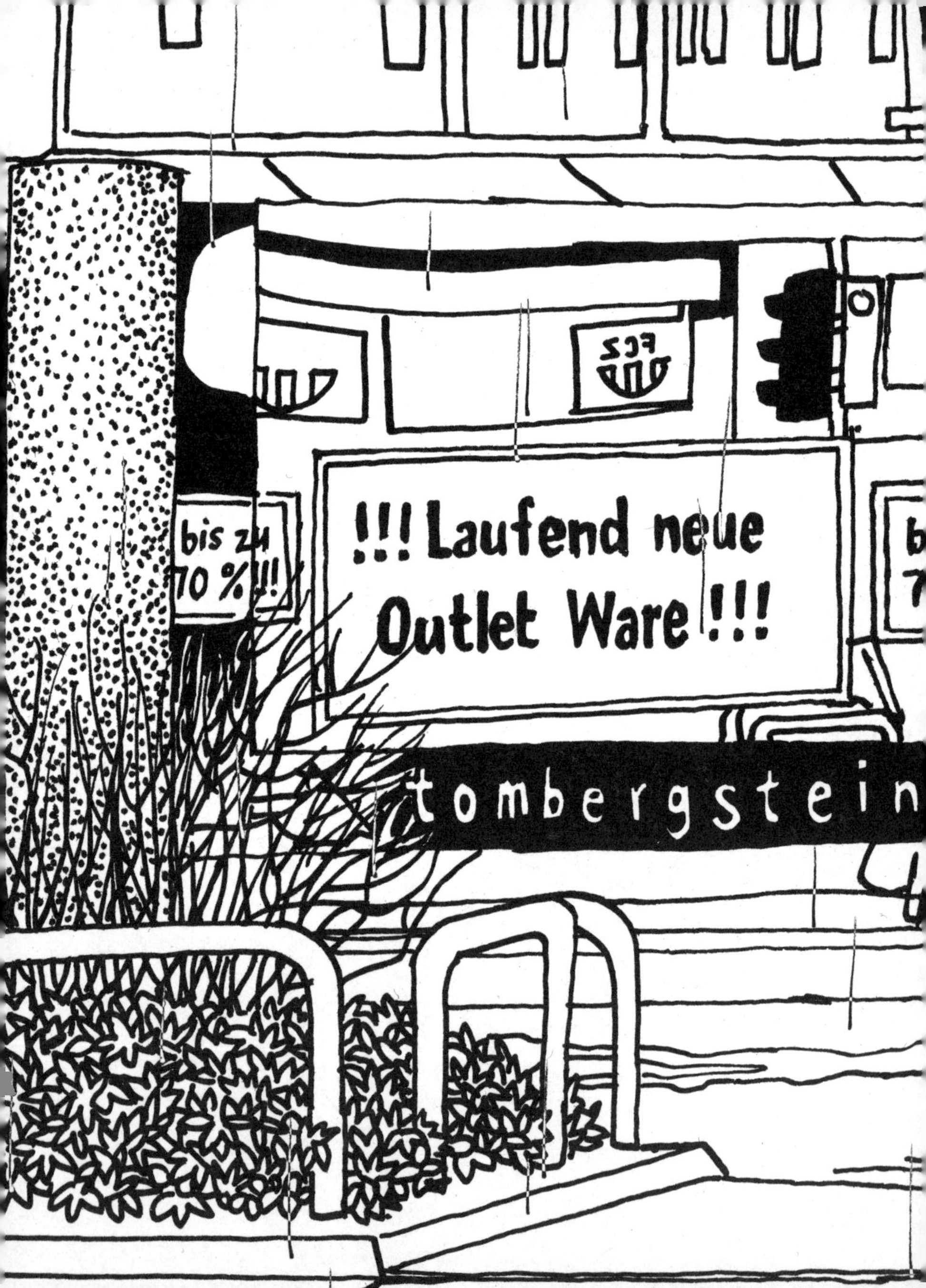

FC2
bis zu
70 %!!!
!!! Laufend neue
Outlet Ware !!!
b
7
tombergstein

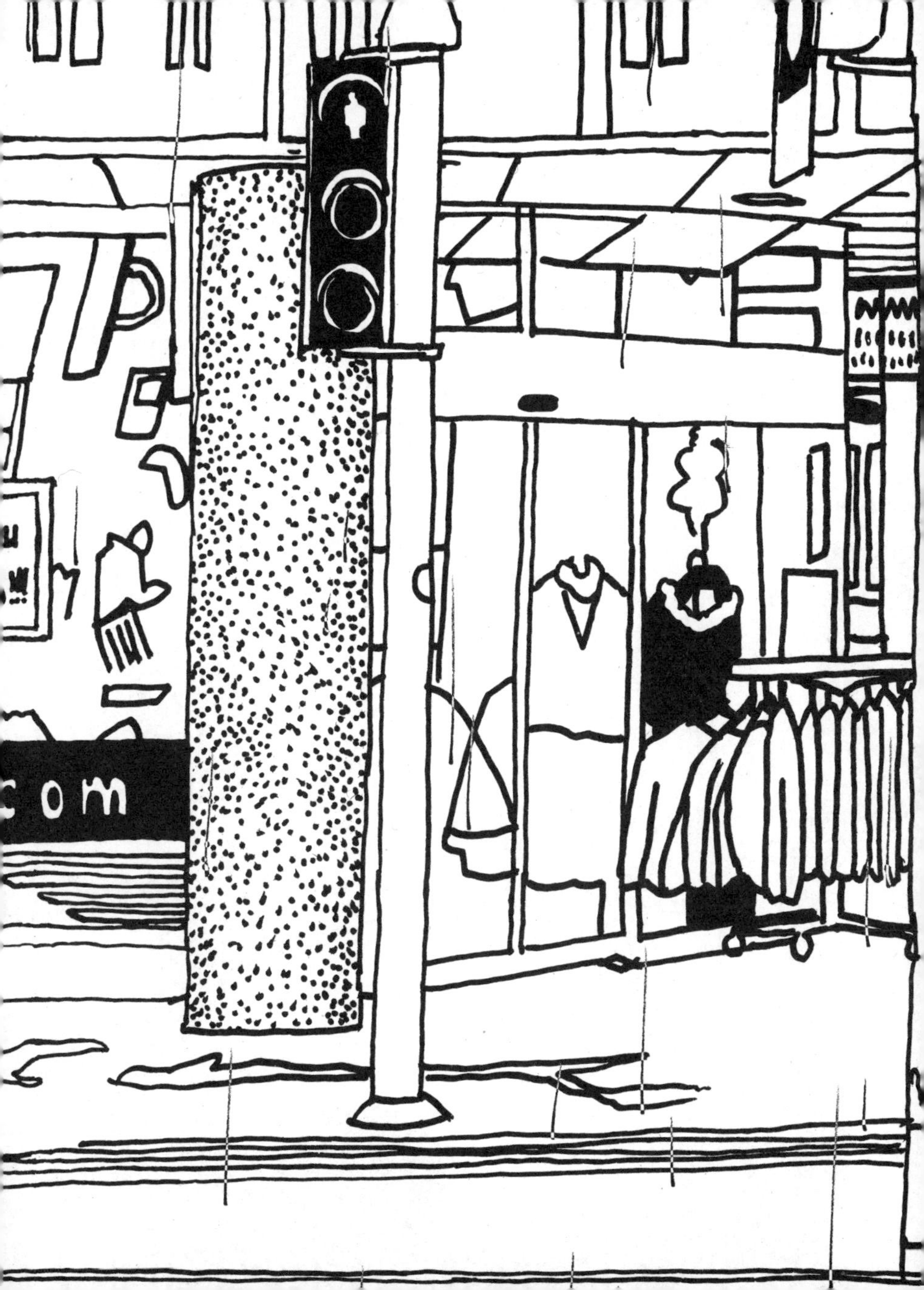

com

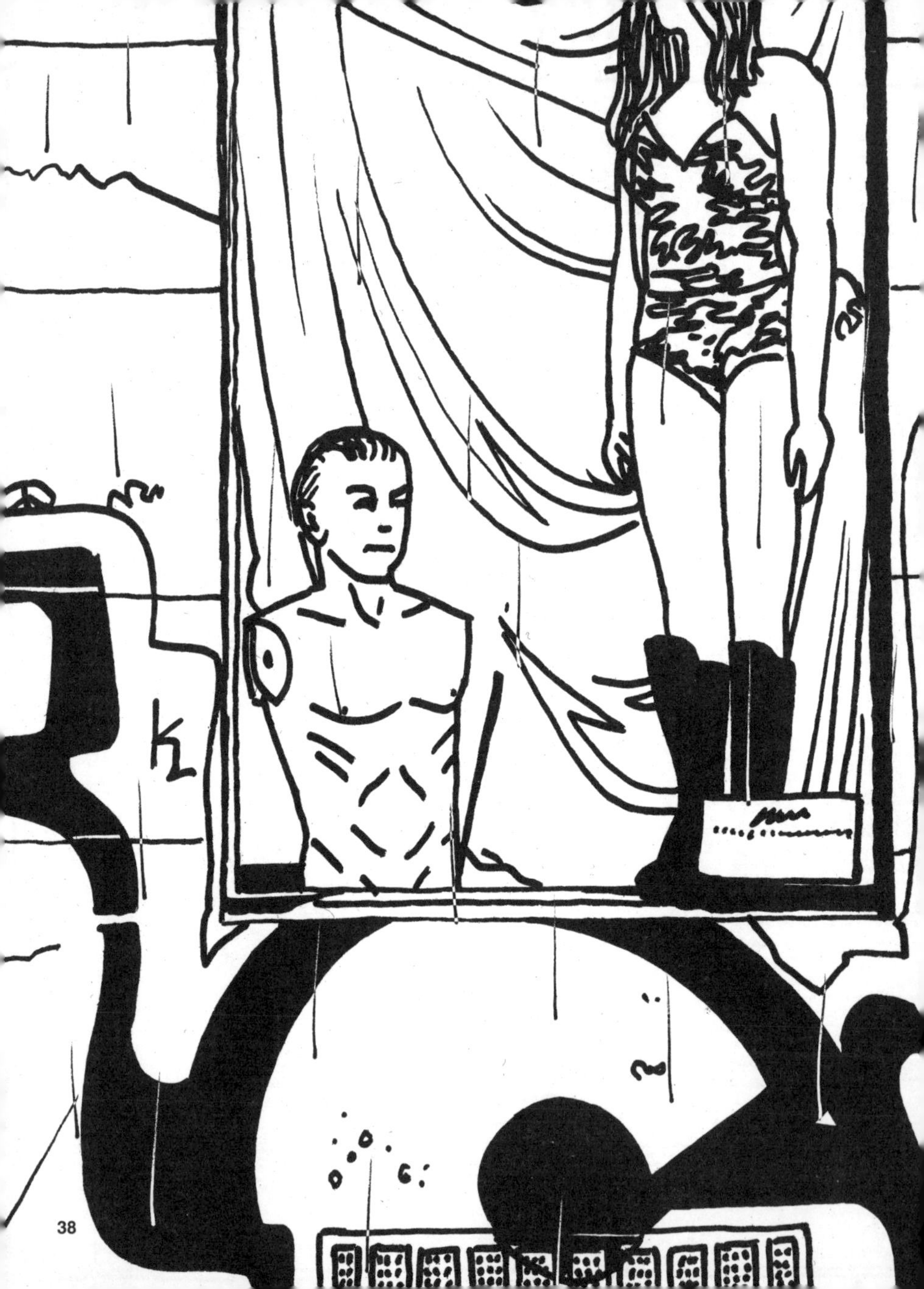

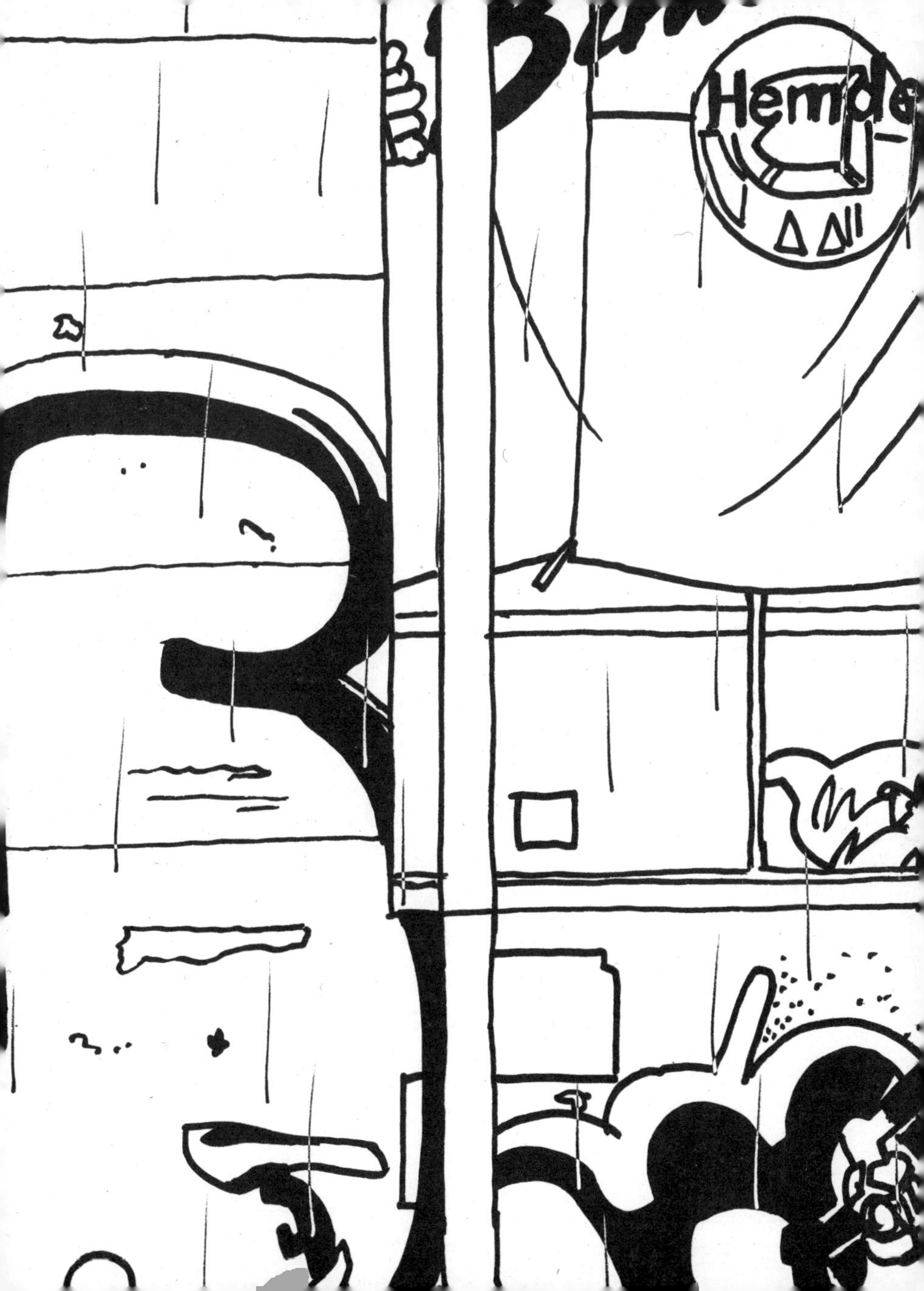

Herrde
Δ Δll

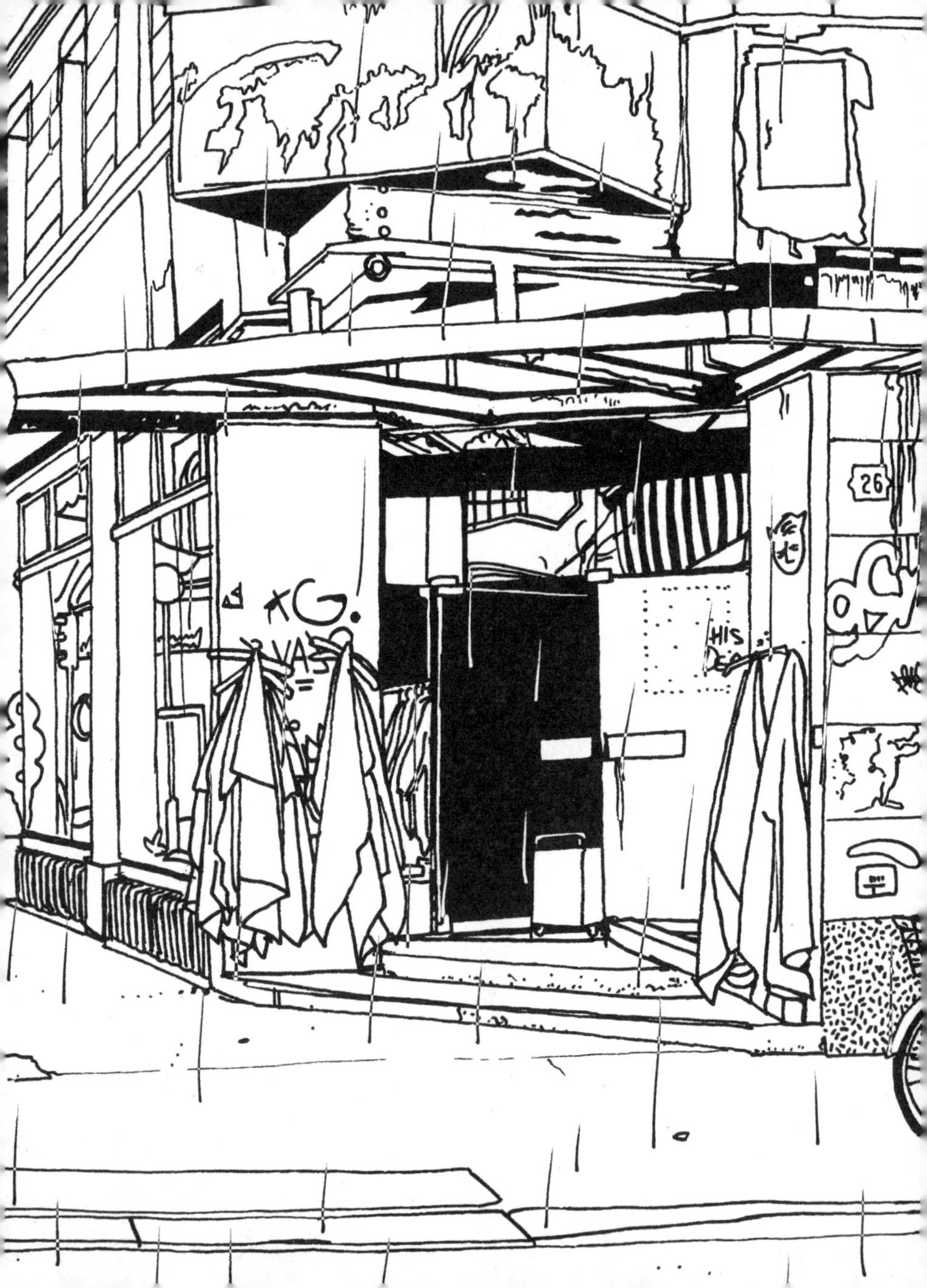

KG.
VAS
HIS
26

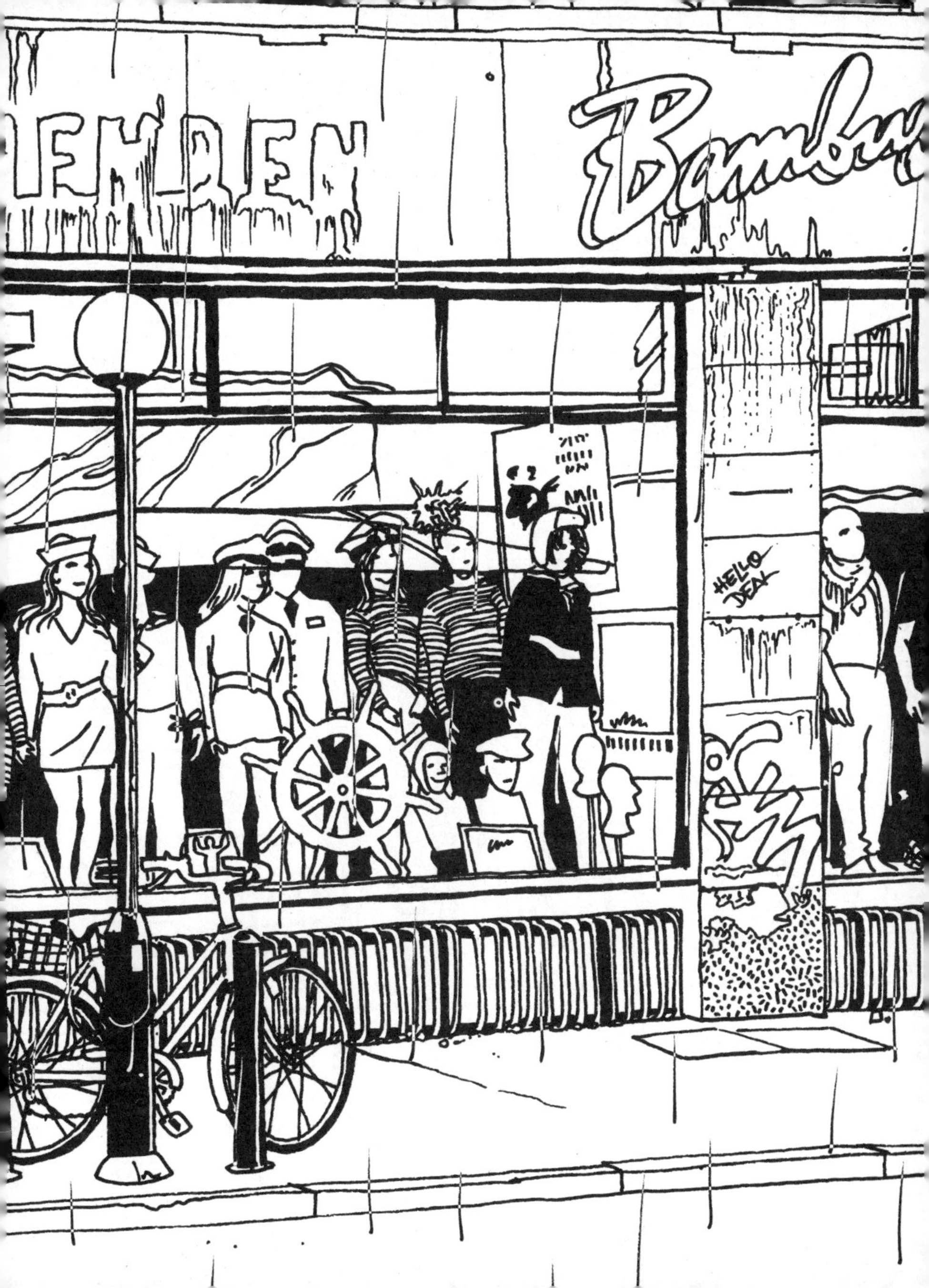

EMDEN
Bambu
HELLO
DEAL

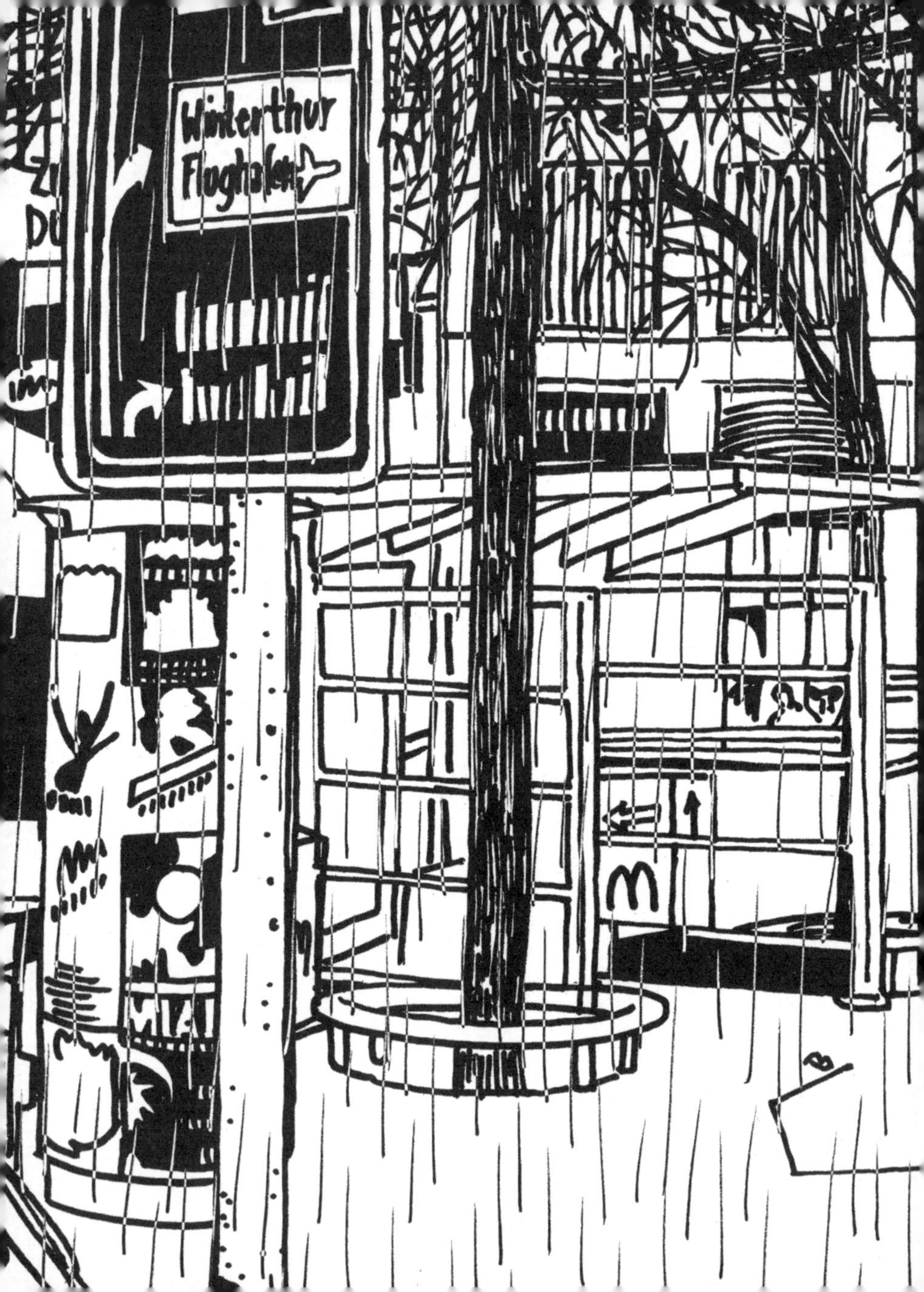
Winterthur
Flughafen

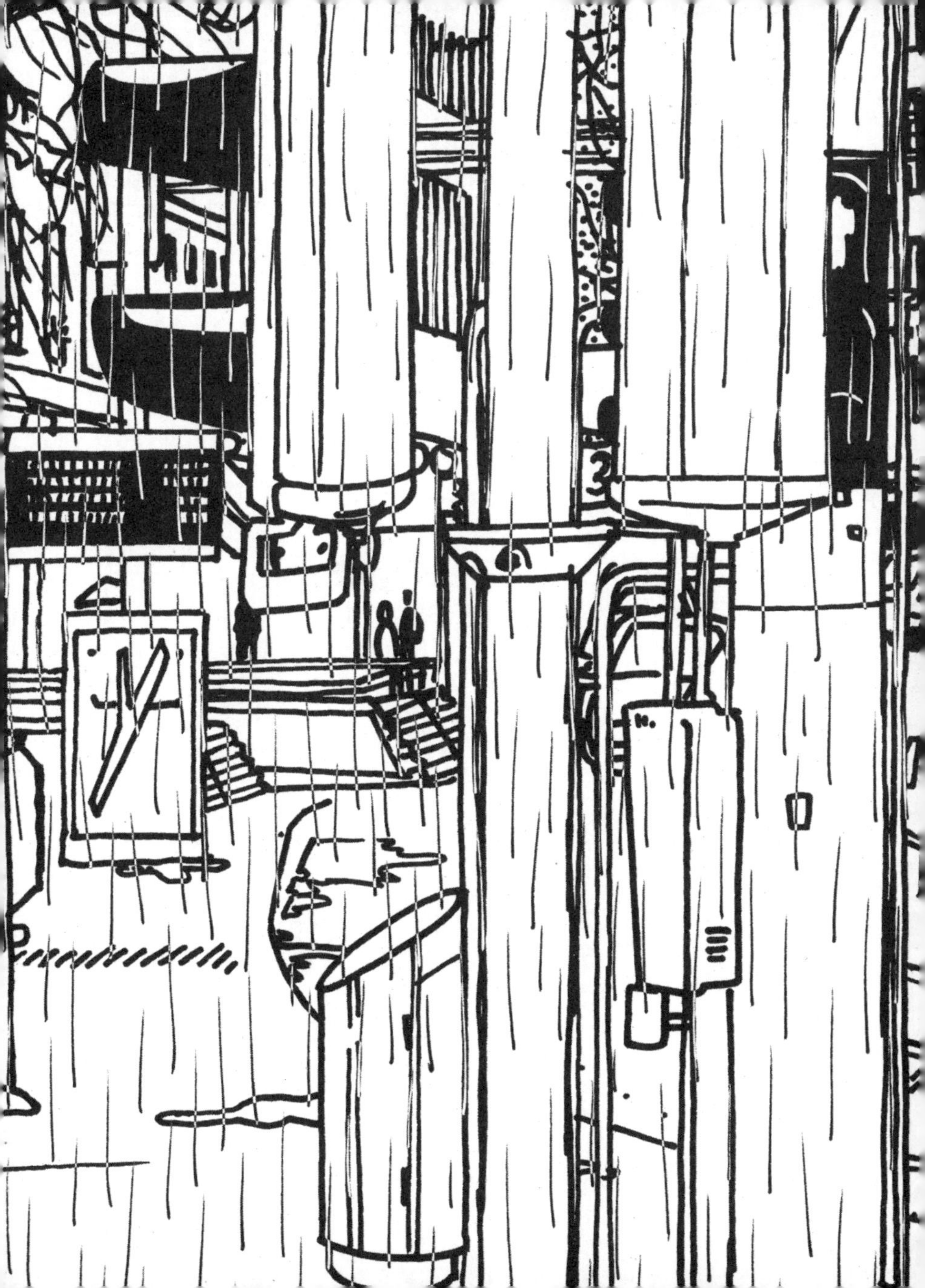

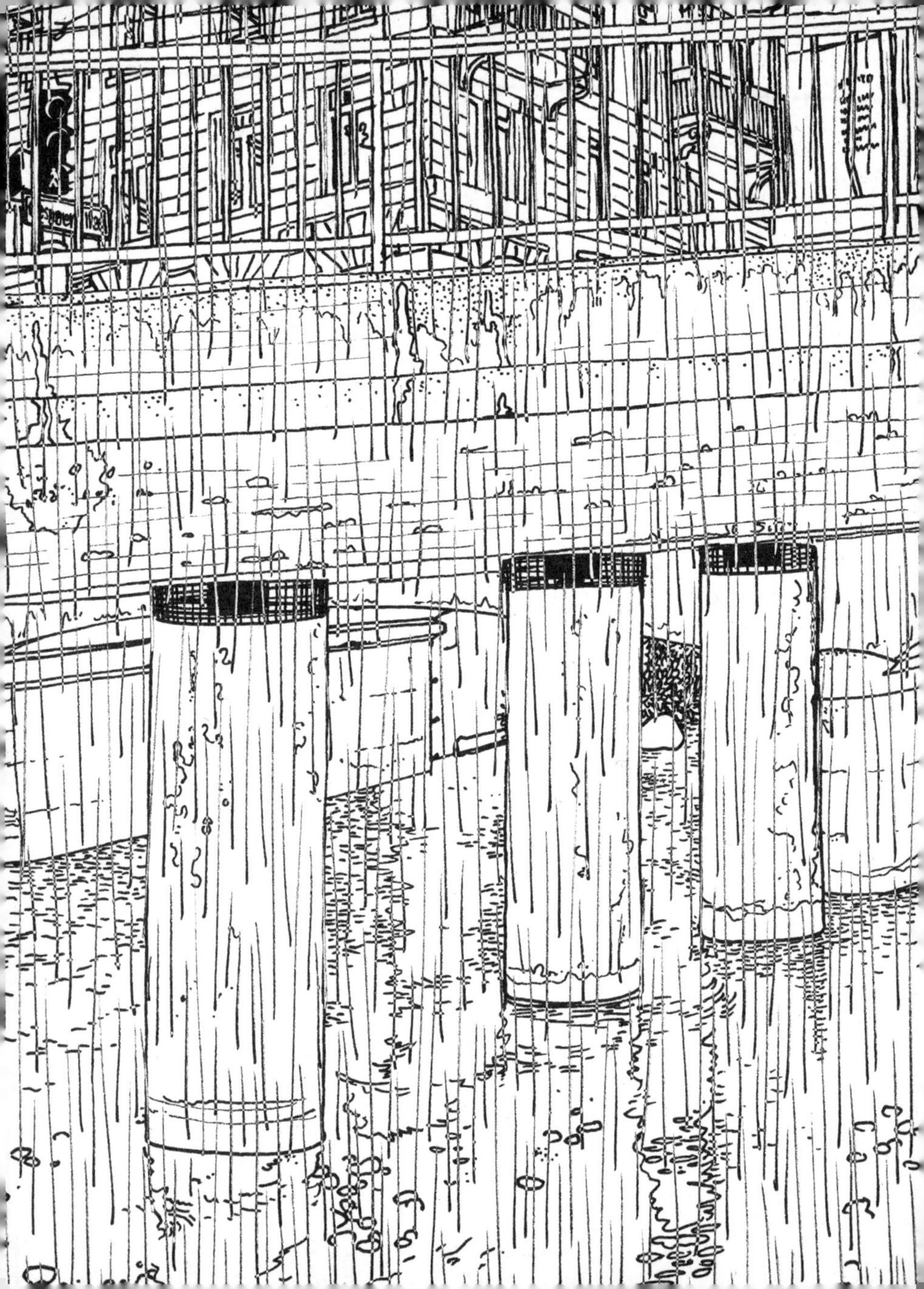

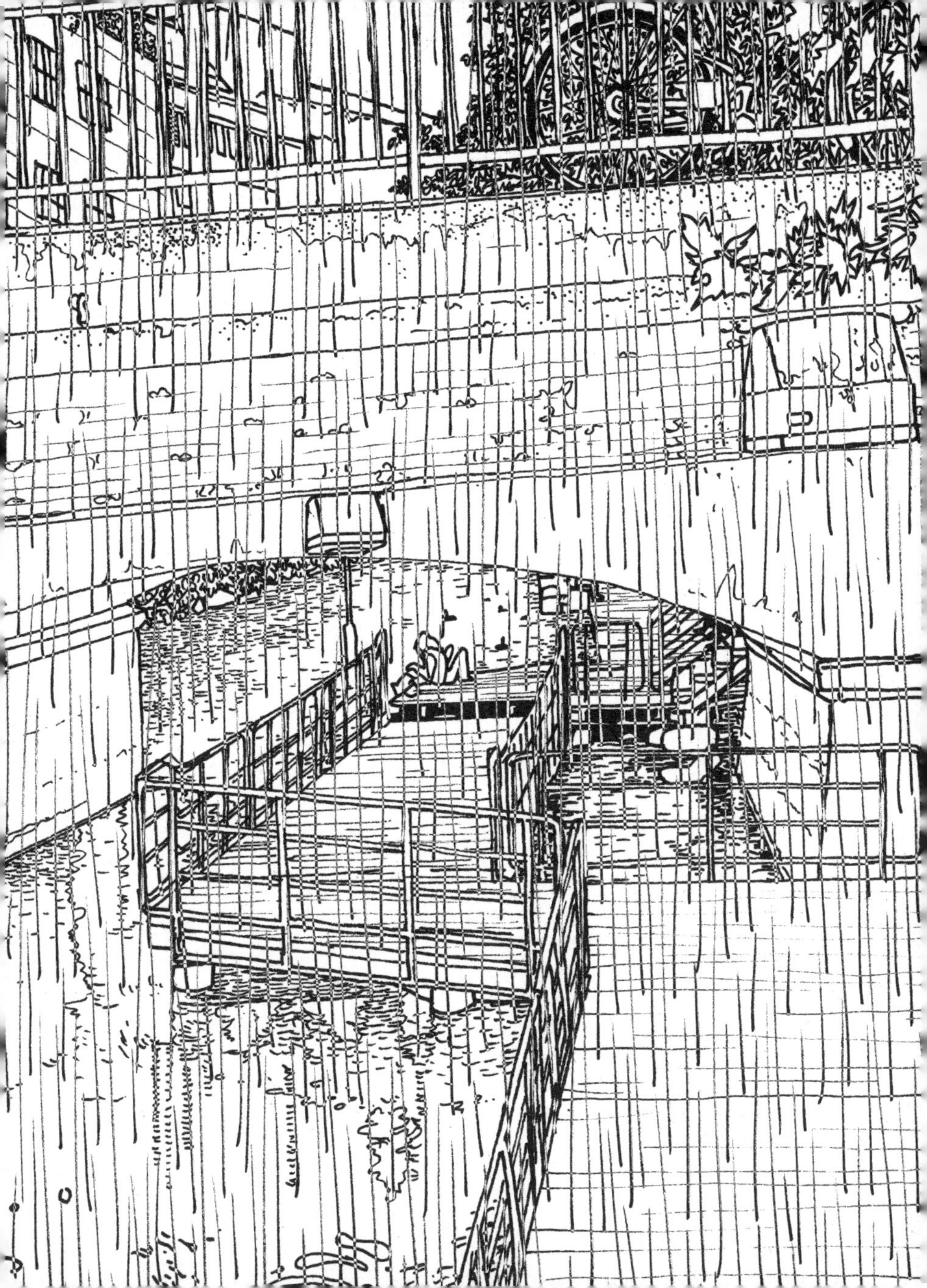

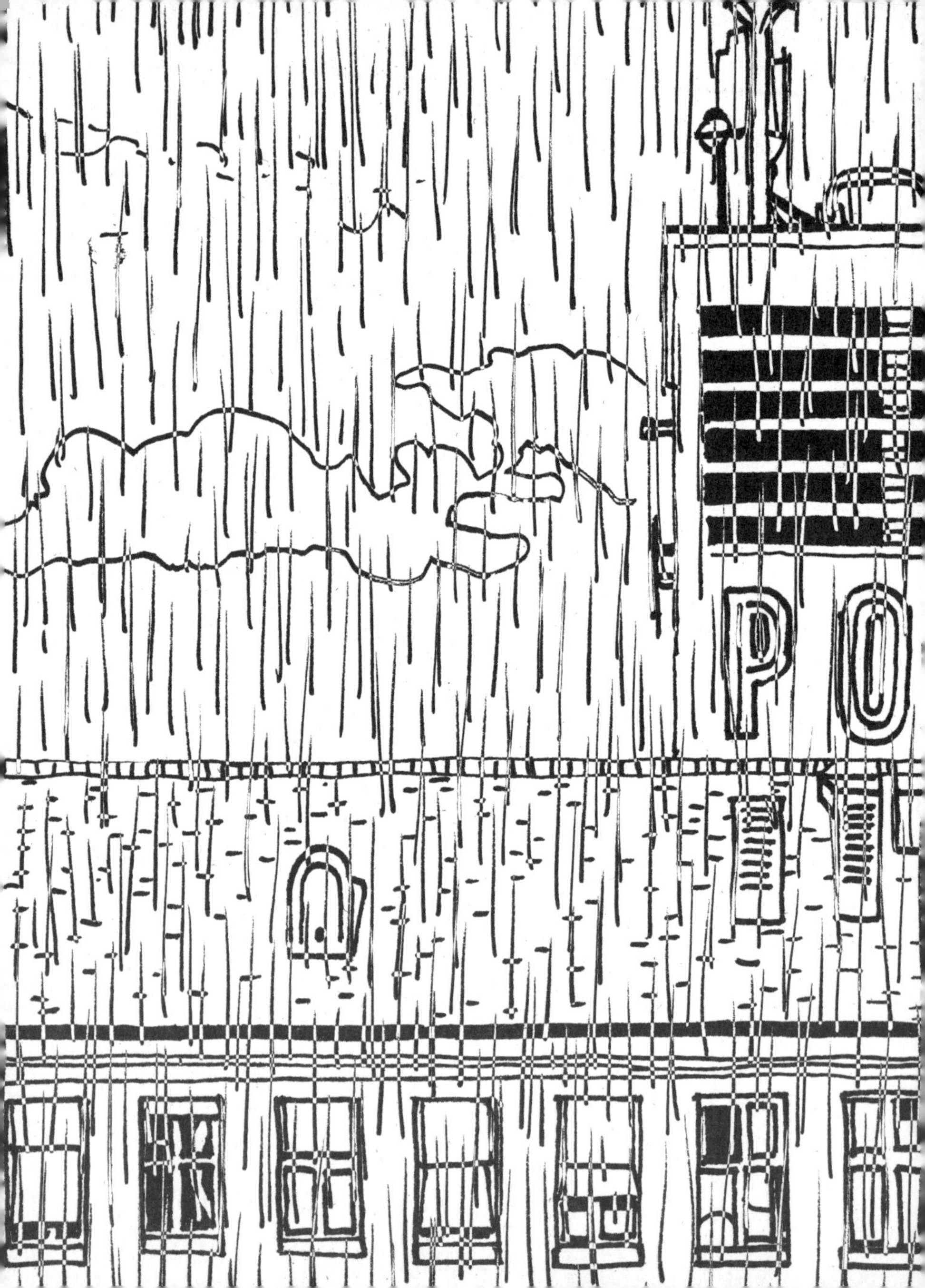

P O

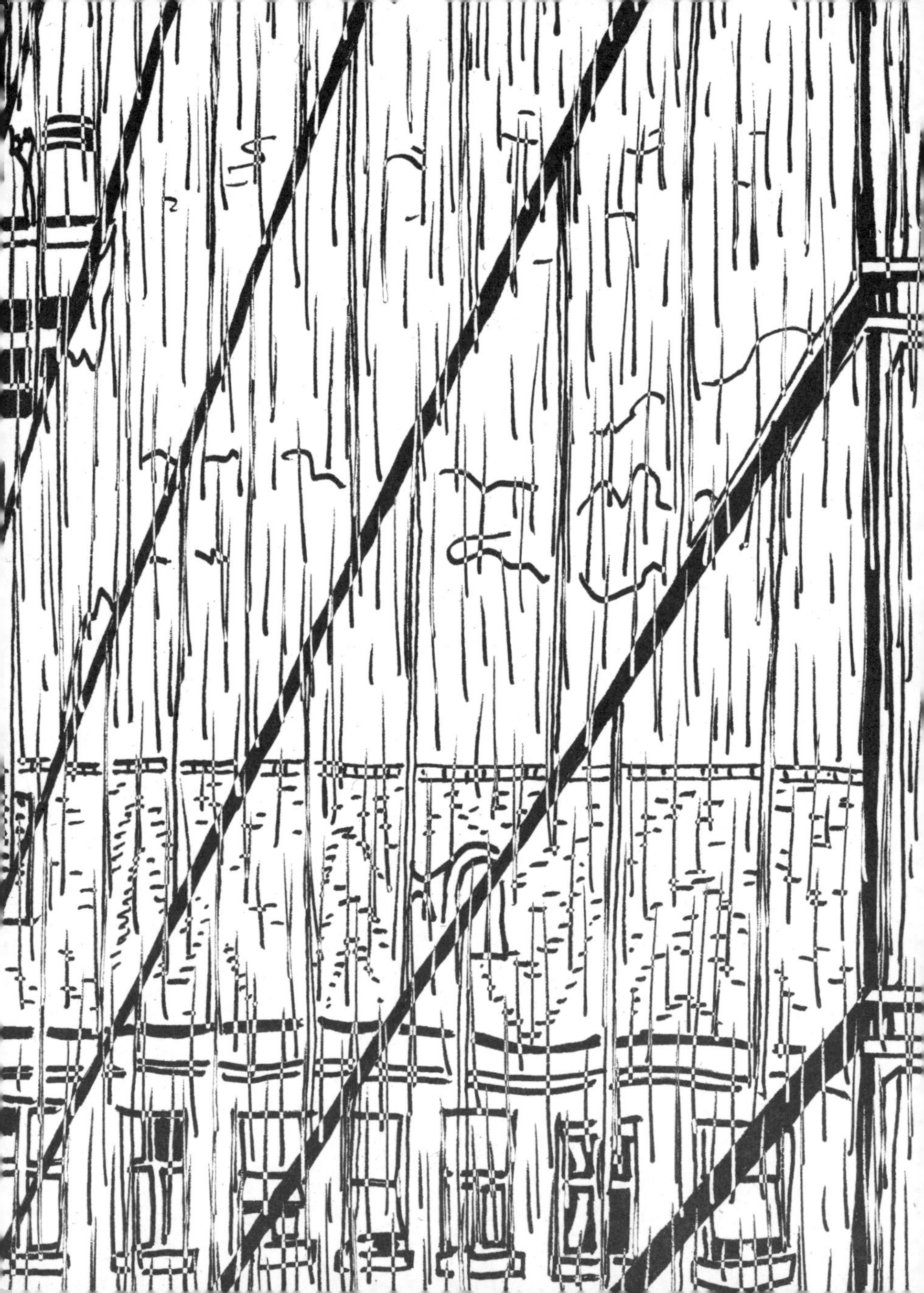

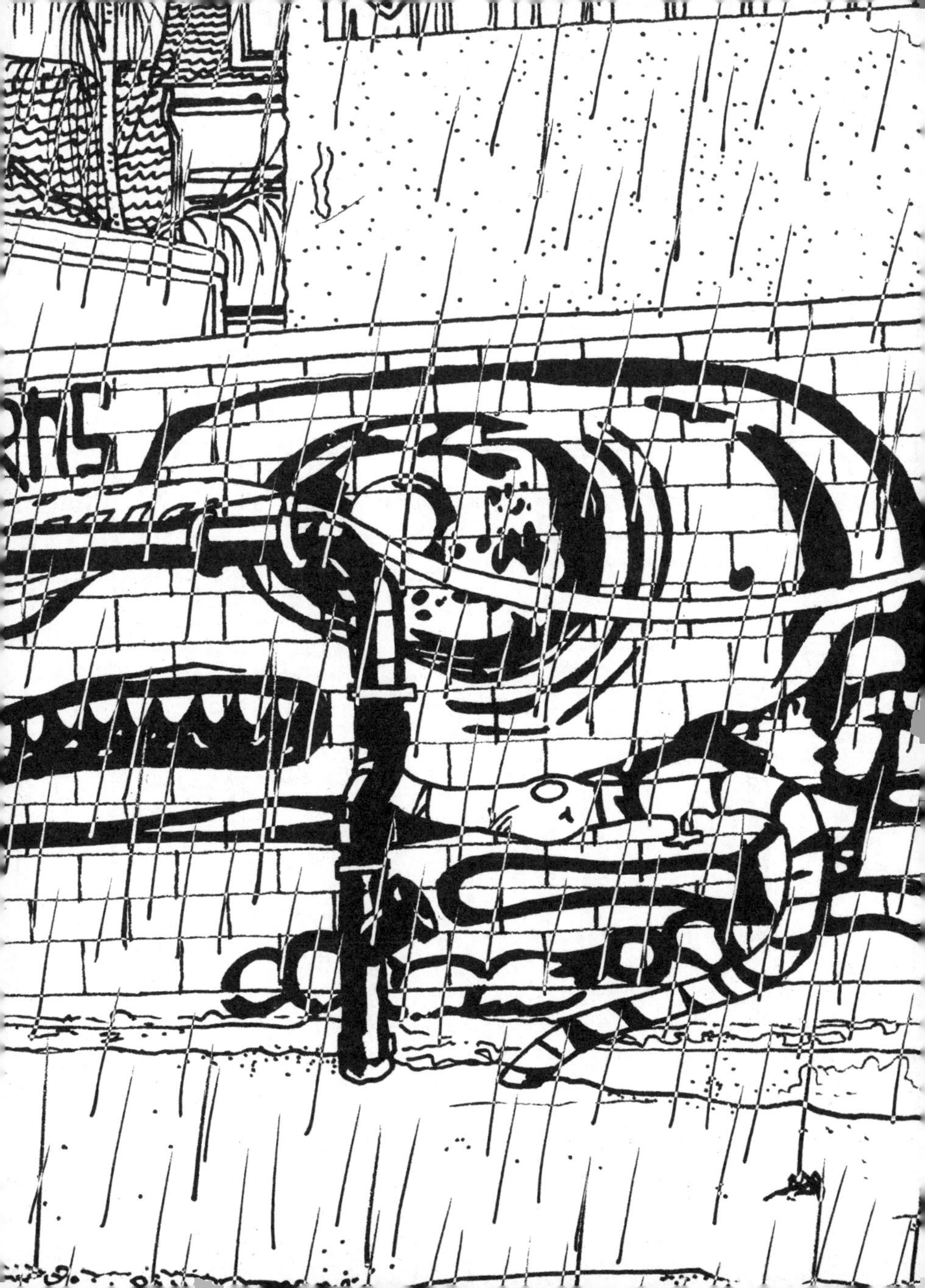

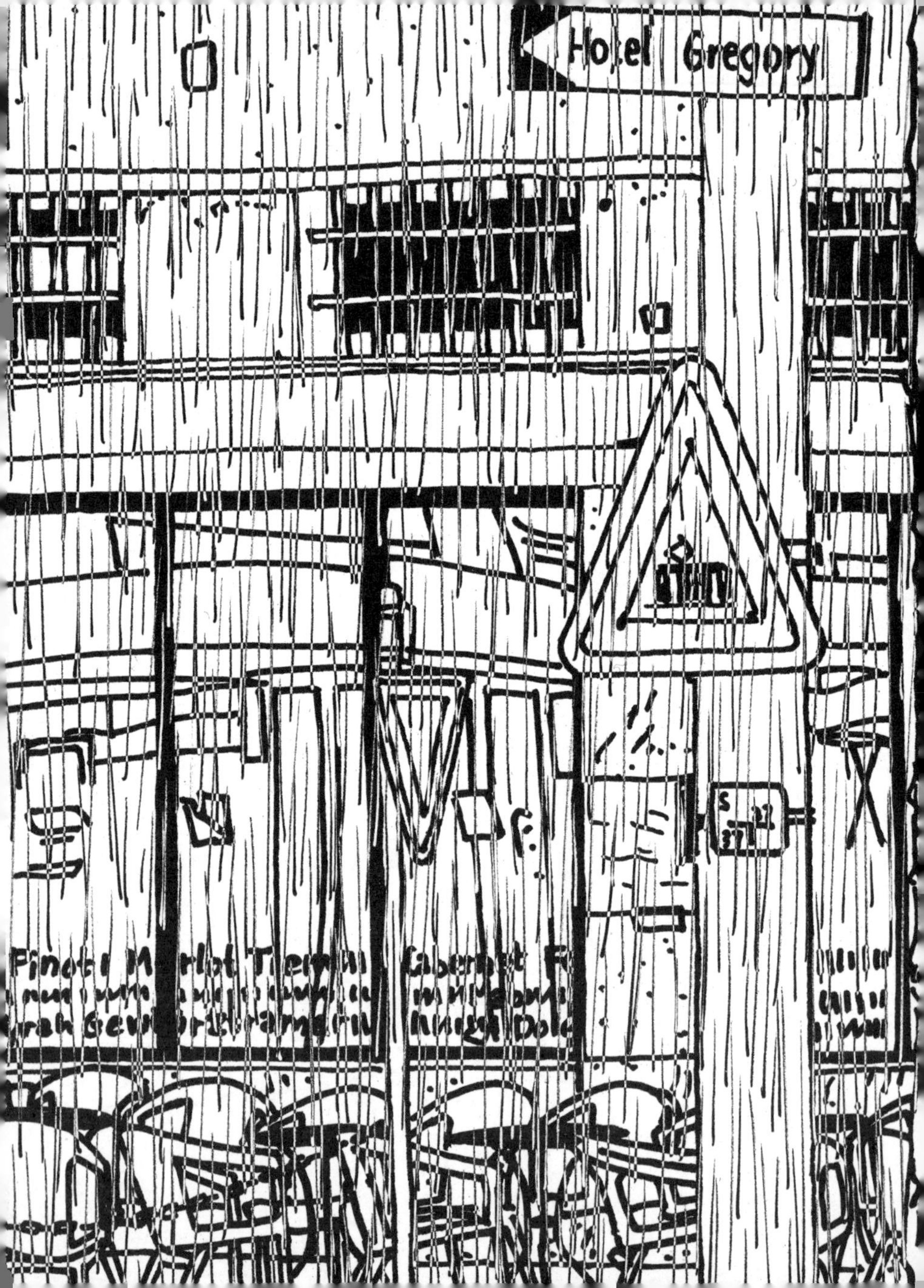

Hotel Gregory

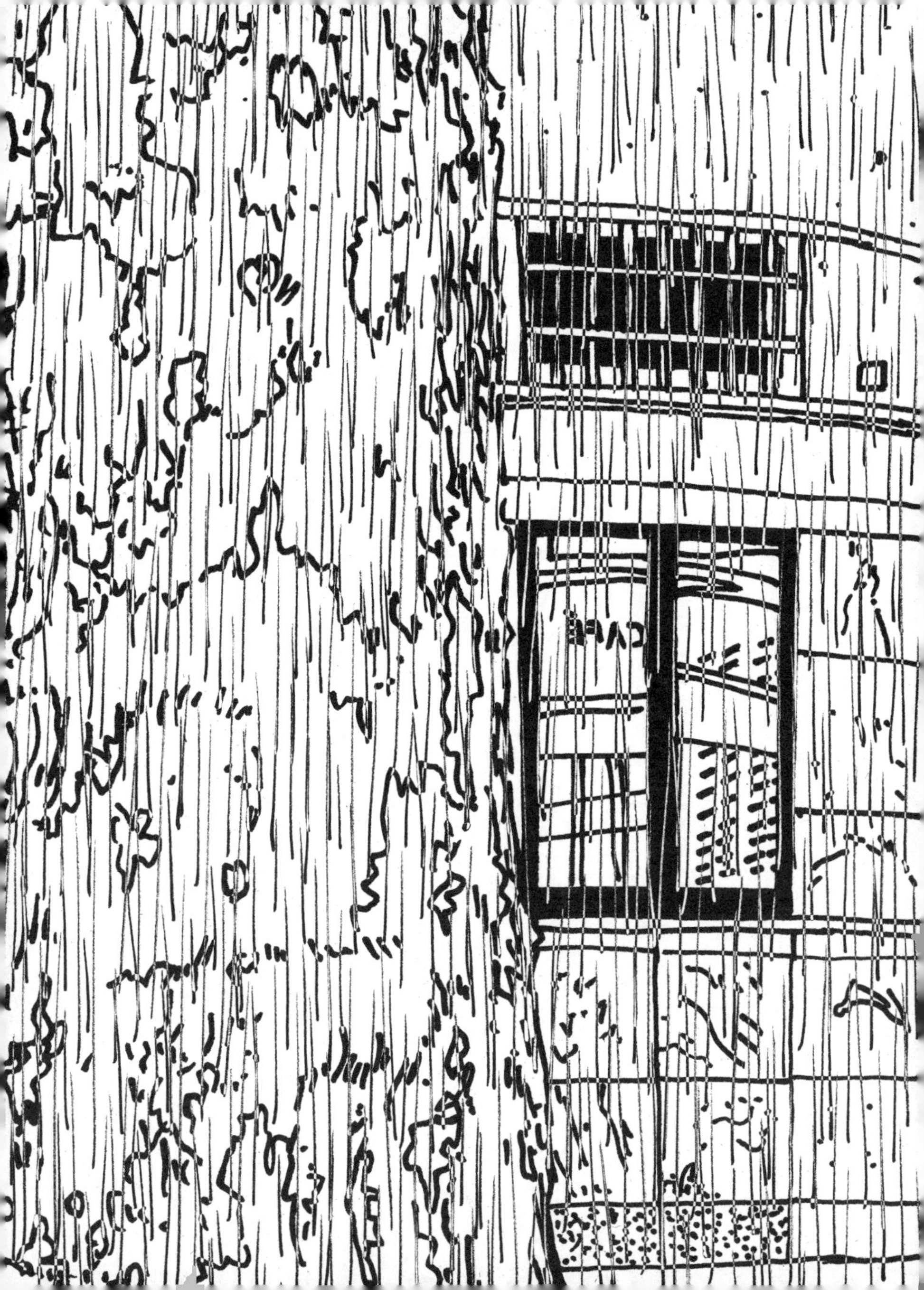
CAFÉ

HANDY
MART
SOLO
MART

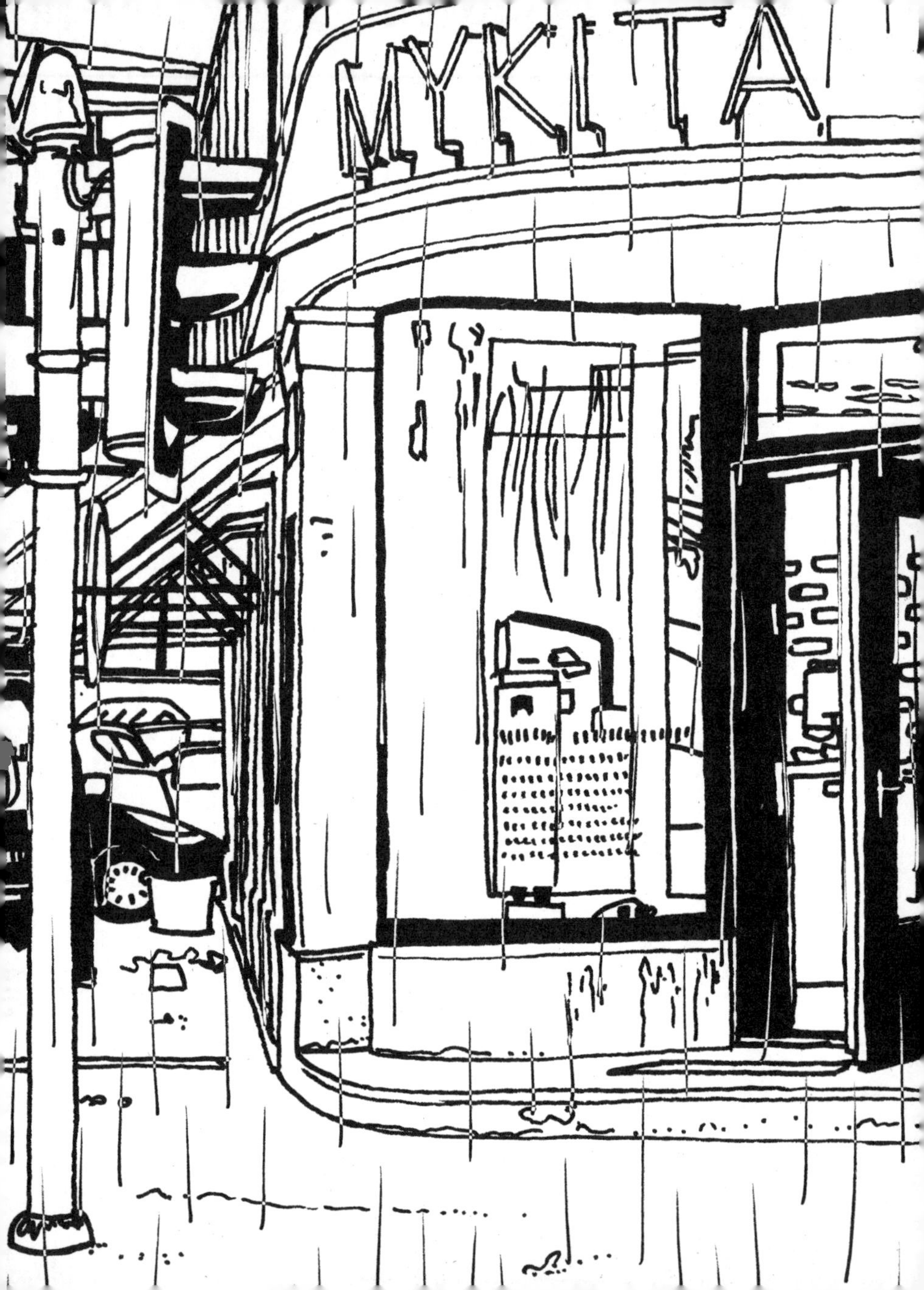

MYKITA

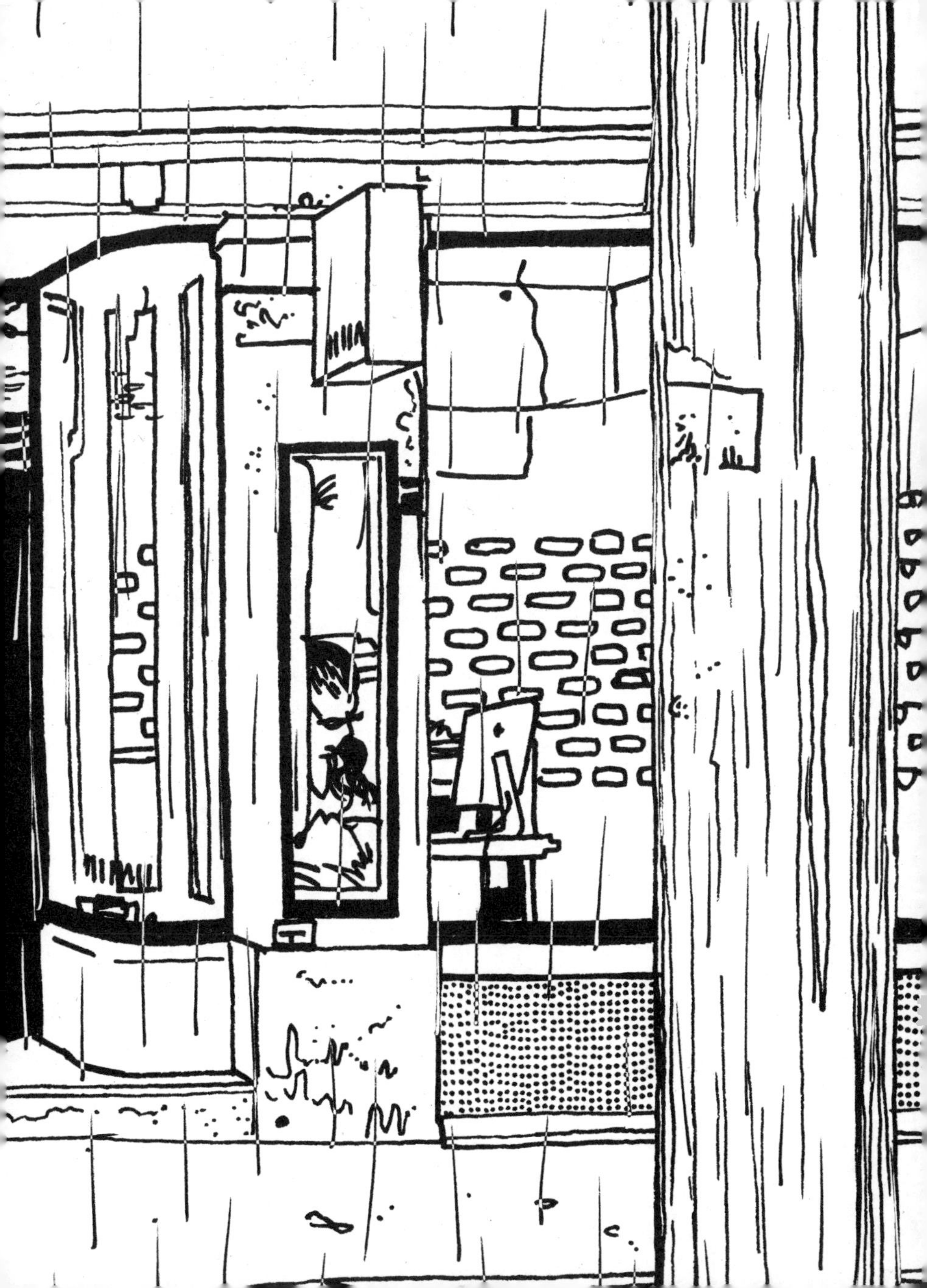

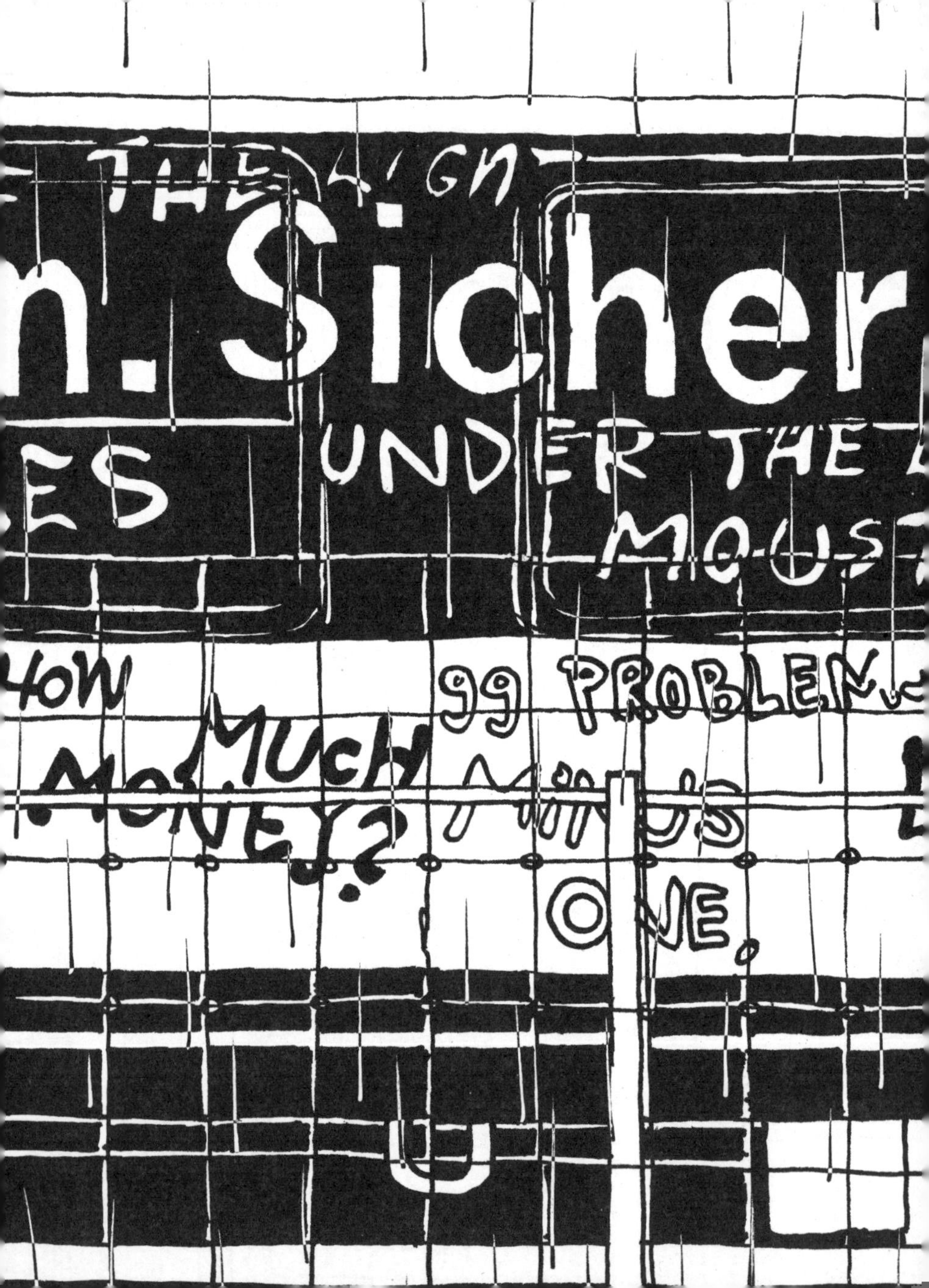
THE SIGN
m. Sicher
ES
UNDER THE
MOUS
HOW
99 PROBLEM
MUCH
MONEY?
MINUS
ONE.

im Job.
SHIT IS THE
DARK
IS THE
LIFE IS STILL GOOD
LUCKY
MOTHERF*CKR

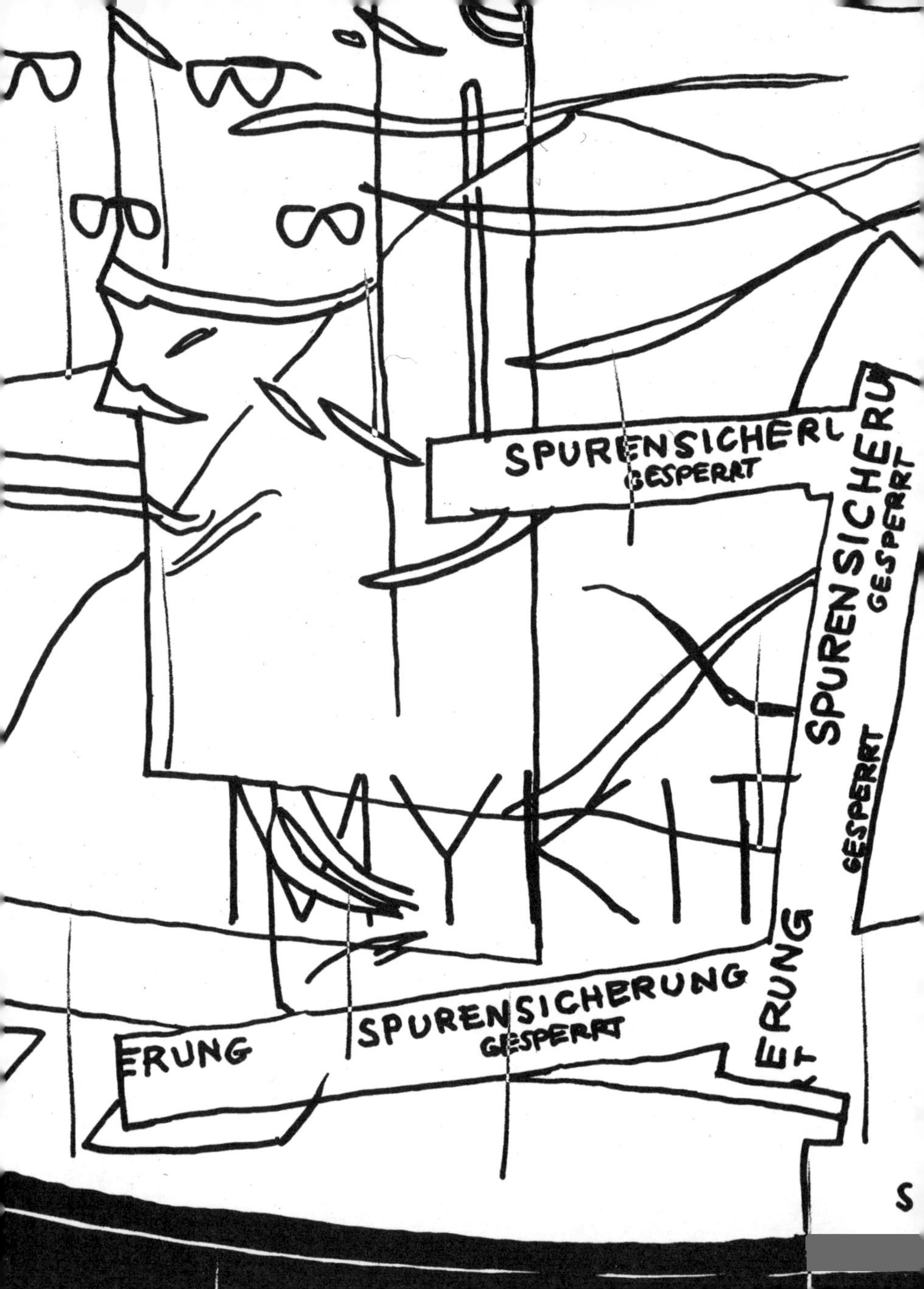
SPURENSICHERL
GESPERRT
SPURENSICHER
GESPERRT
SPURENSICHER
GESPERRT
GESPERRT
MYKIT
ERUNG
SPURENSICHERUNG
GESPERRT
ERUNG
S

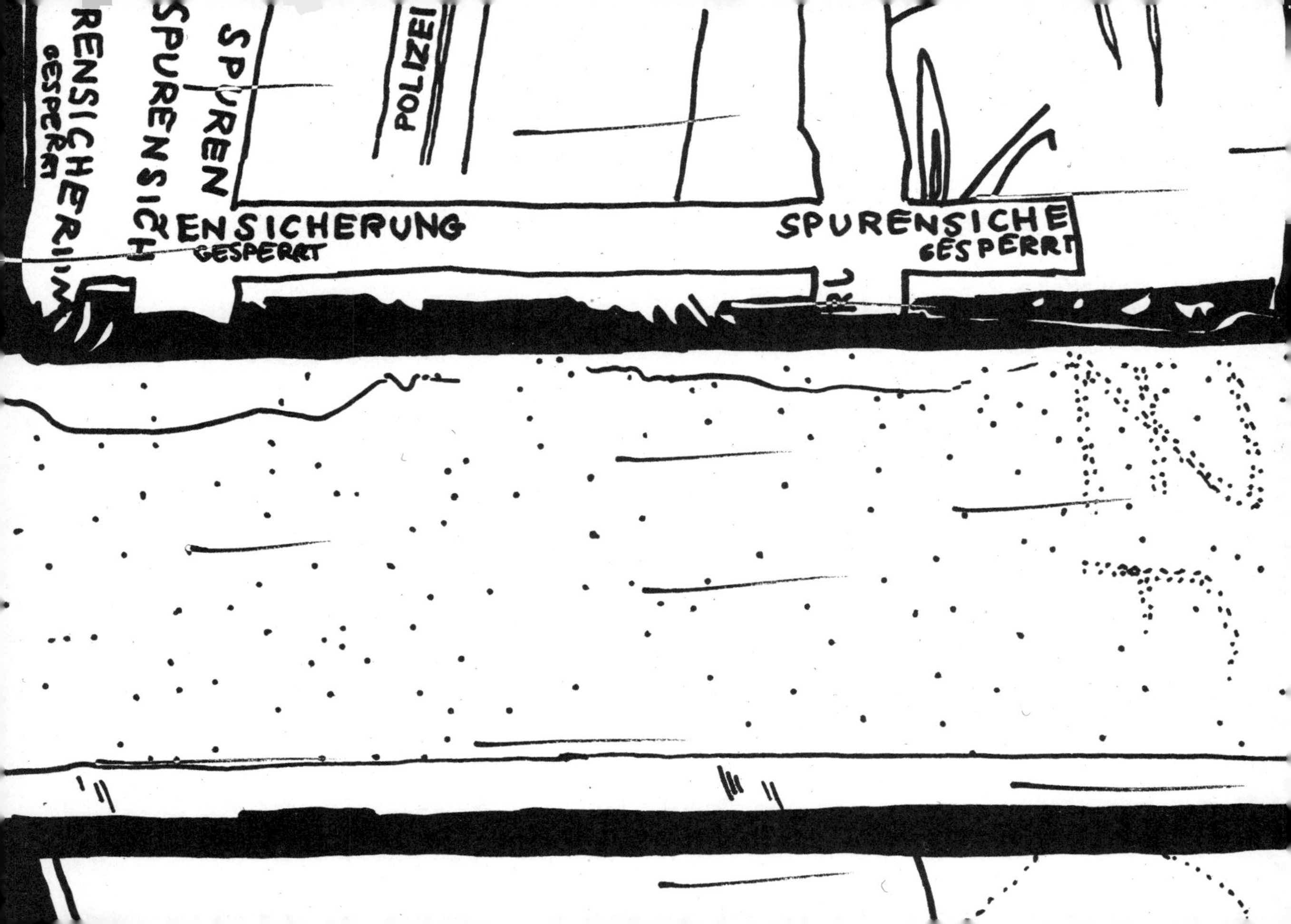

SPUREN
SPURENSICH
RENSICHERUN GESPERRT
ENSICHERUNG GESPERRT
POLIZEI
SPURENSICHE GESPERRT

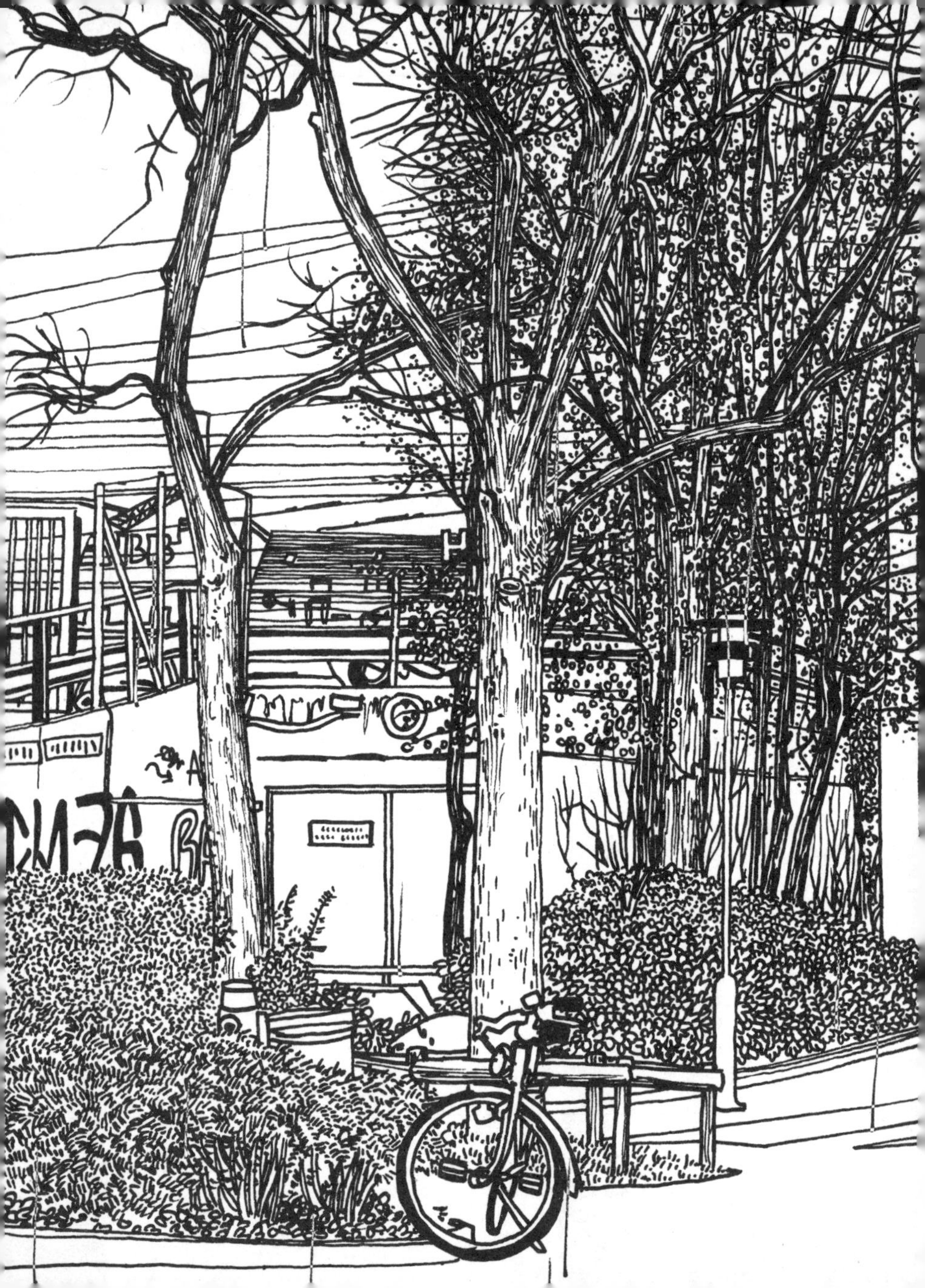

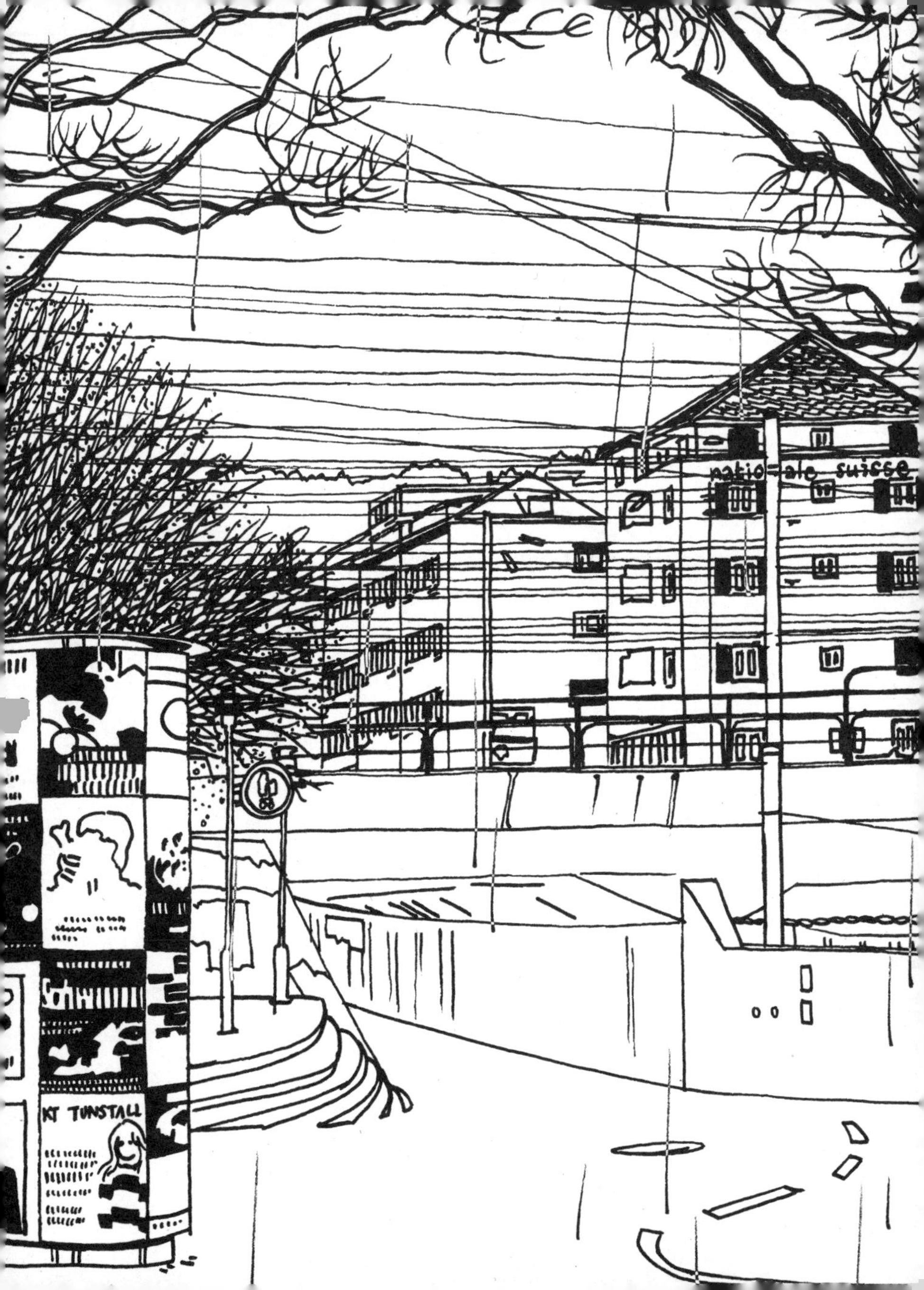

nationale suisse
Schwi
KT TUNSTALL

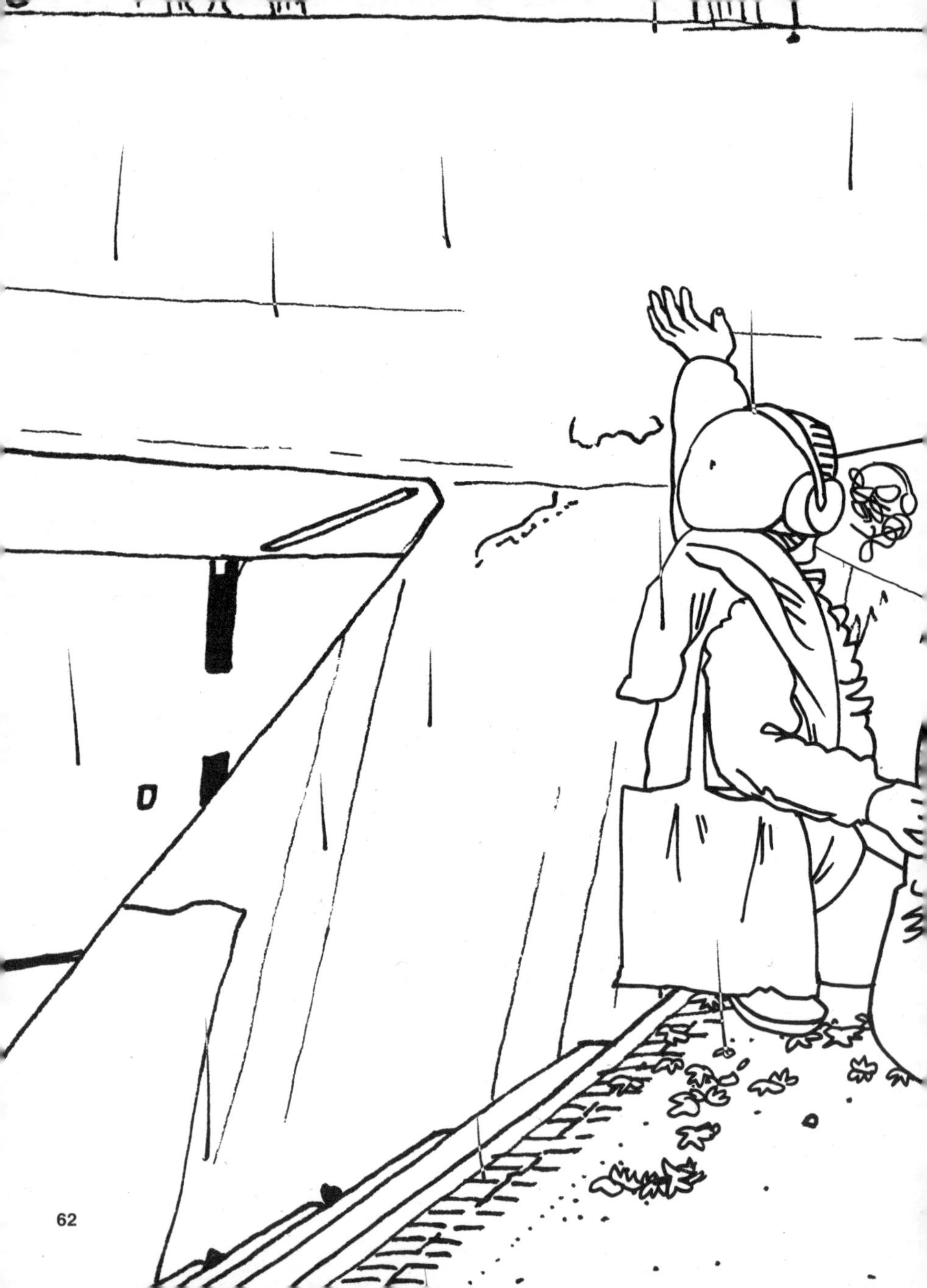

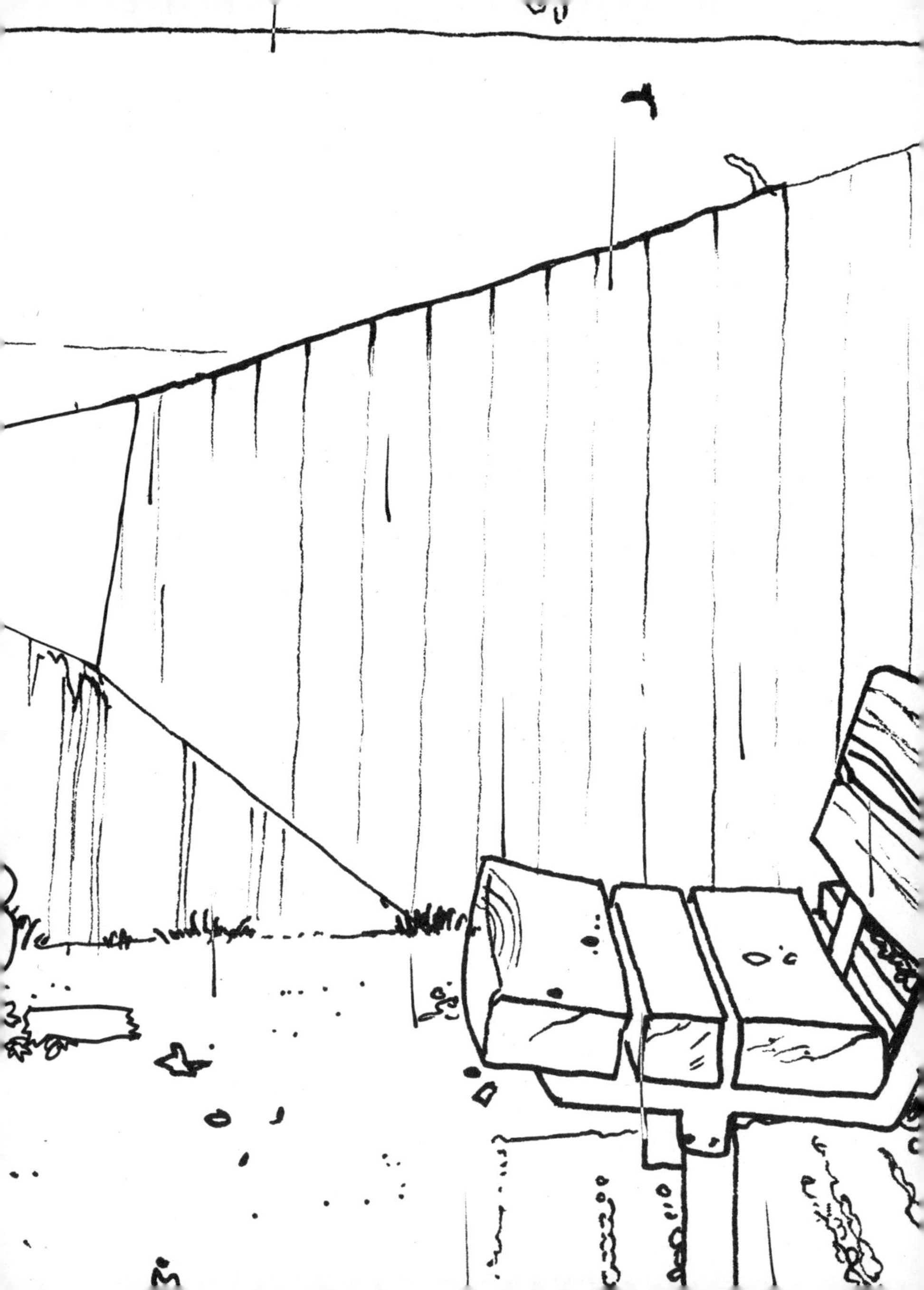

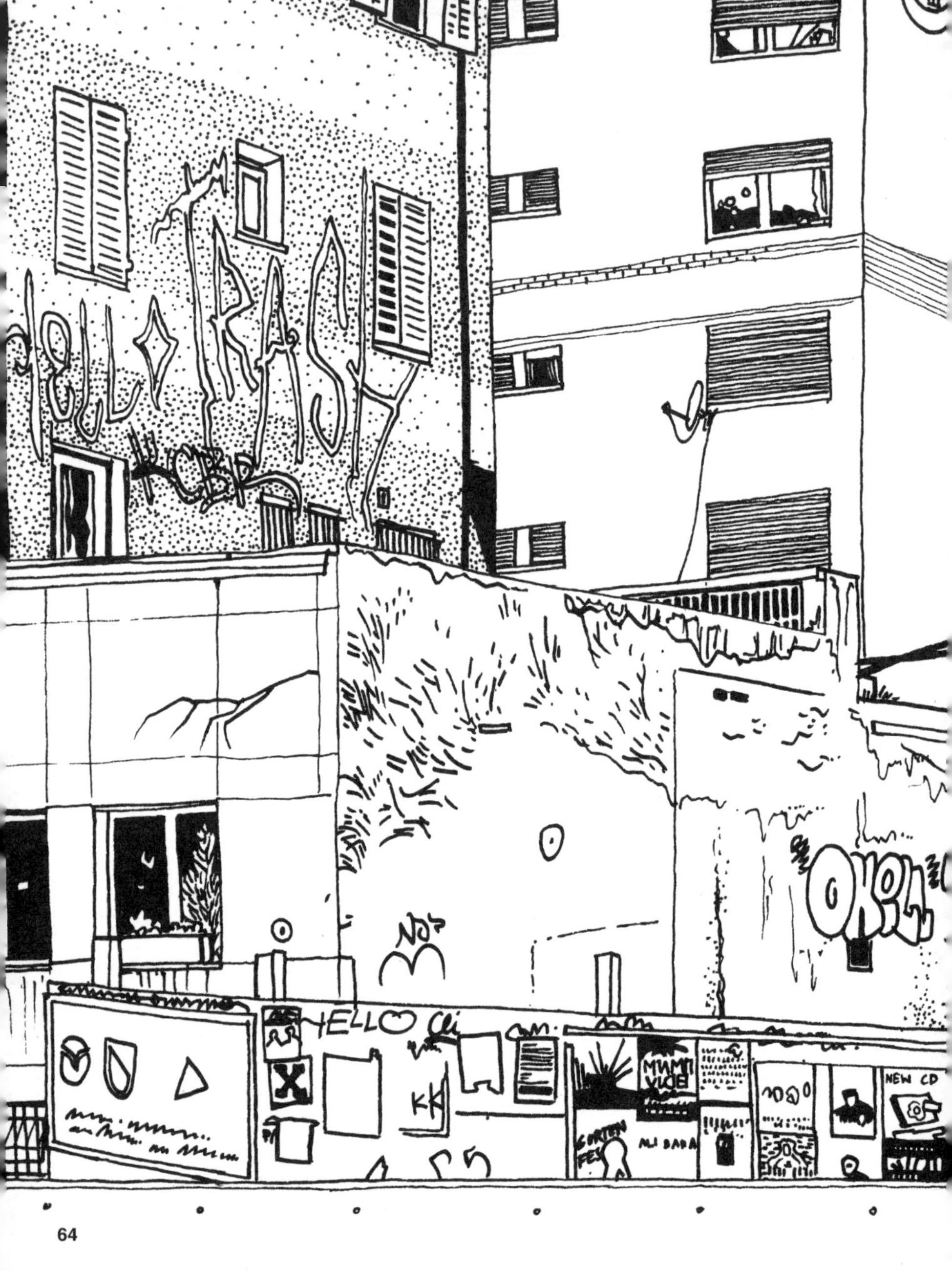
HELLO
NEW CD
MIAMI VICE

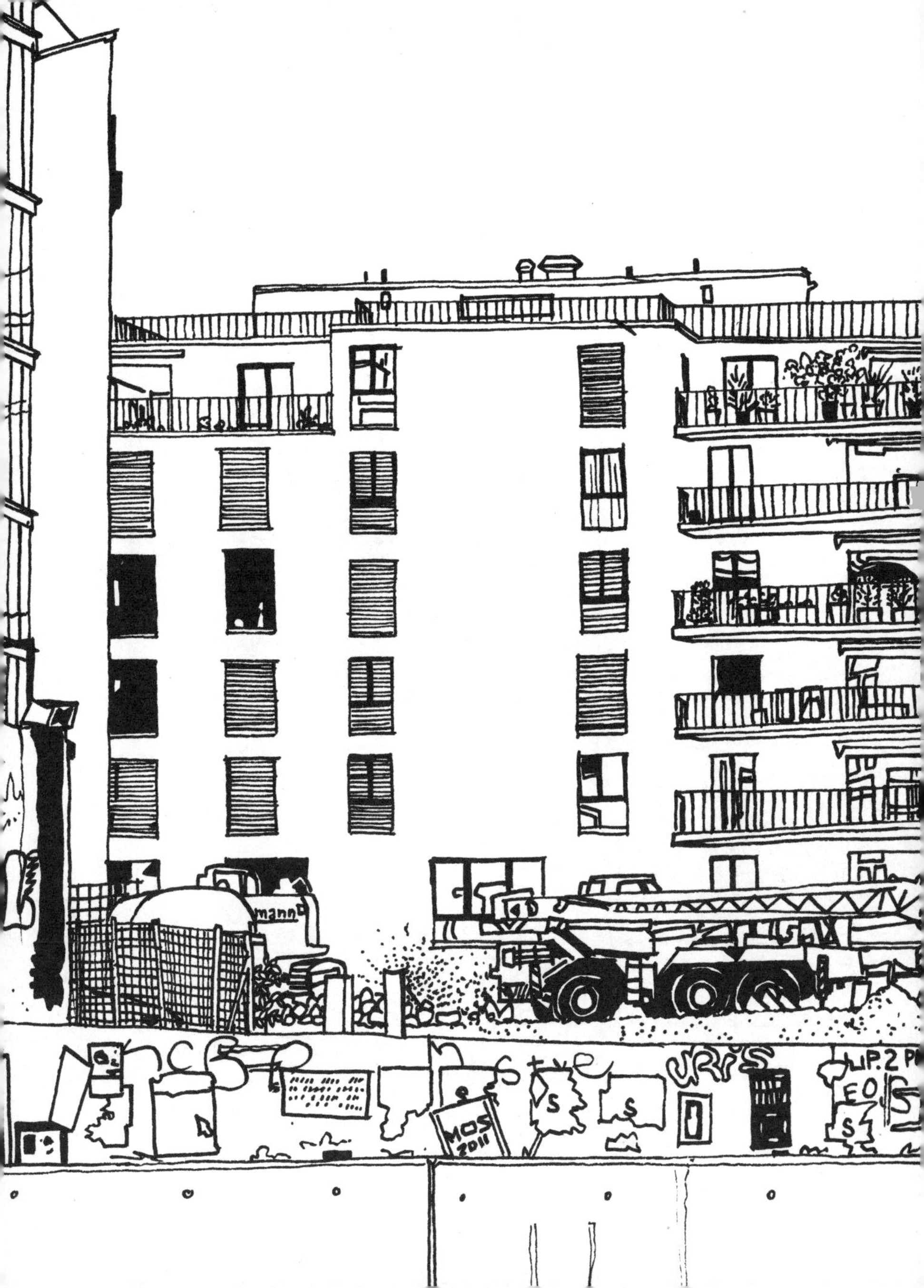
mann
MOS 2011
S
S
URI'S
LIP.2 P
EO
S
S

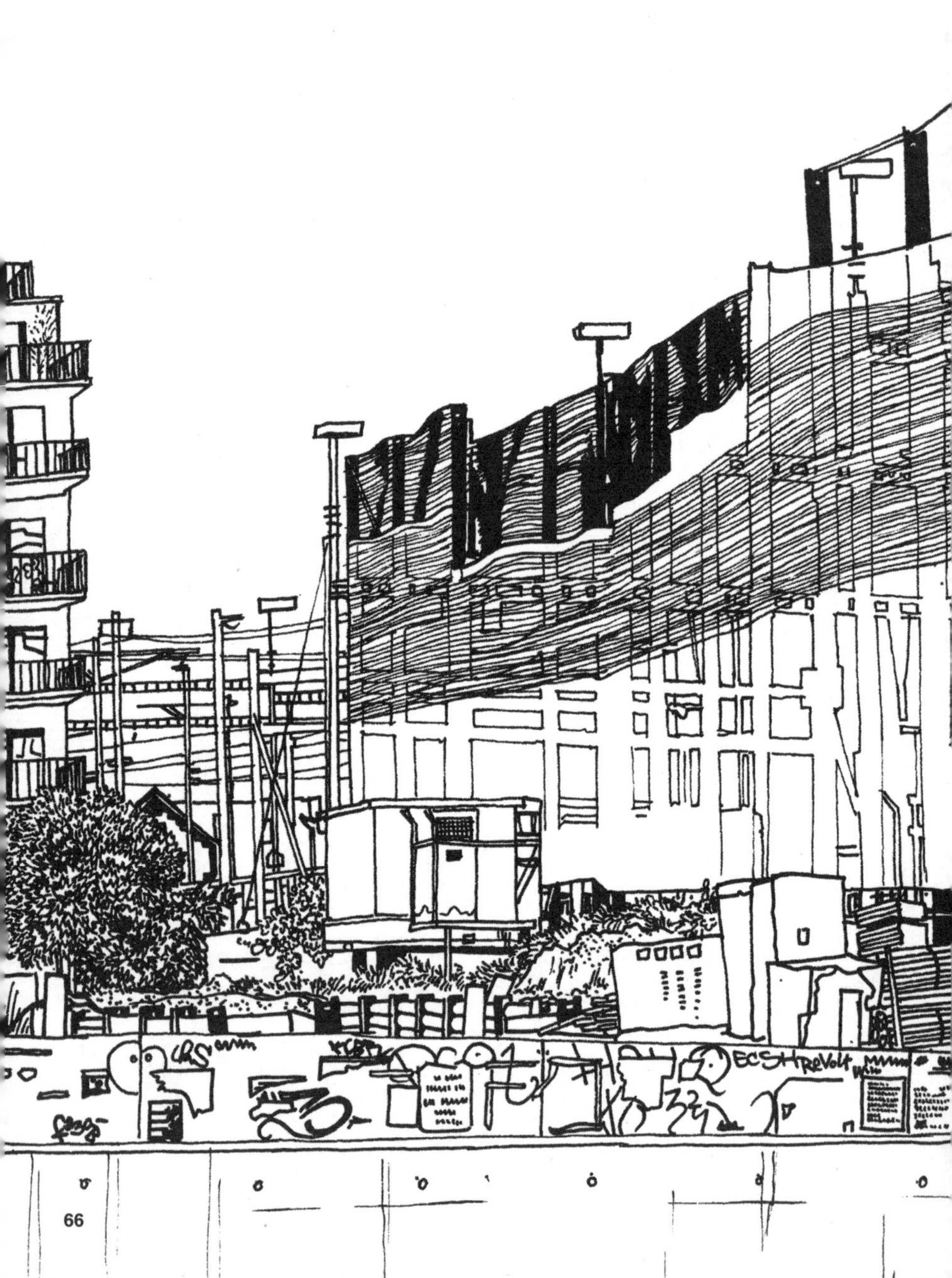

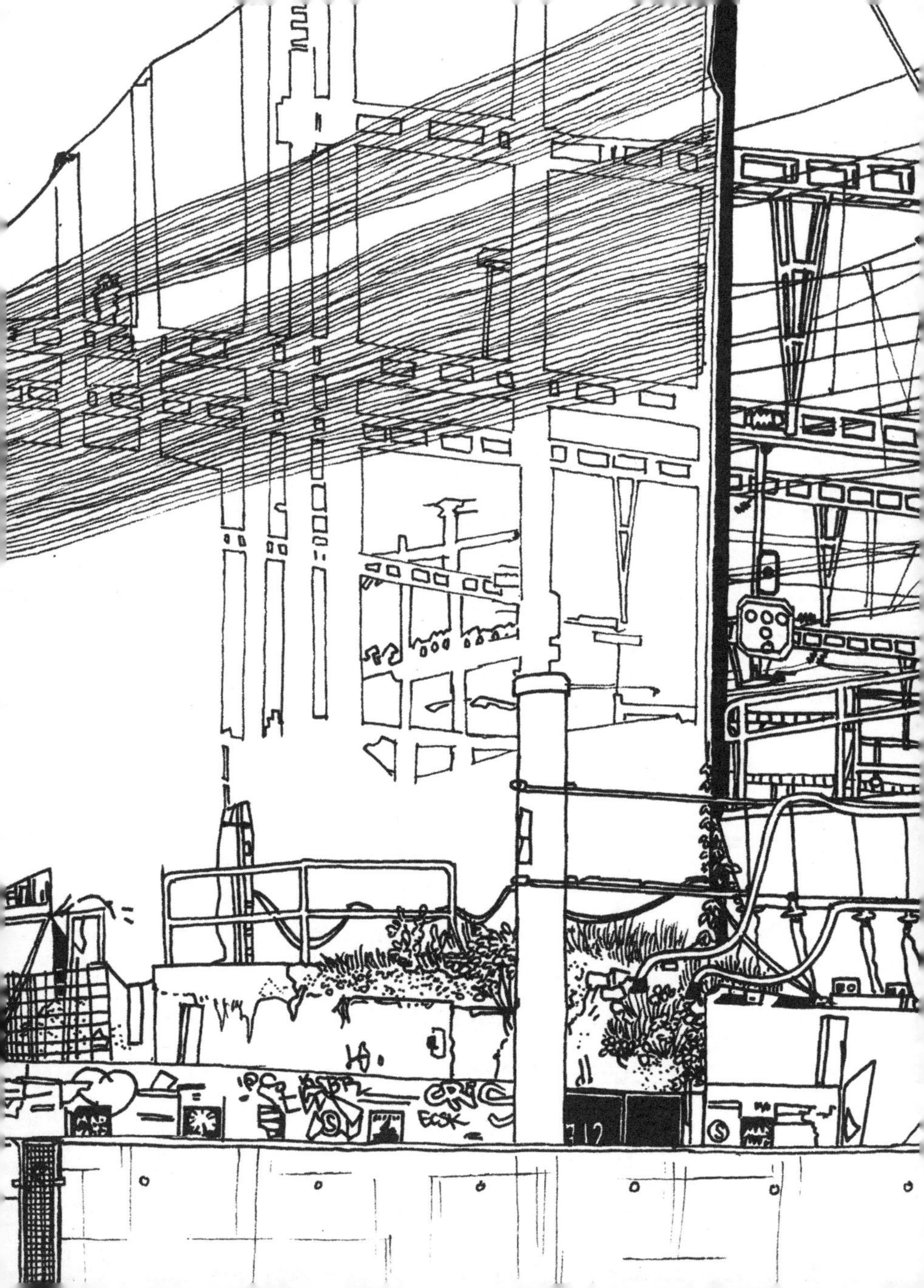

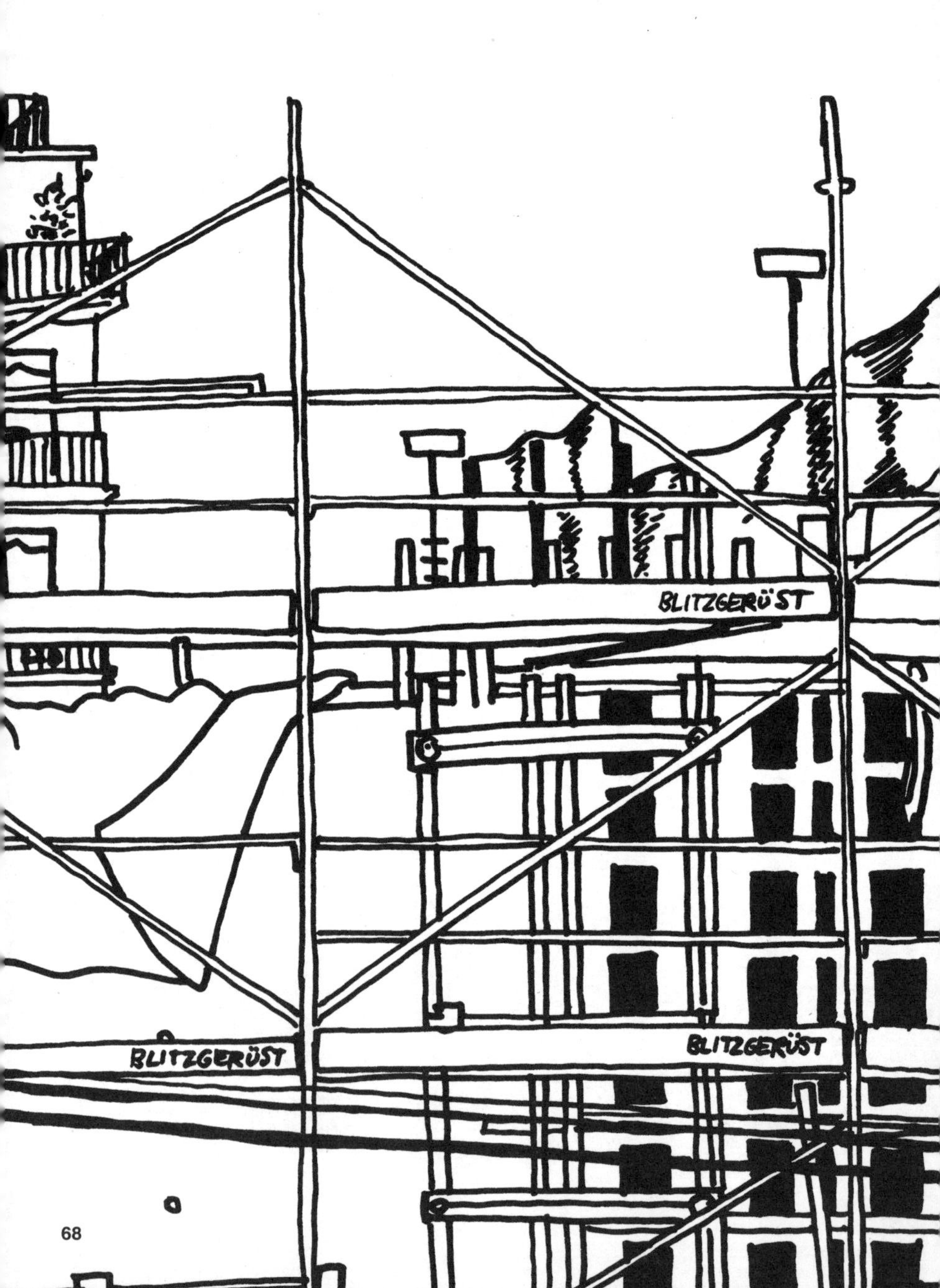

68

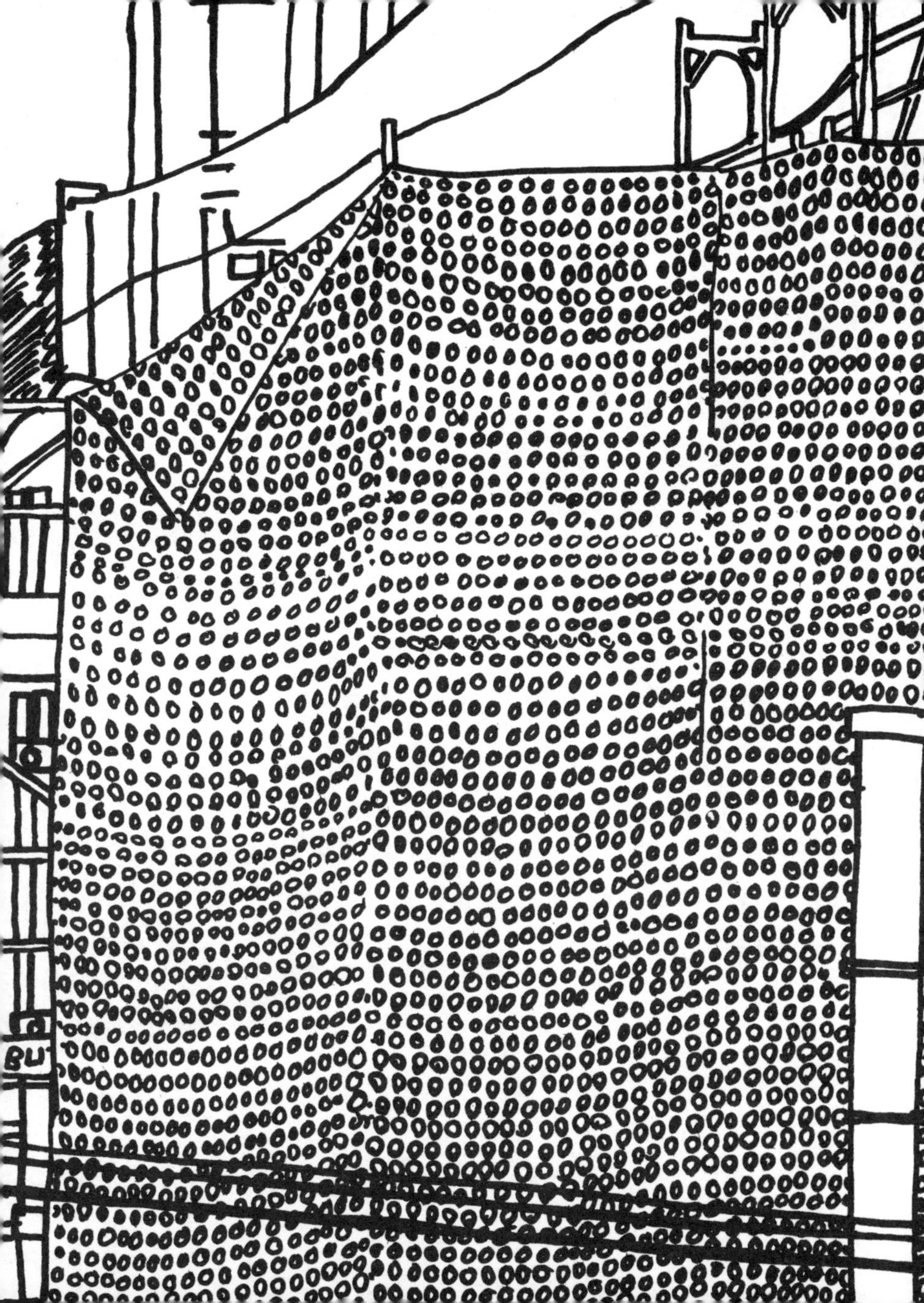

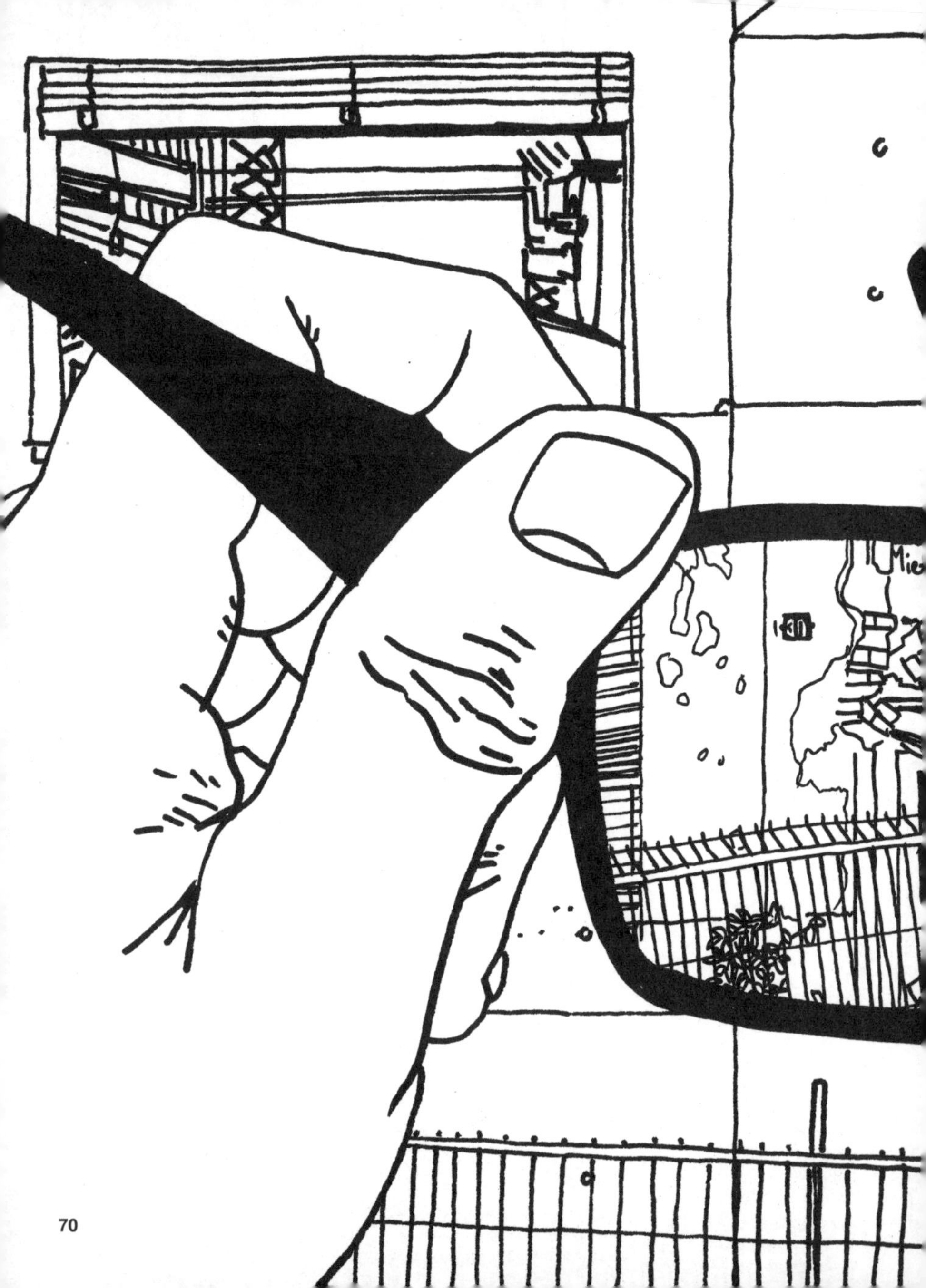
Mie

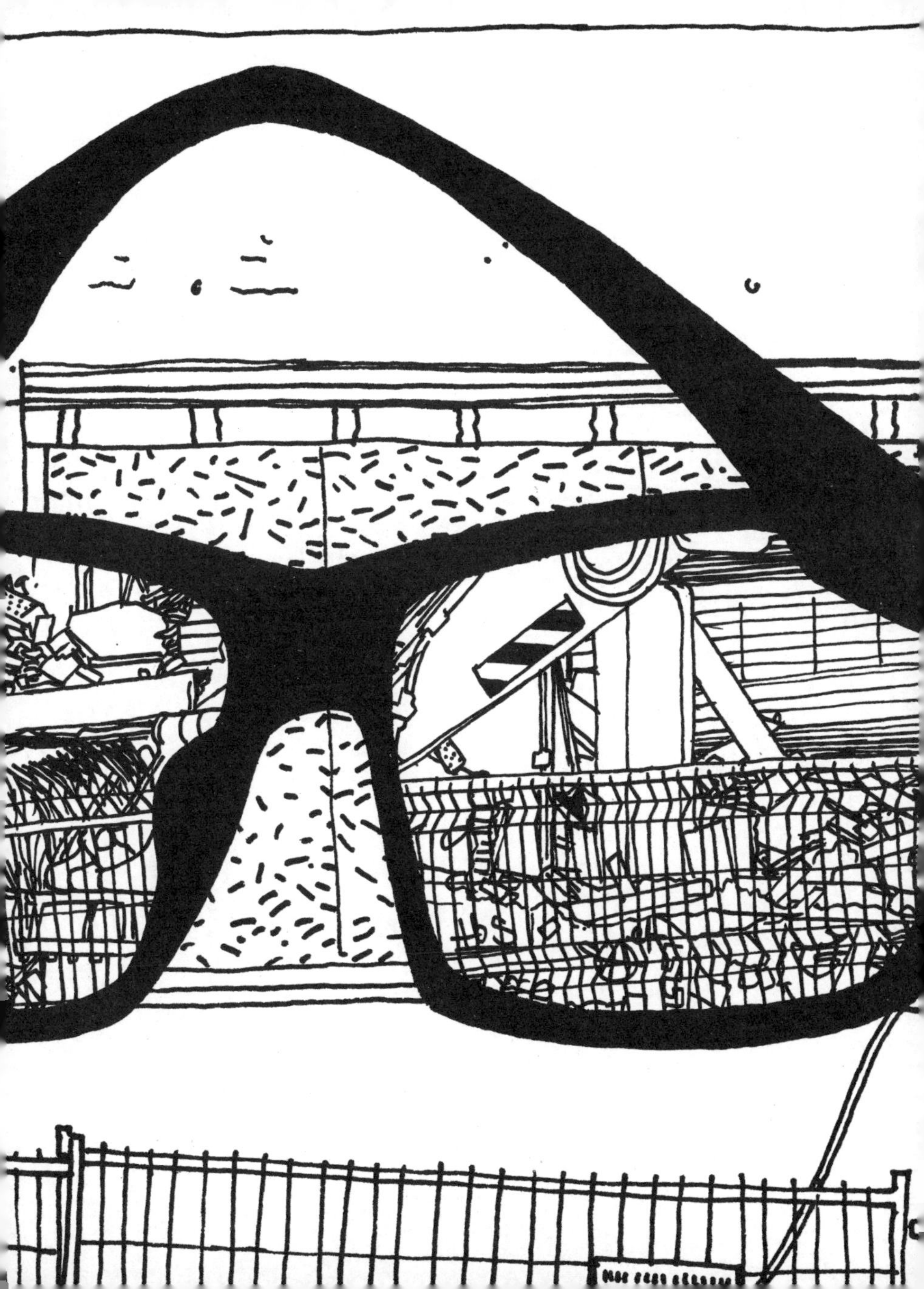

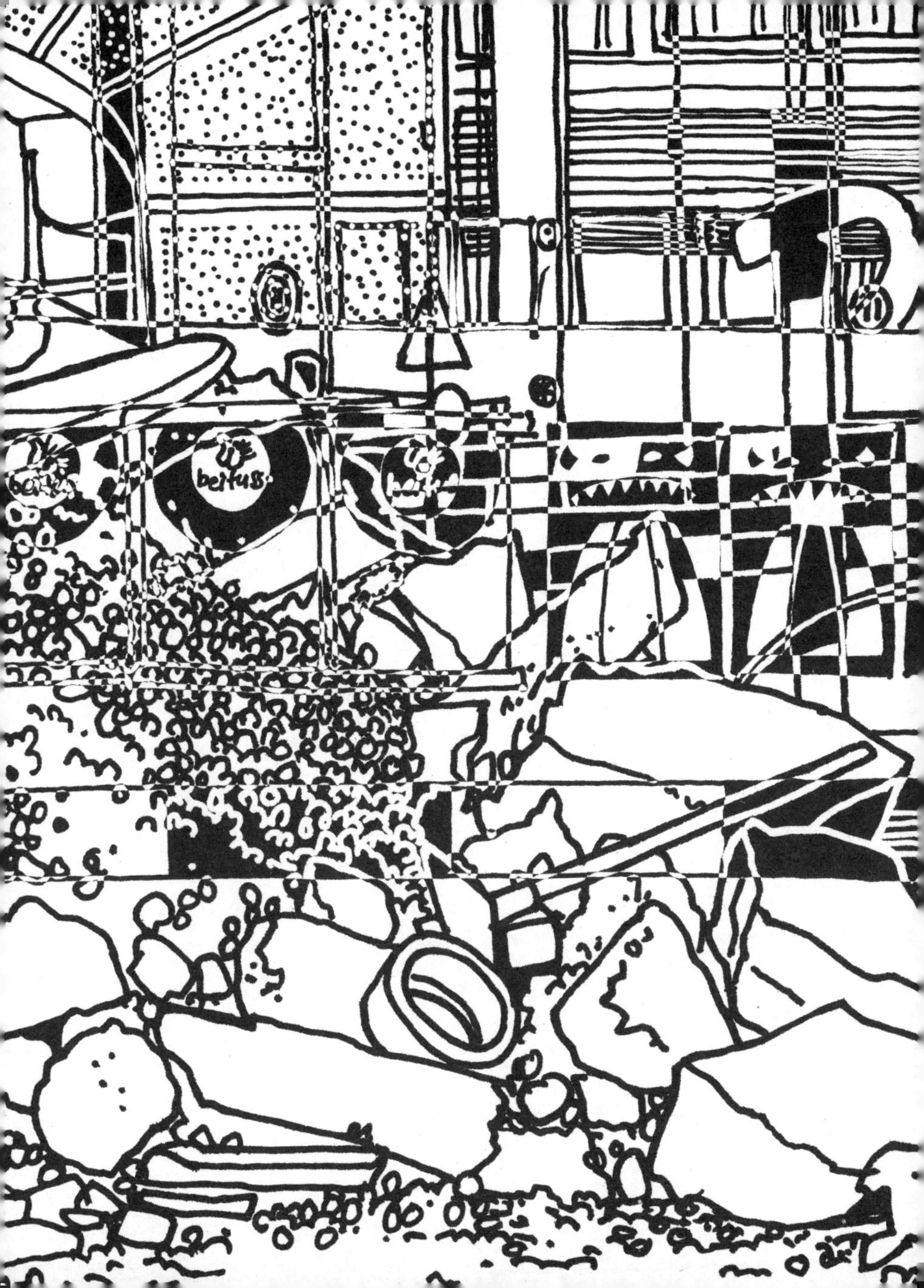

beltus

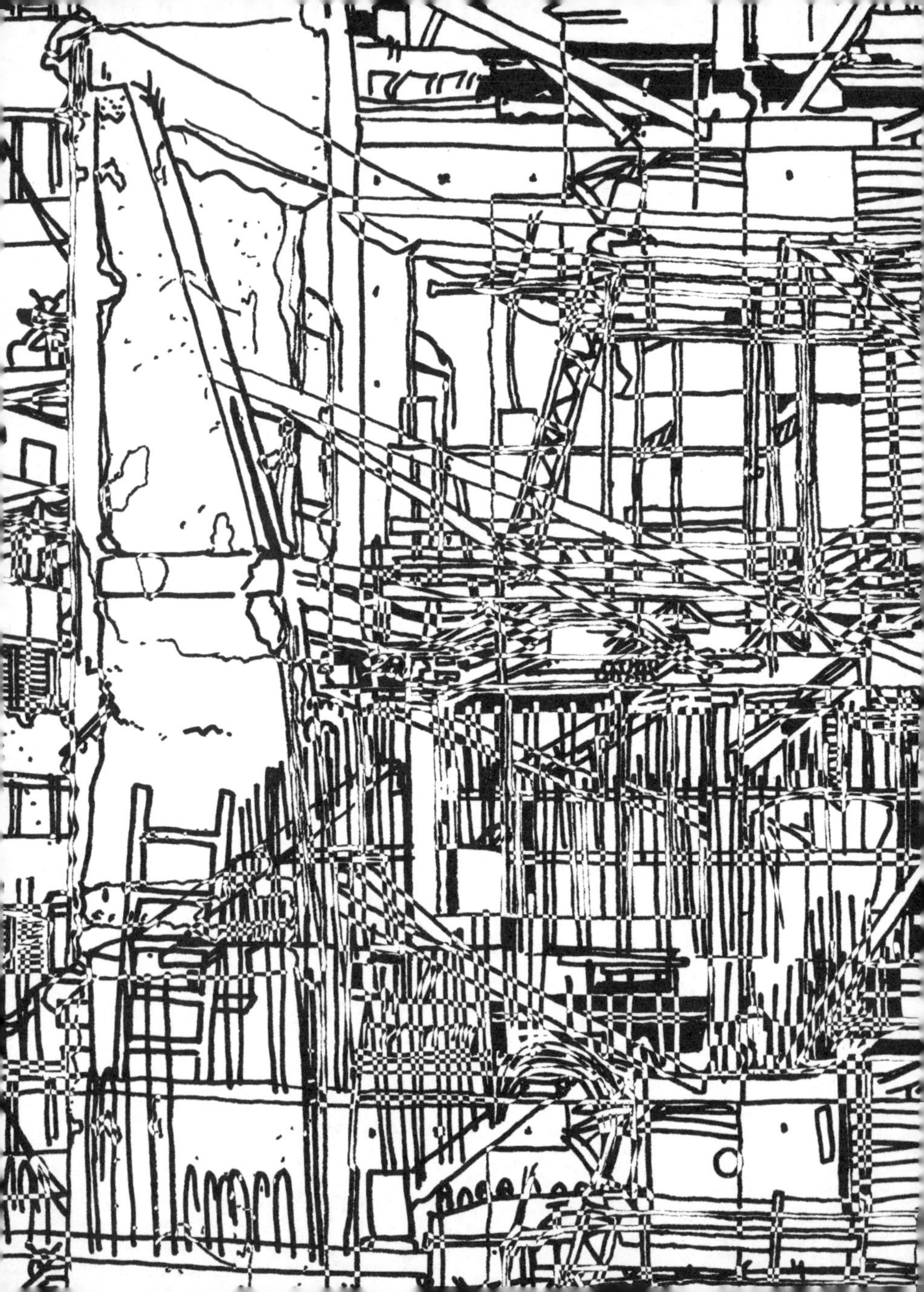

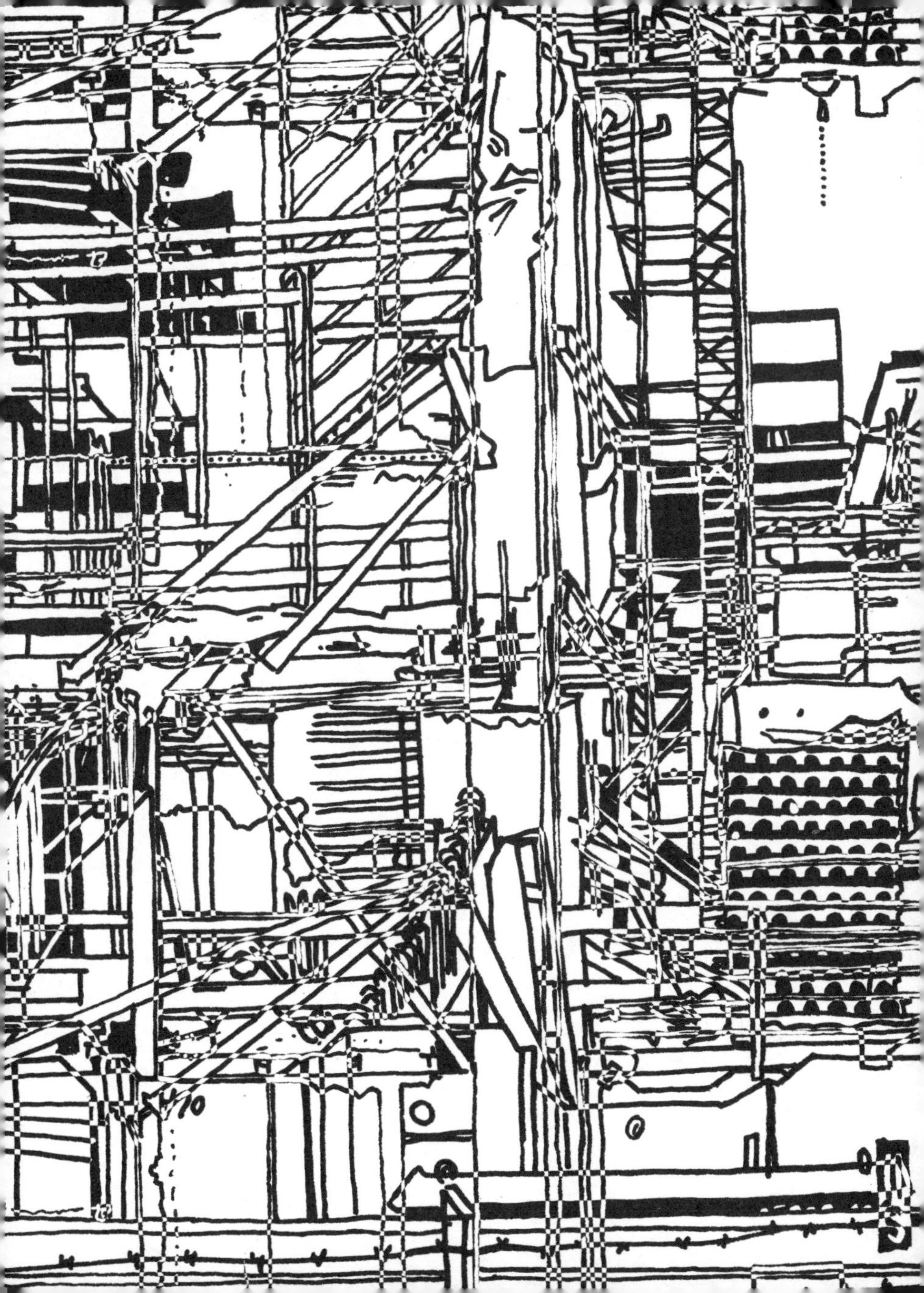

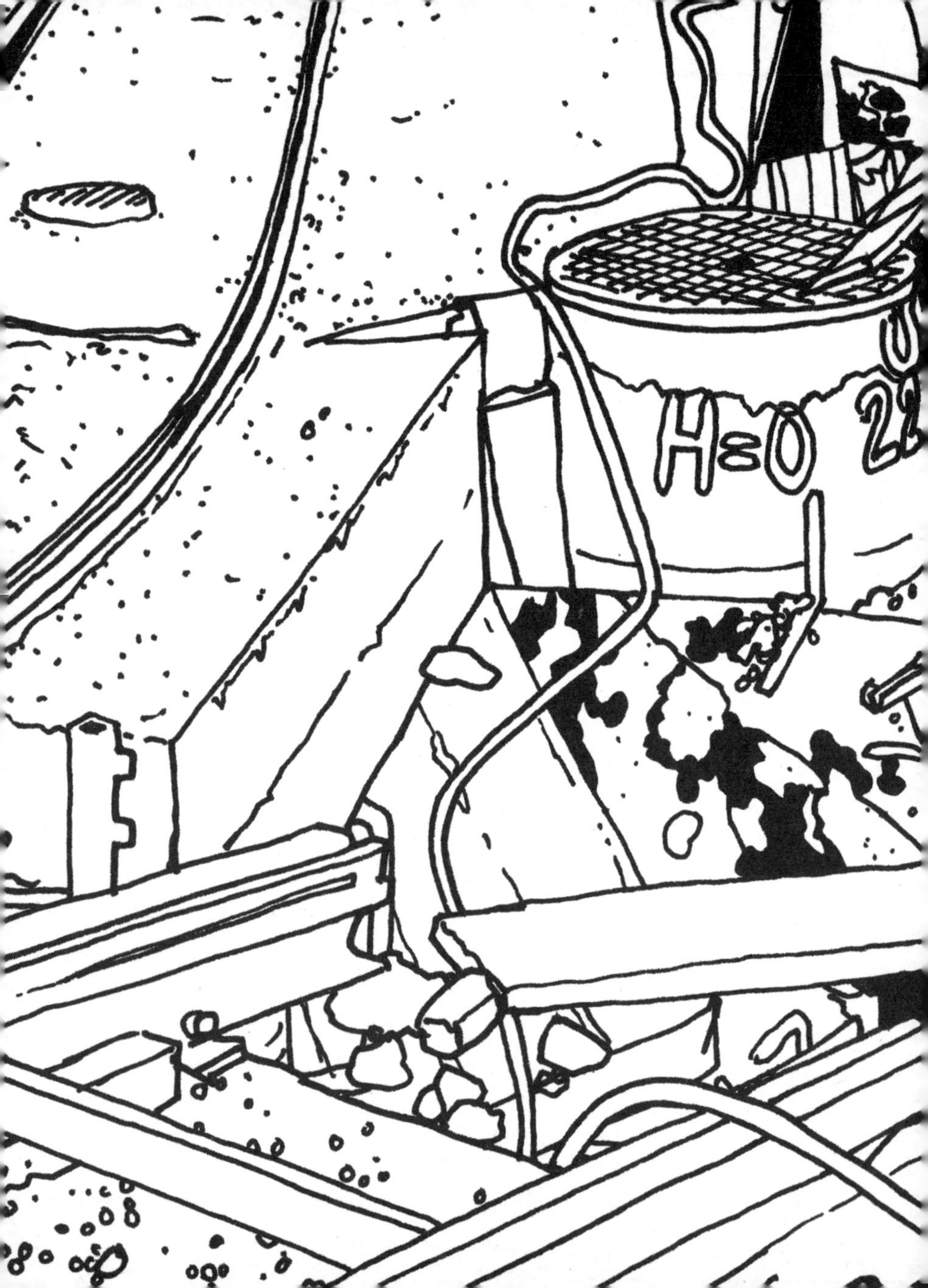
H₂O 22

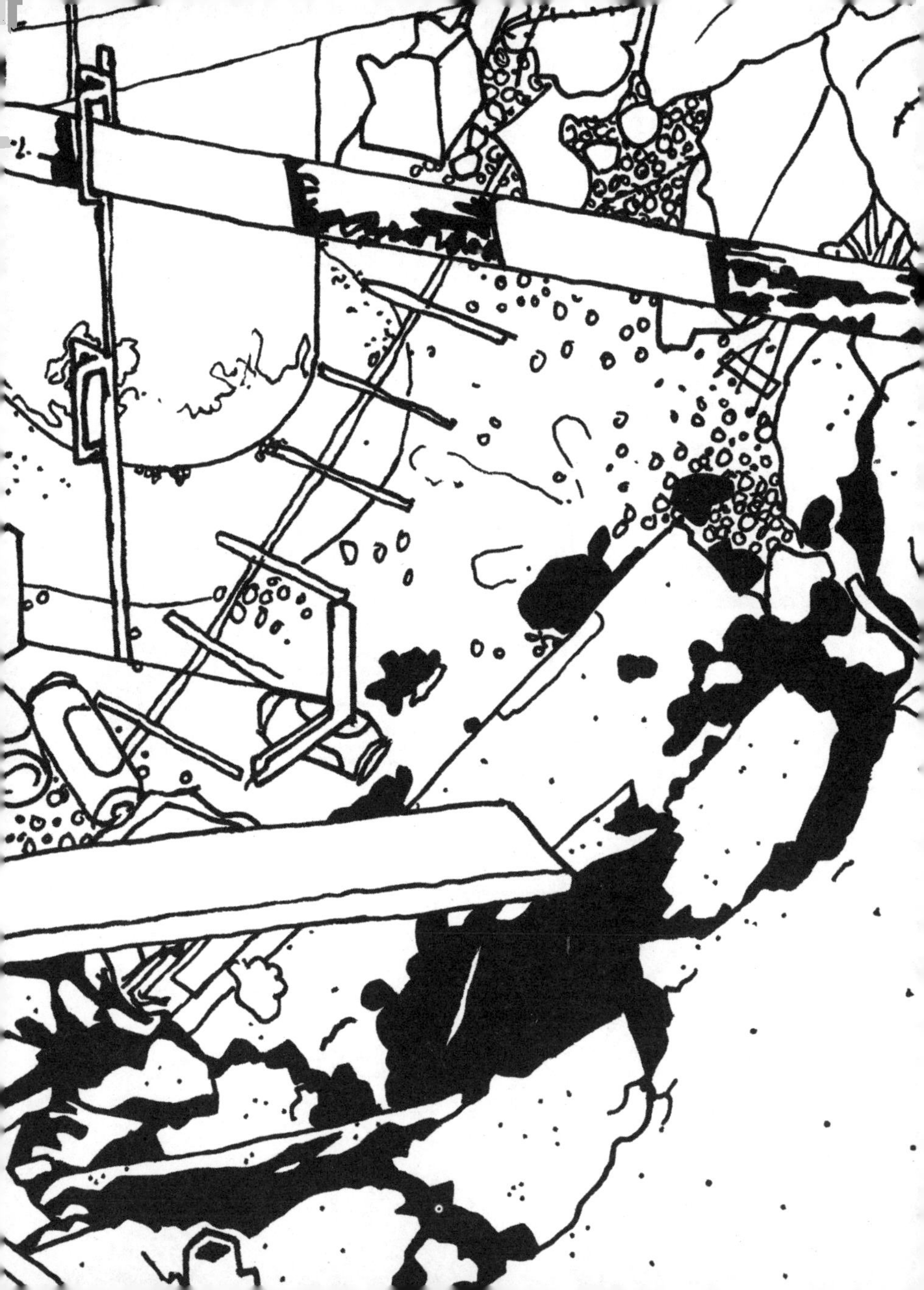

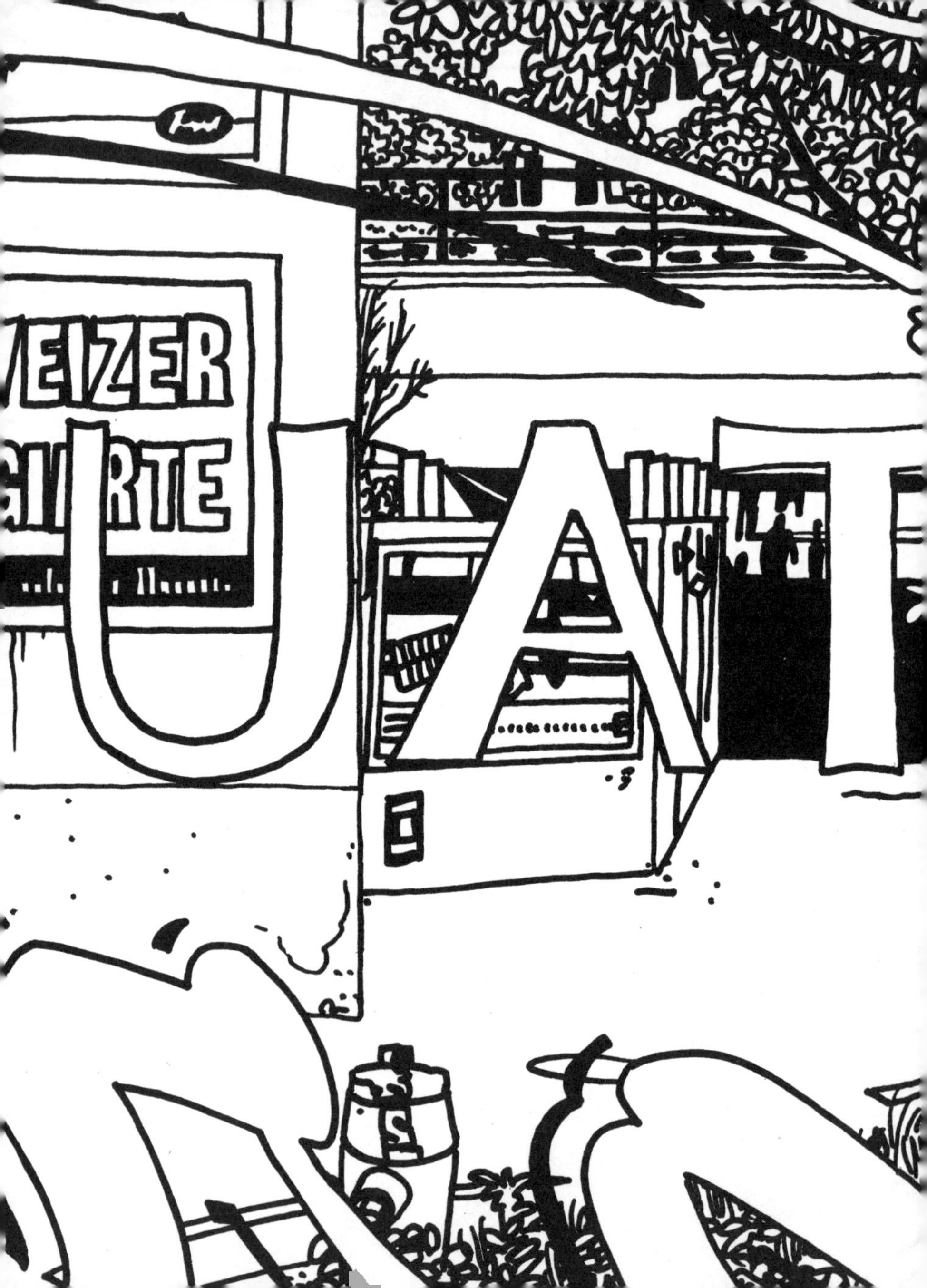

EIZER
GÜRTE

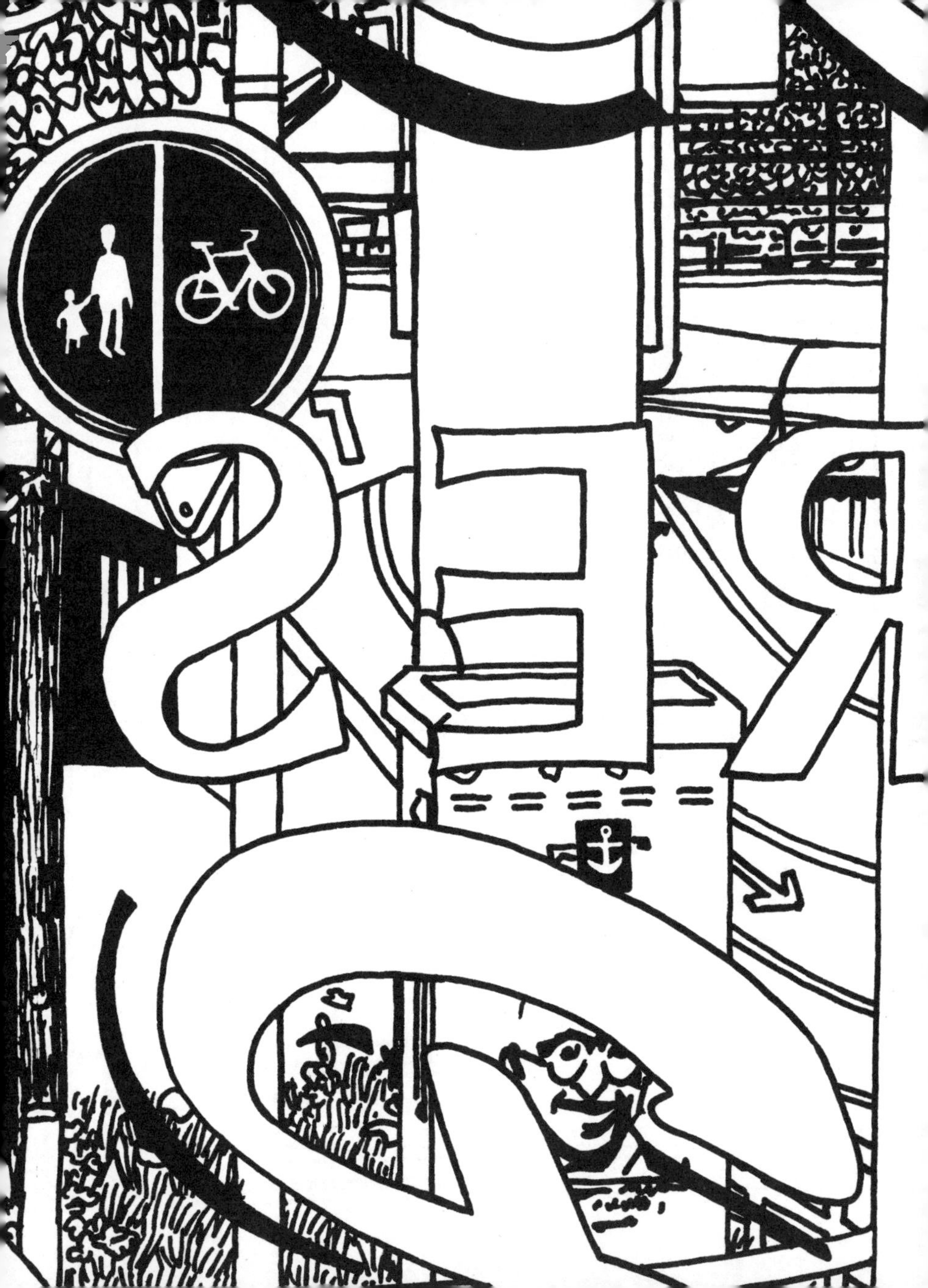

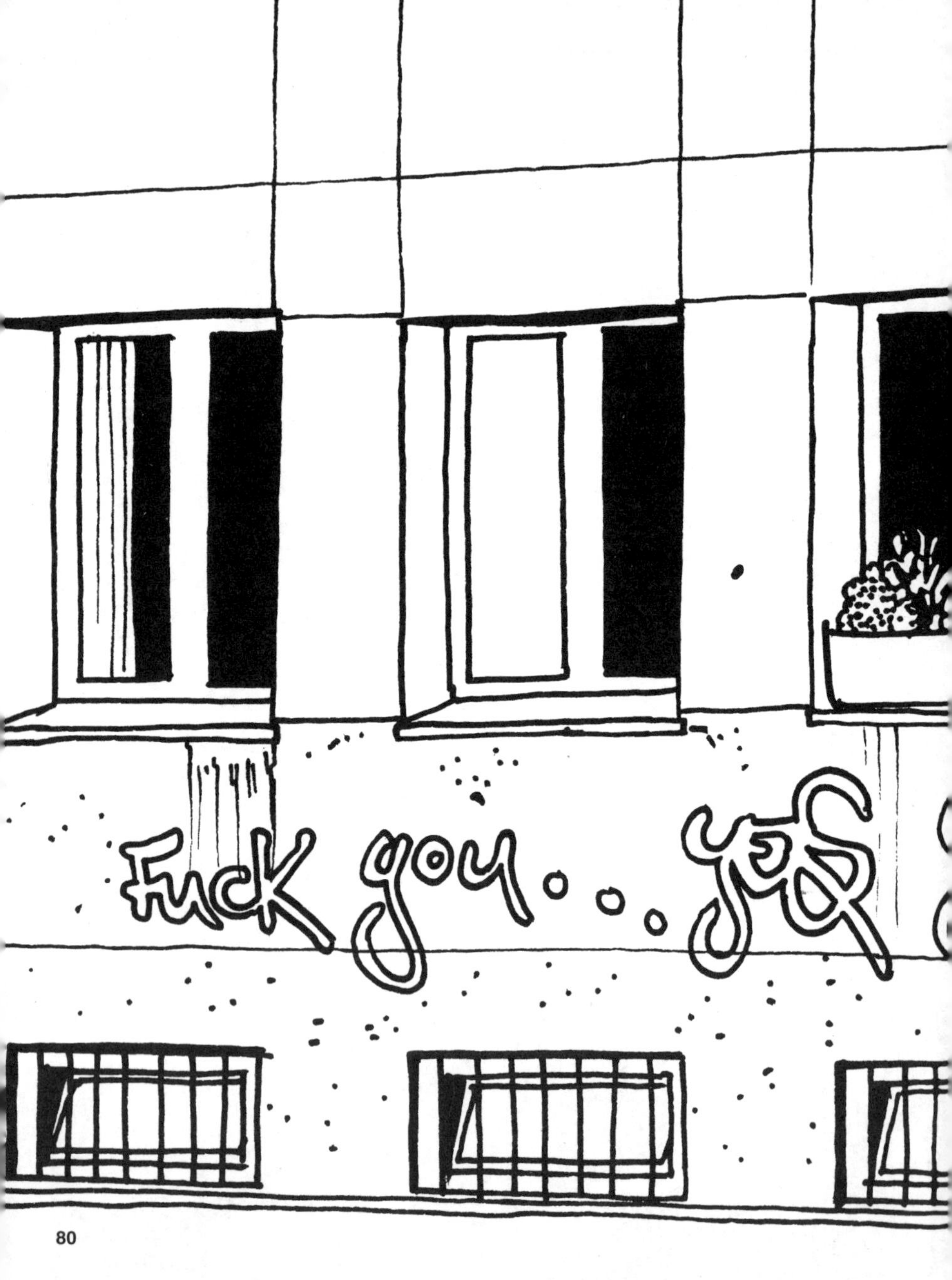

Fuck you... yes

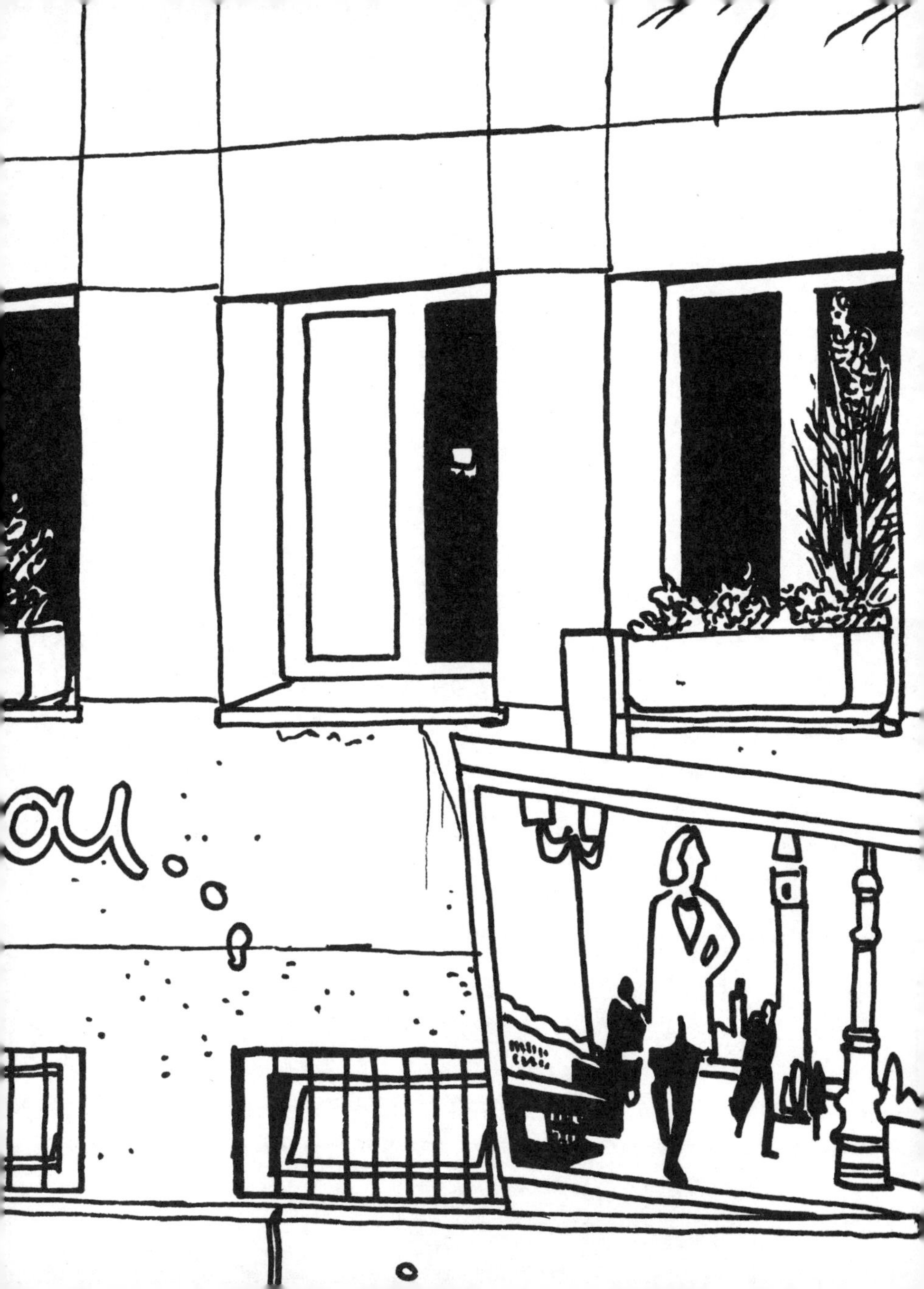

au

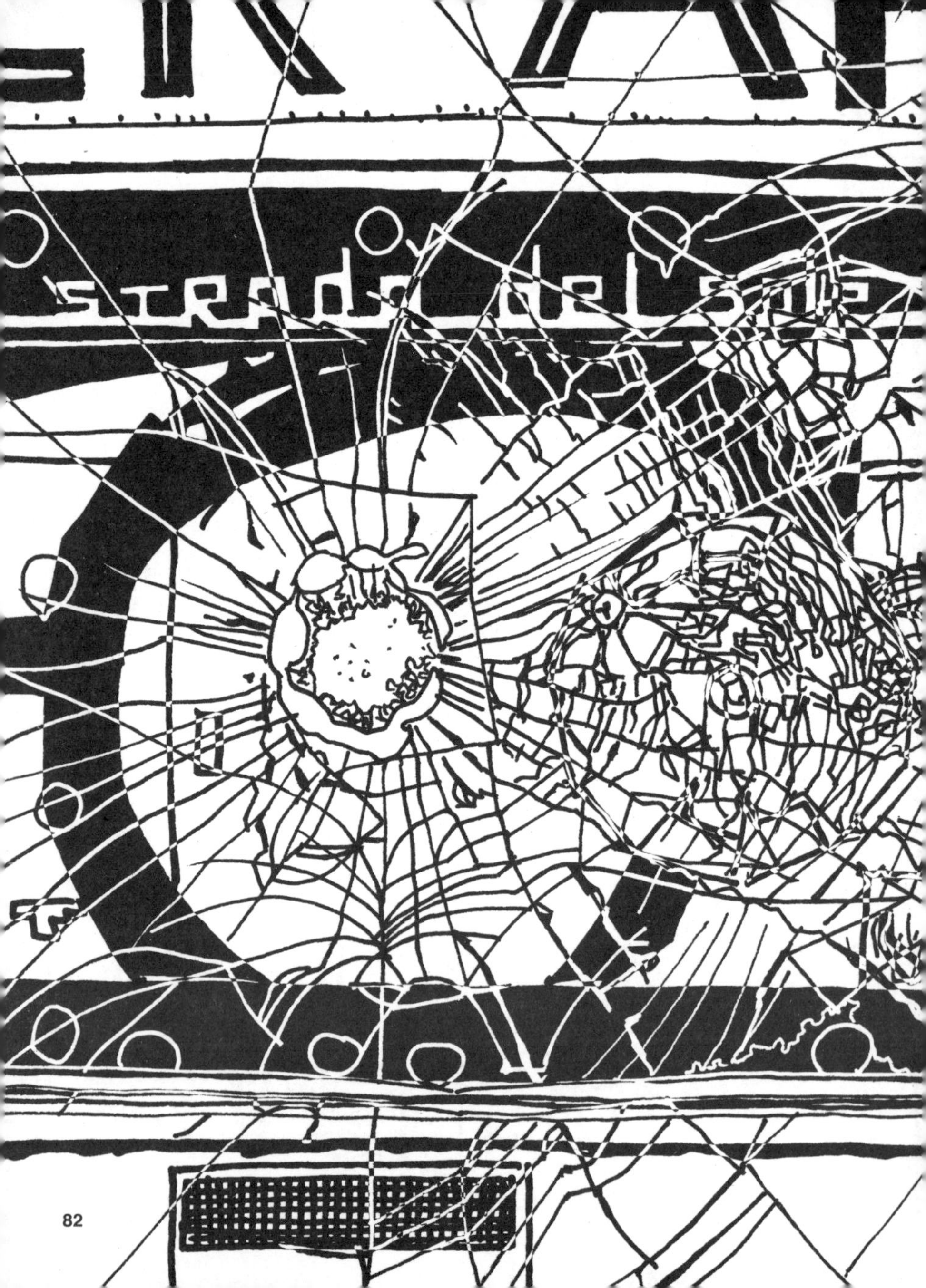
strada del sur

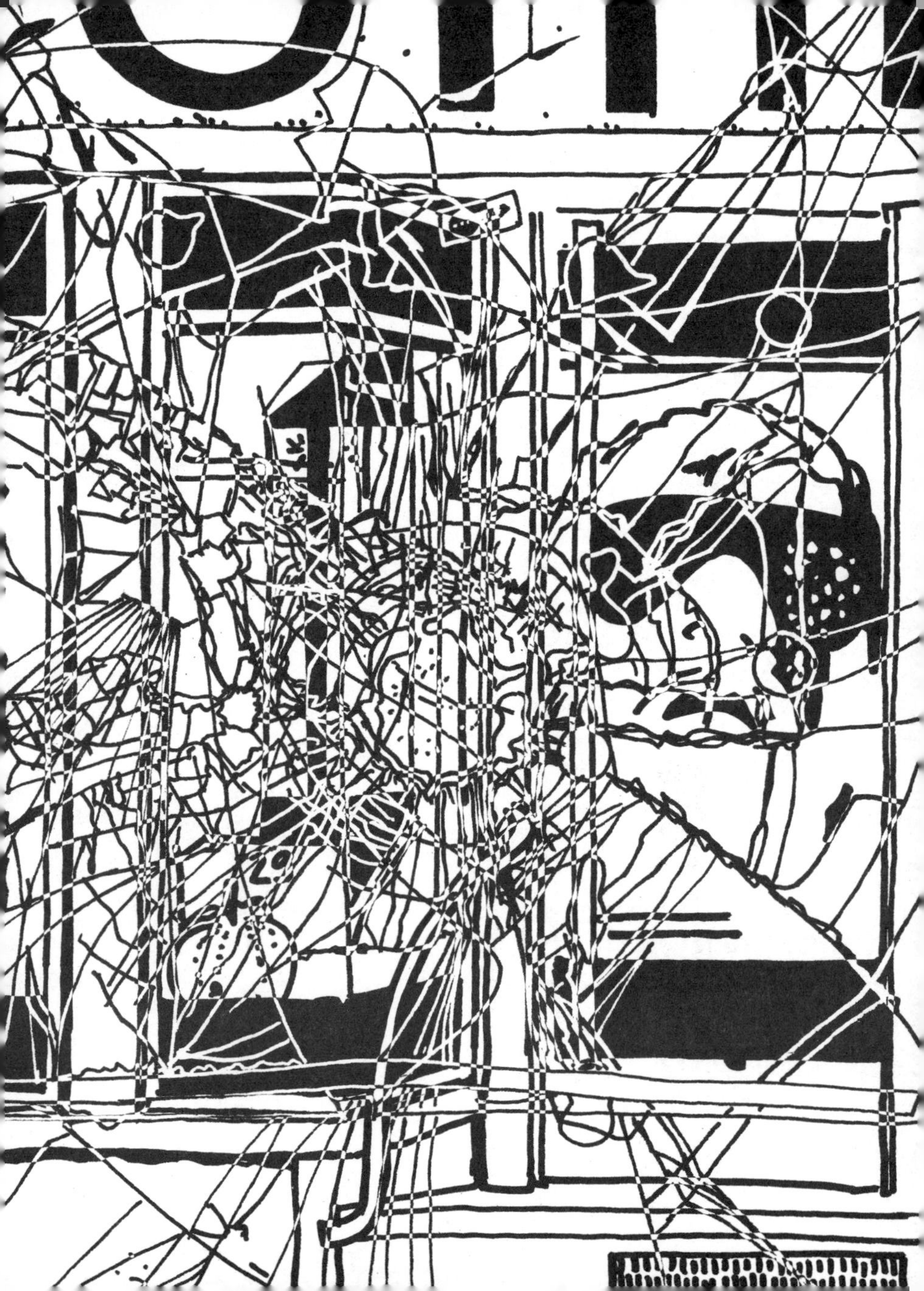

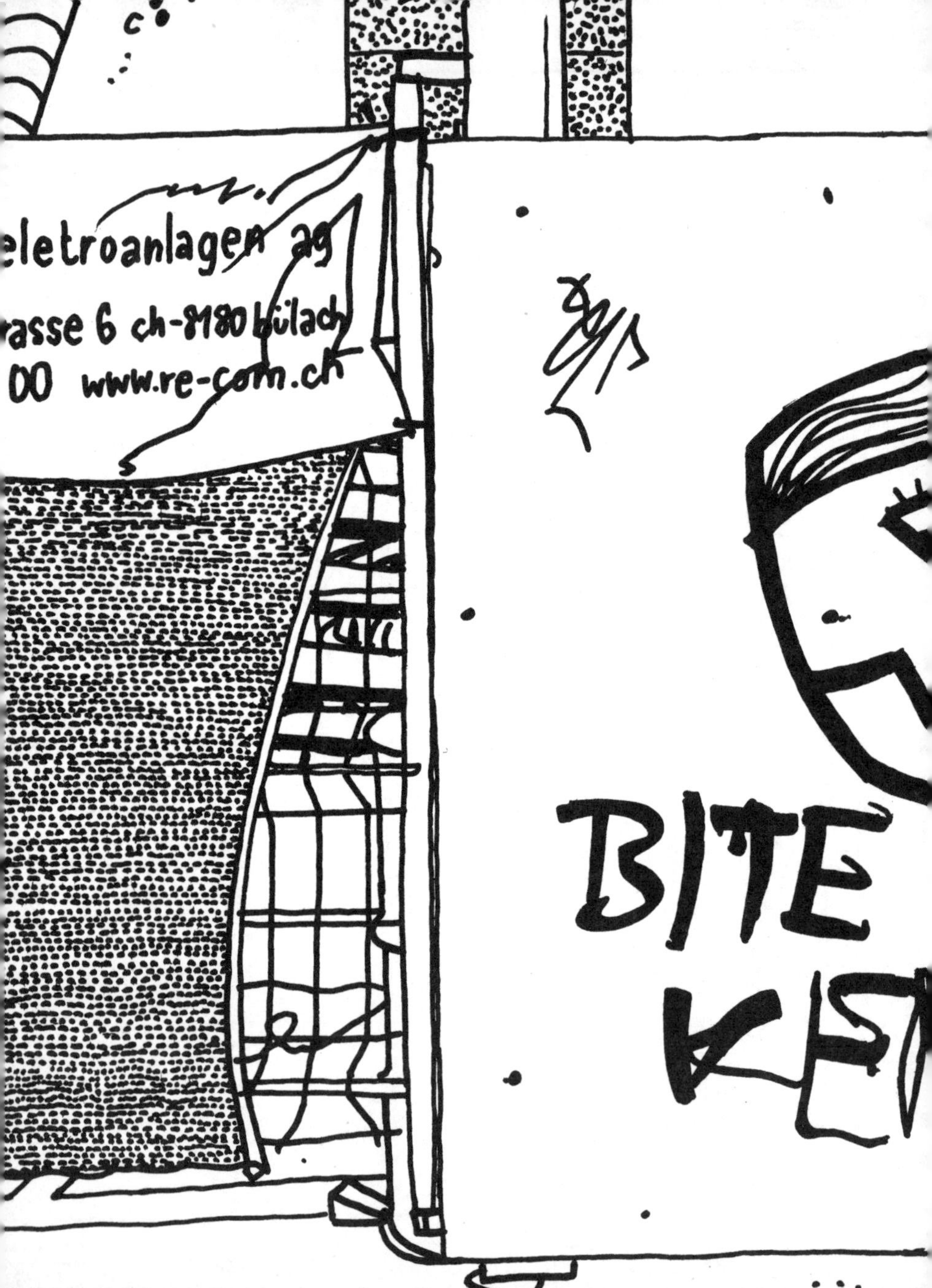
eletroanlagen ag
asse 6 ch-8180 bülach
00 www.re-com.ch
BITE
KST

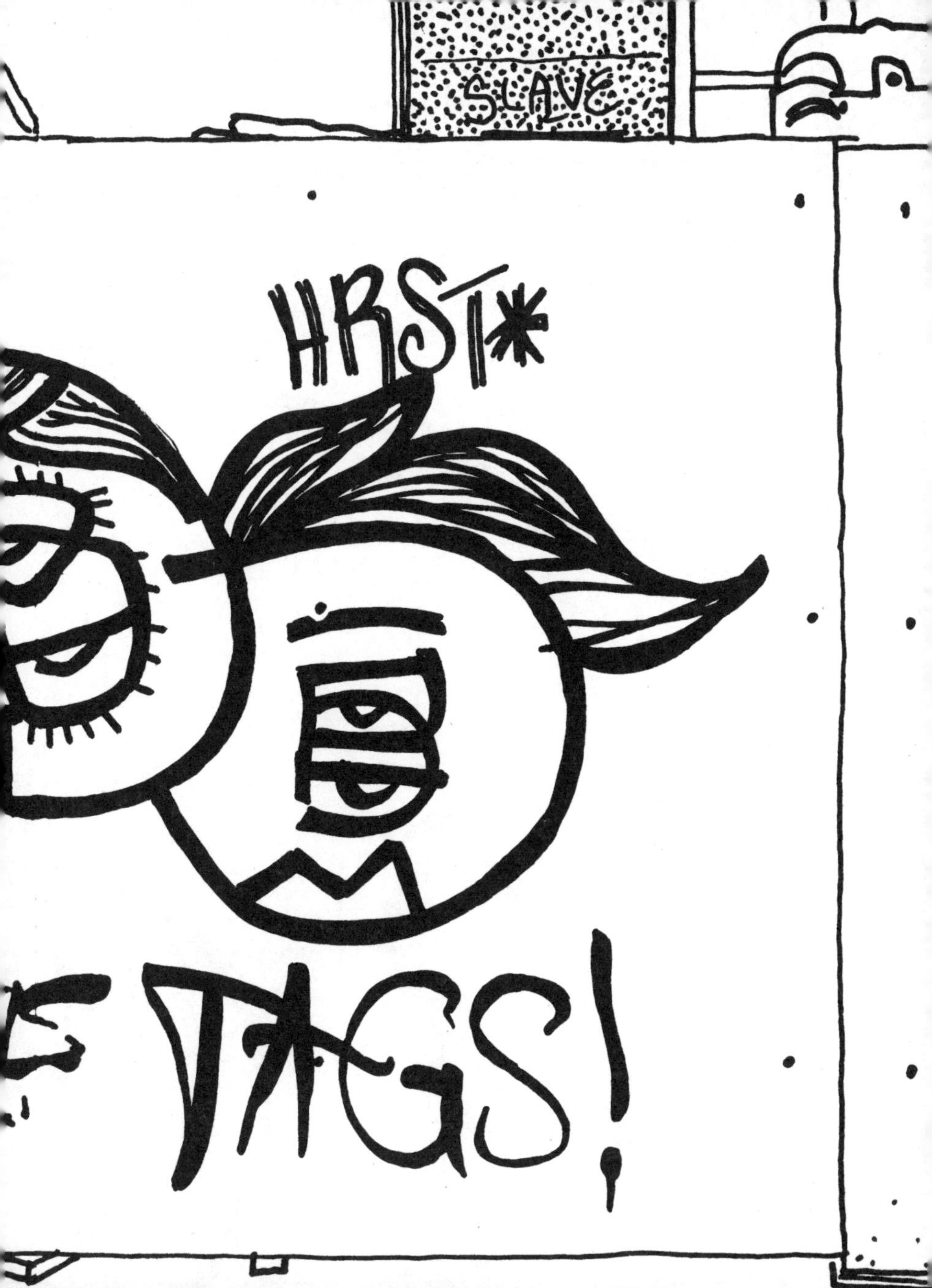
SLAVE.
HRST*
TAGS!

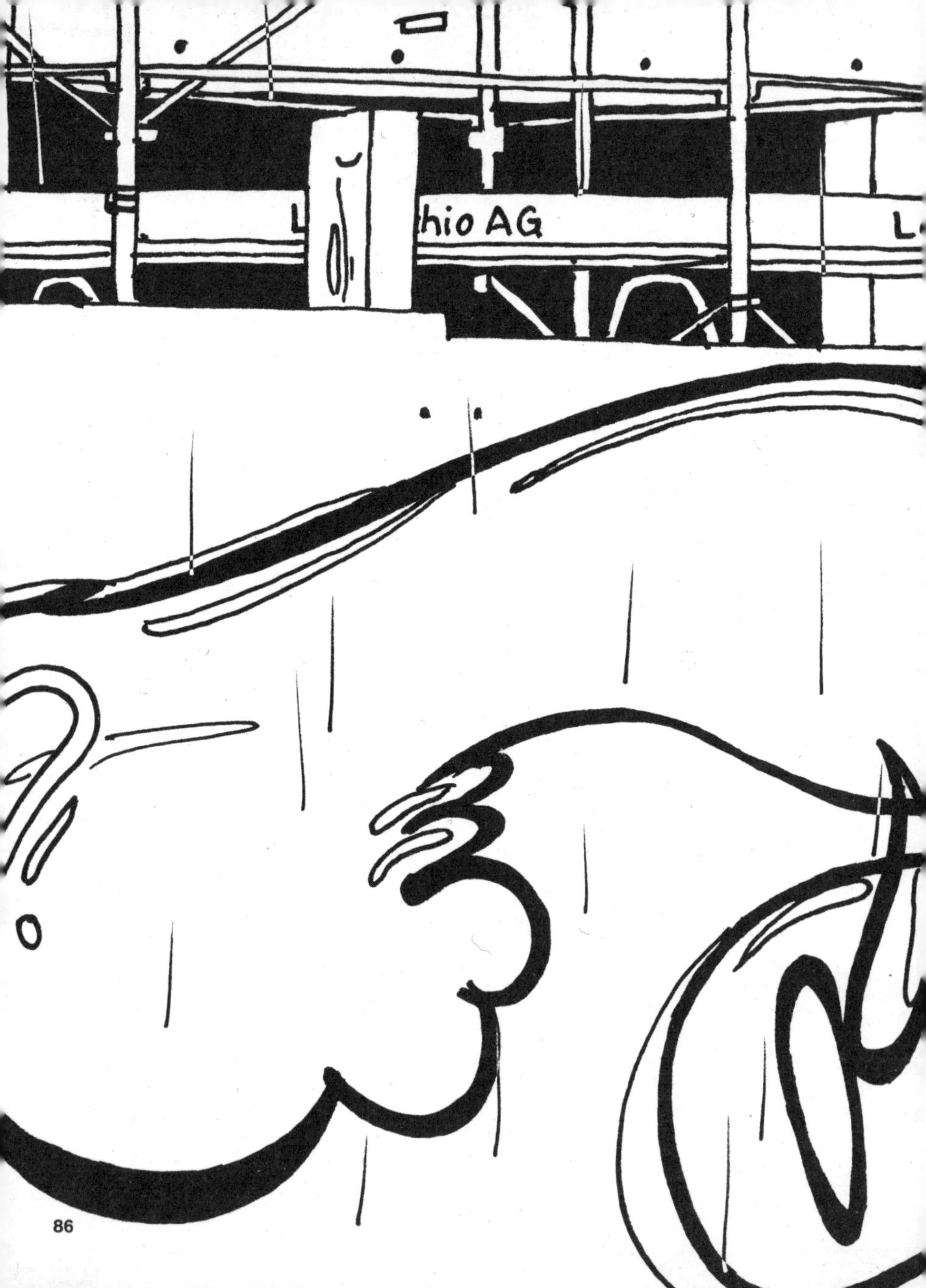

hio AG

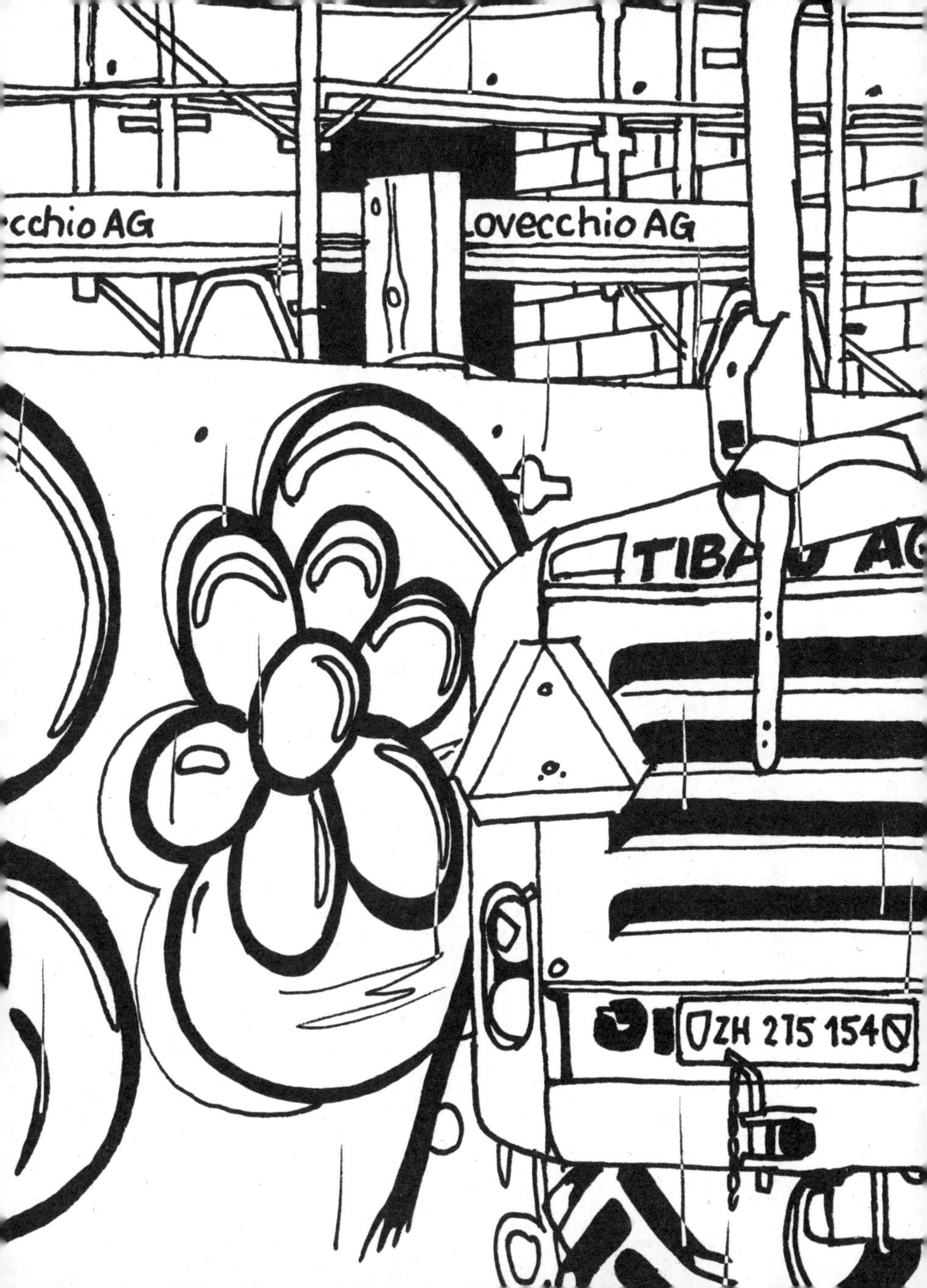
cchio AG
Lovecchio AG
TIBA AG
ZH 275 154

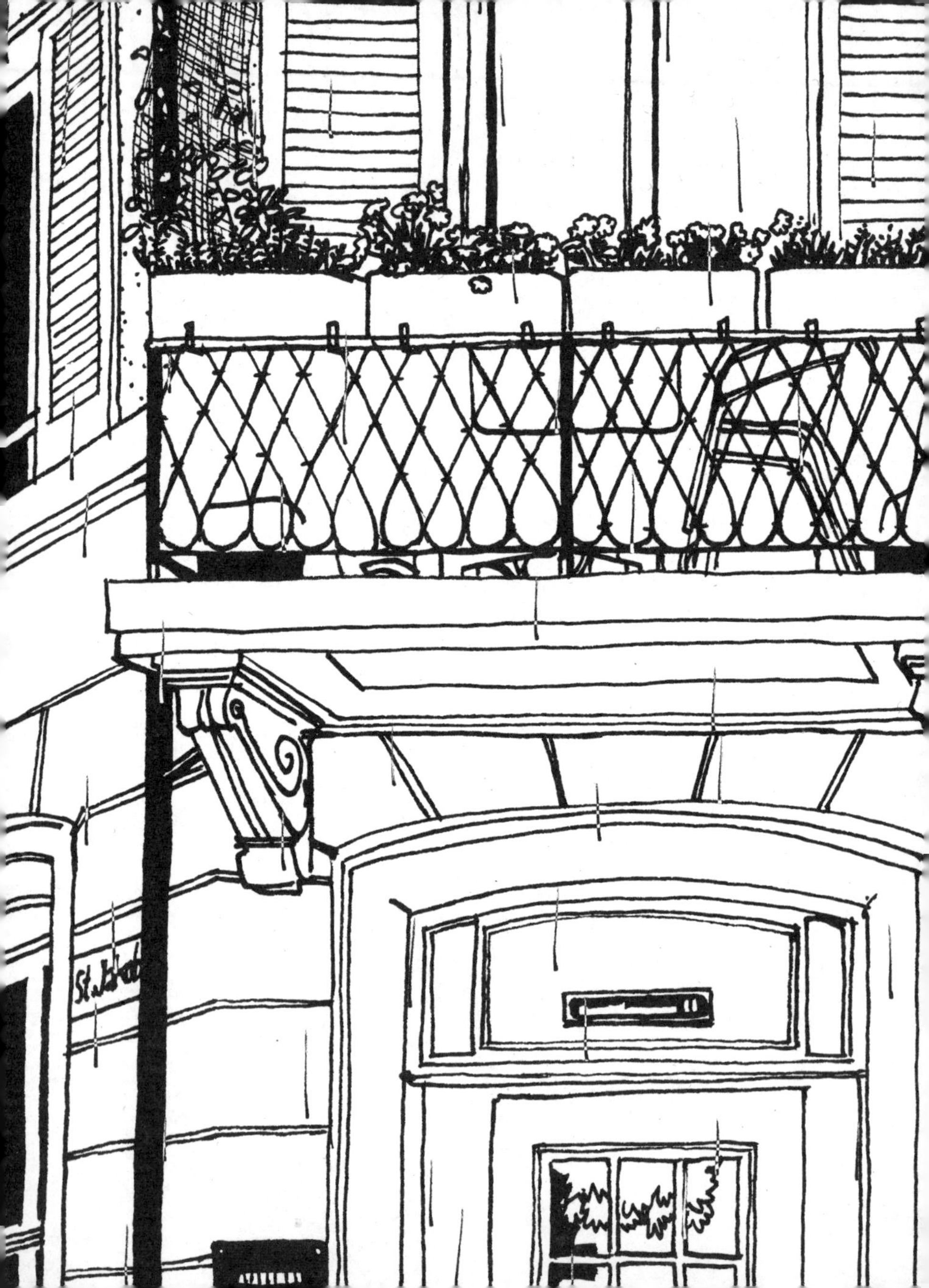

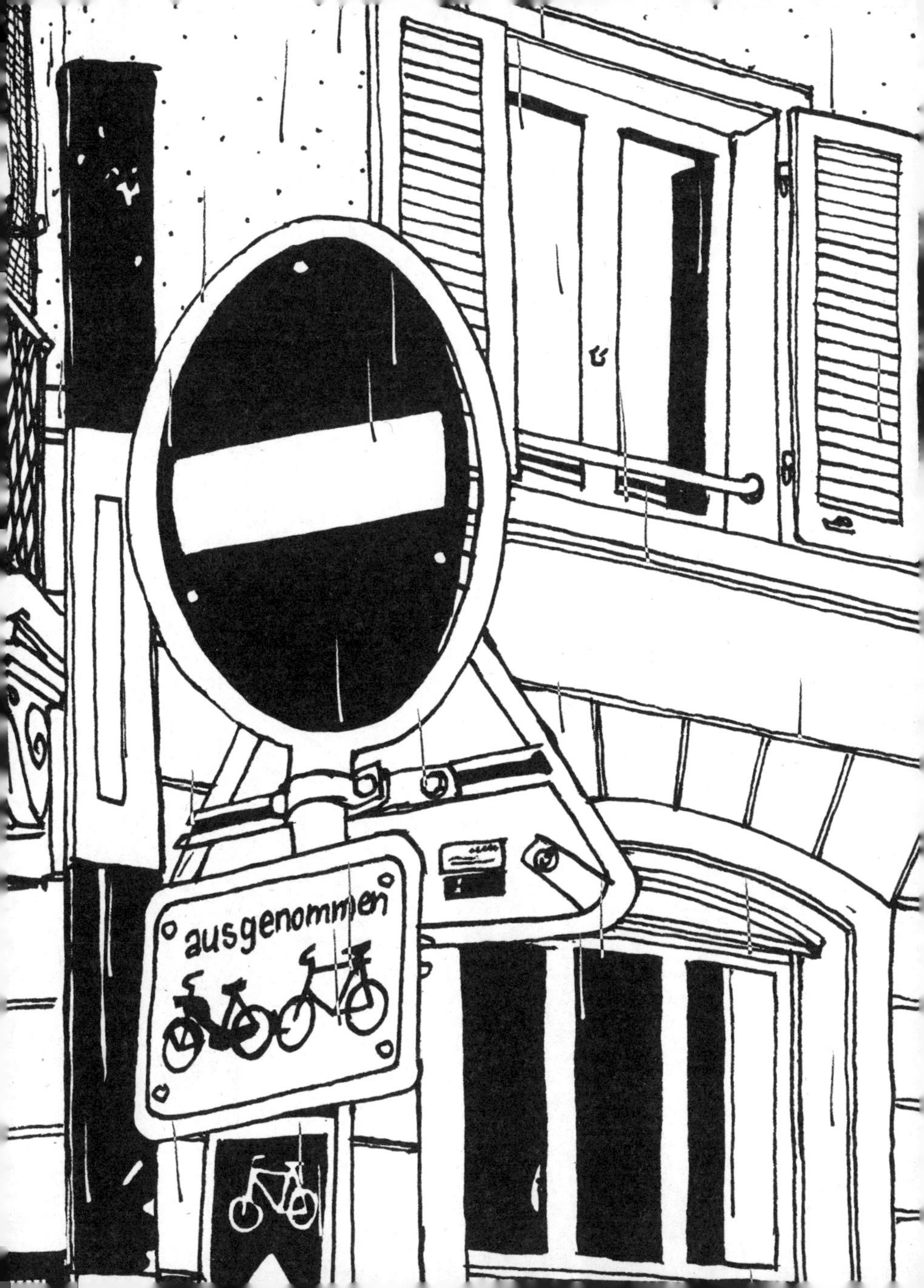

ausgenommen

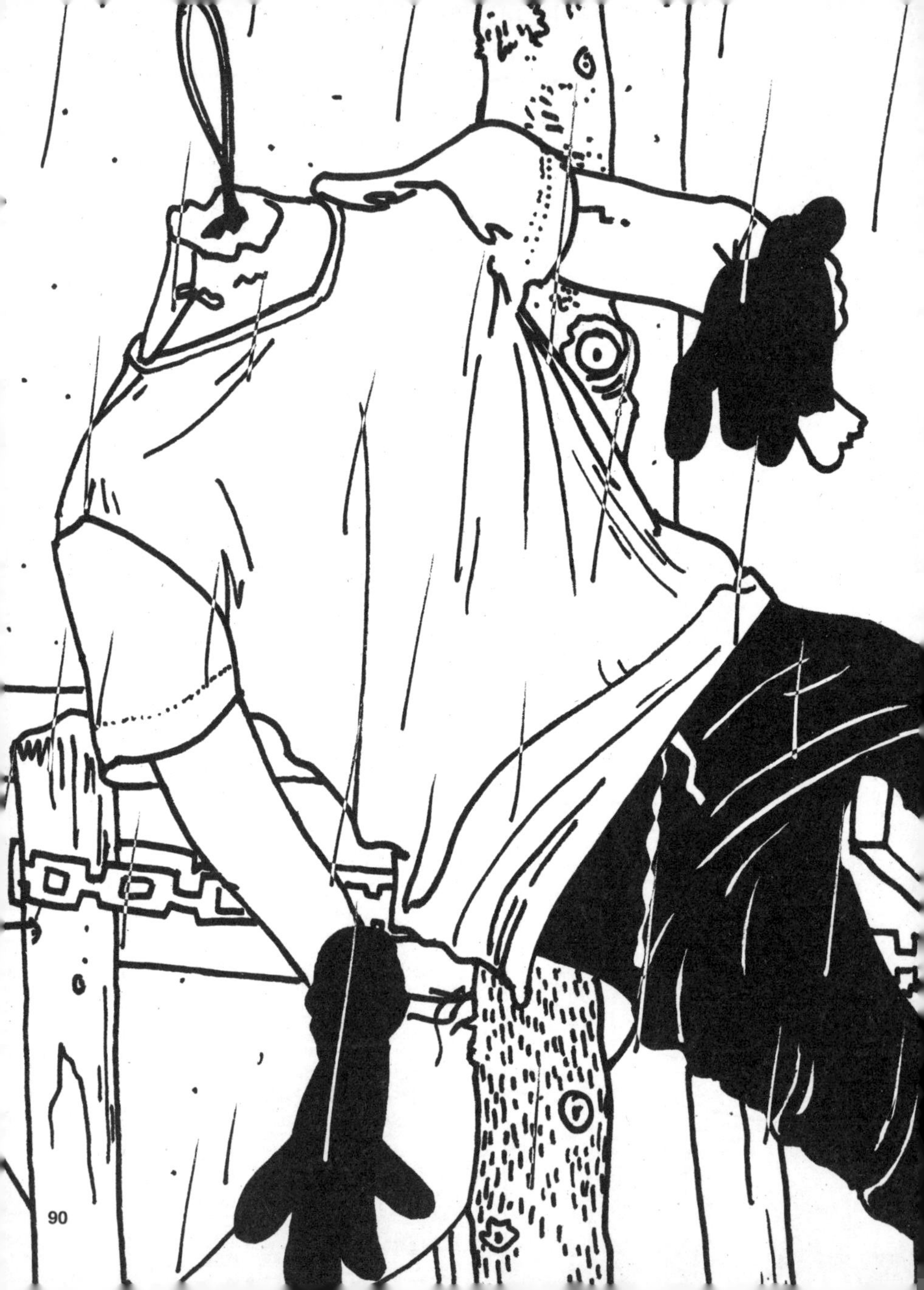

ST
ZO

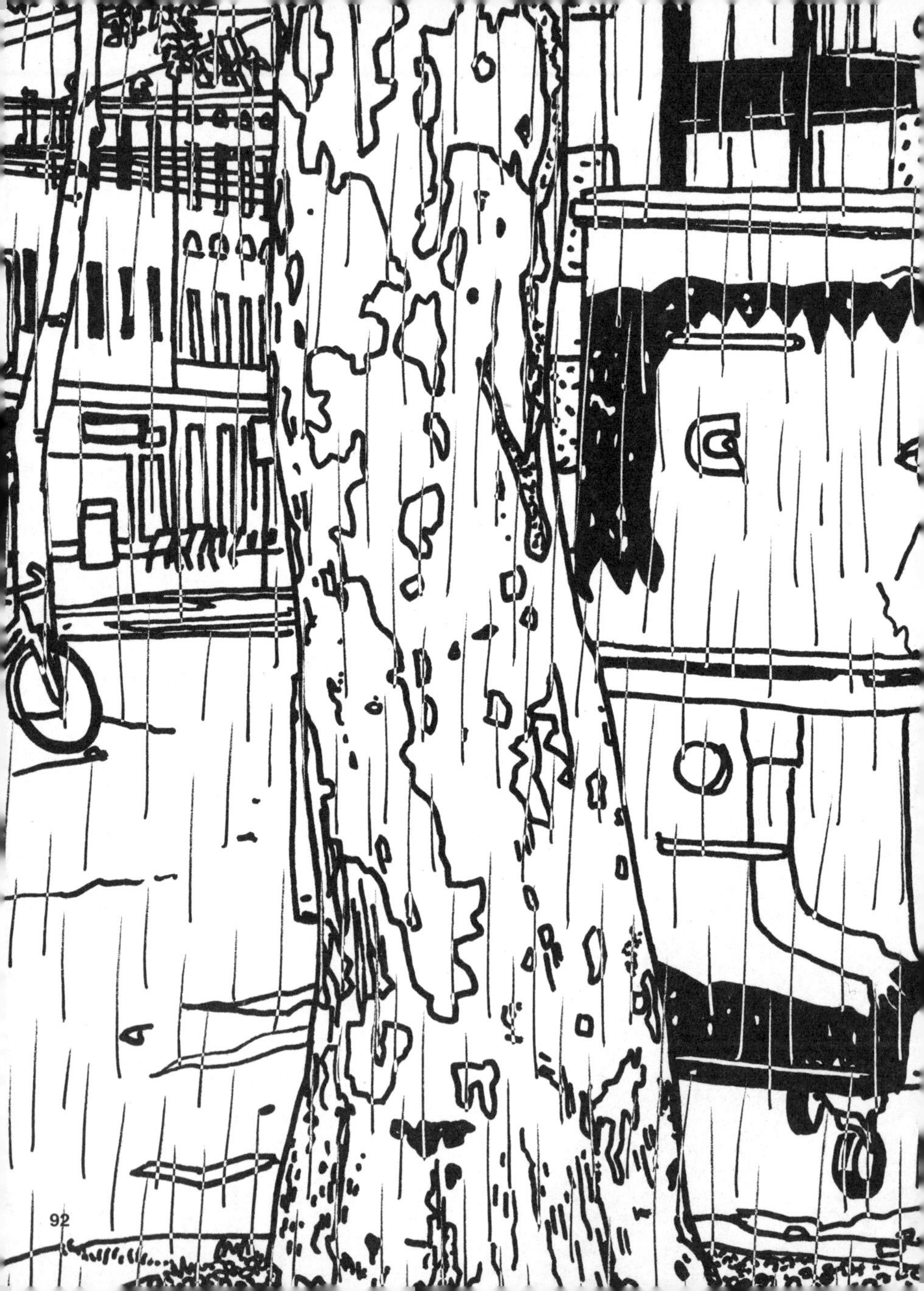

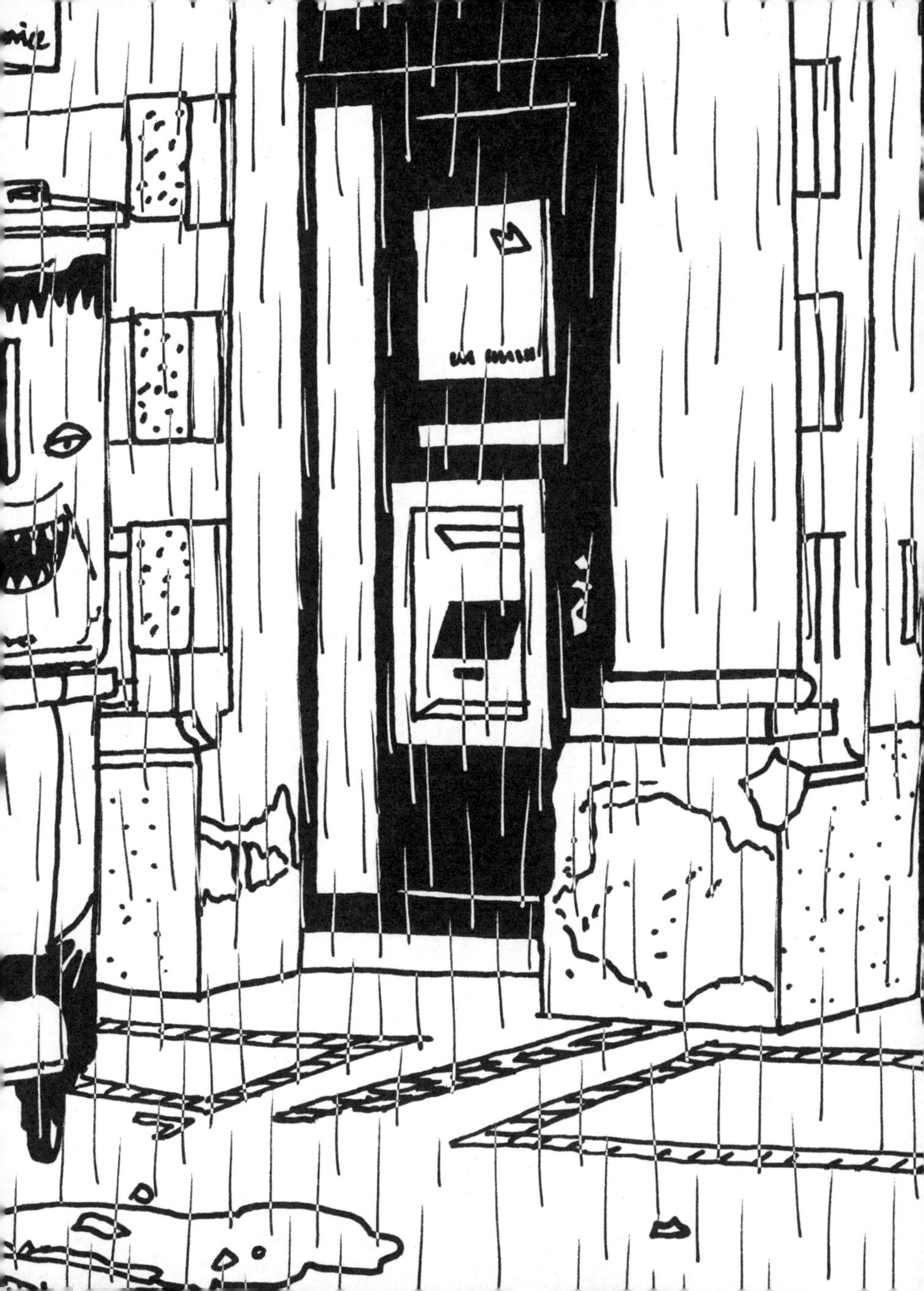

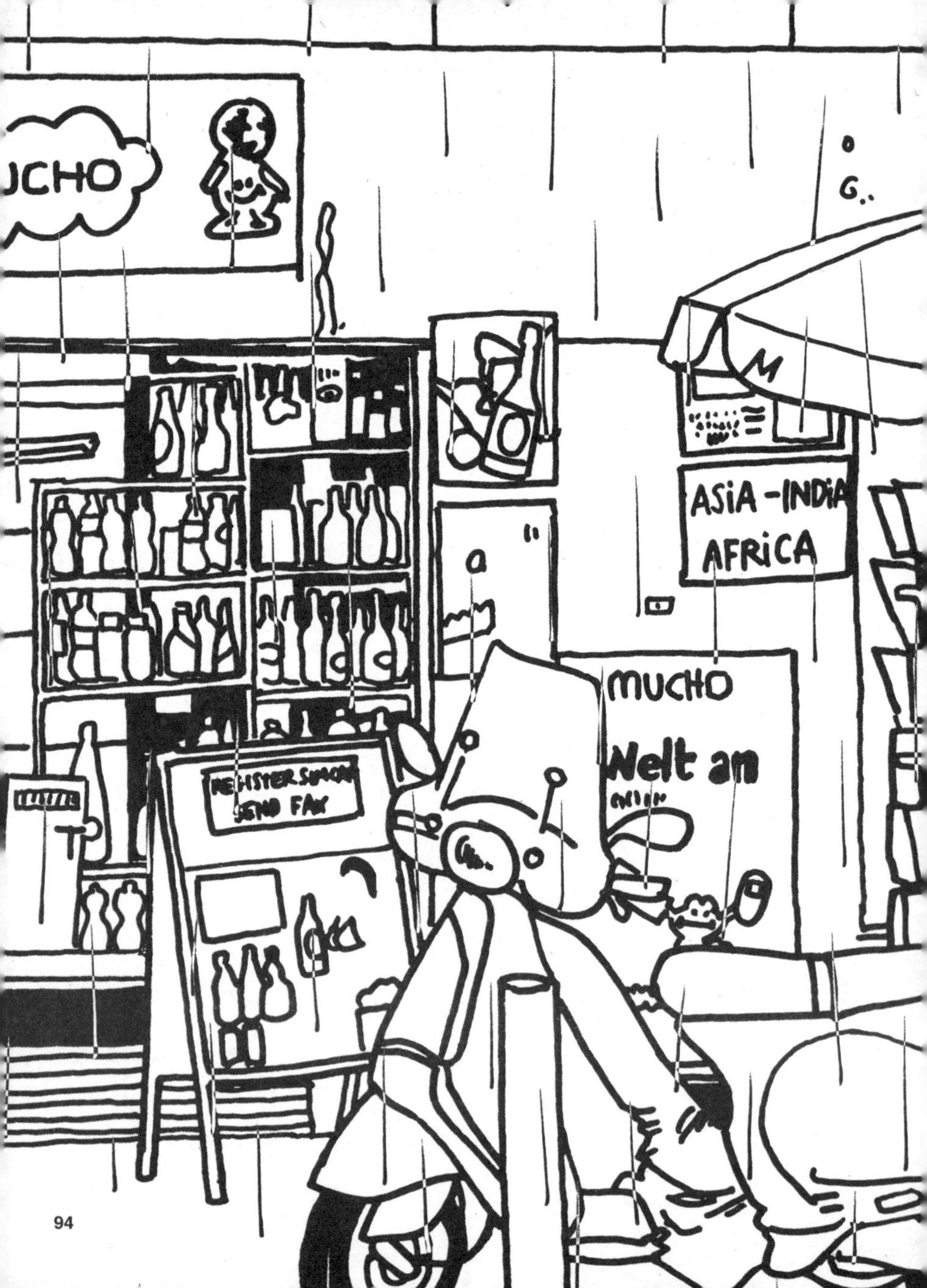

UCHO
MUCHO
Welt an
ASIA - INDIA
AFRICA
M
94

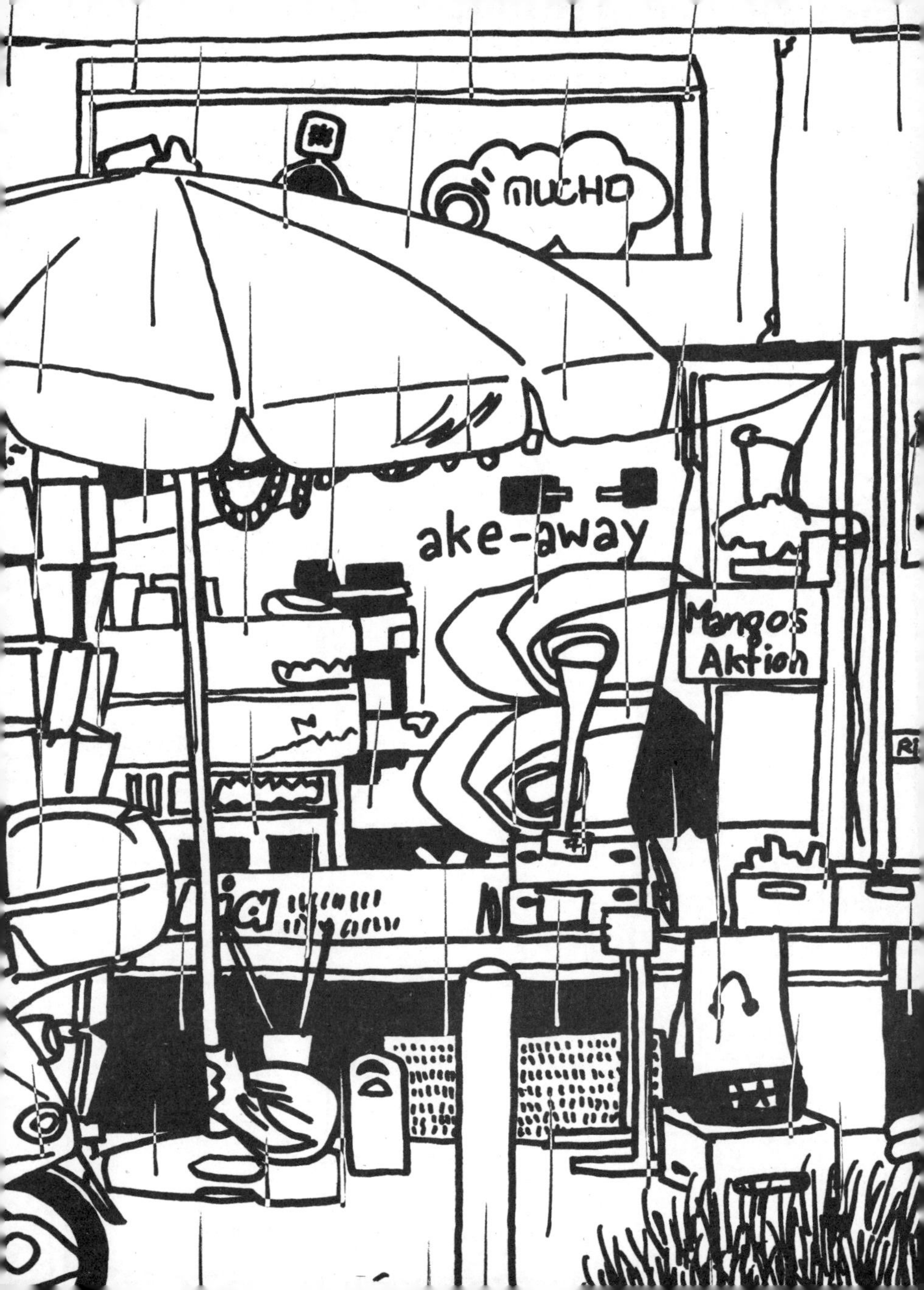
mucho
ake-away
Mangos
Aktion

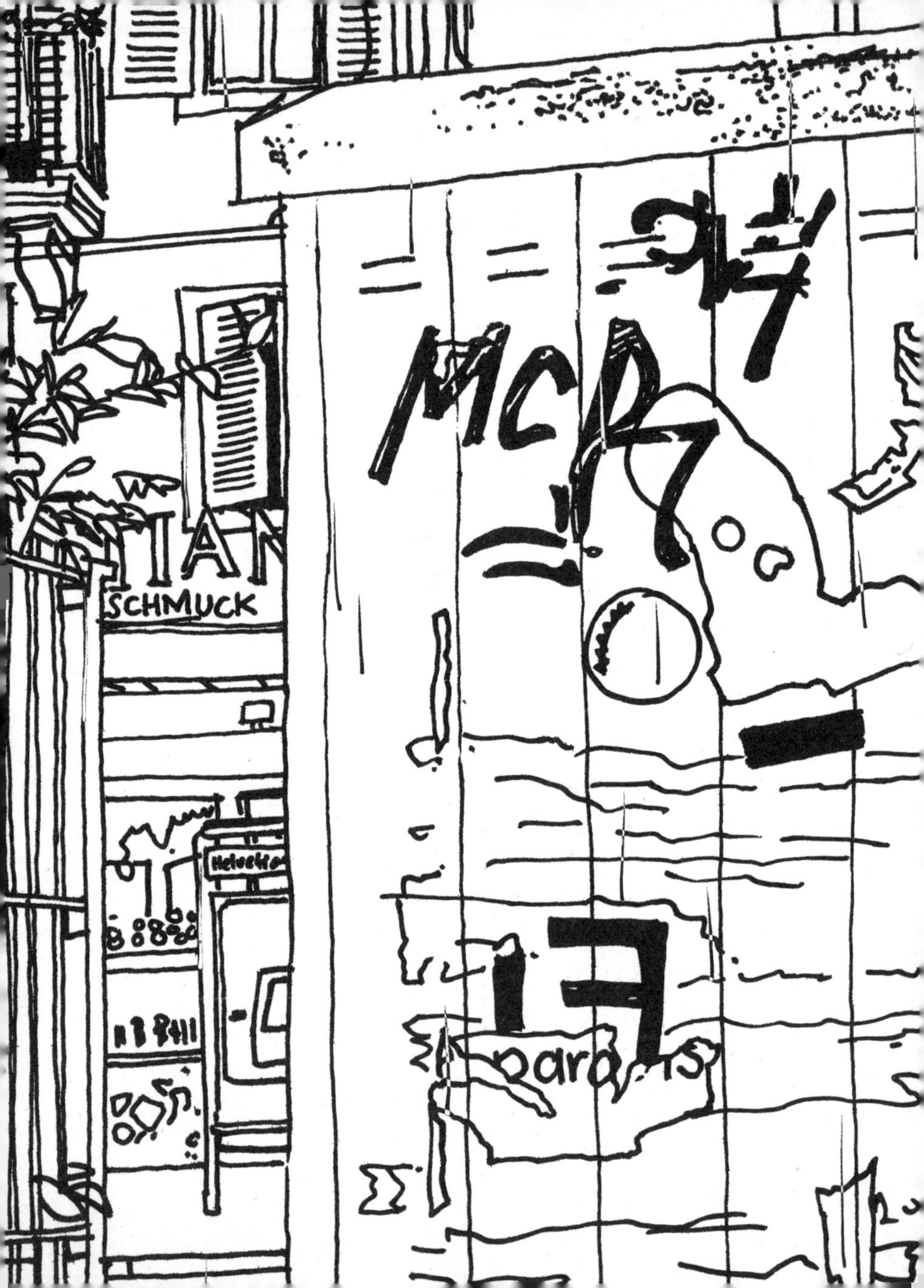

SCHMUCK
MCR

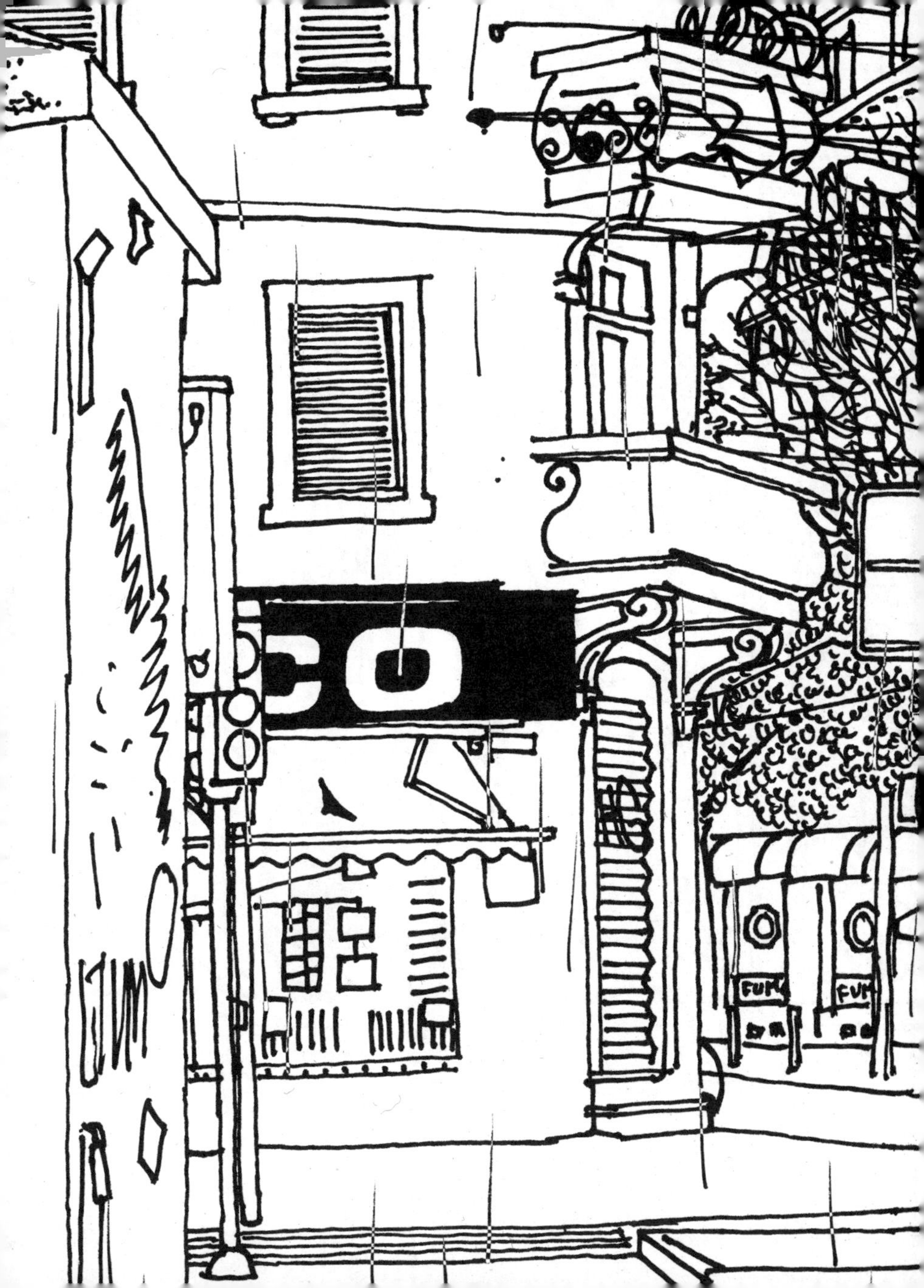

CO
FUM
FUM

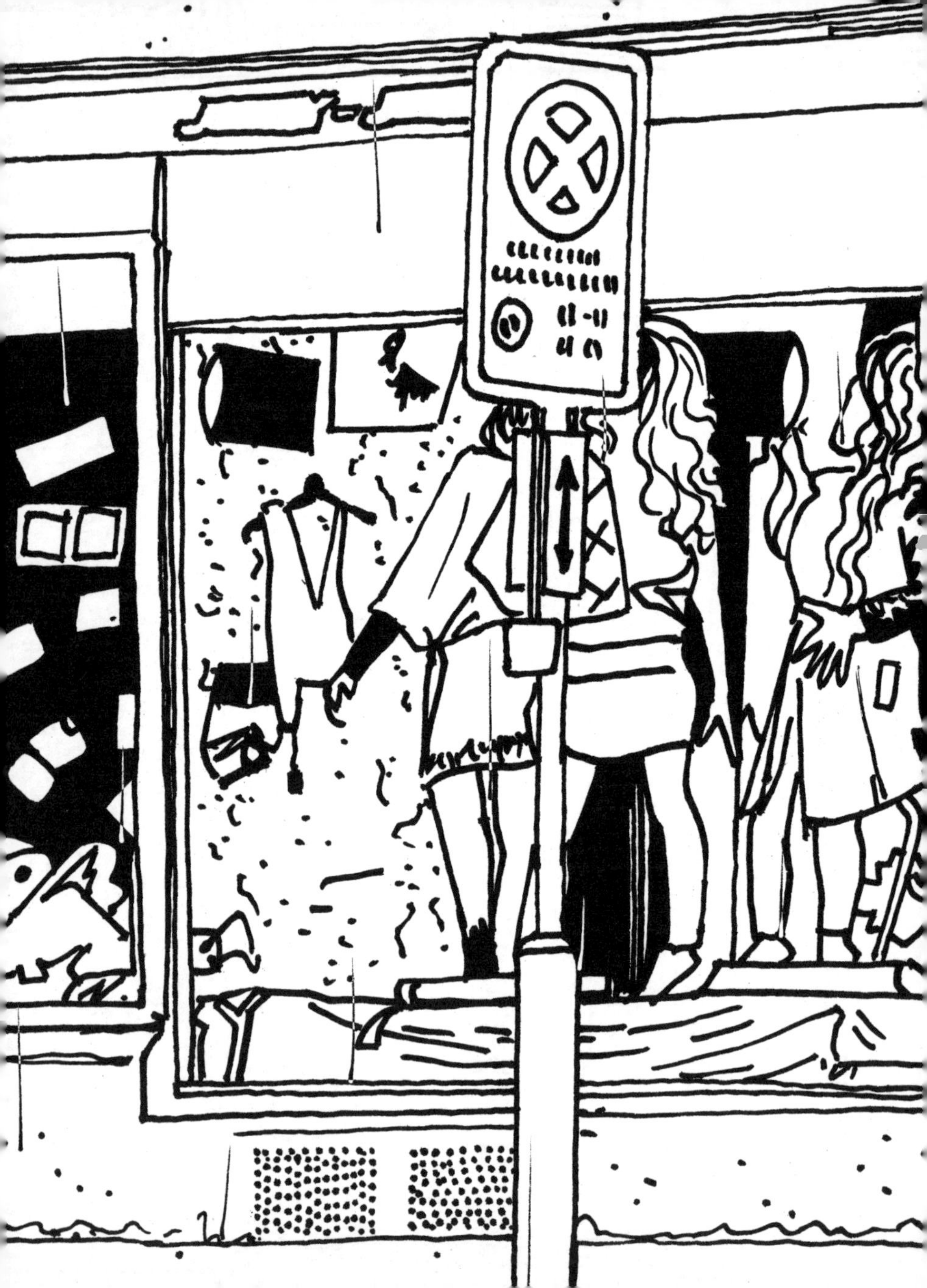

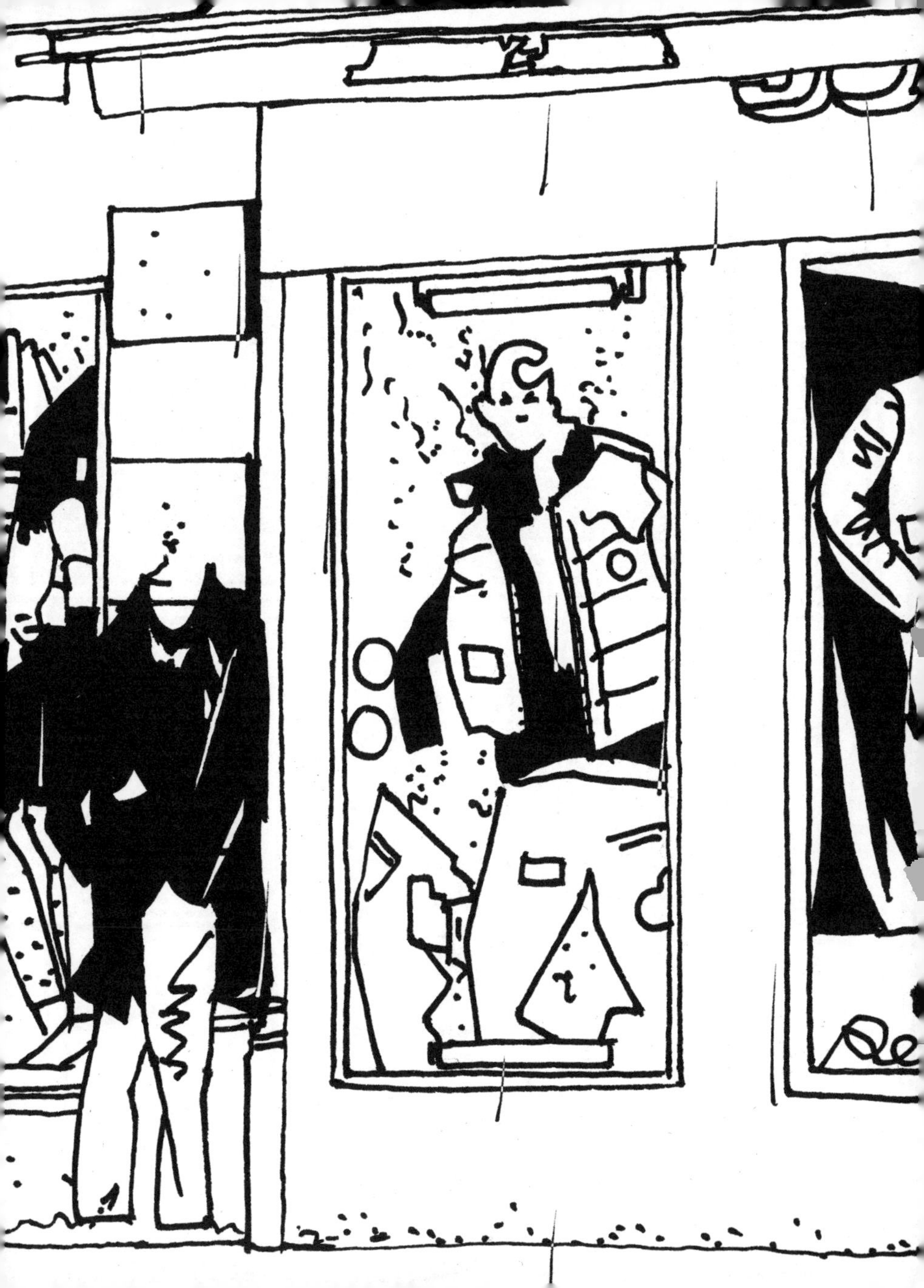

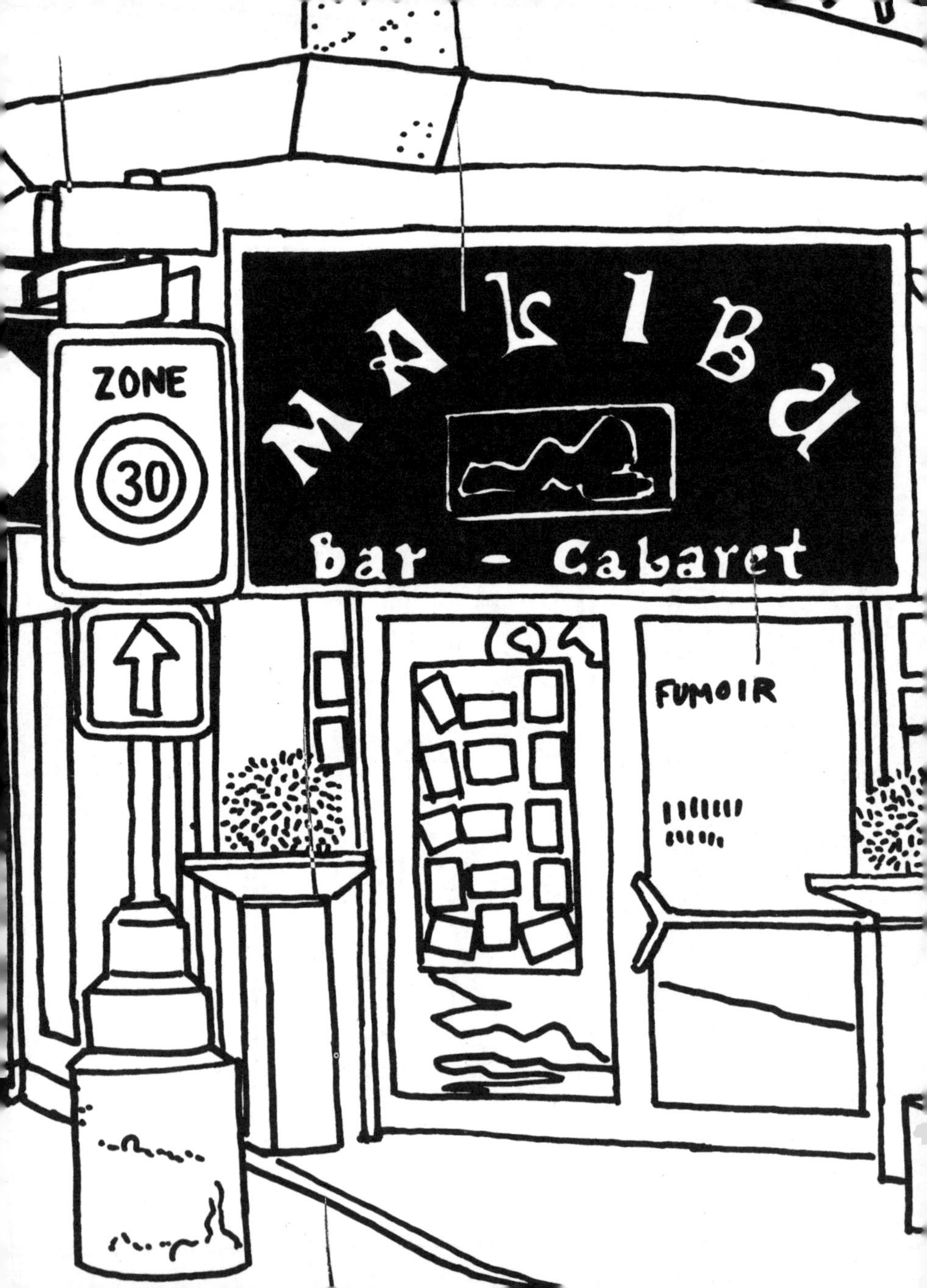

MALIBU
bar - Cabaret
ZONE
30
FUMOIR

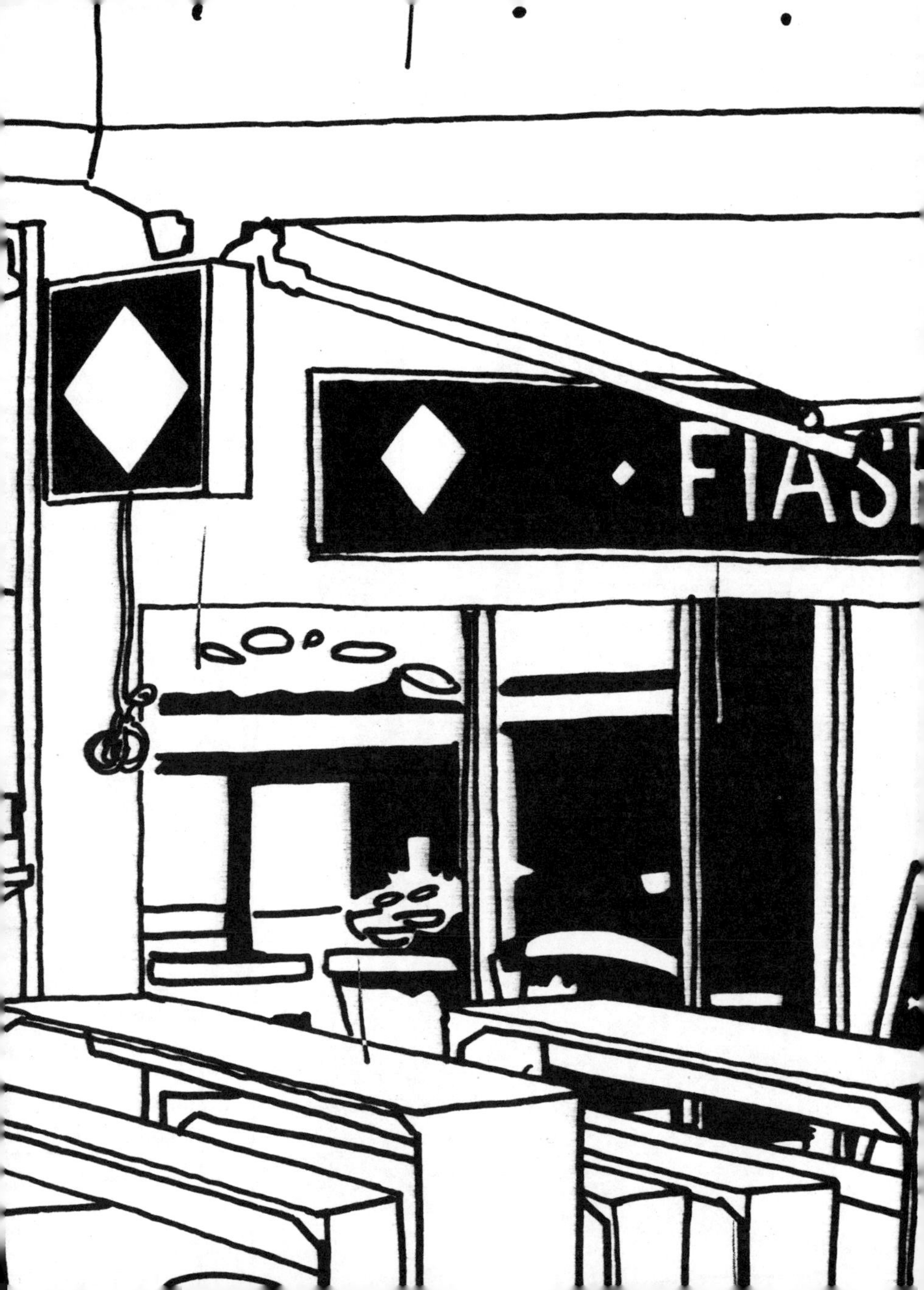

· FIAS

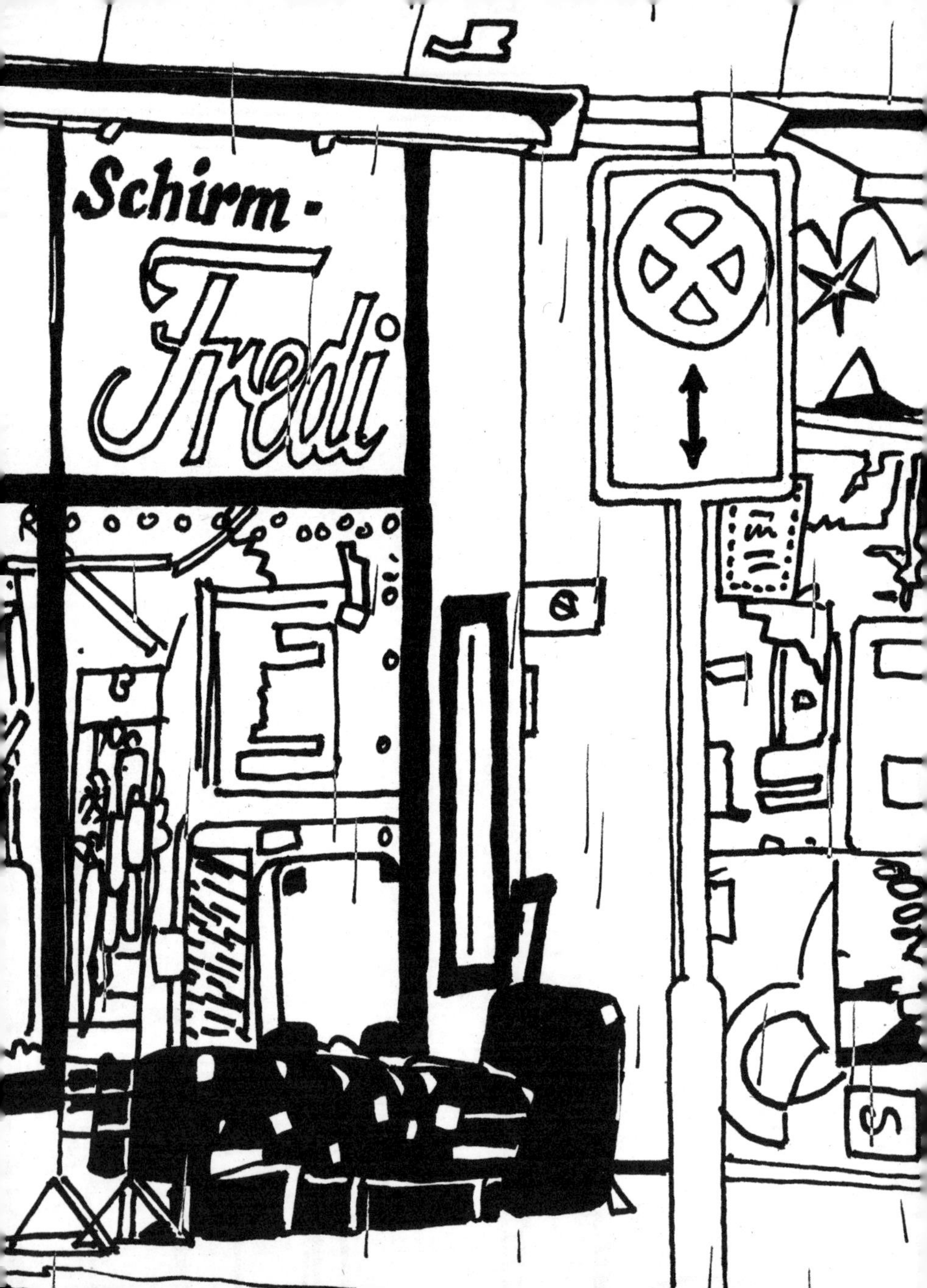
Schirm-
Fredi

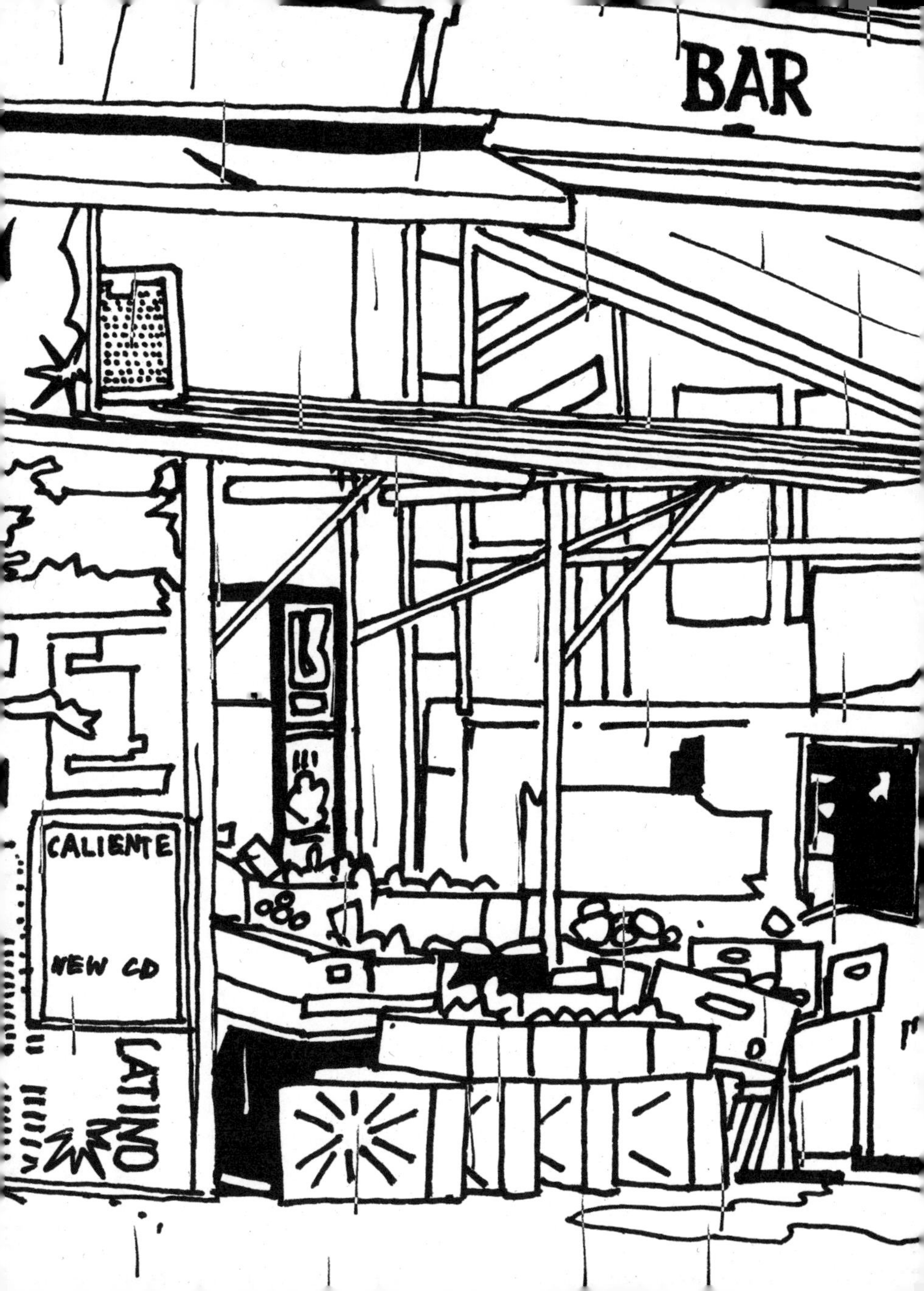

BAR
CALIENTE
NEW CD
LATINO

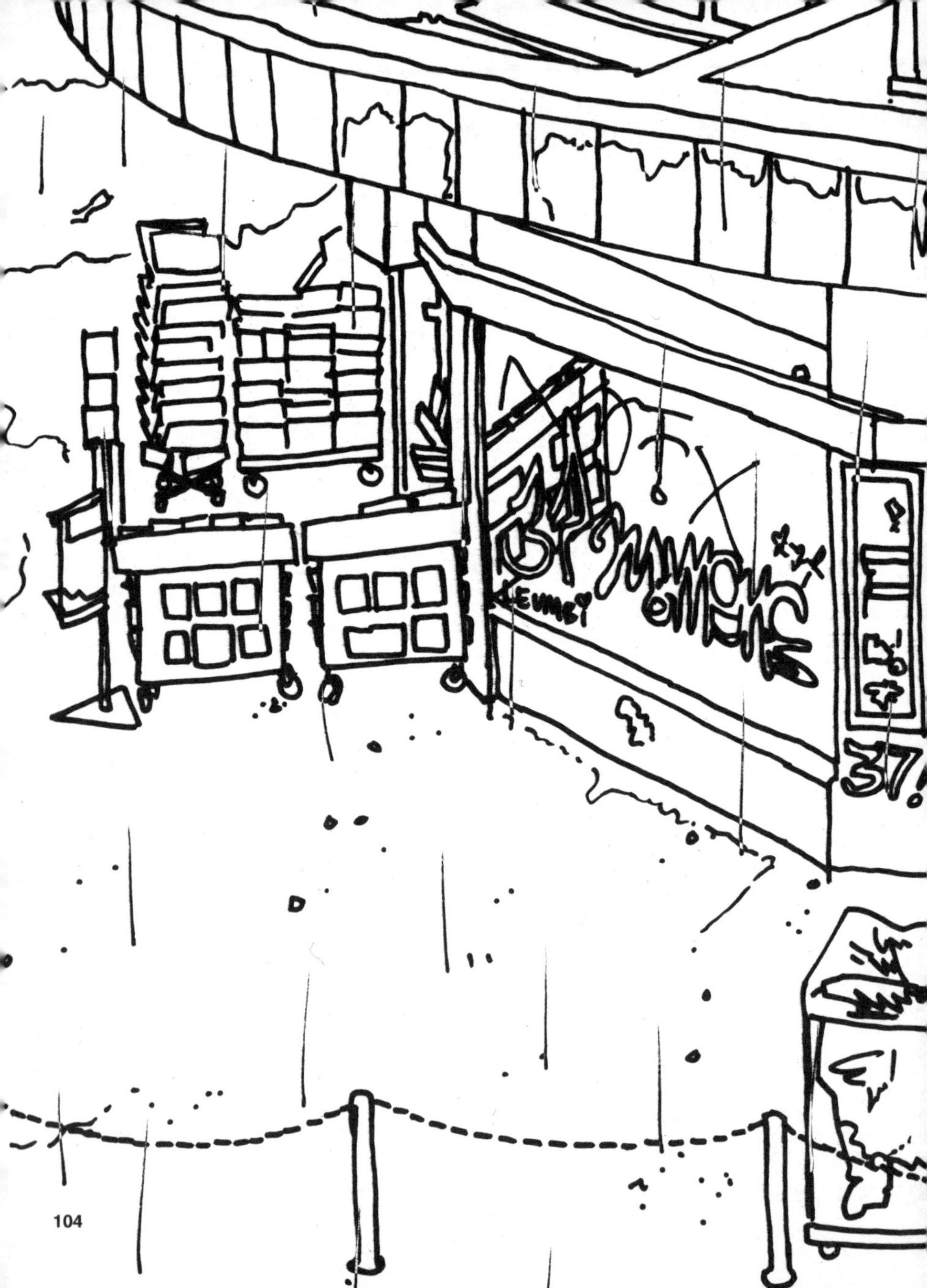

LEUMEY
37!

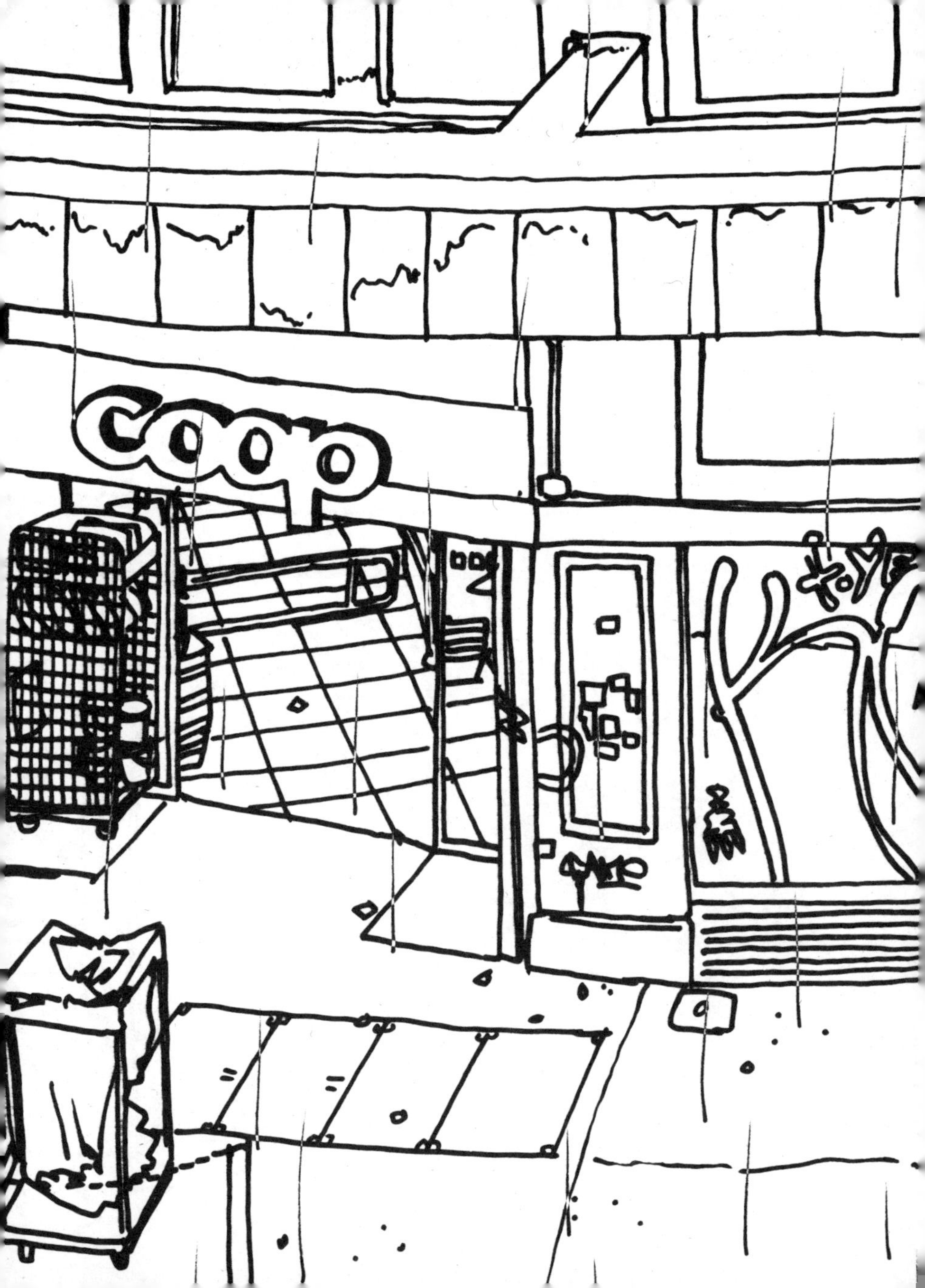

coop

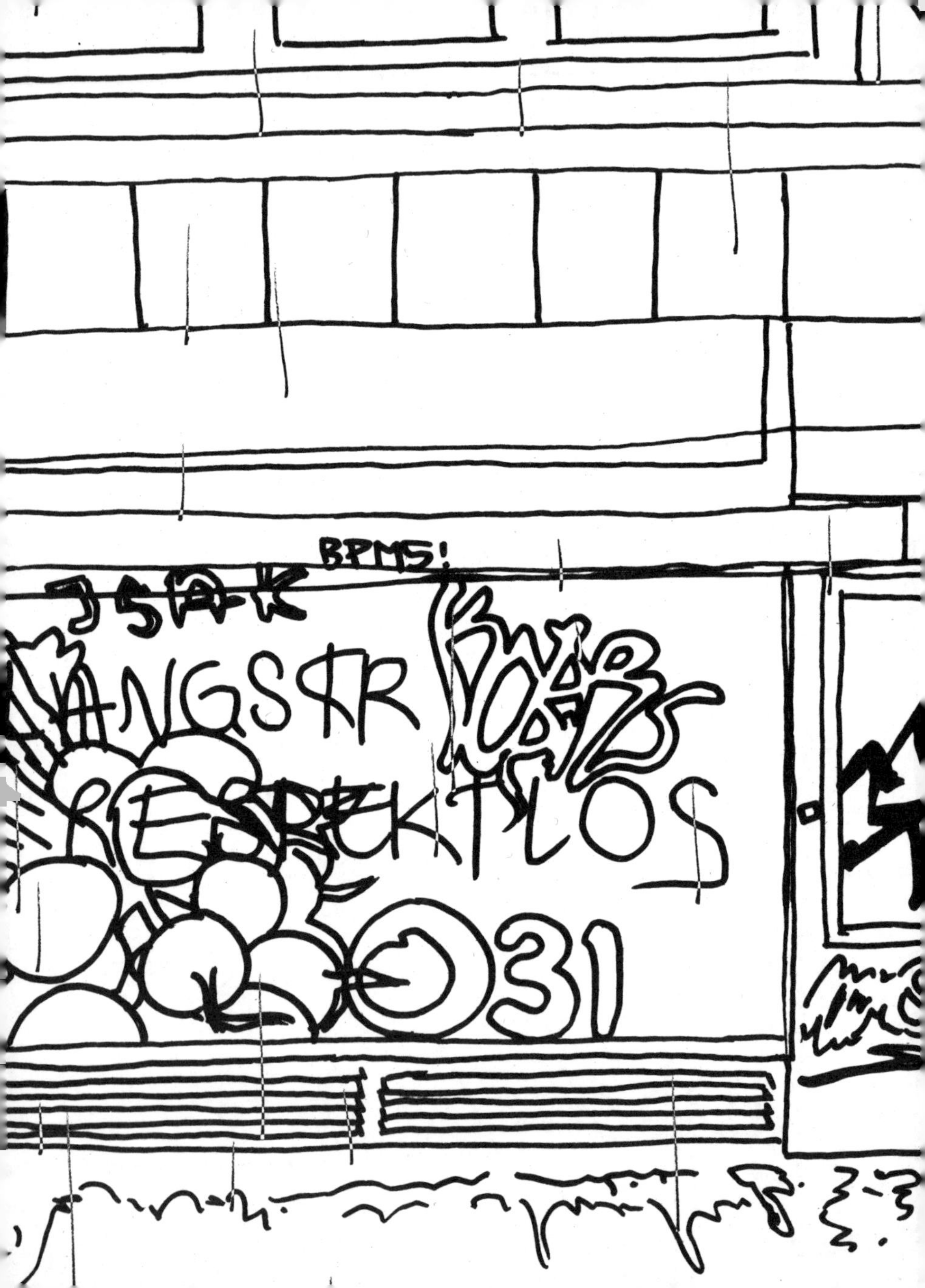

BPMS!
JSPK
ANGSTR
RESPEKTLOS
31

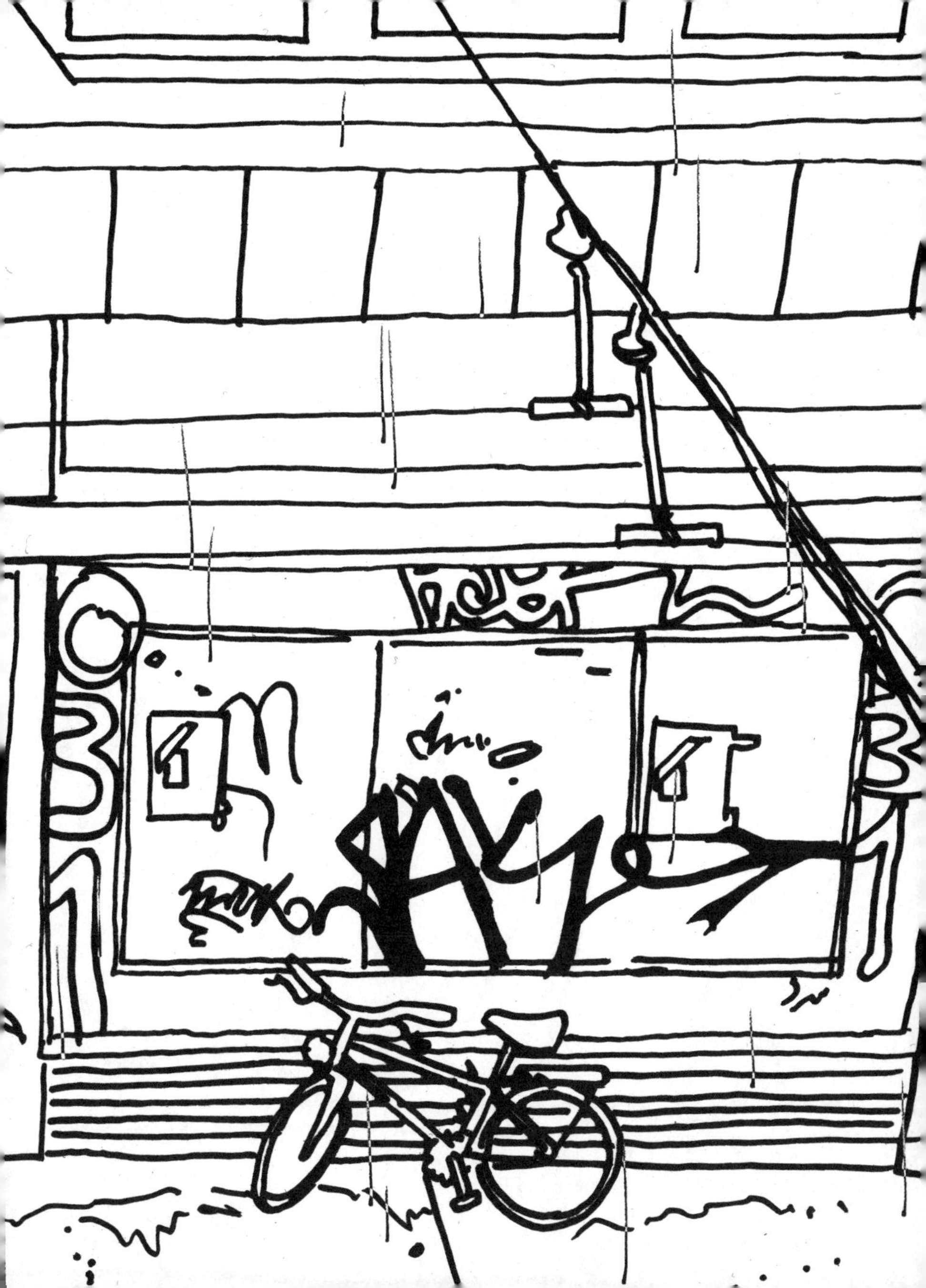

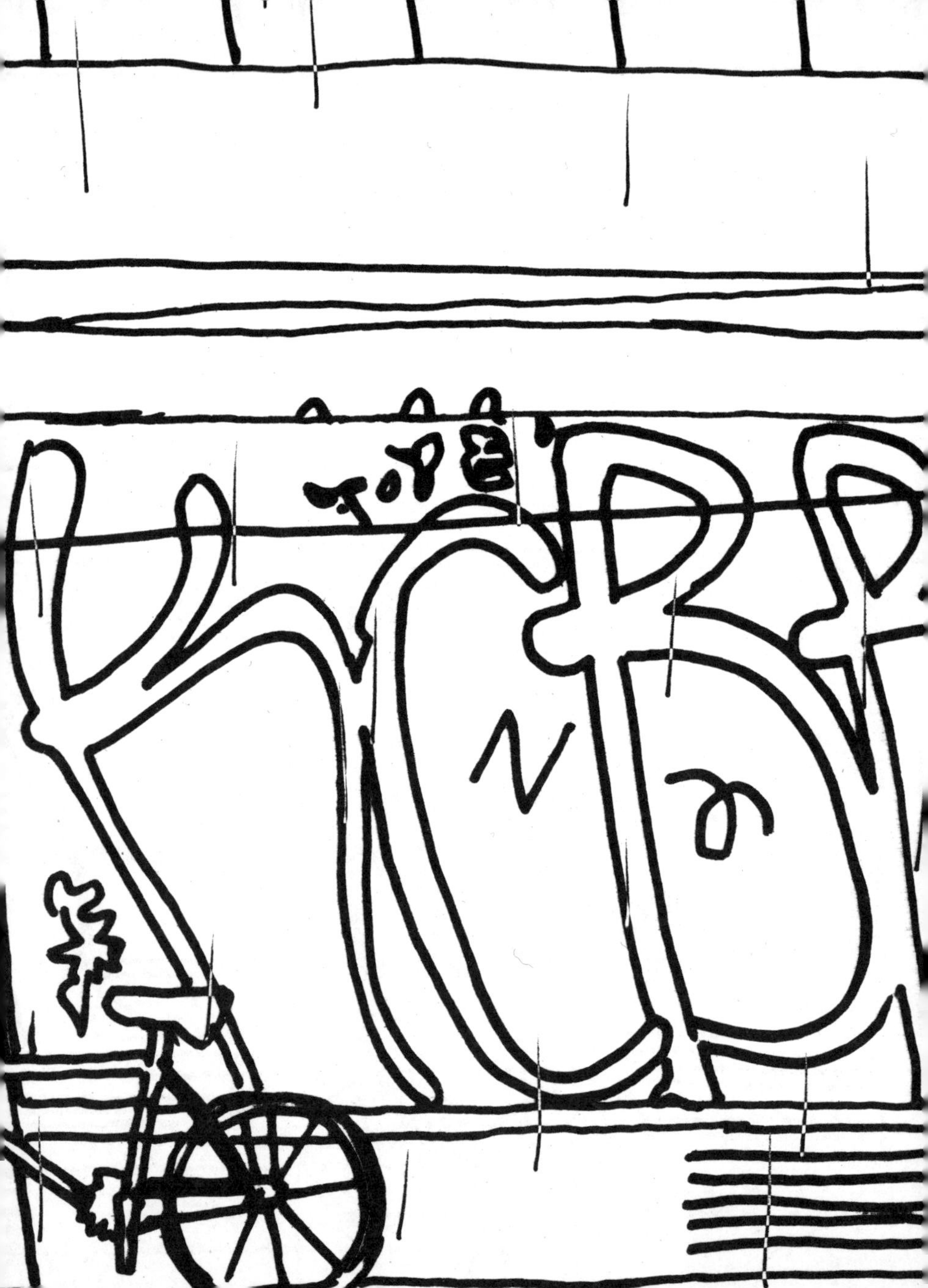

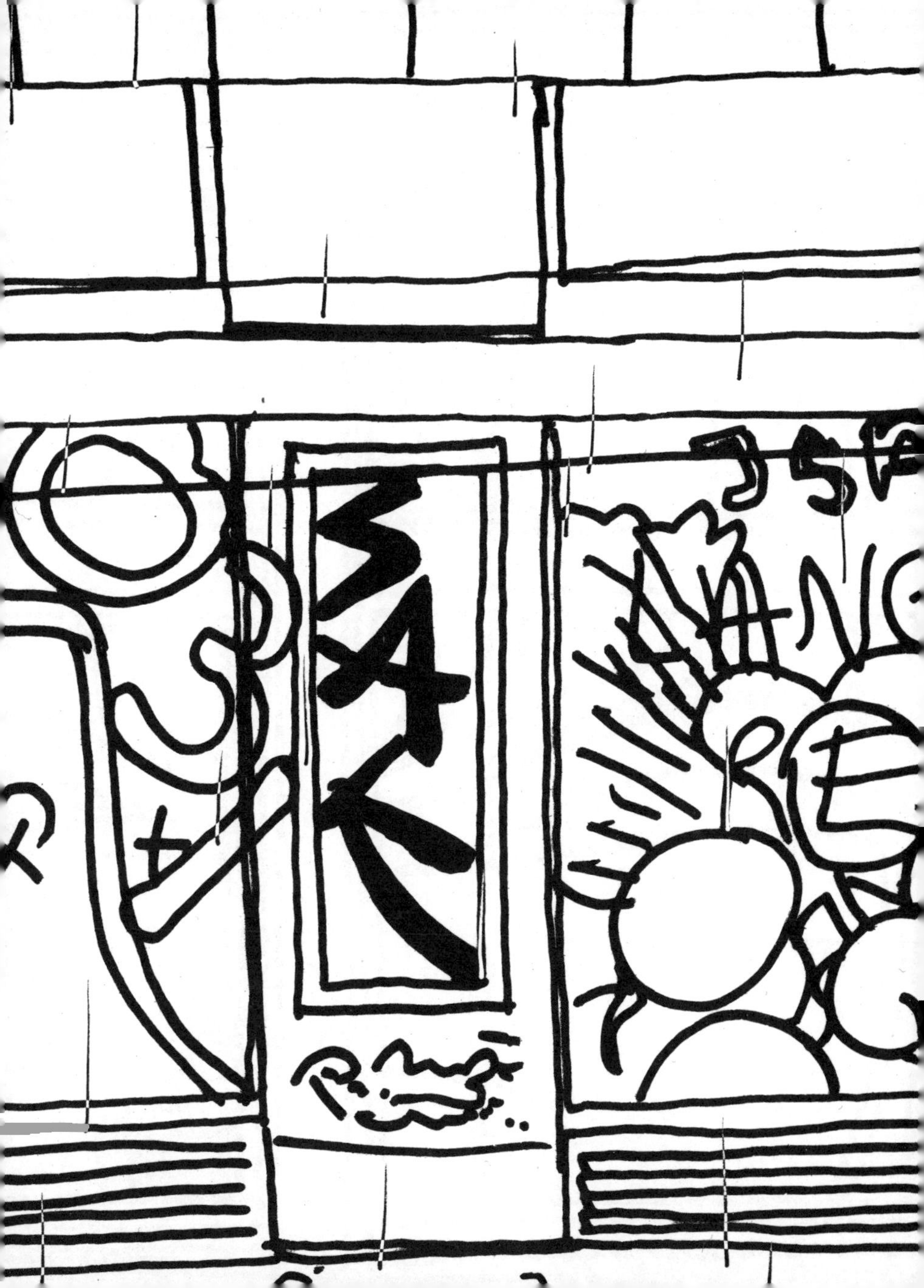

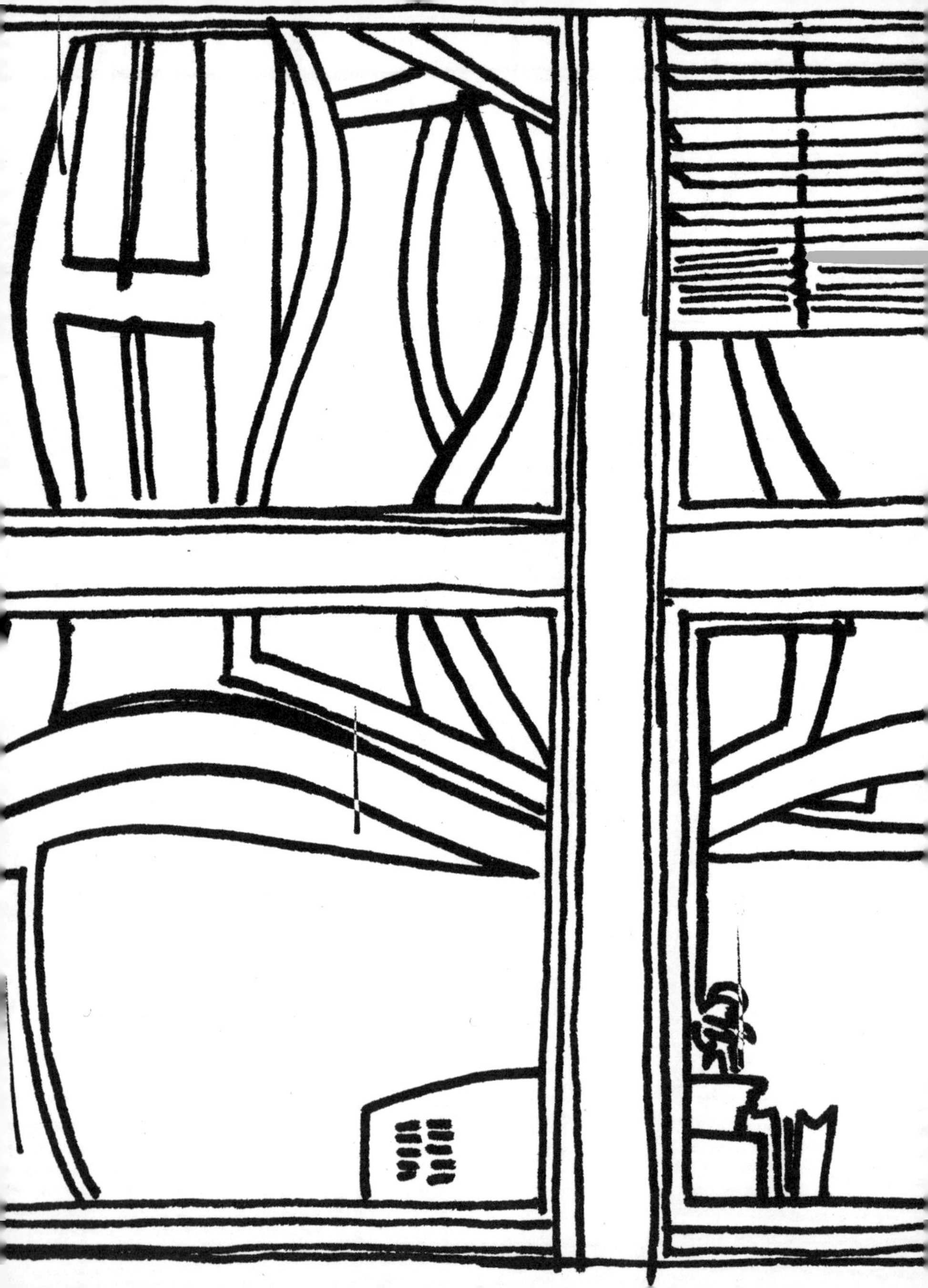

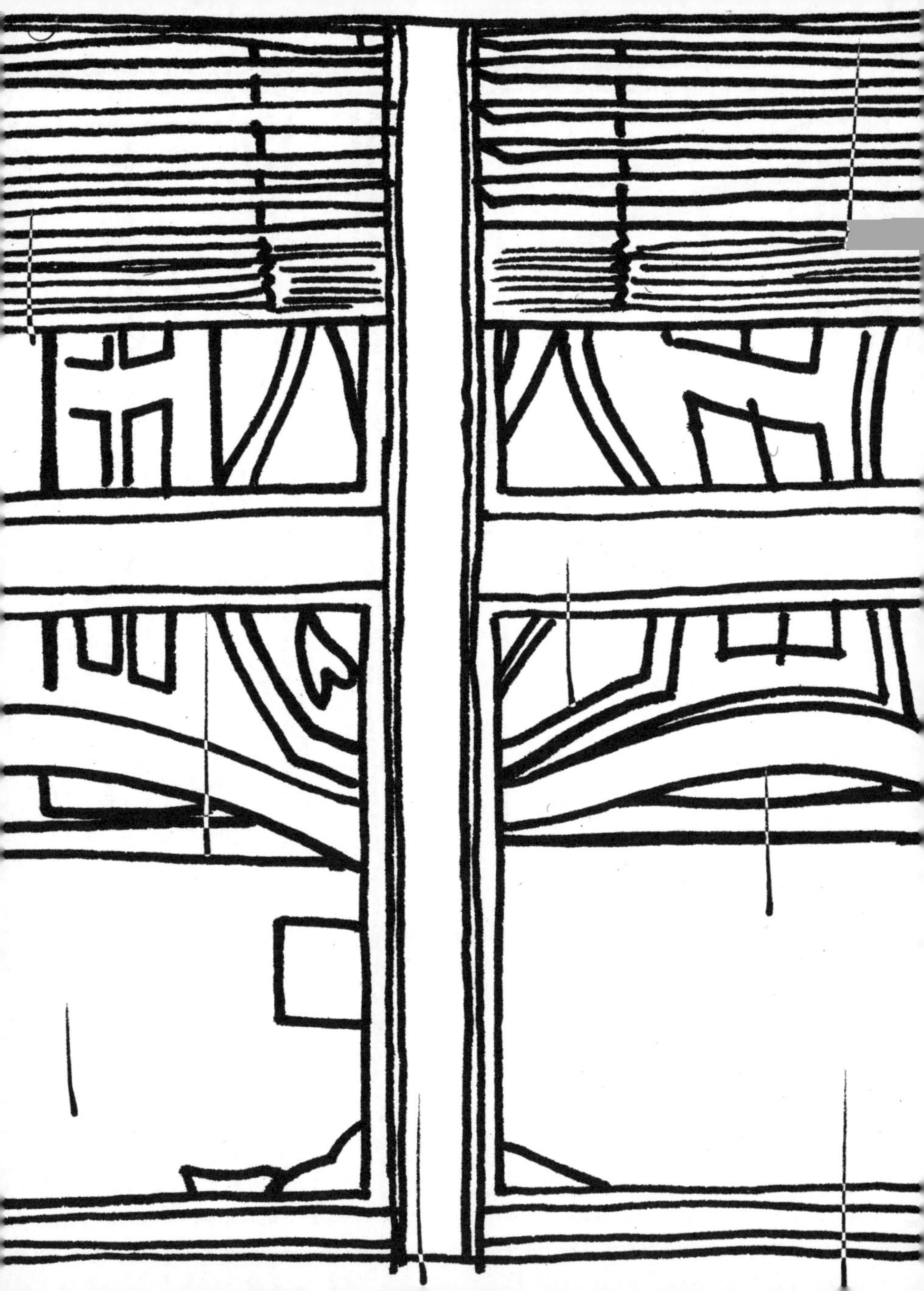

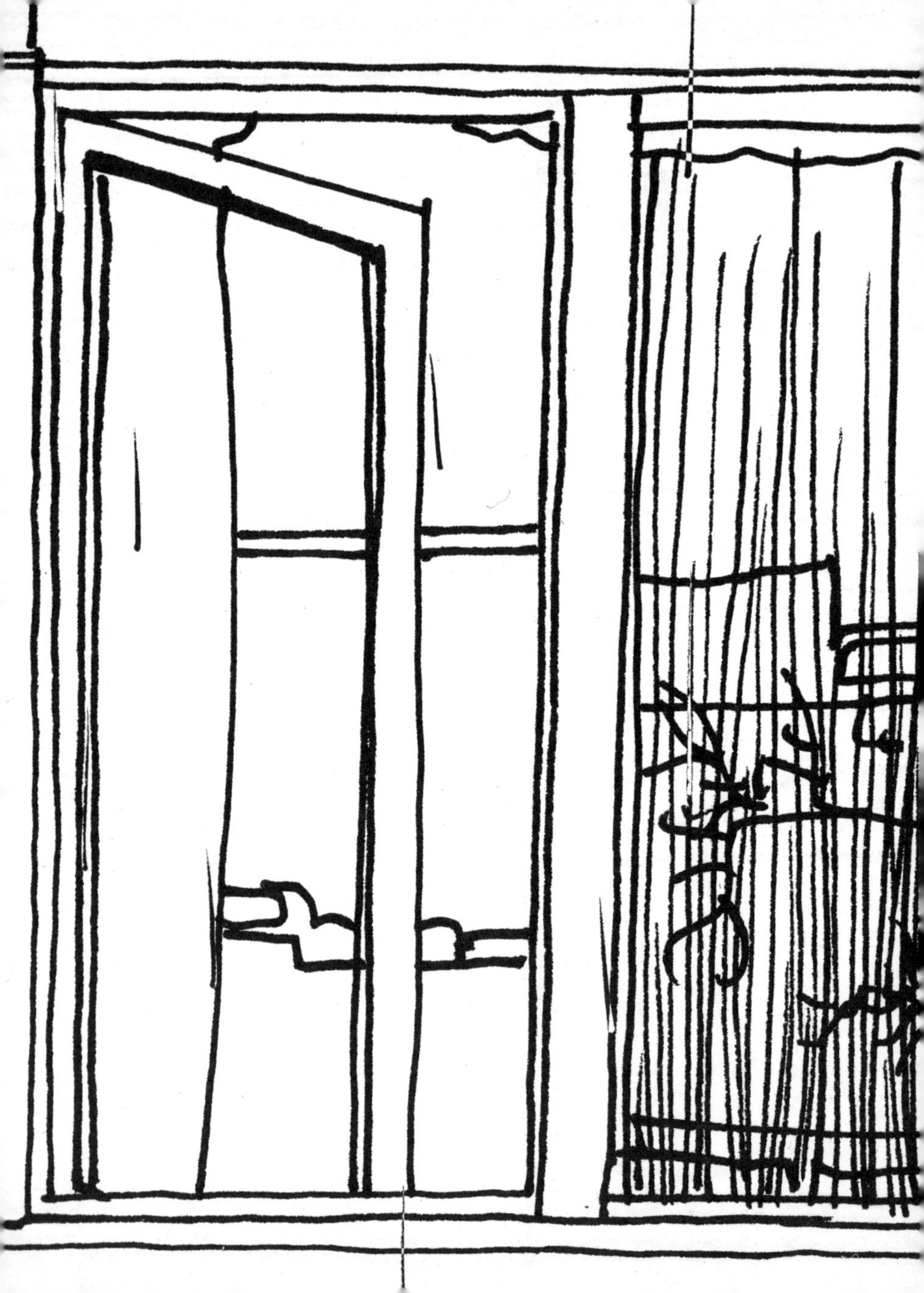

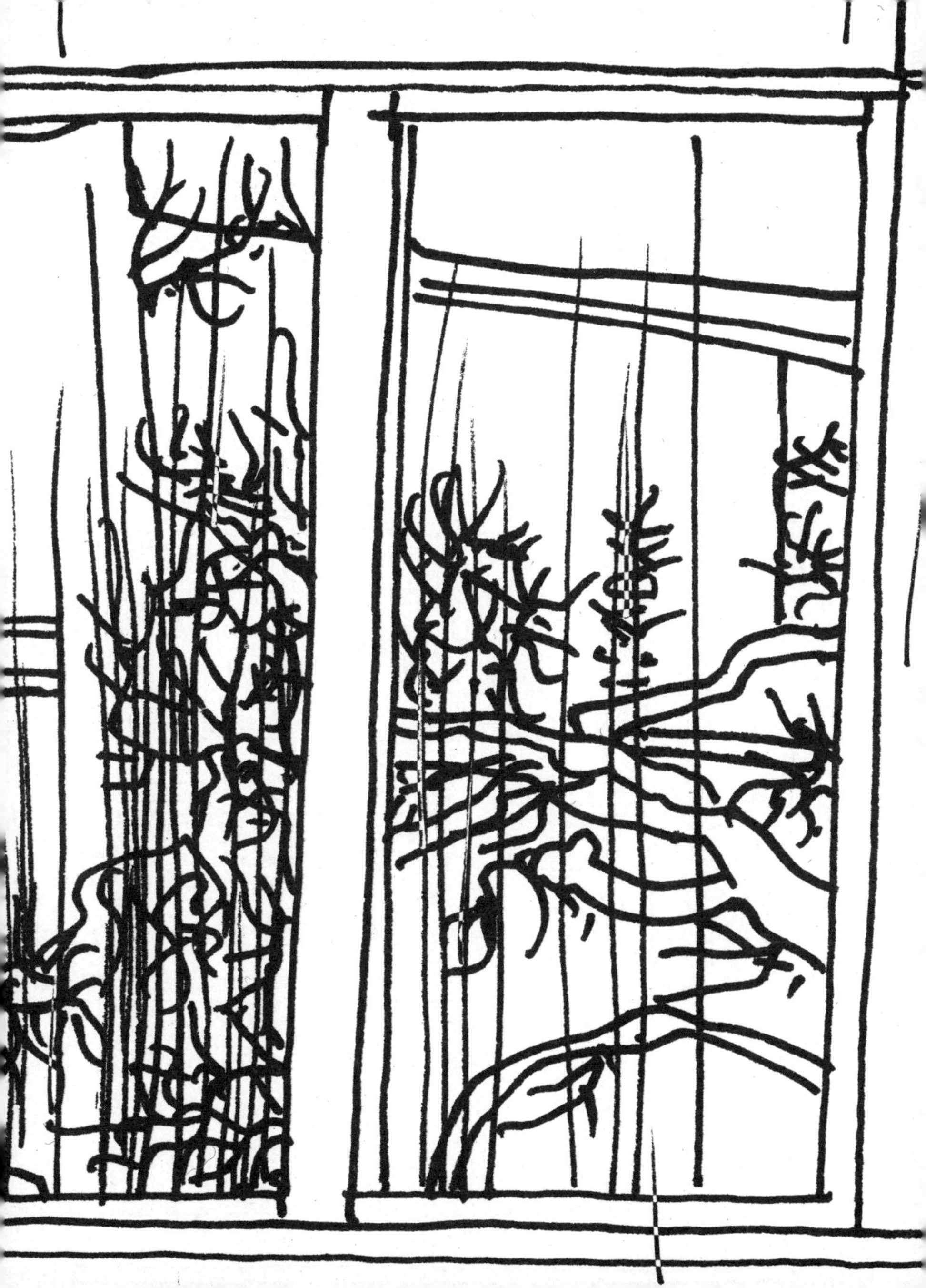

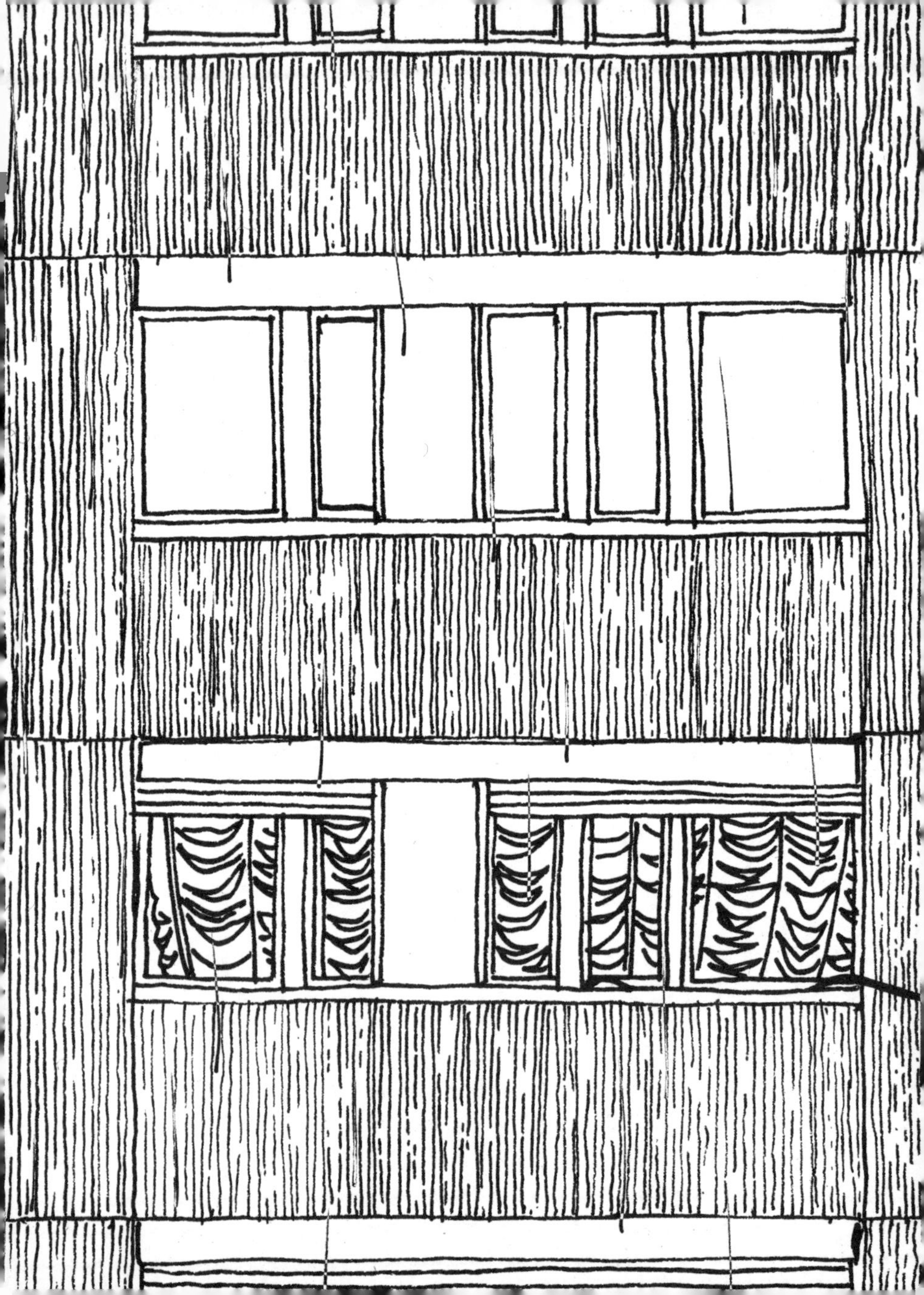

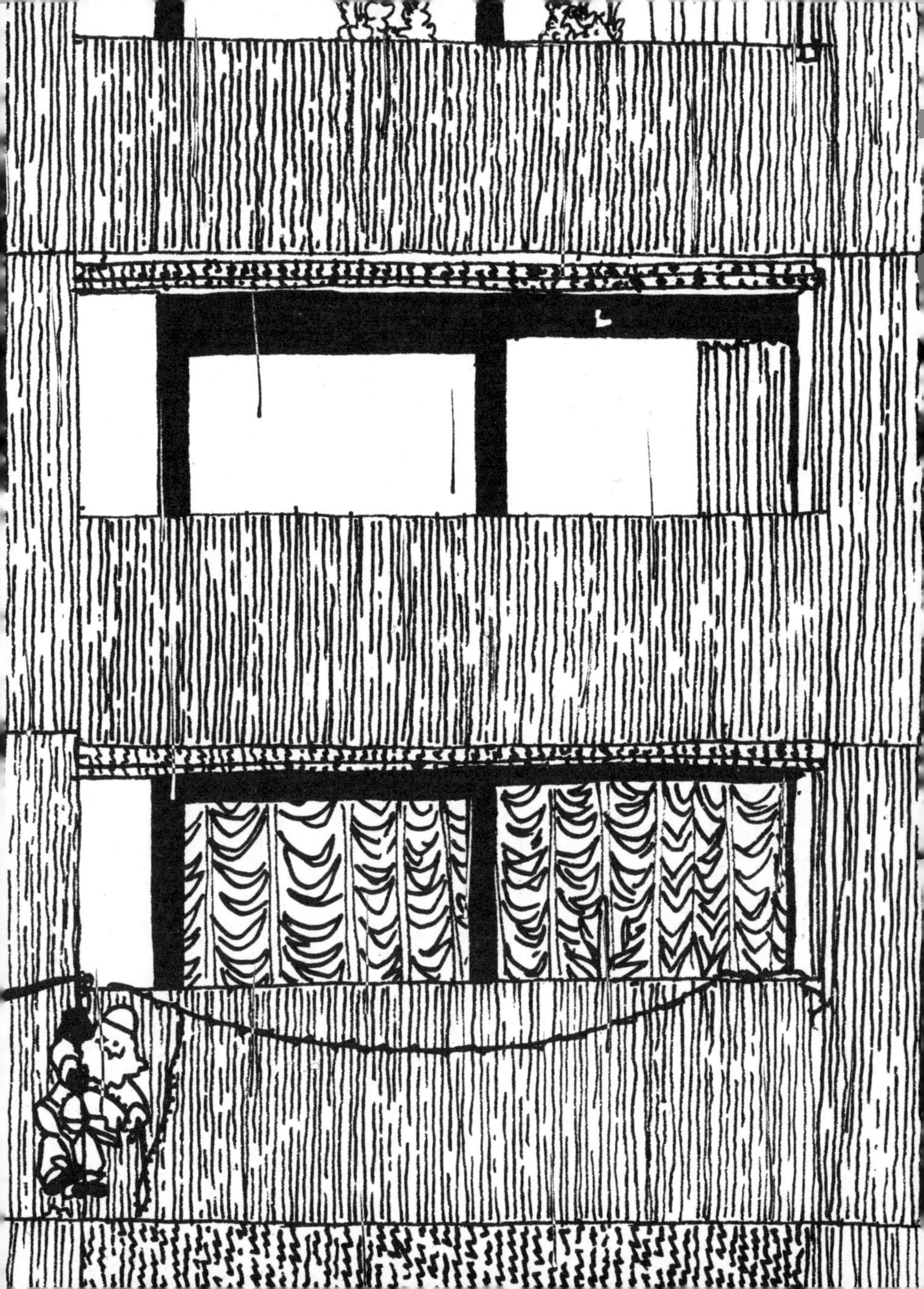

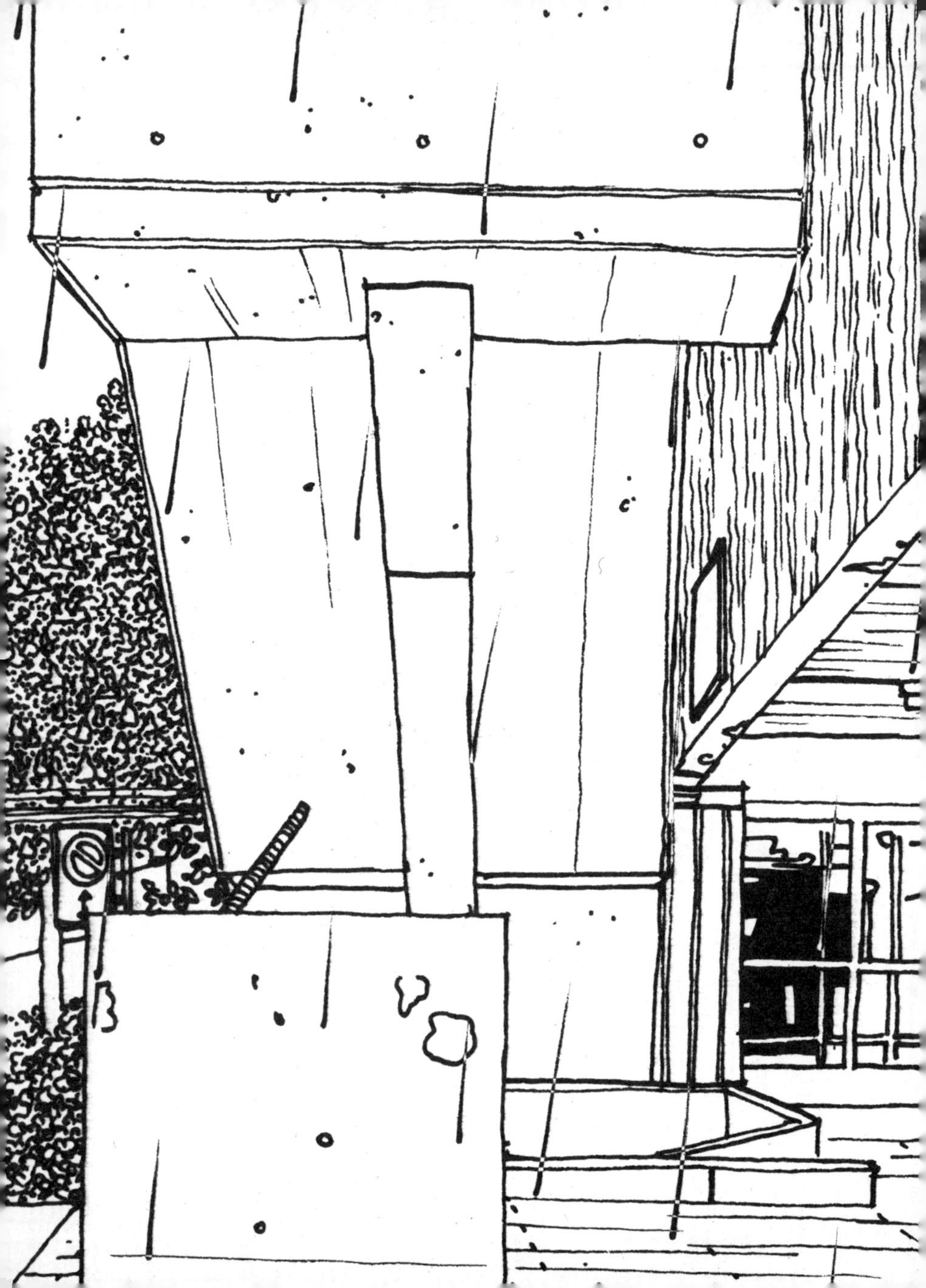

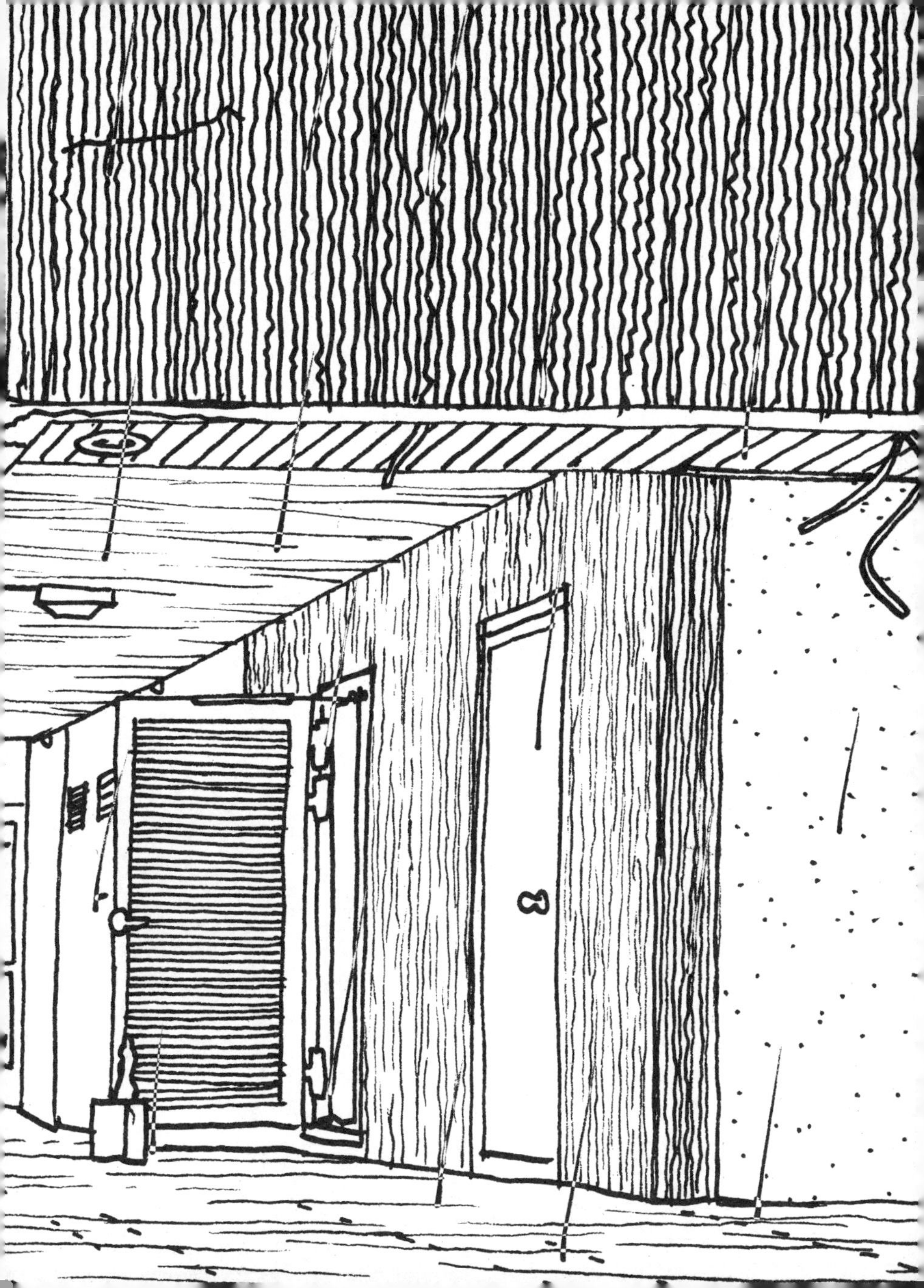

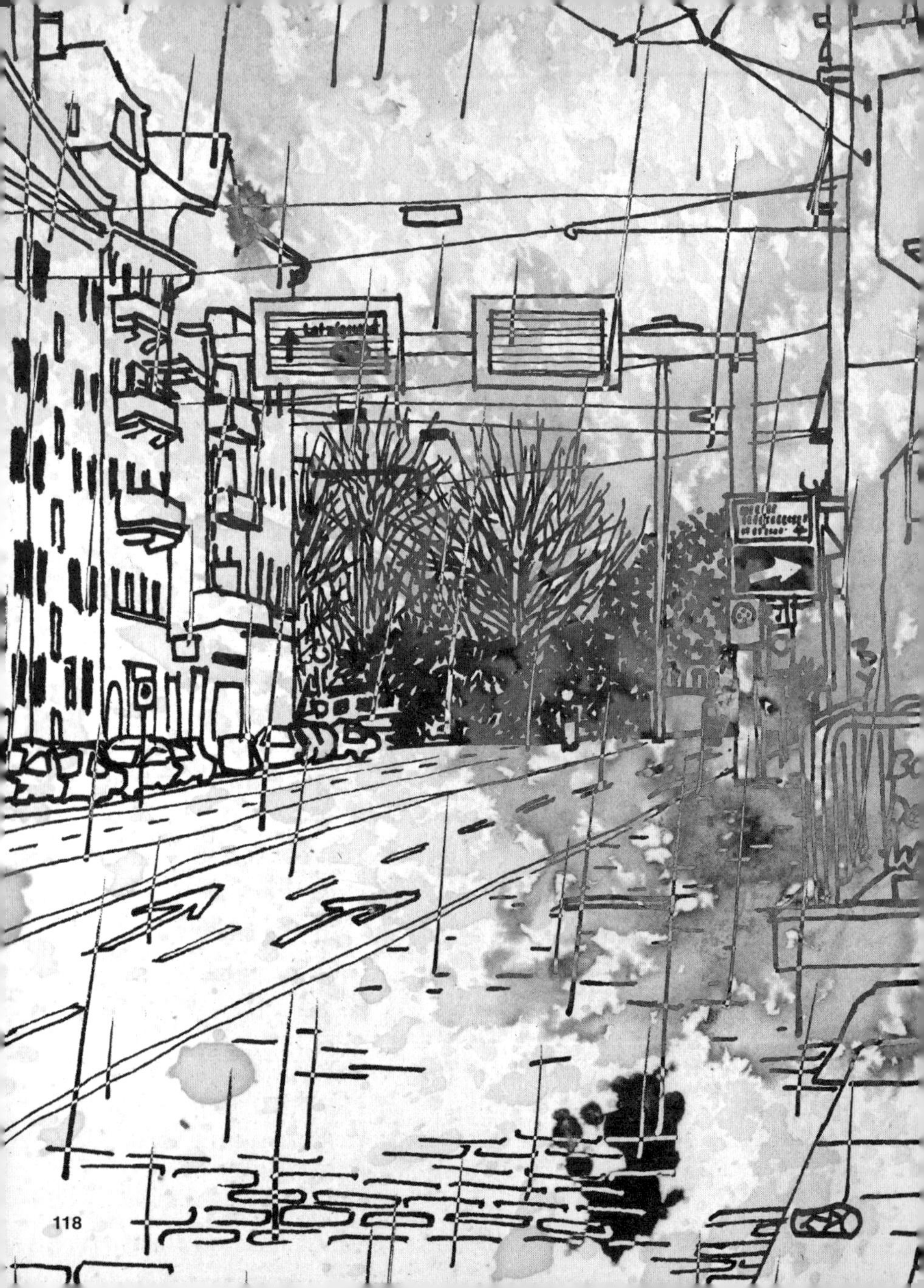

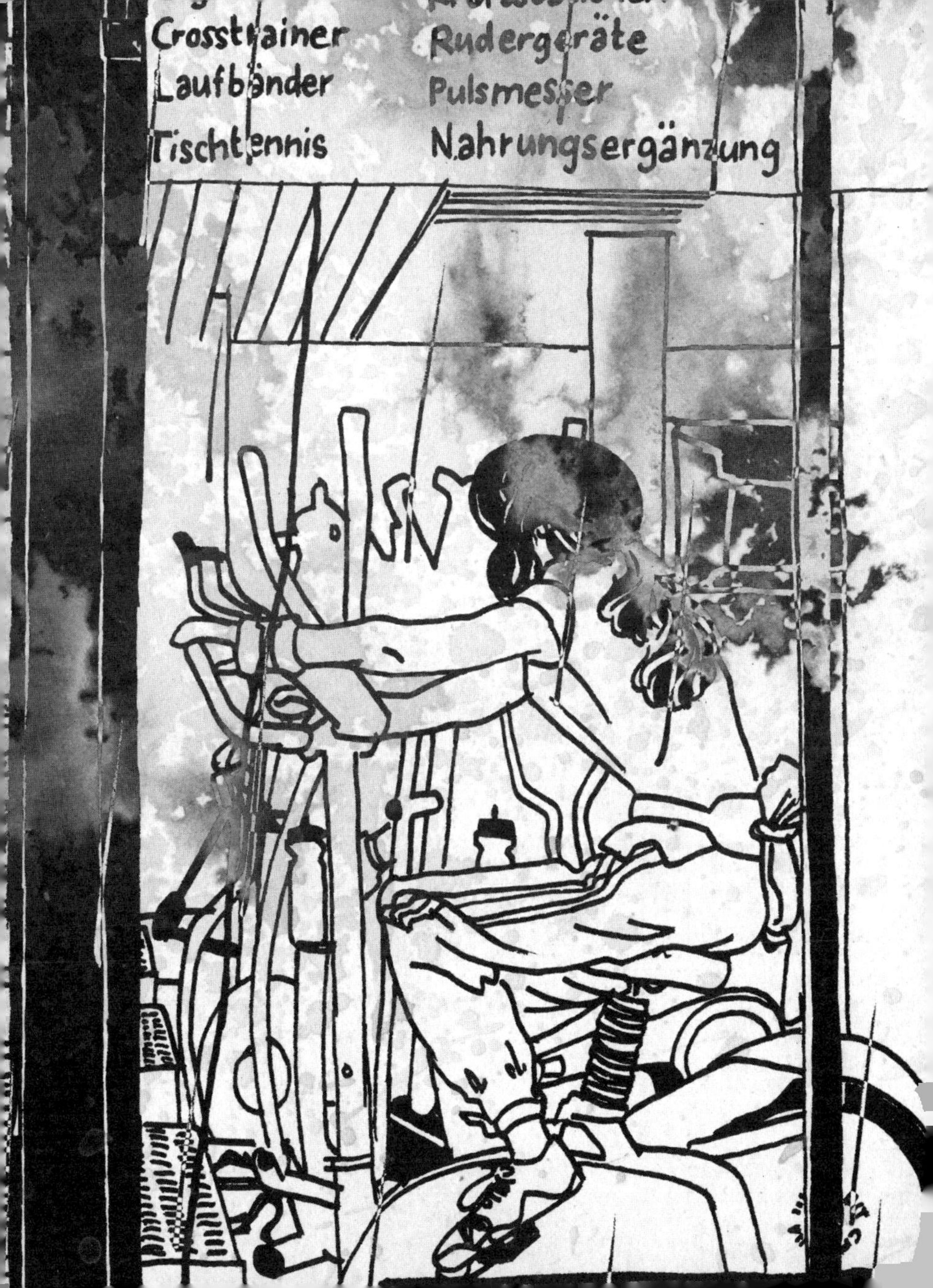

Crosstrainer
Laufbänder
Tischtennis
Rudergeräte
Pulsmesser
Nahrungsergänzung

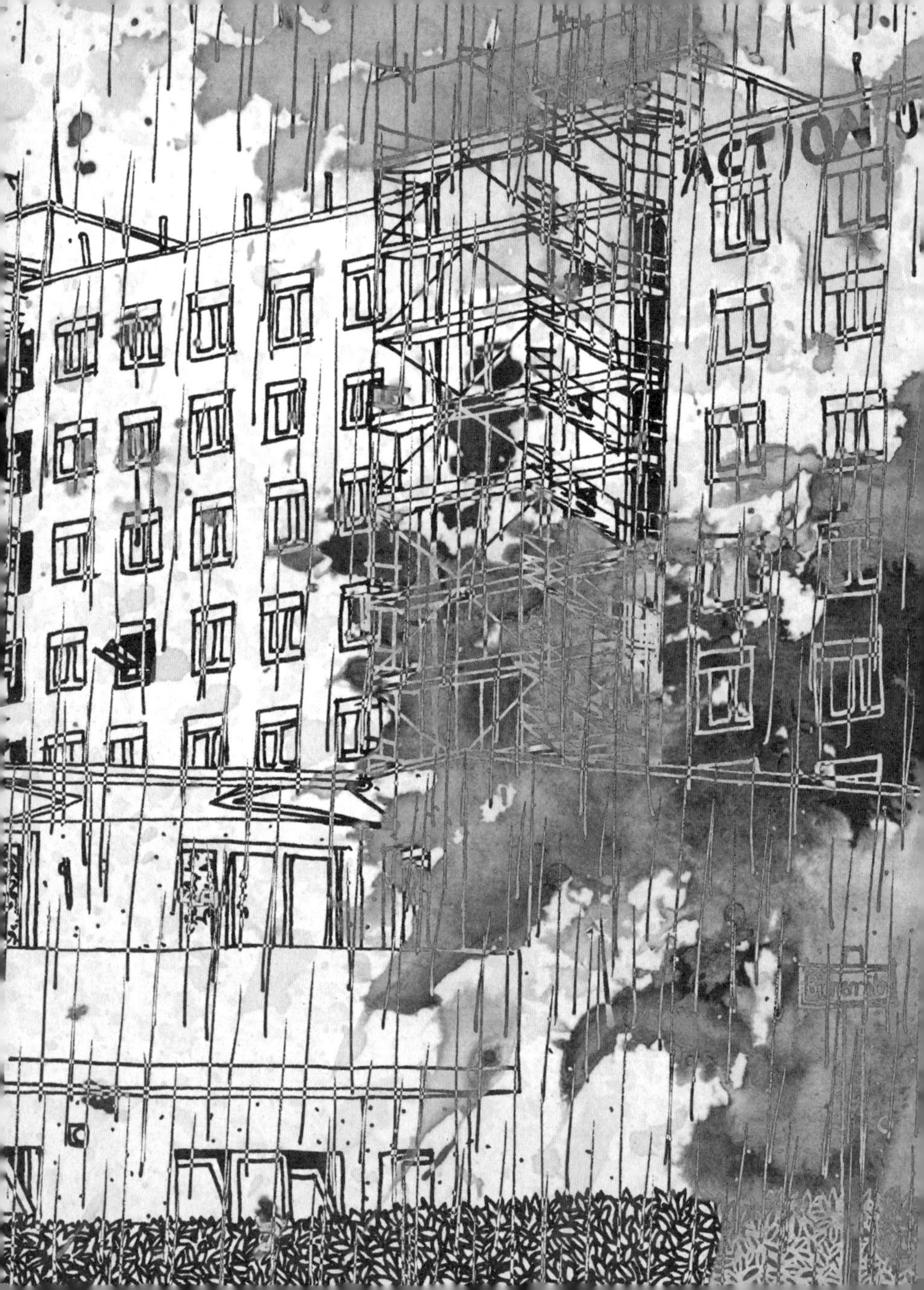
ACTION

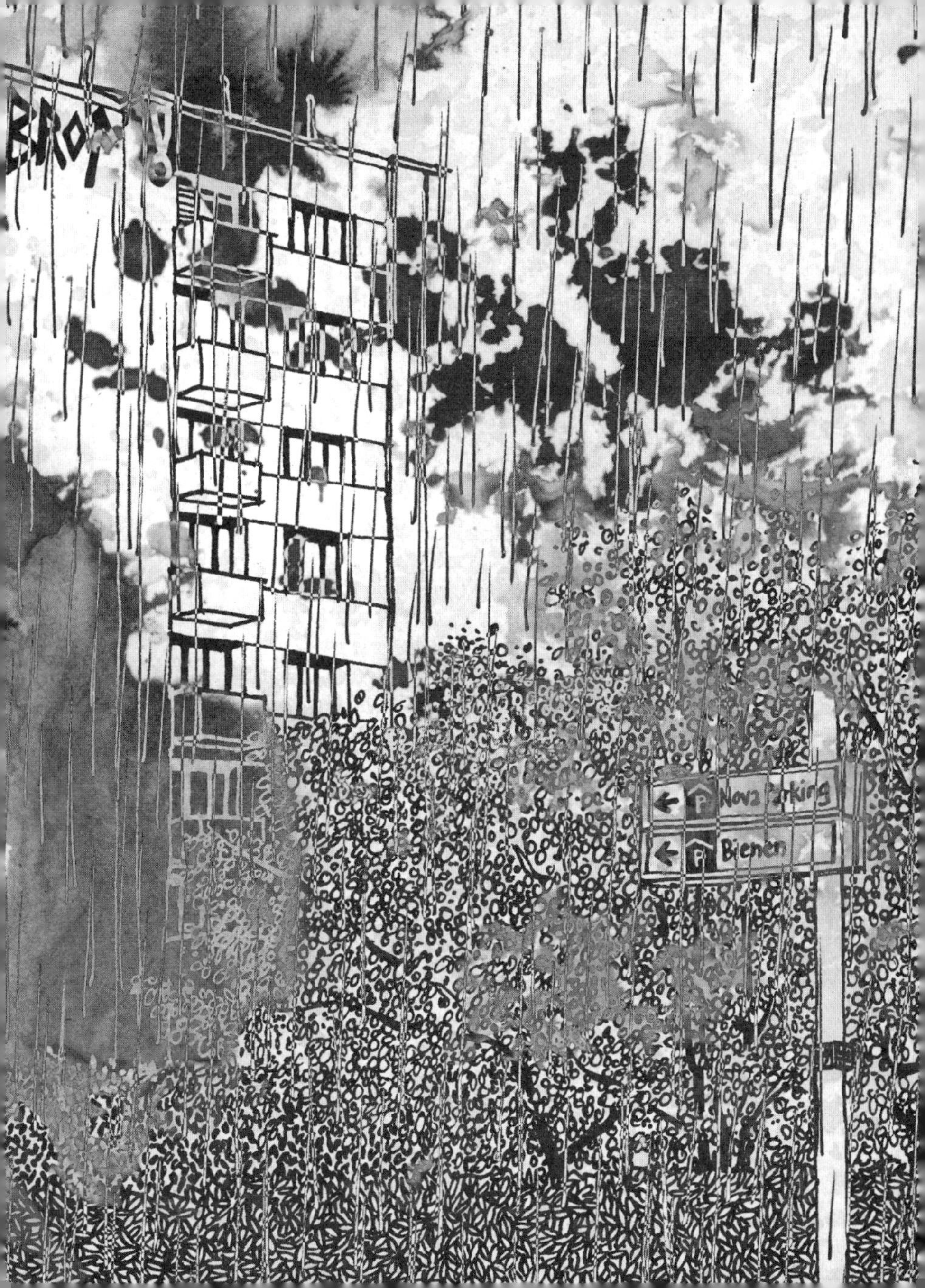
BROT
Nova Parking
Bienen

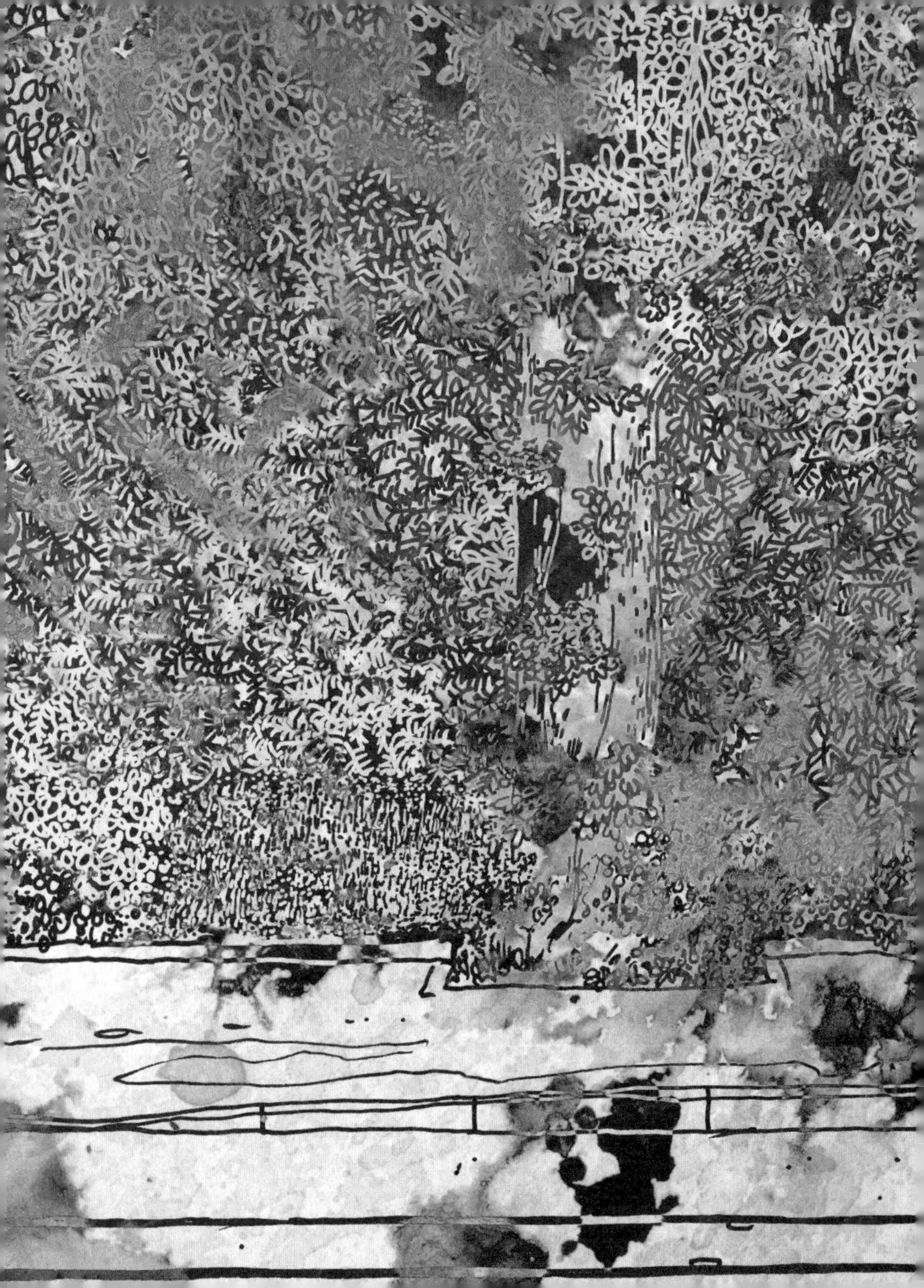

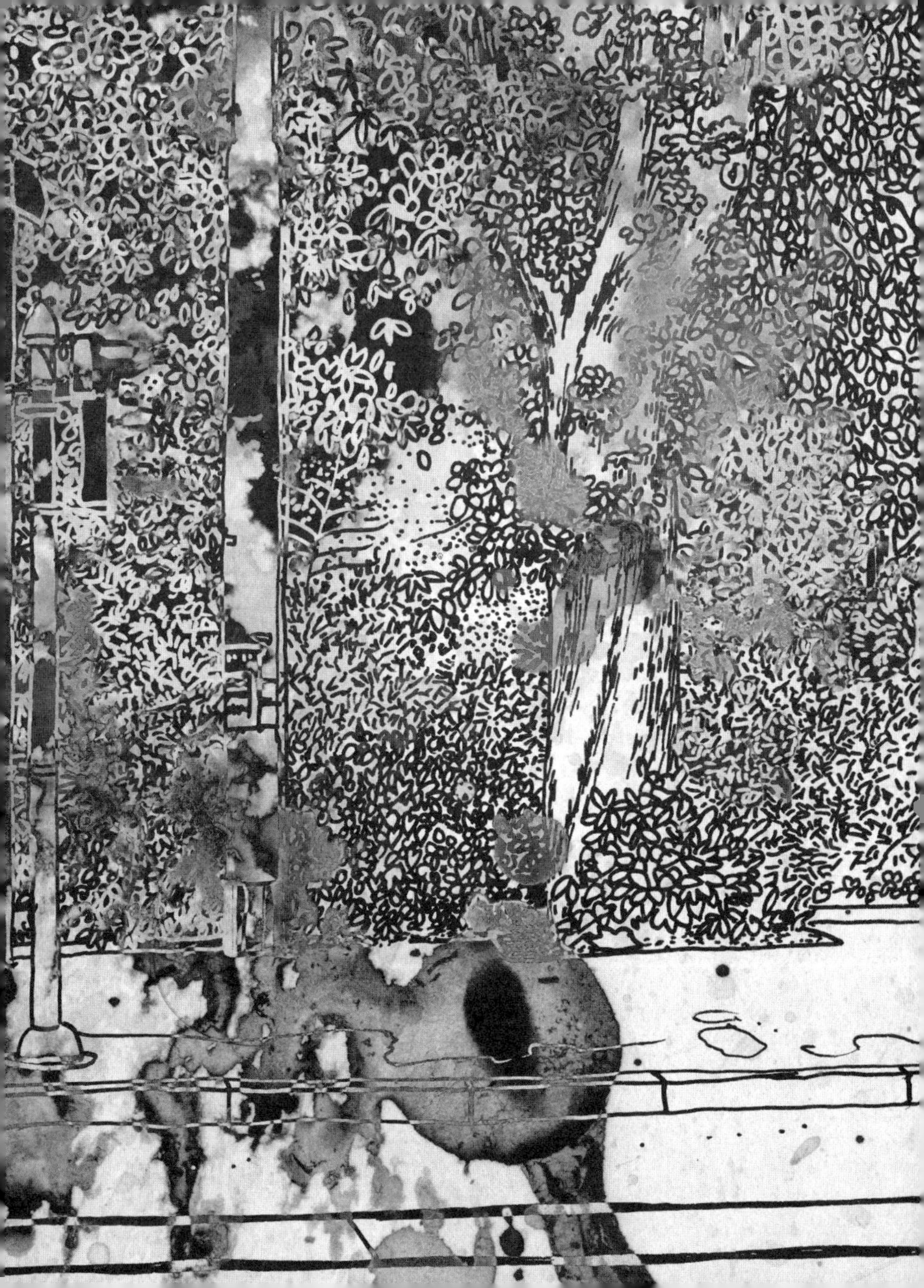

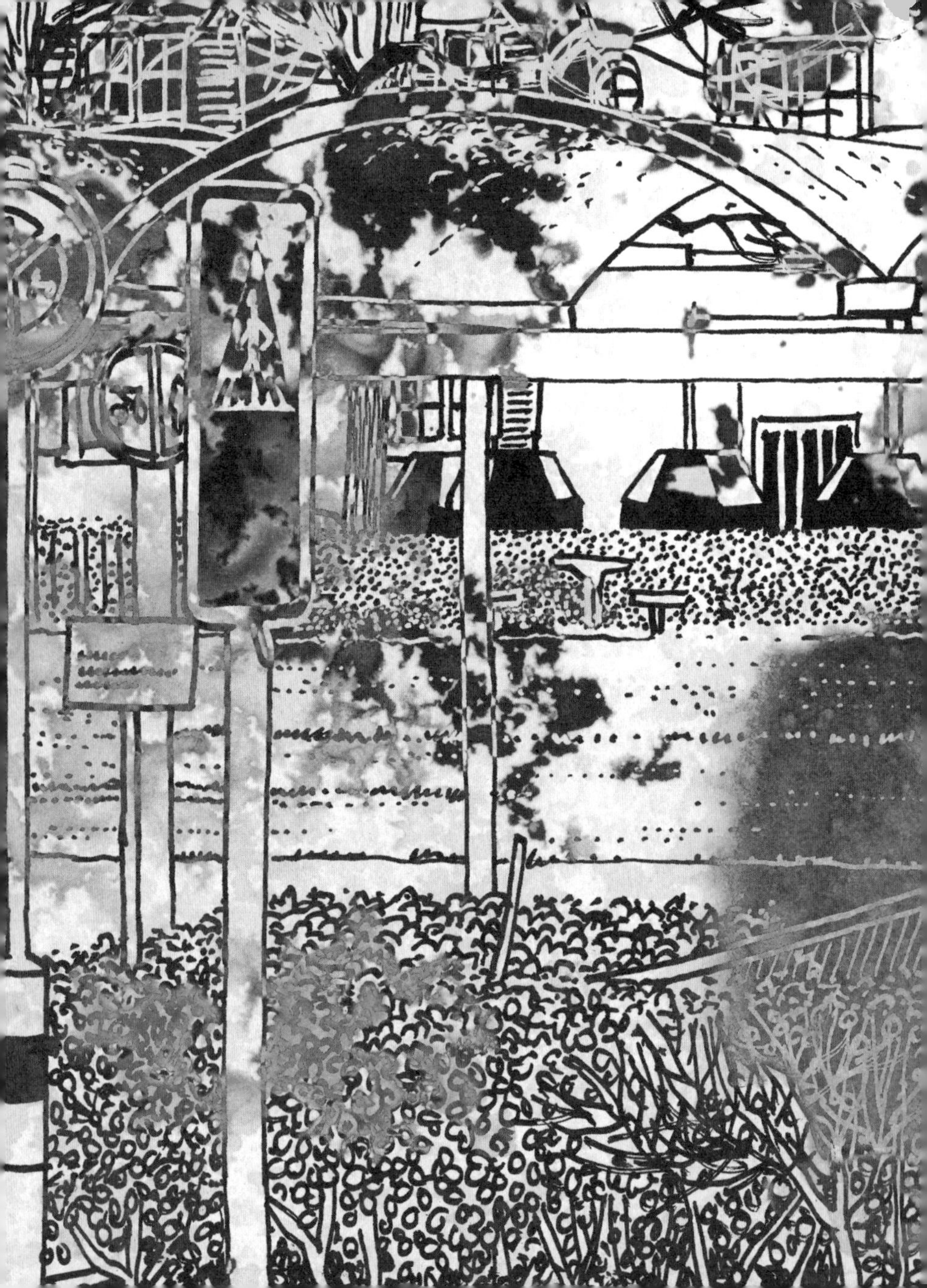

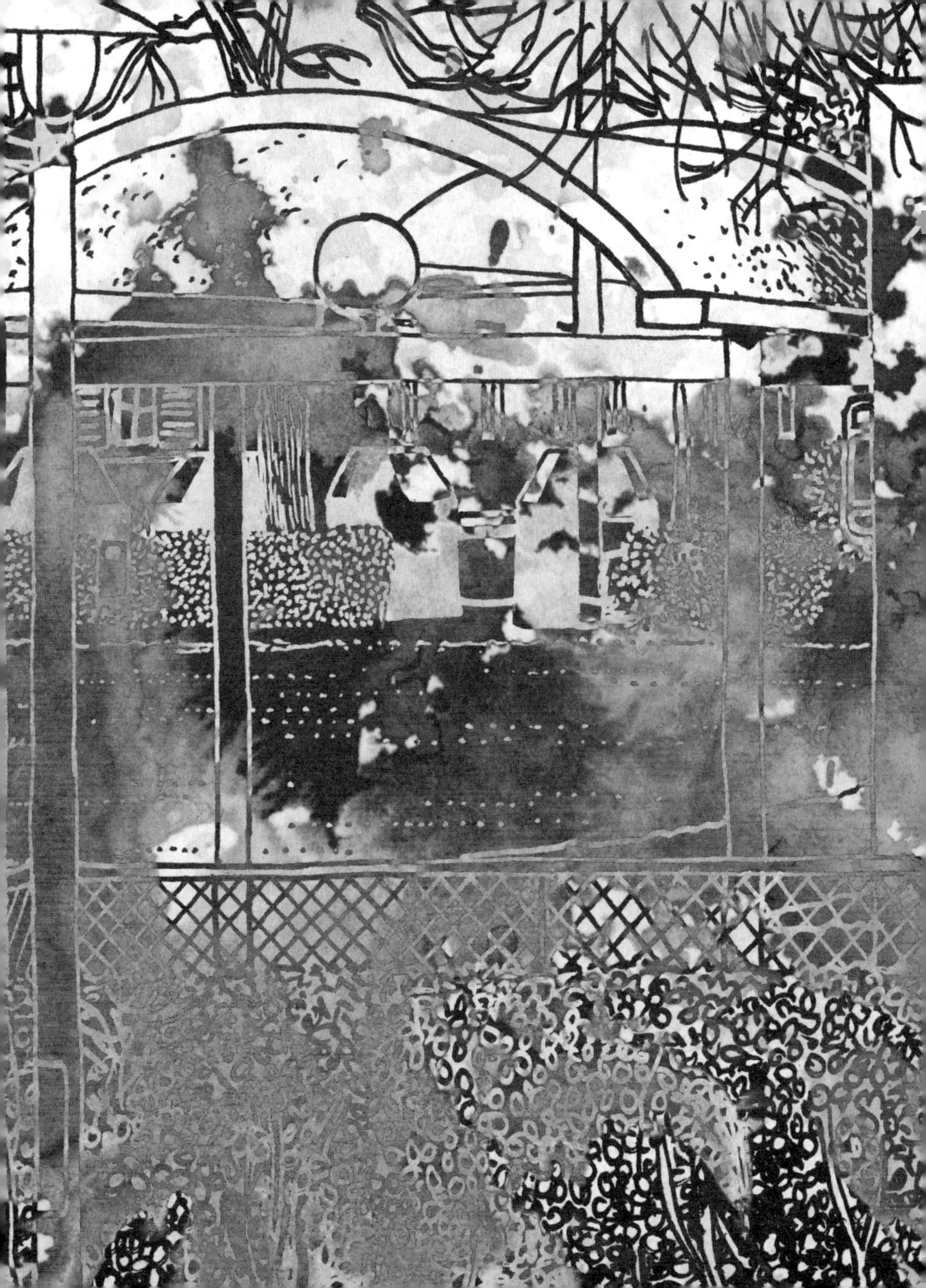

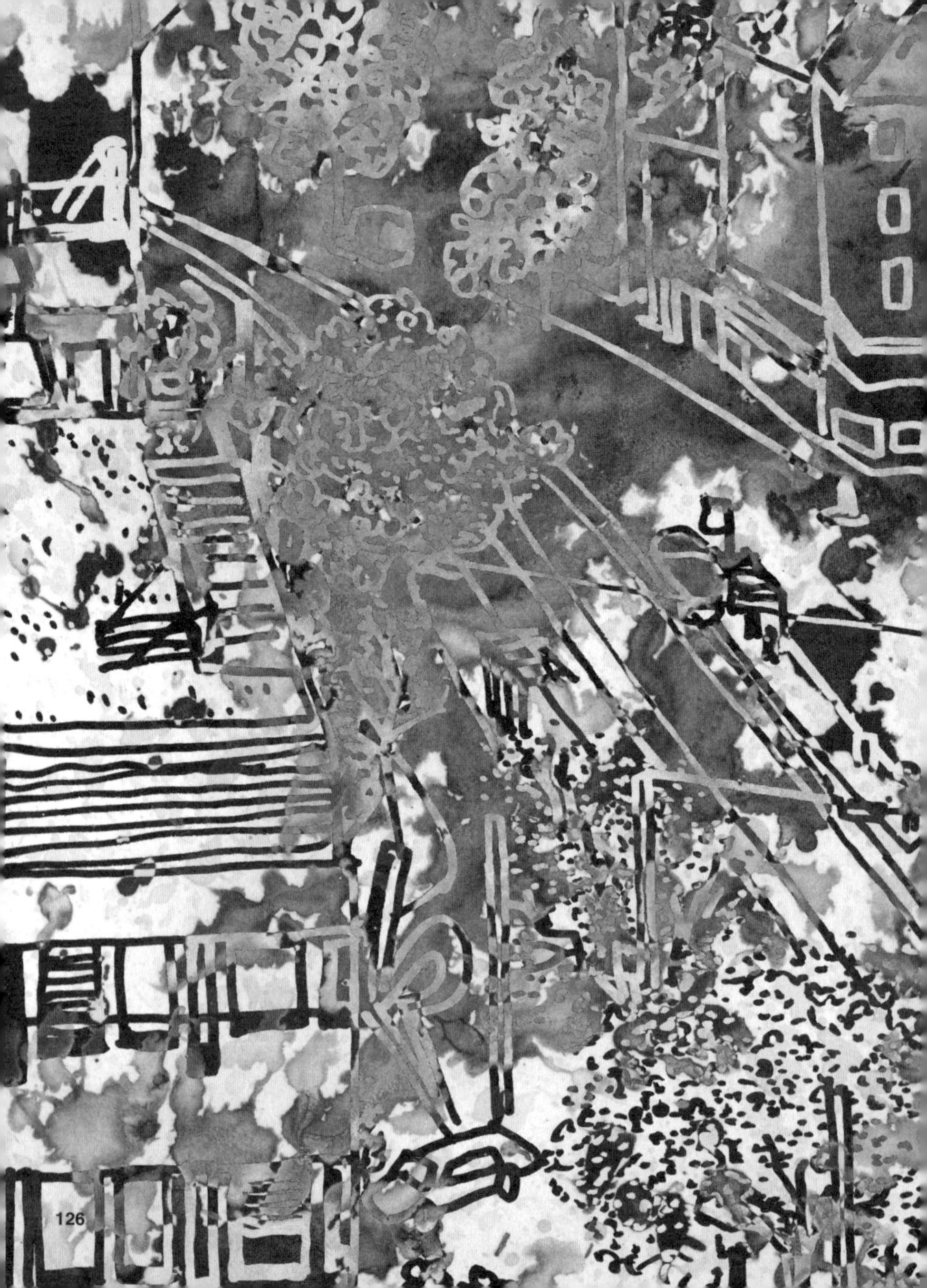

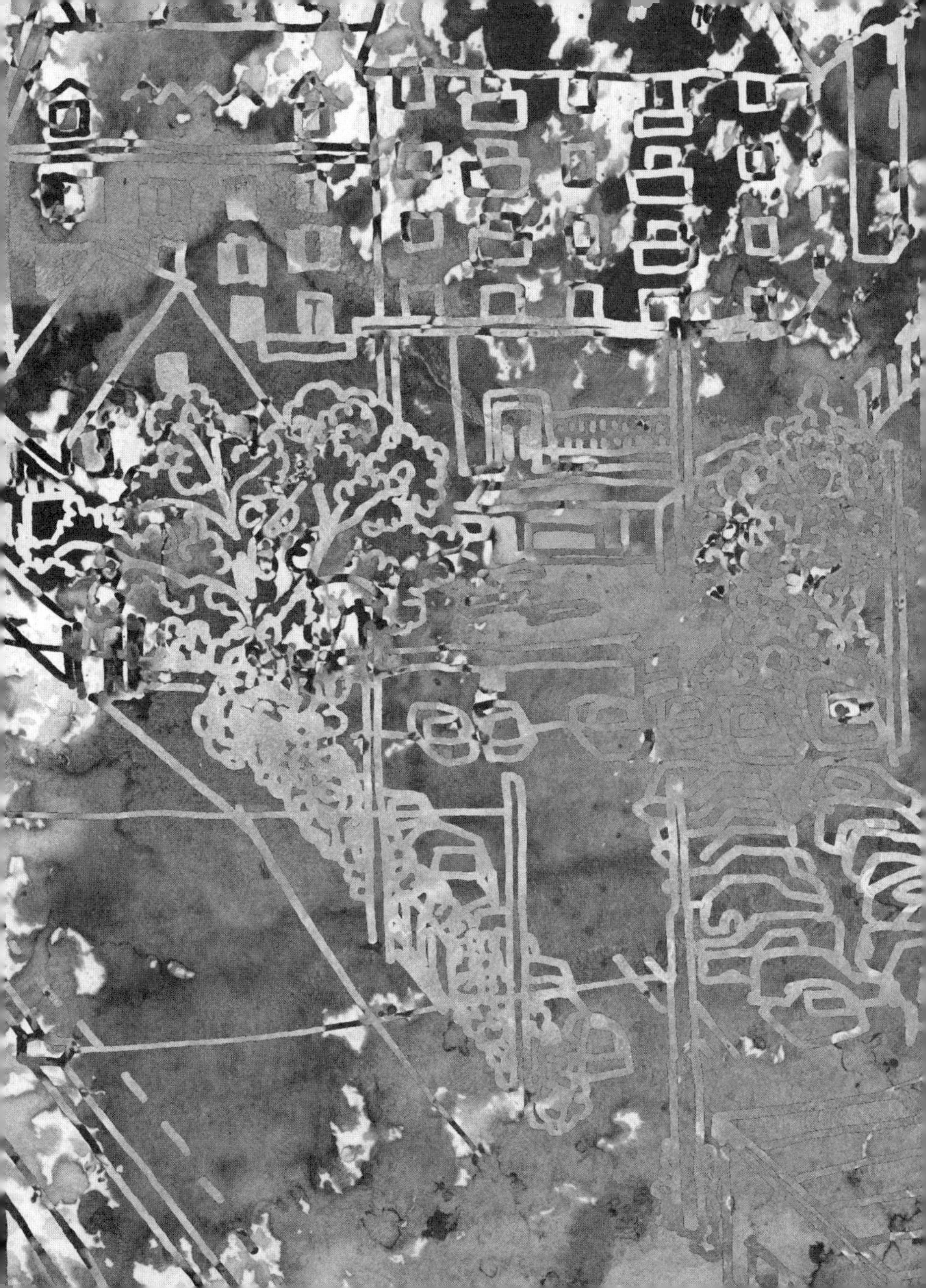

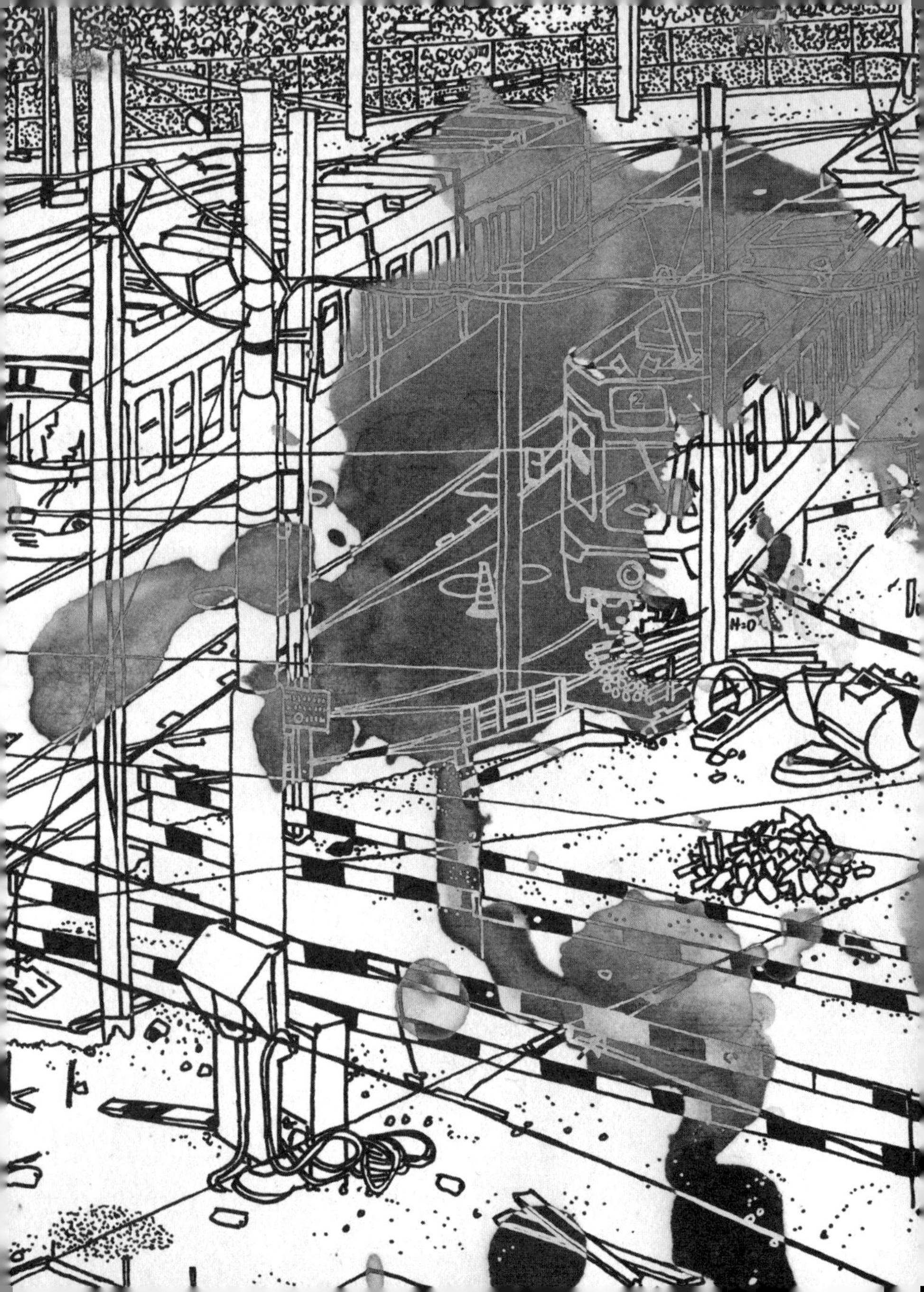

2
H₂O

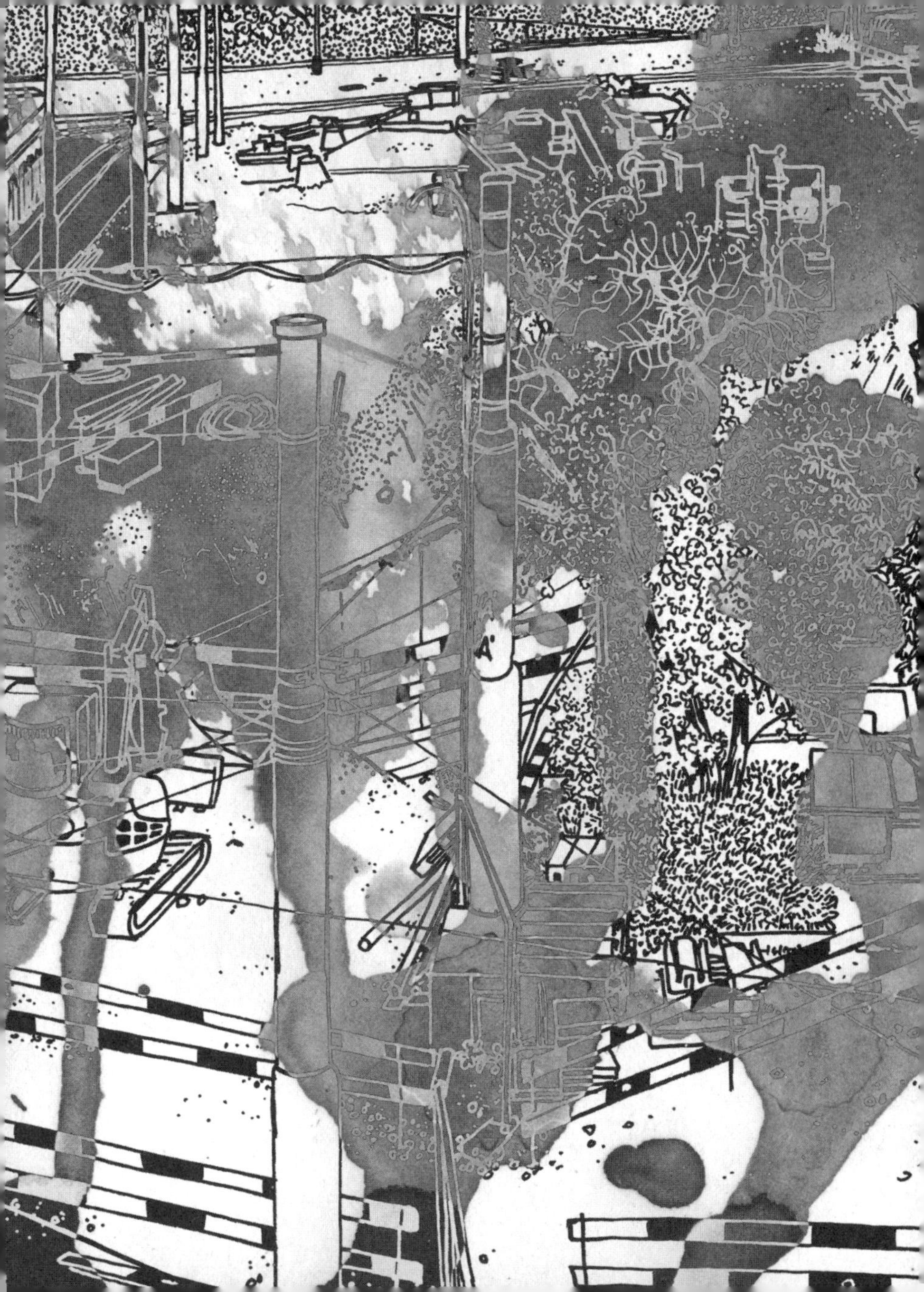

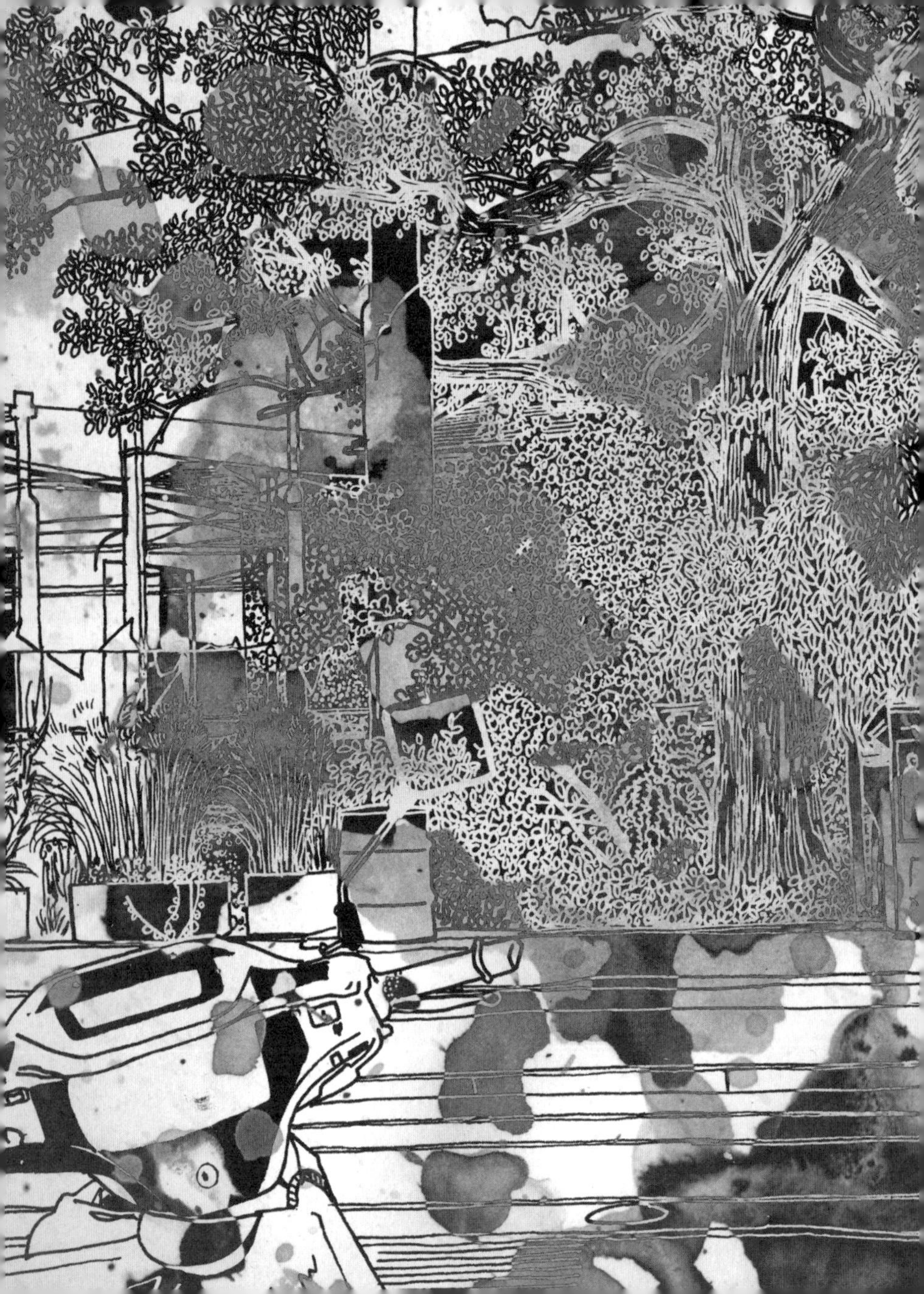

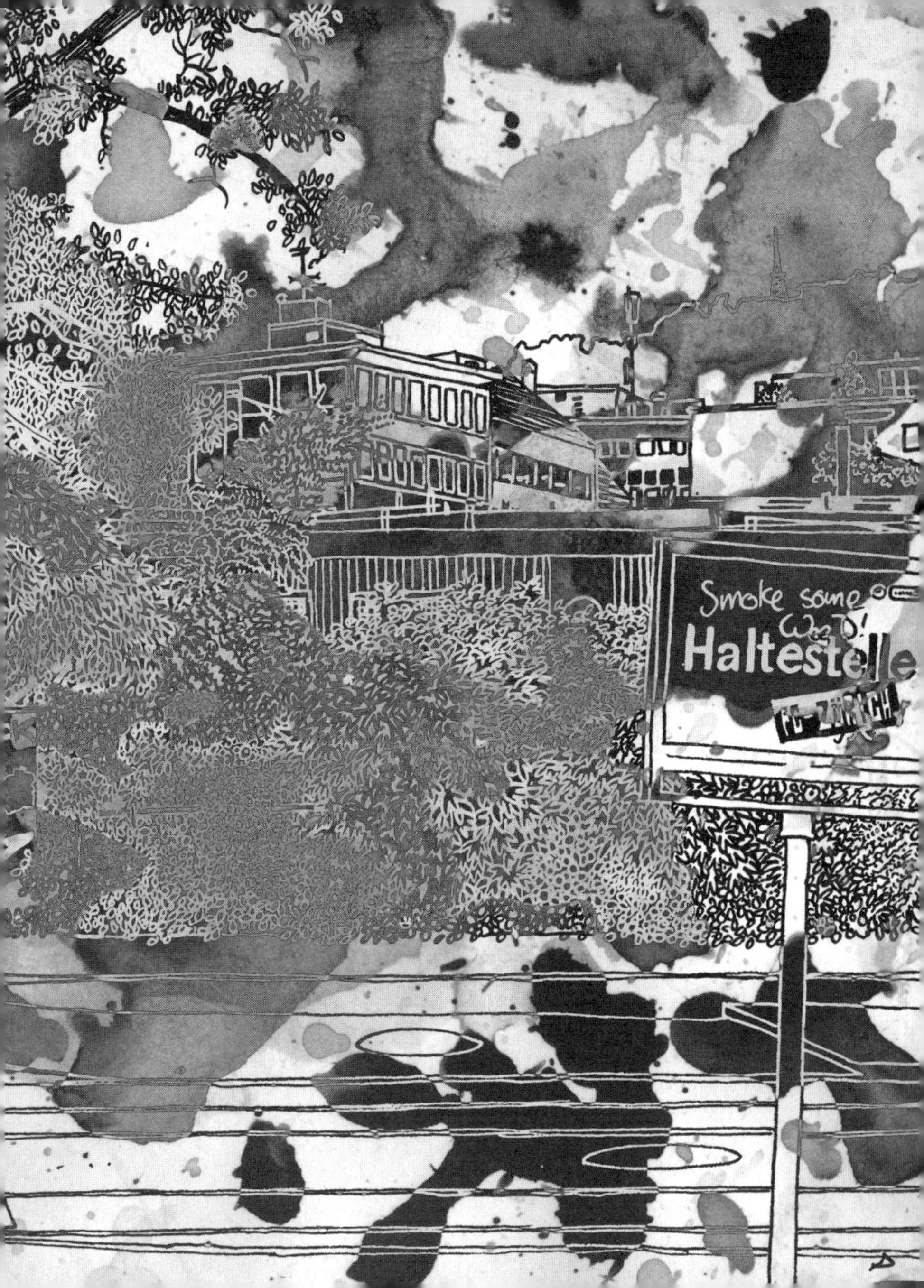

Smoke some Weed!
Haltestelle
Zürich

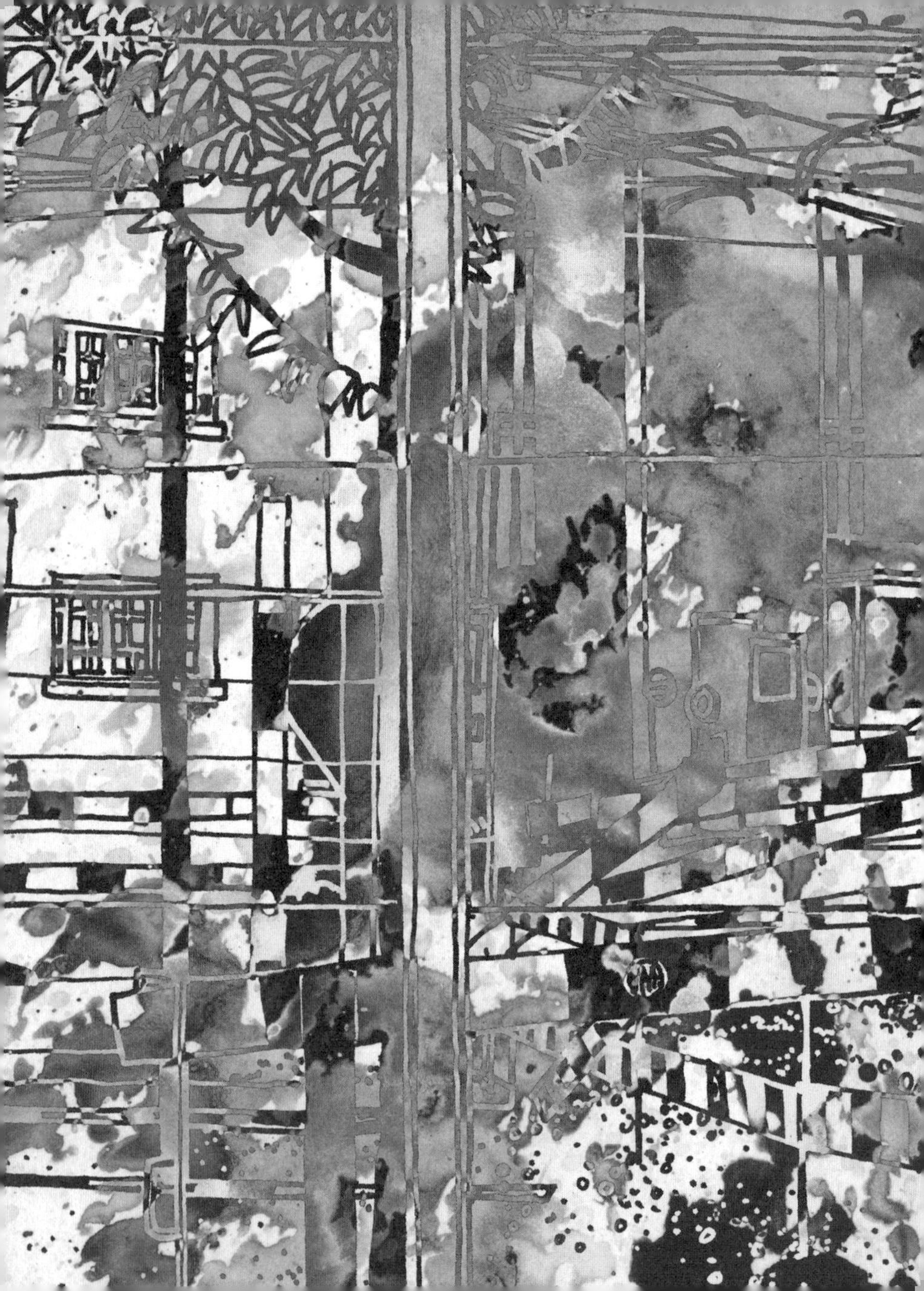

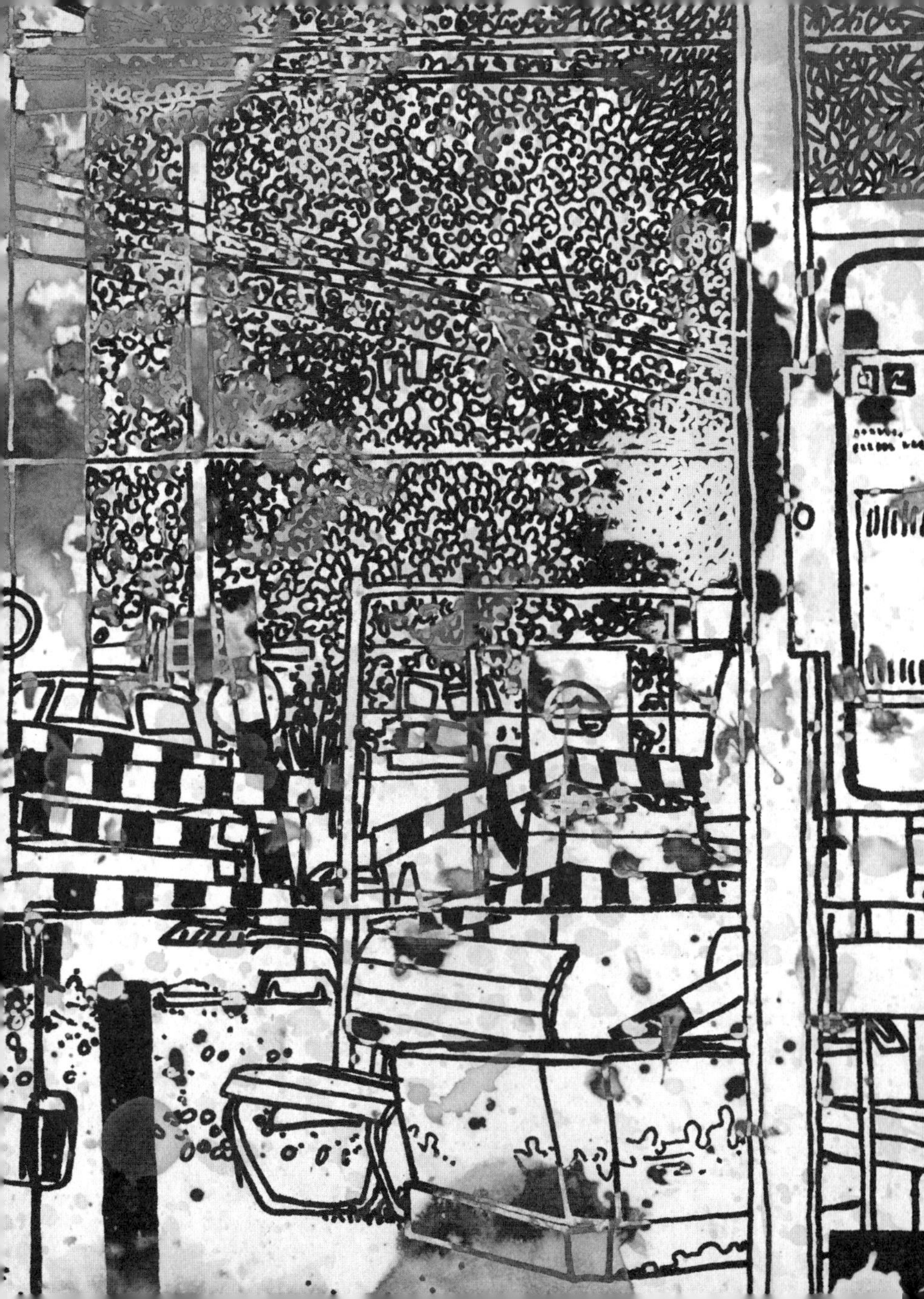

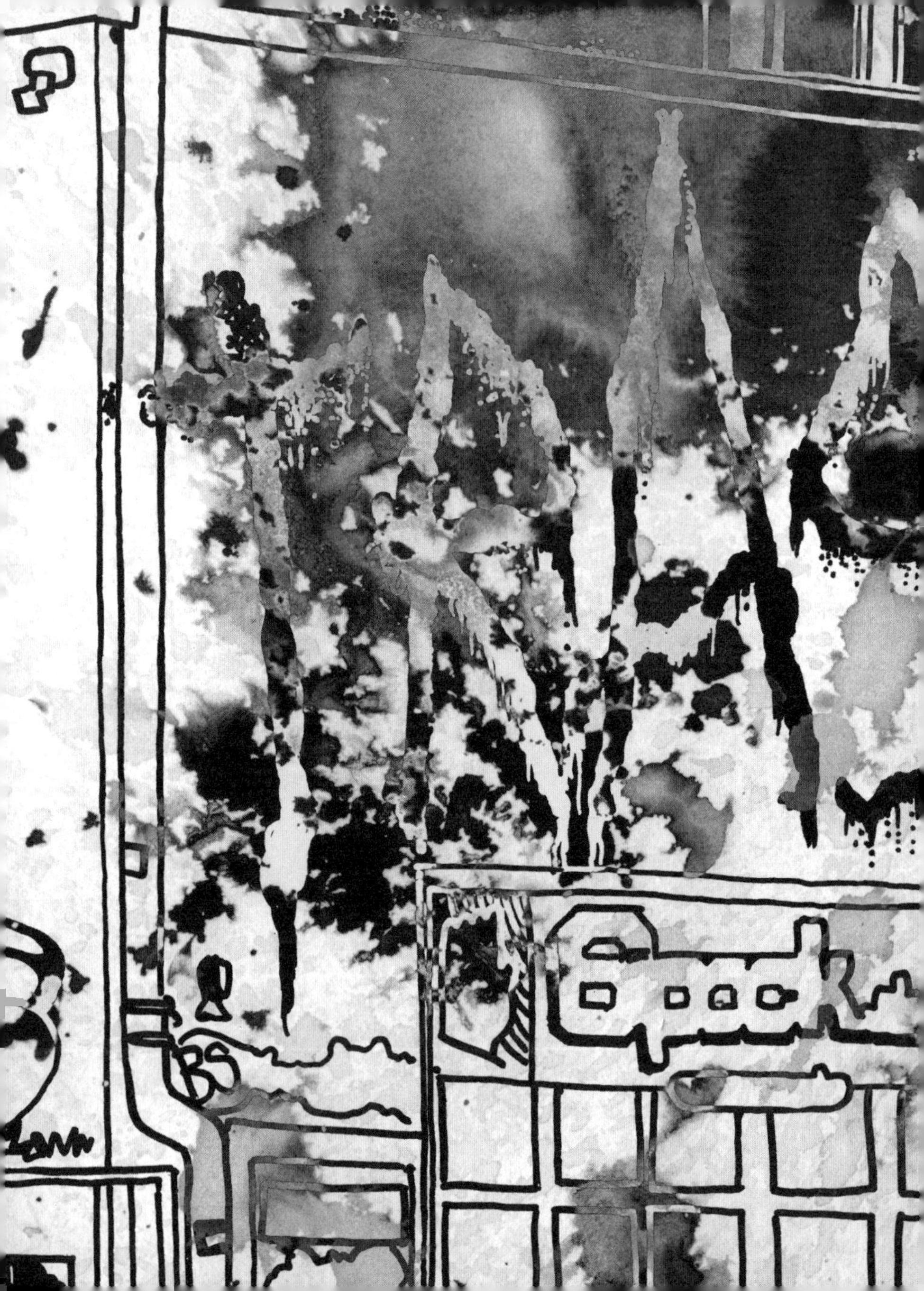

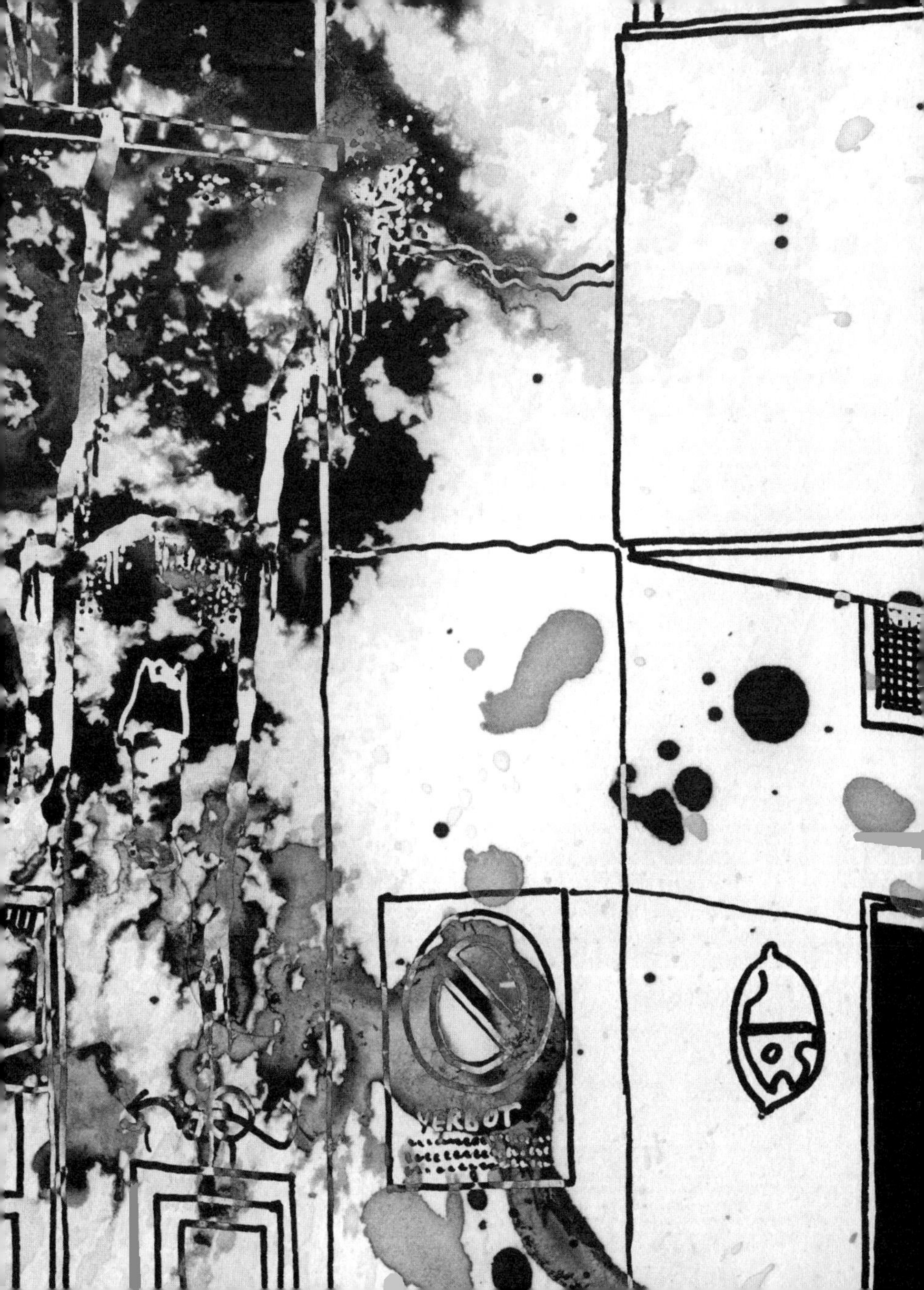
VERBOT

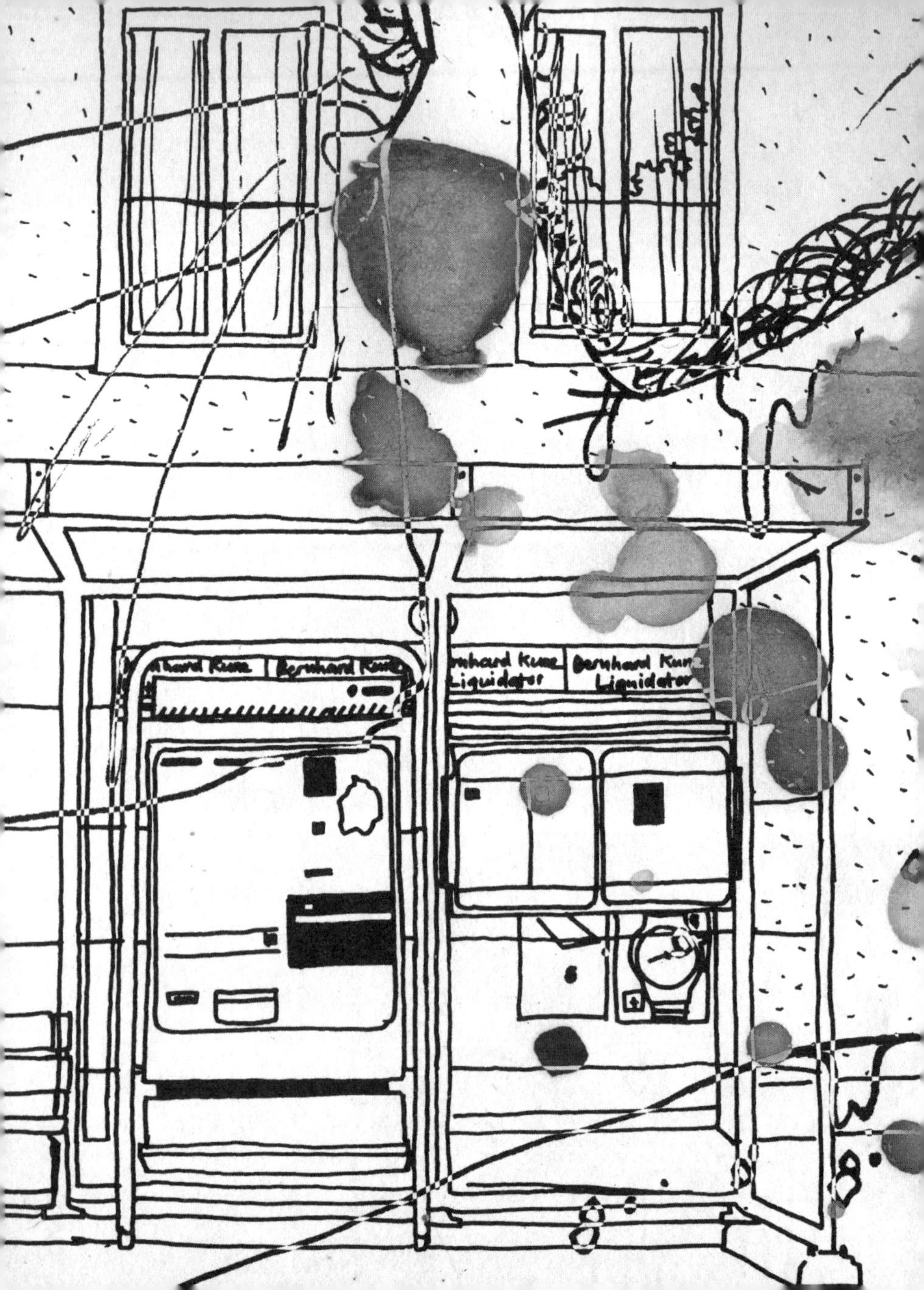
Bernhard Kunz
Bernhard Kunz
Bernhard Kunz
Liquidator
Bernhard Kunz
Liquidator

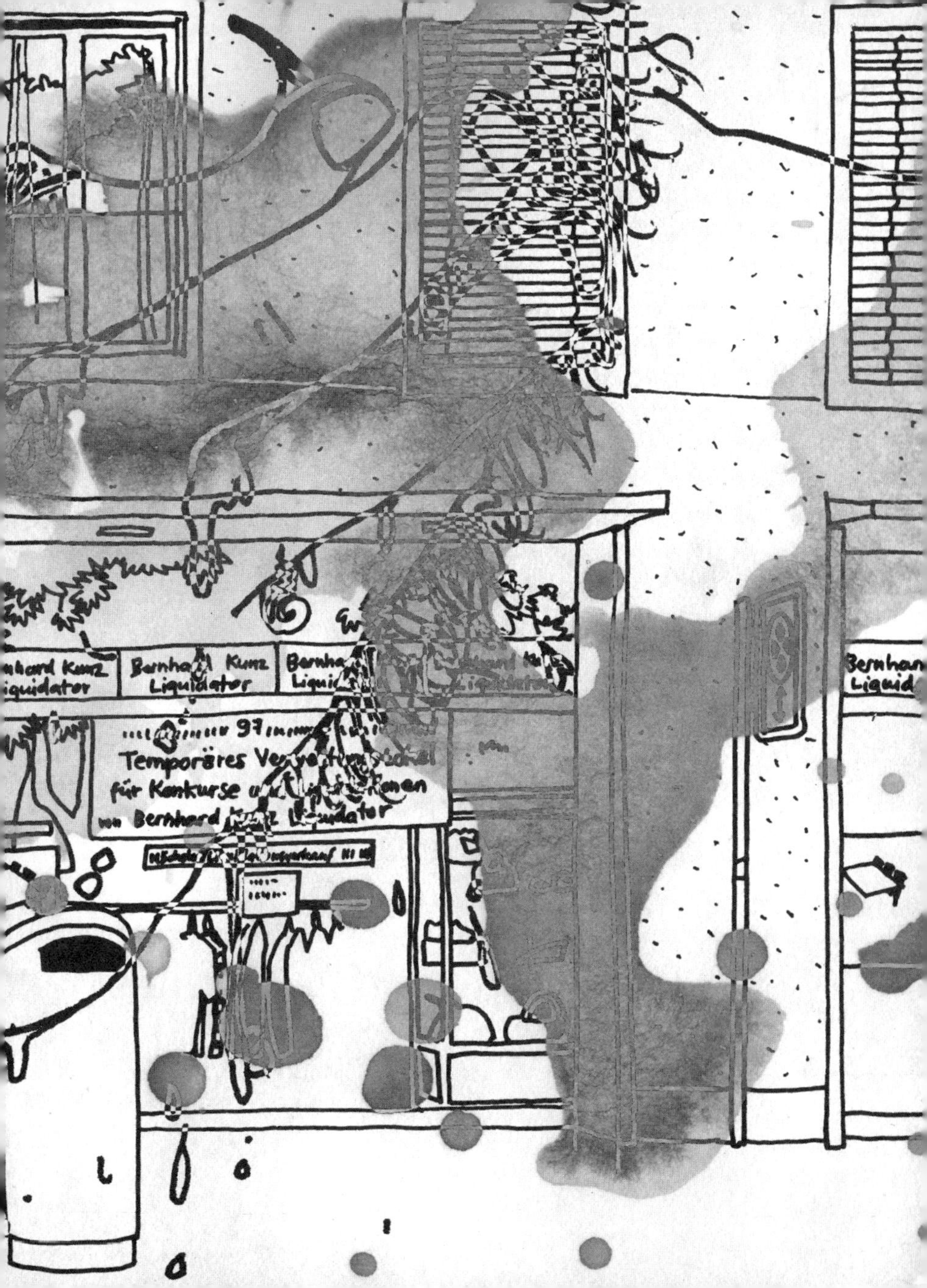

Bernhard Kunz Liquidator
Bernhard Kunz Liquidator
Bernhard Liquidator
Bernhard Liquid
Temporäres Vertretungsbüro
für Konkurse und Liquidationen
von Bernhard Kunz Liquidator

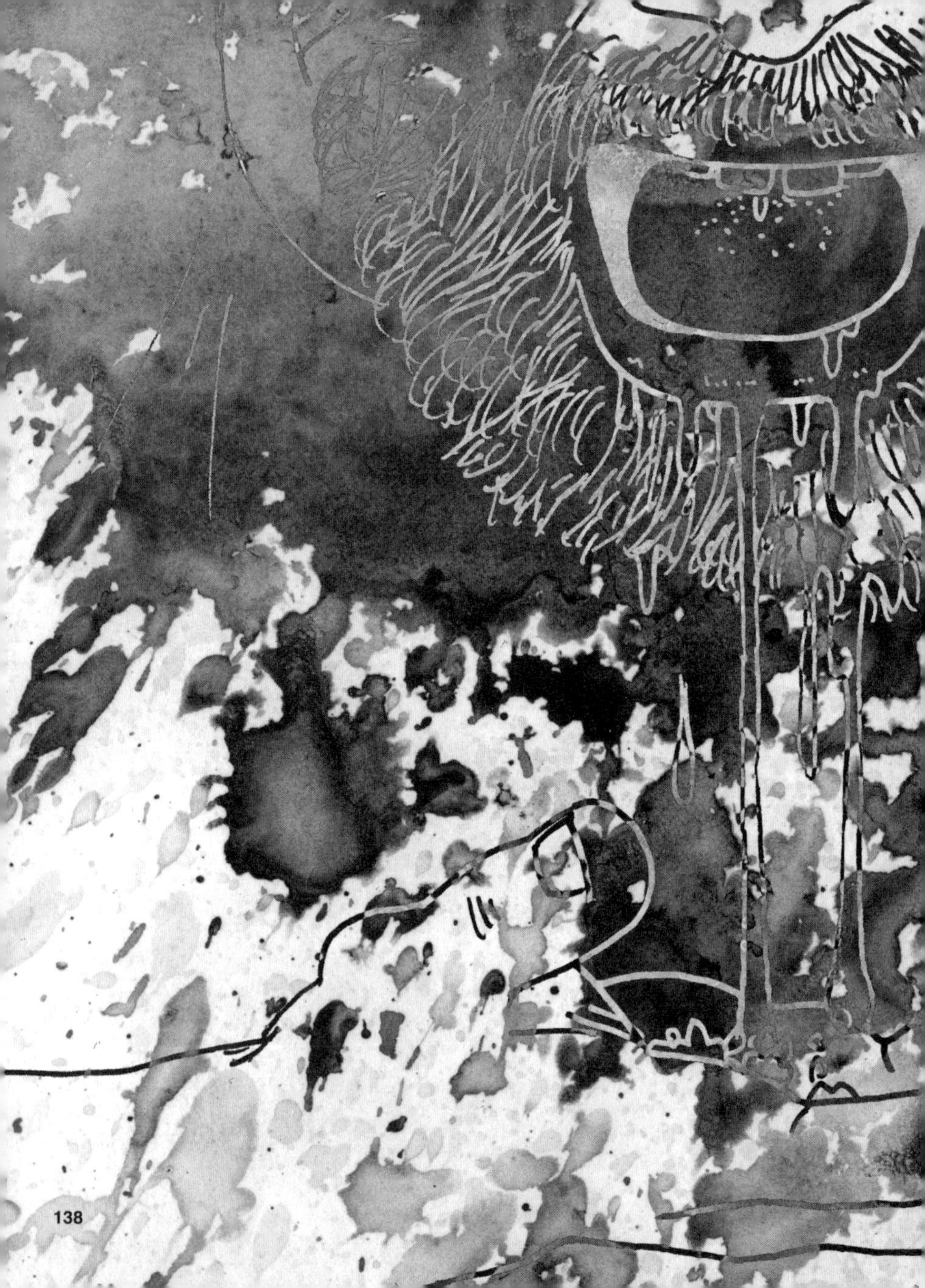

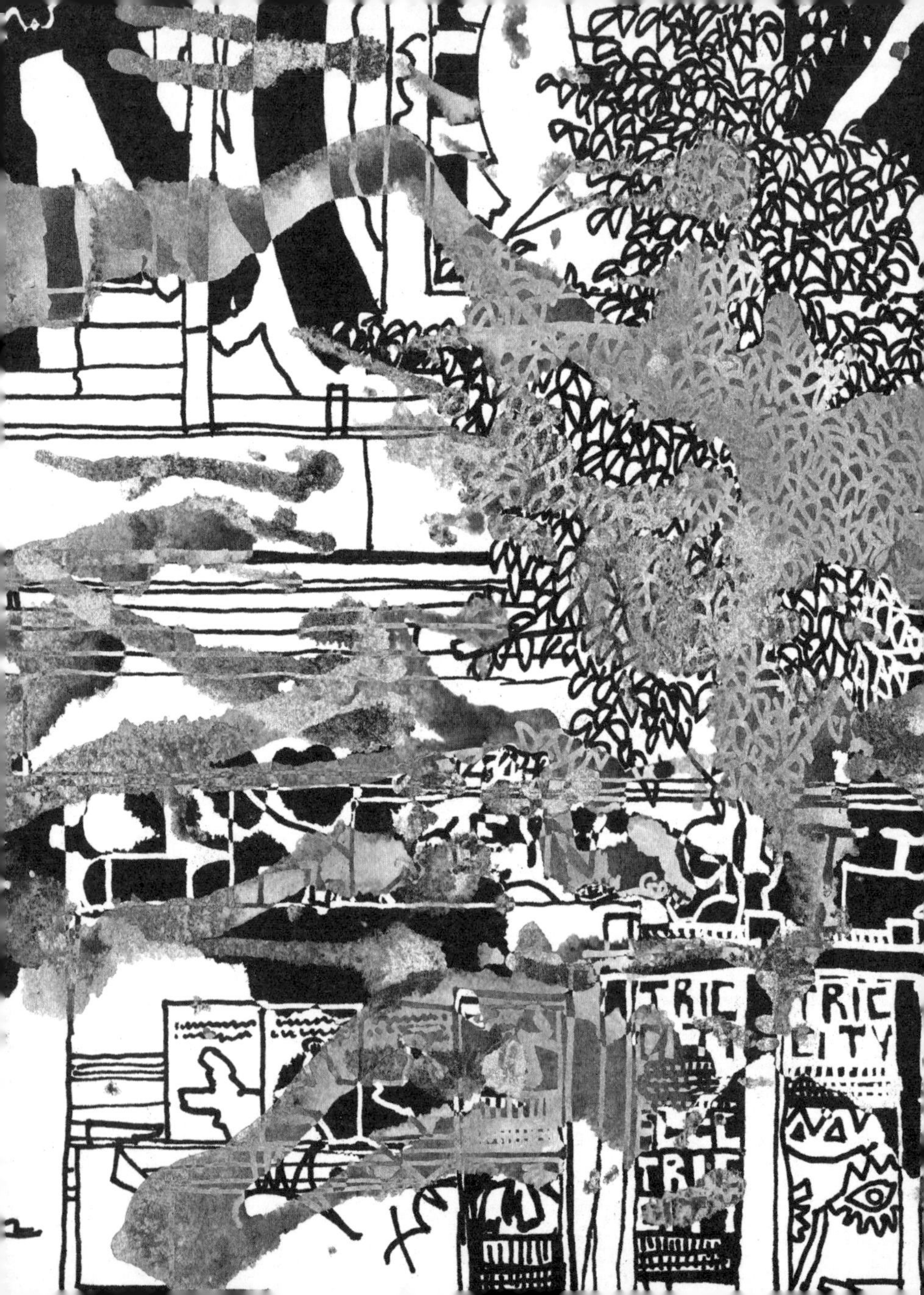
TRIC
CITY
TRIC
CITY
TRIC
CITY

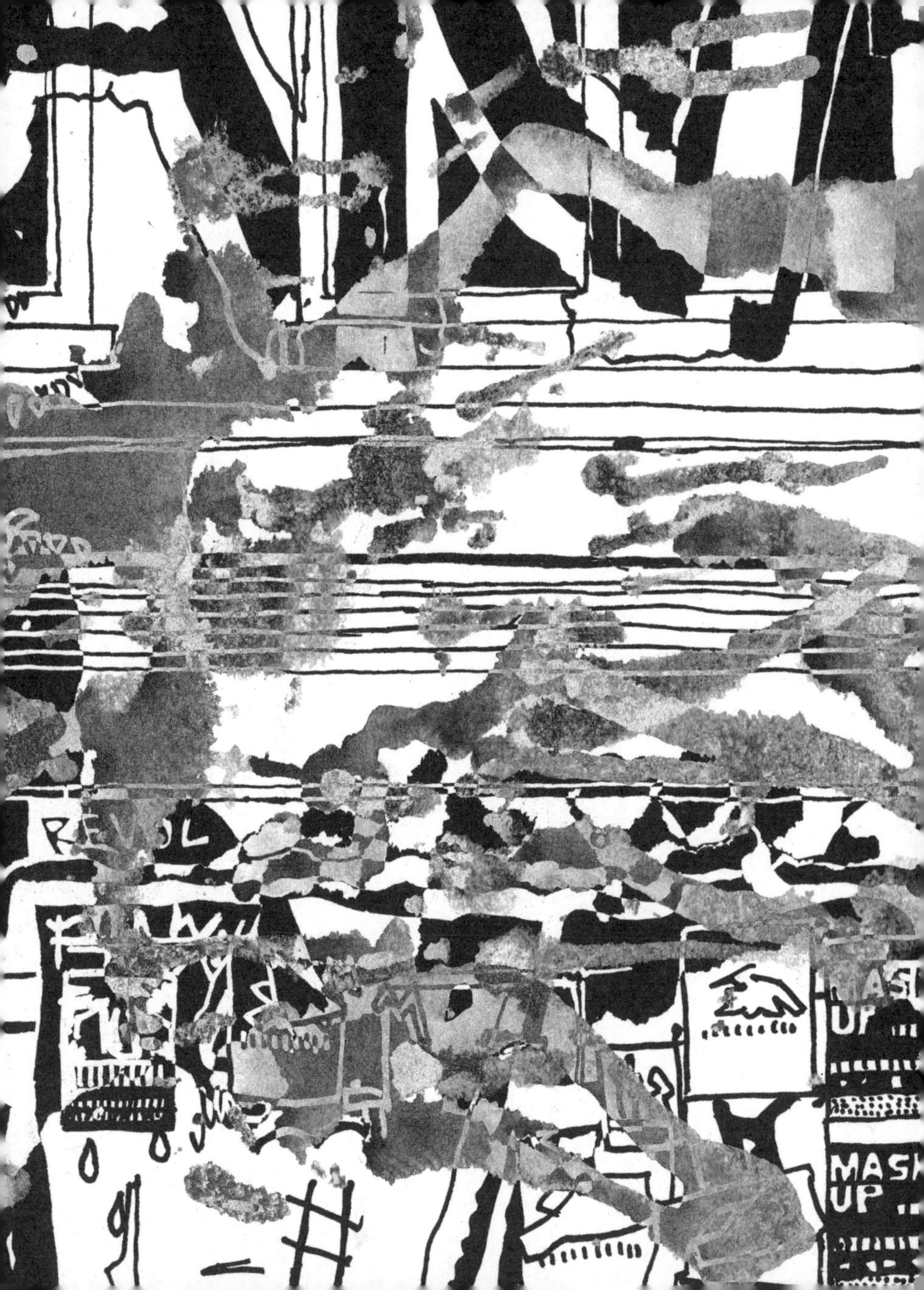
REVOL
MASH
UP
MASH
UP

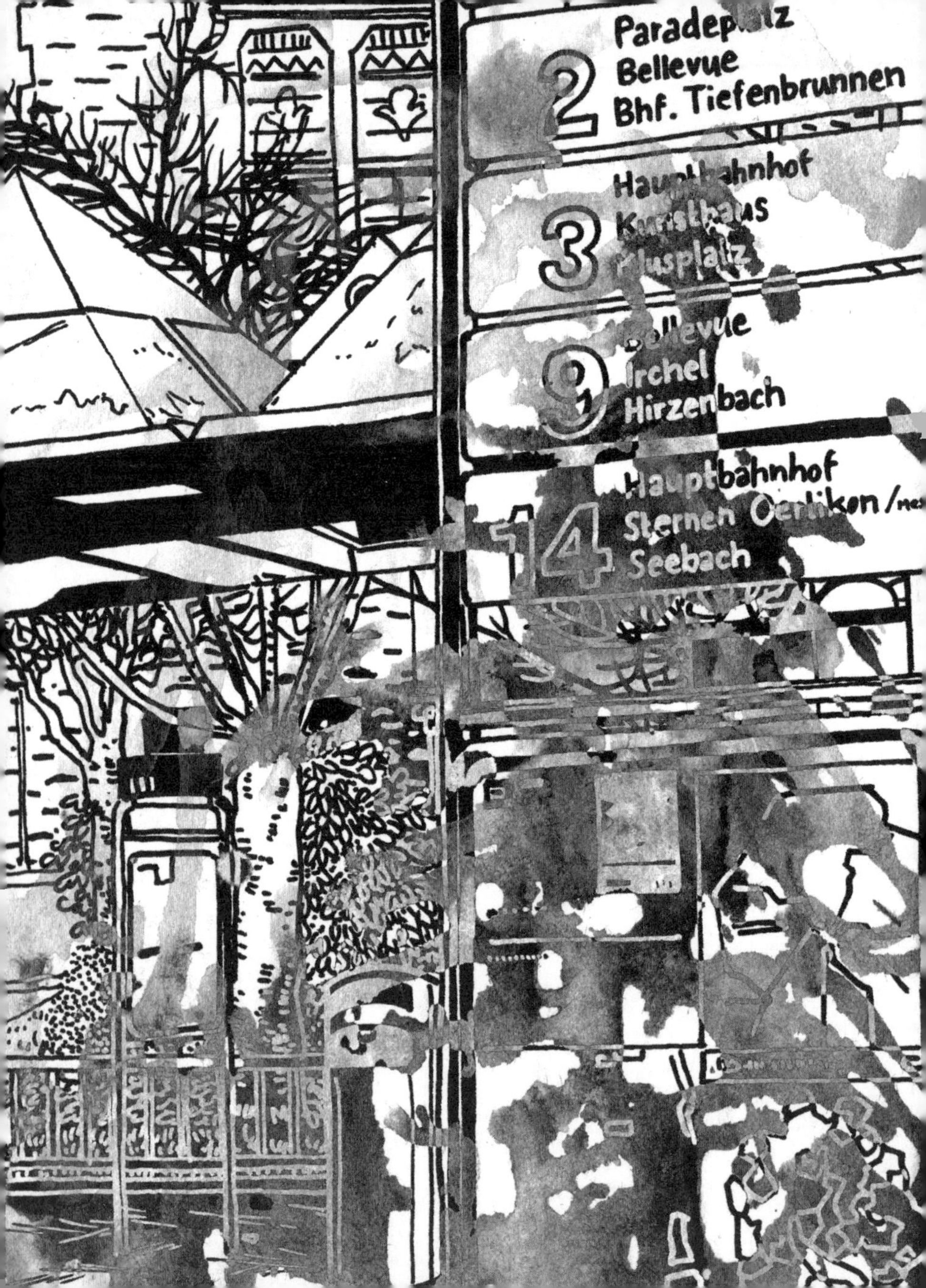

2 Paradeplatz
Bellevue
Bhf. Tiefenbrunnen

3 Hauptbahnhof
Kunsthaus
Klusplatz

9 Bellevue
Irchel
Hirzenbach

14 Hauptbahnhof
Sternen Oerlikon / ne
Seebach

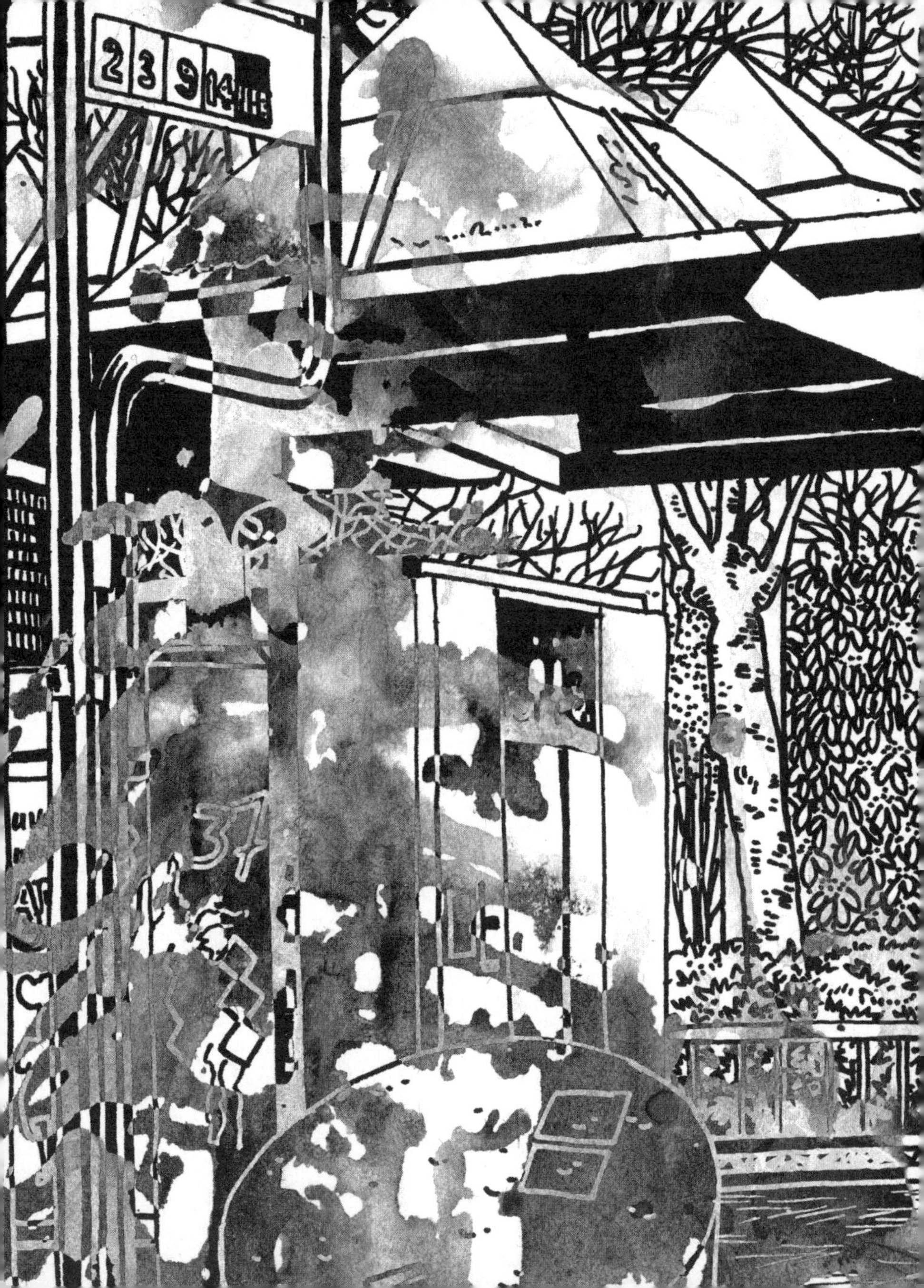

239
37

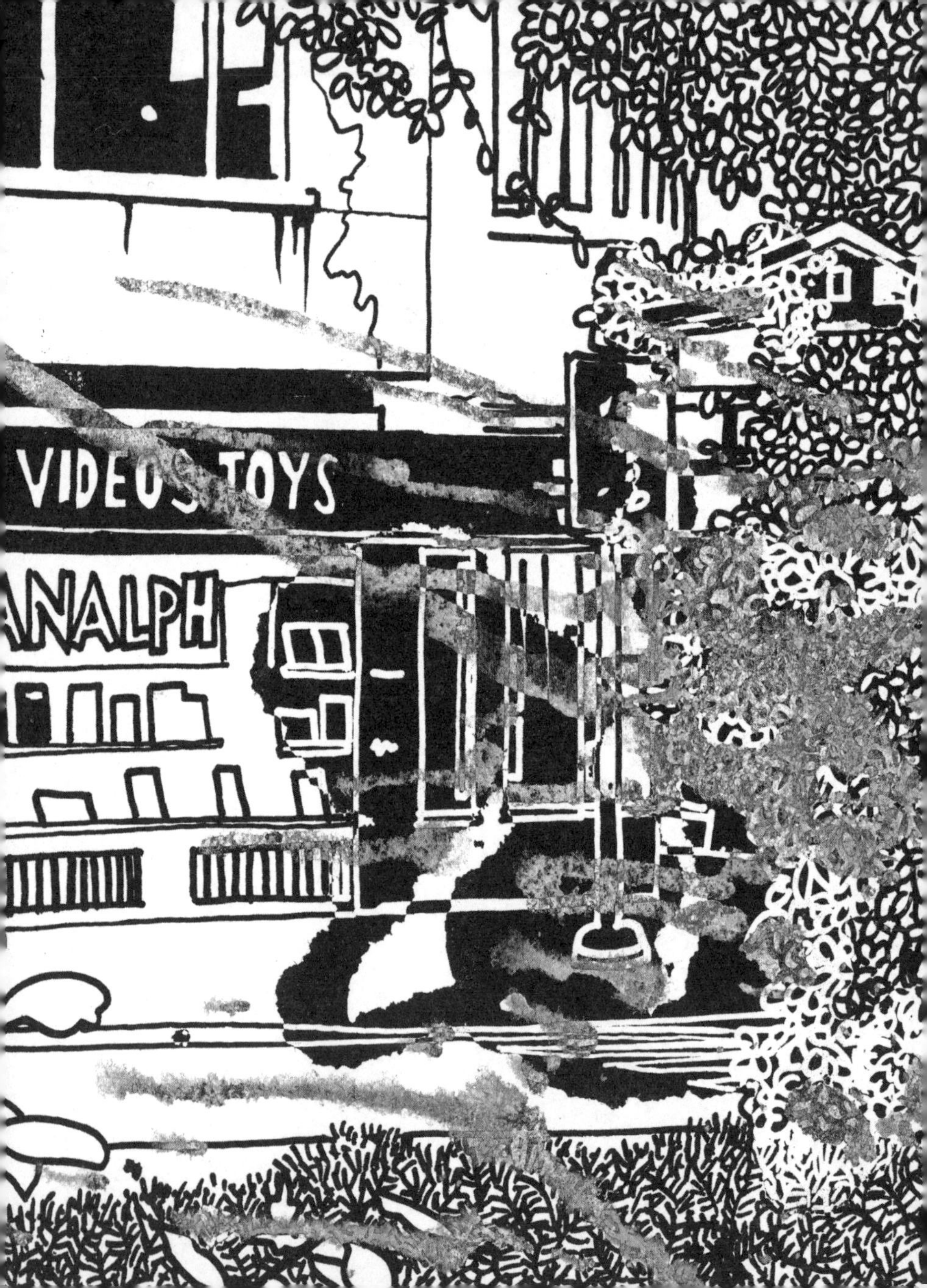

VIDEOS TOYS
ANALPH

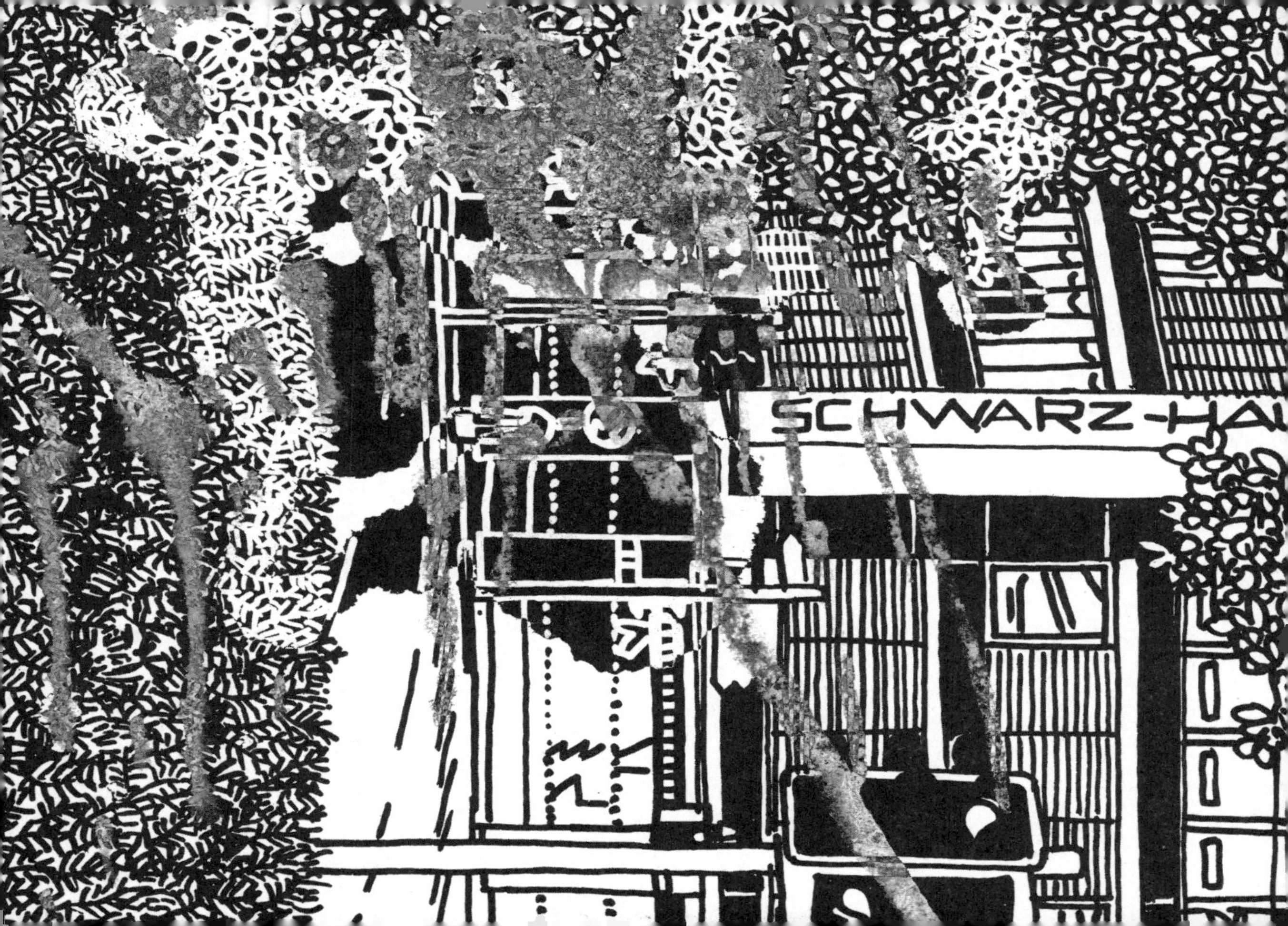
SCHWARZ-HA

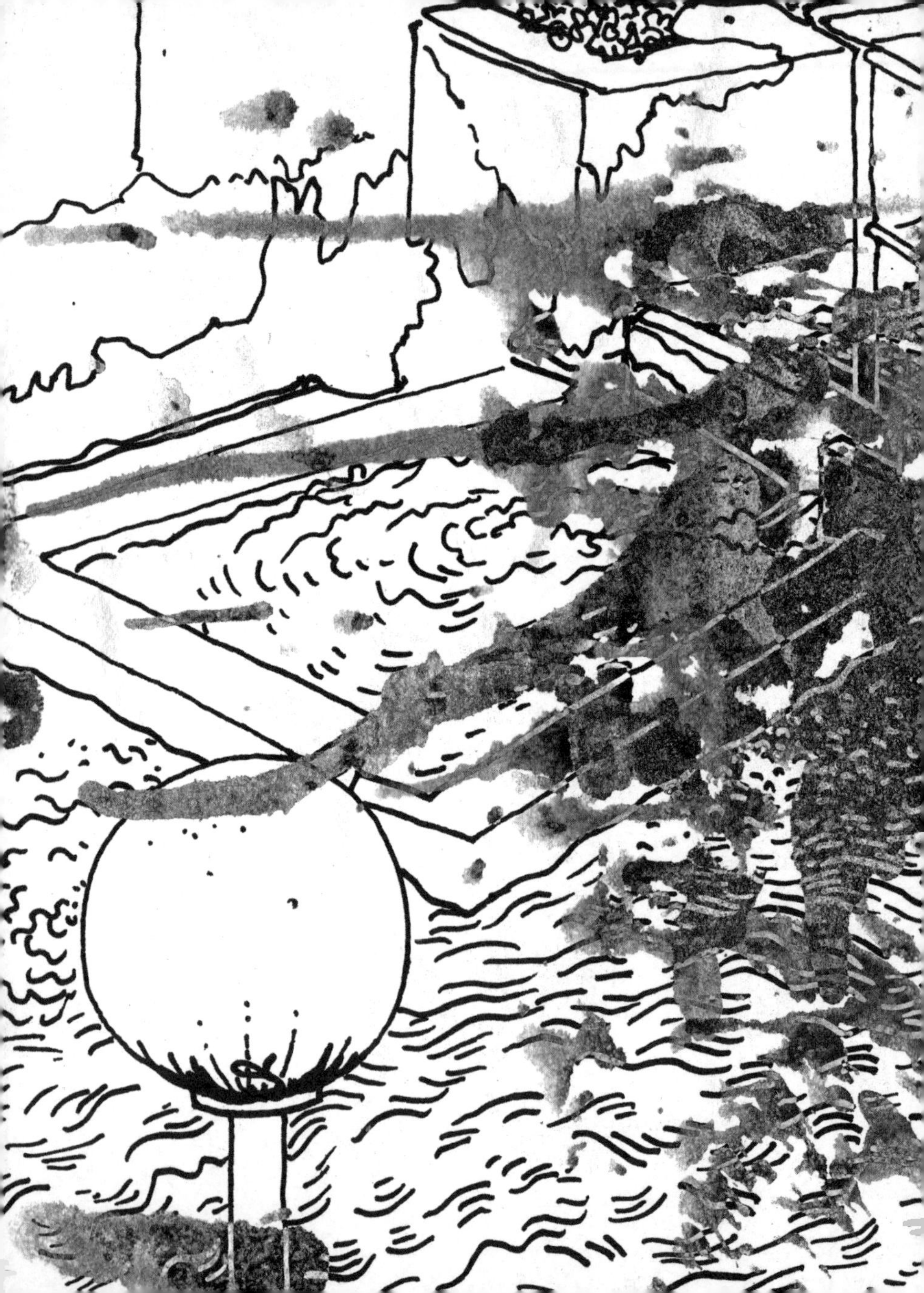

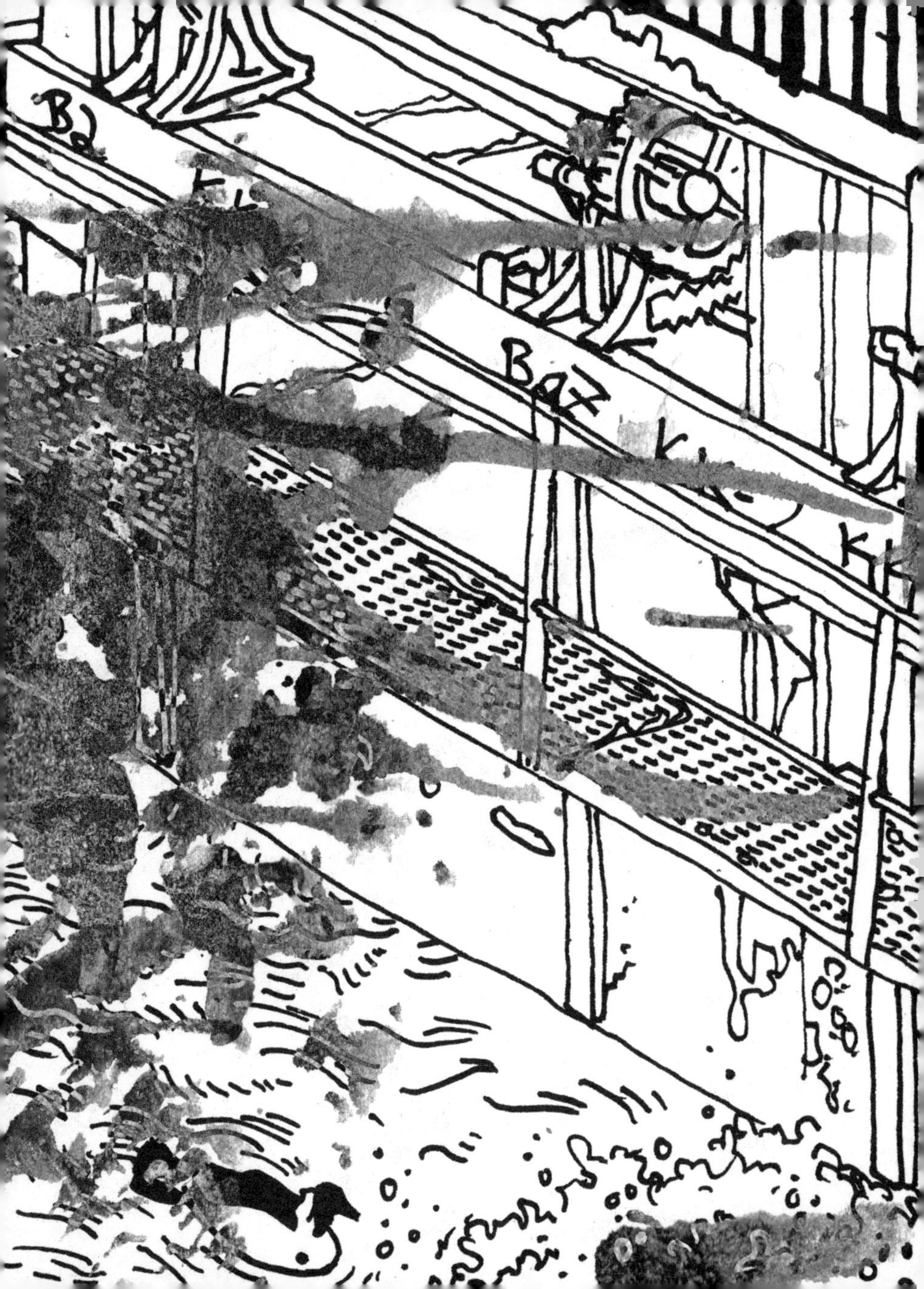

BAZ

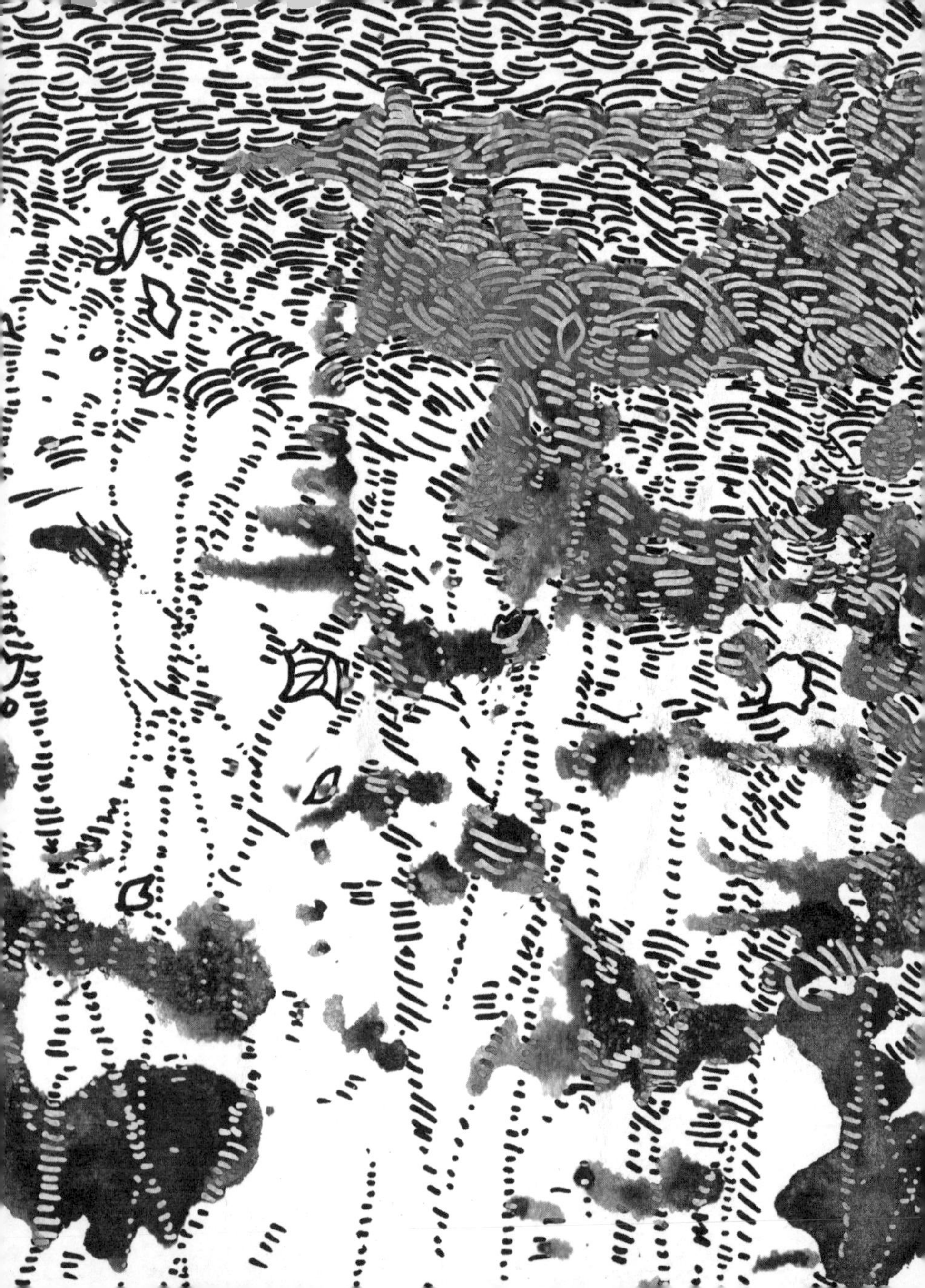

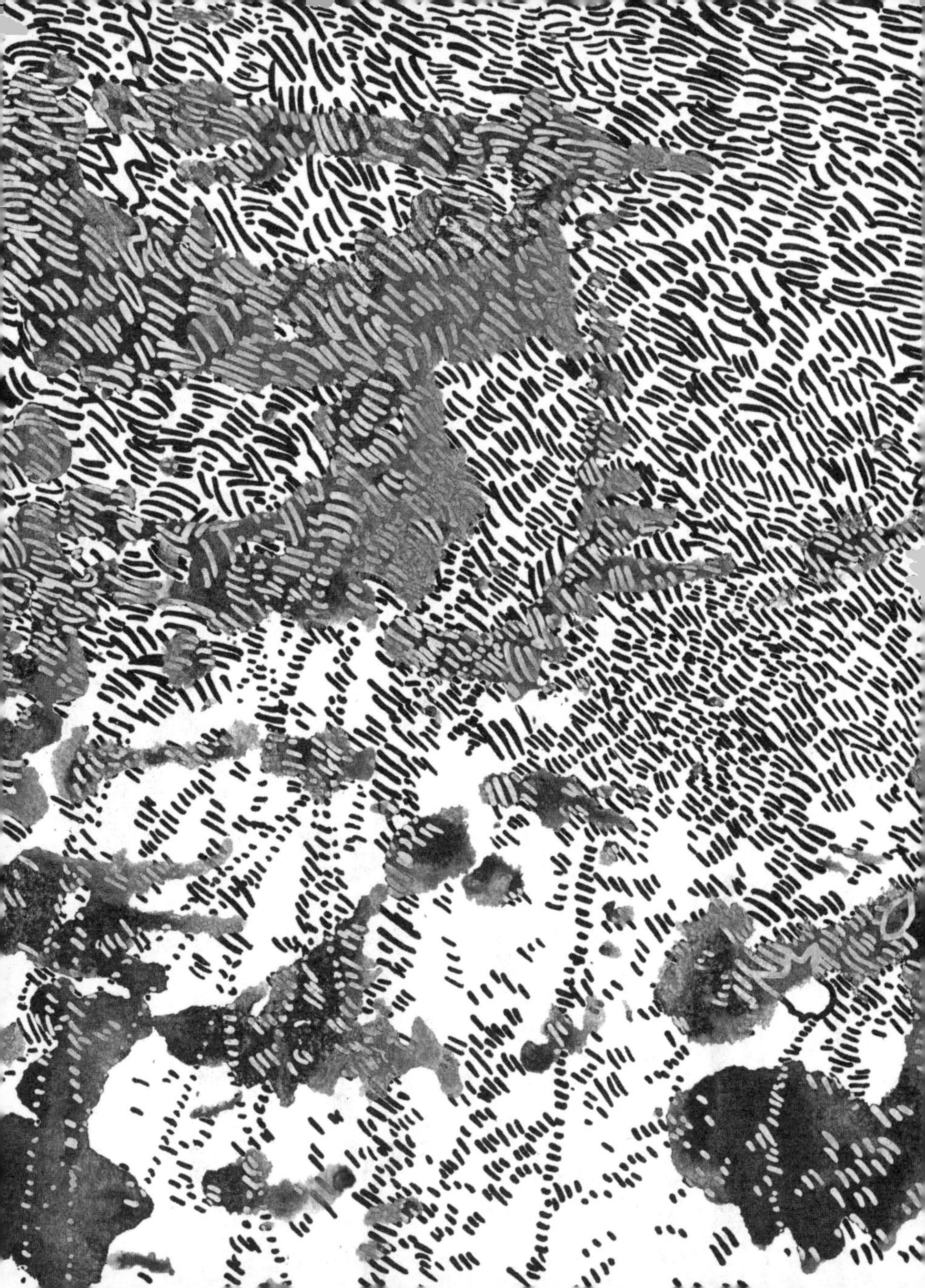

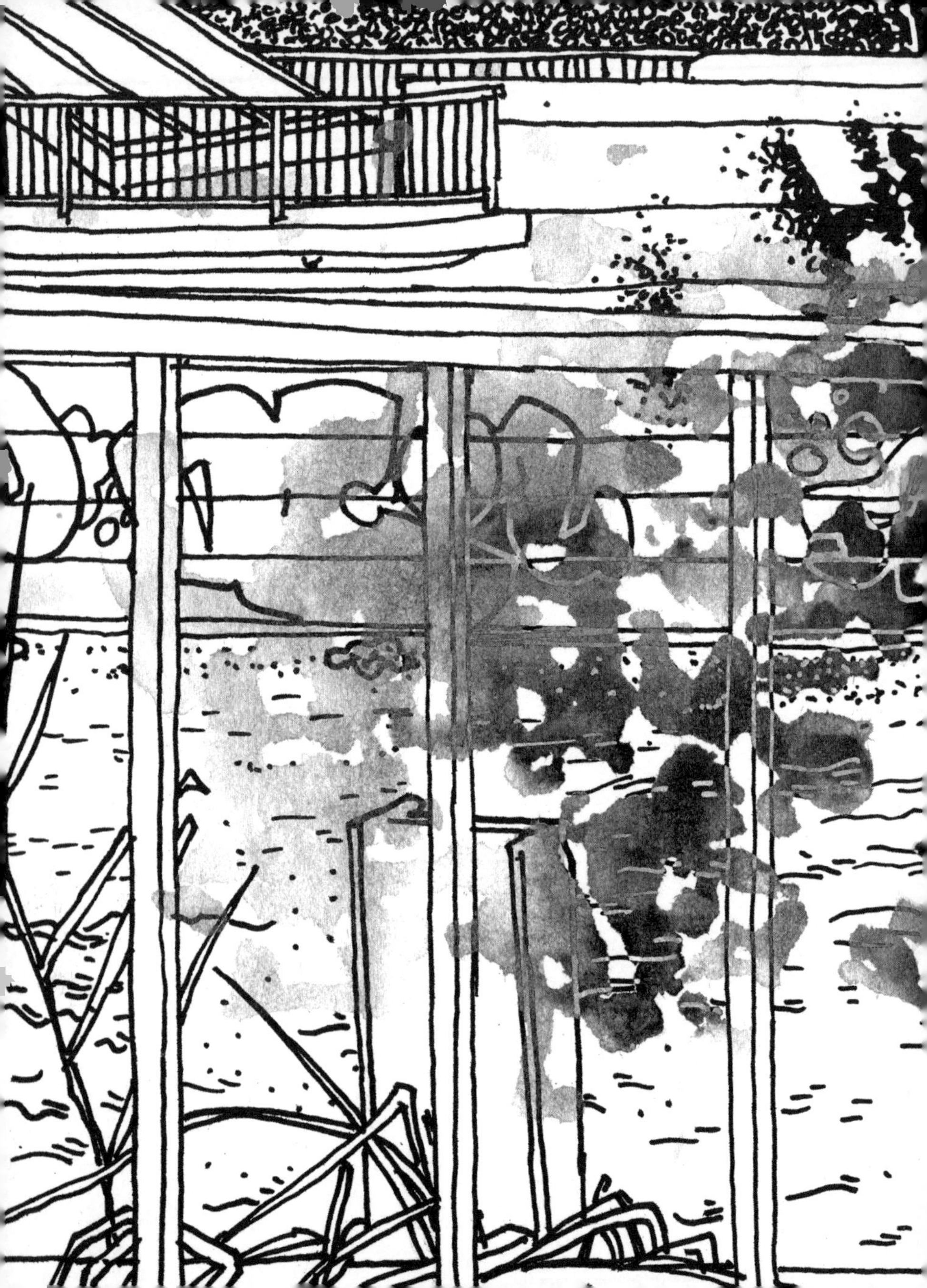

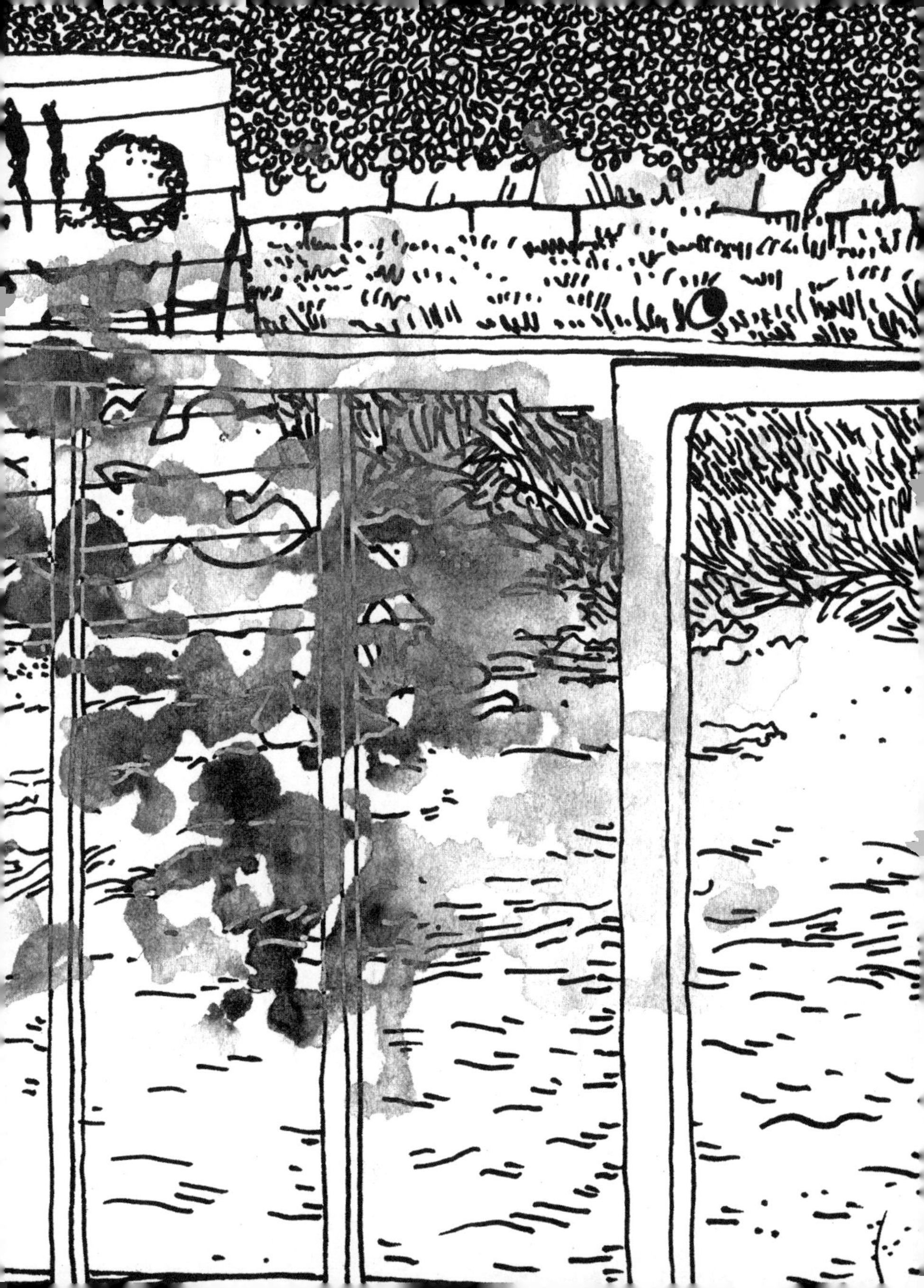

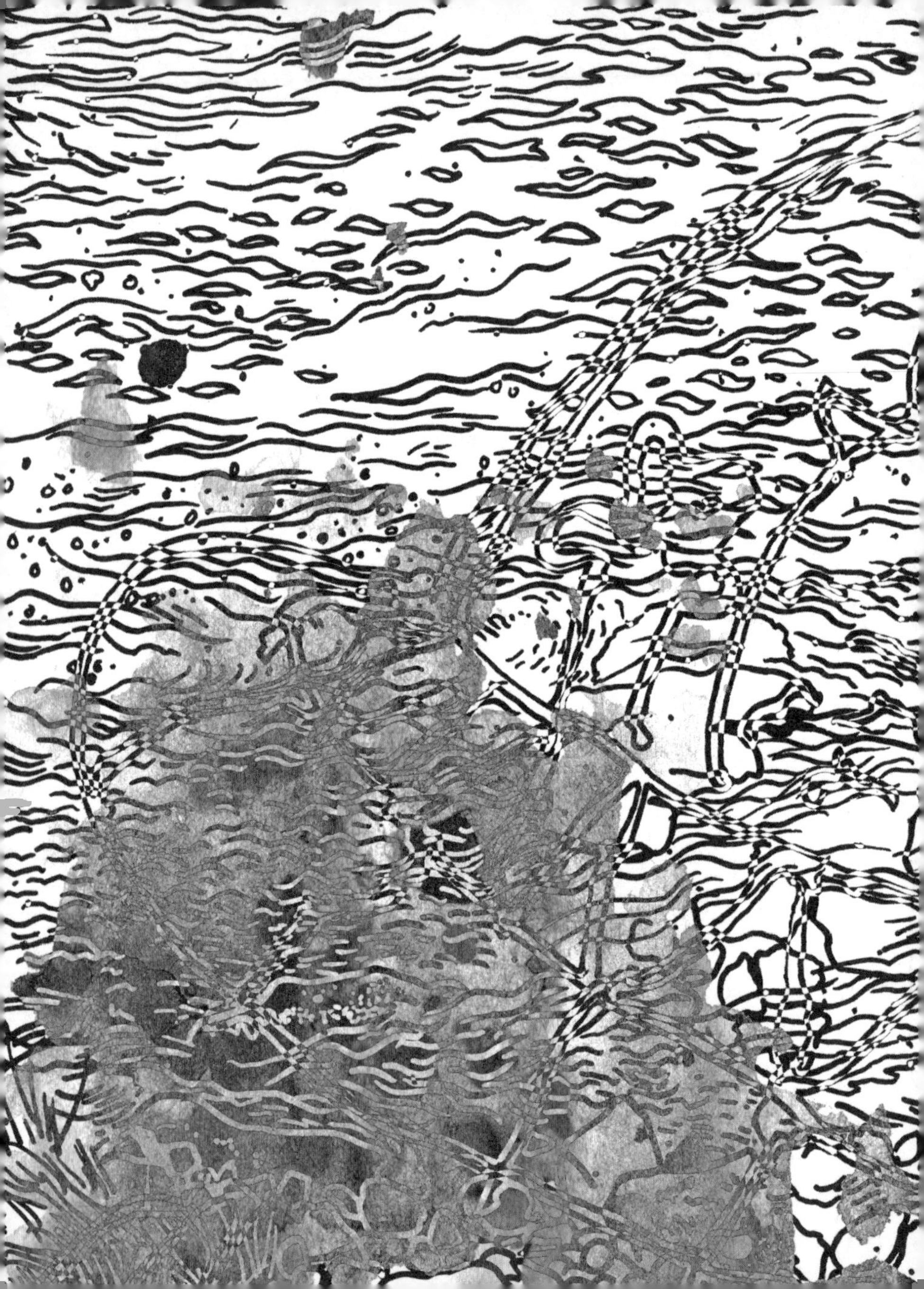

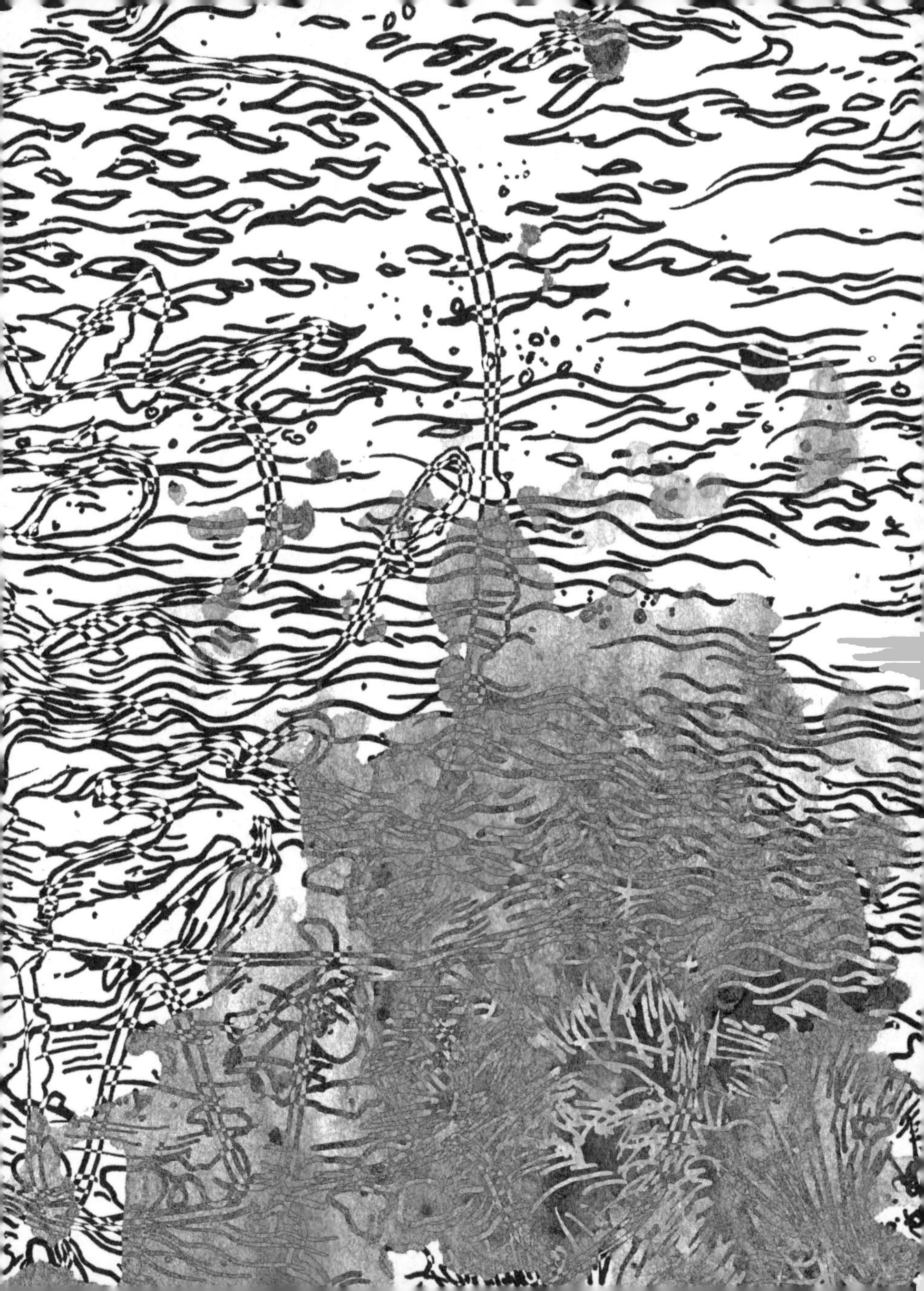

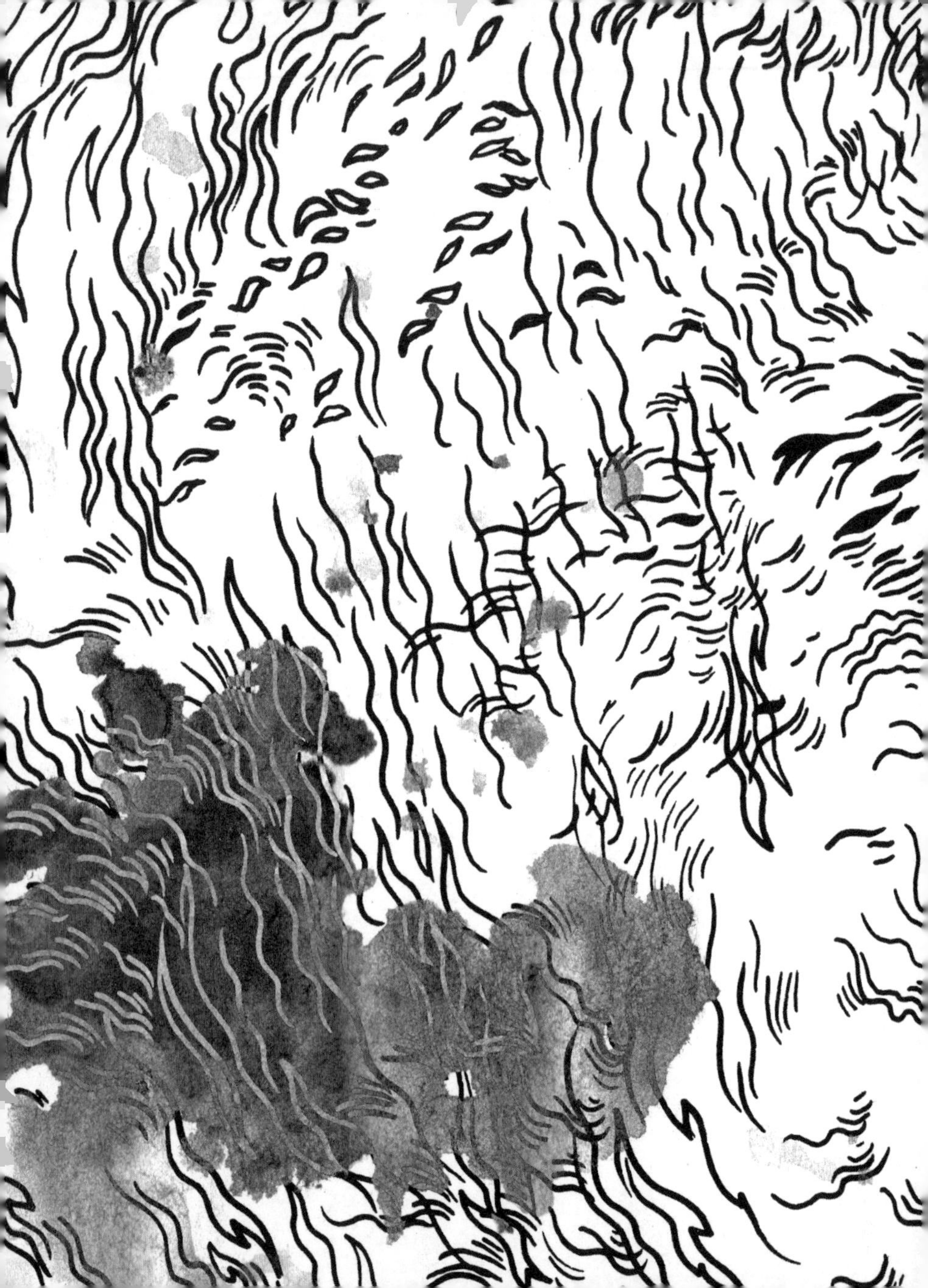

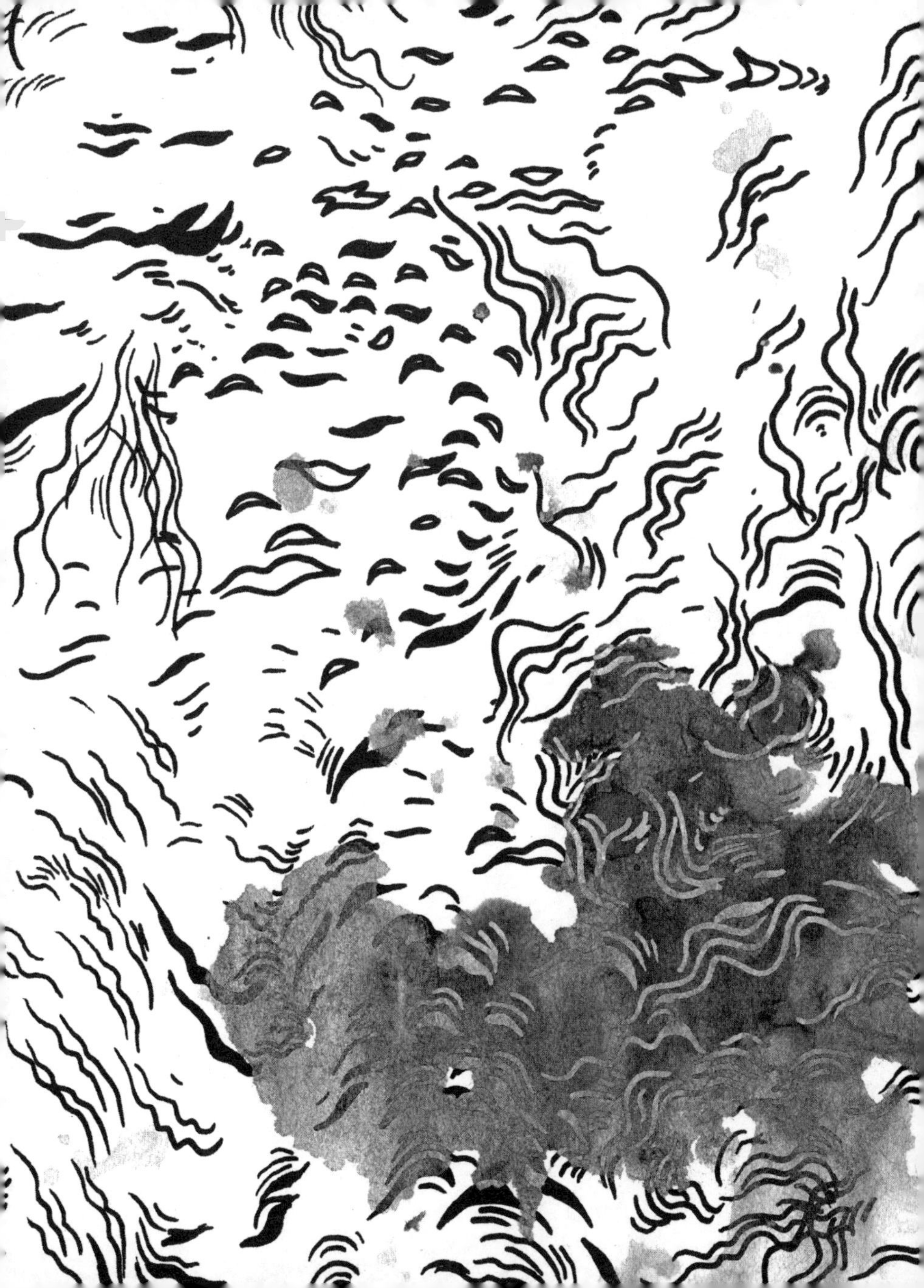

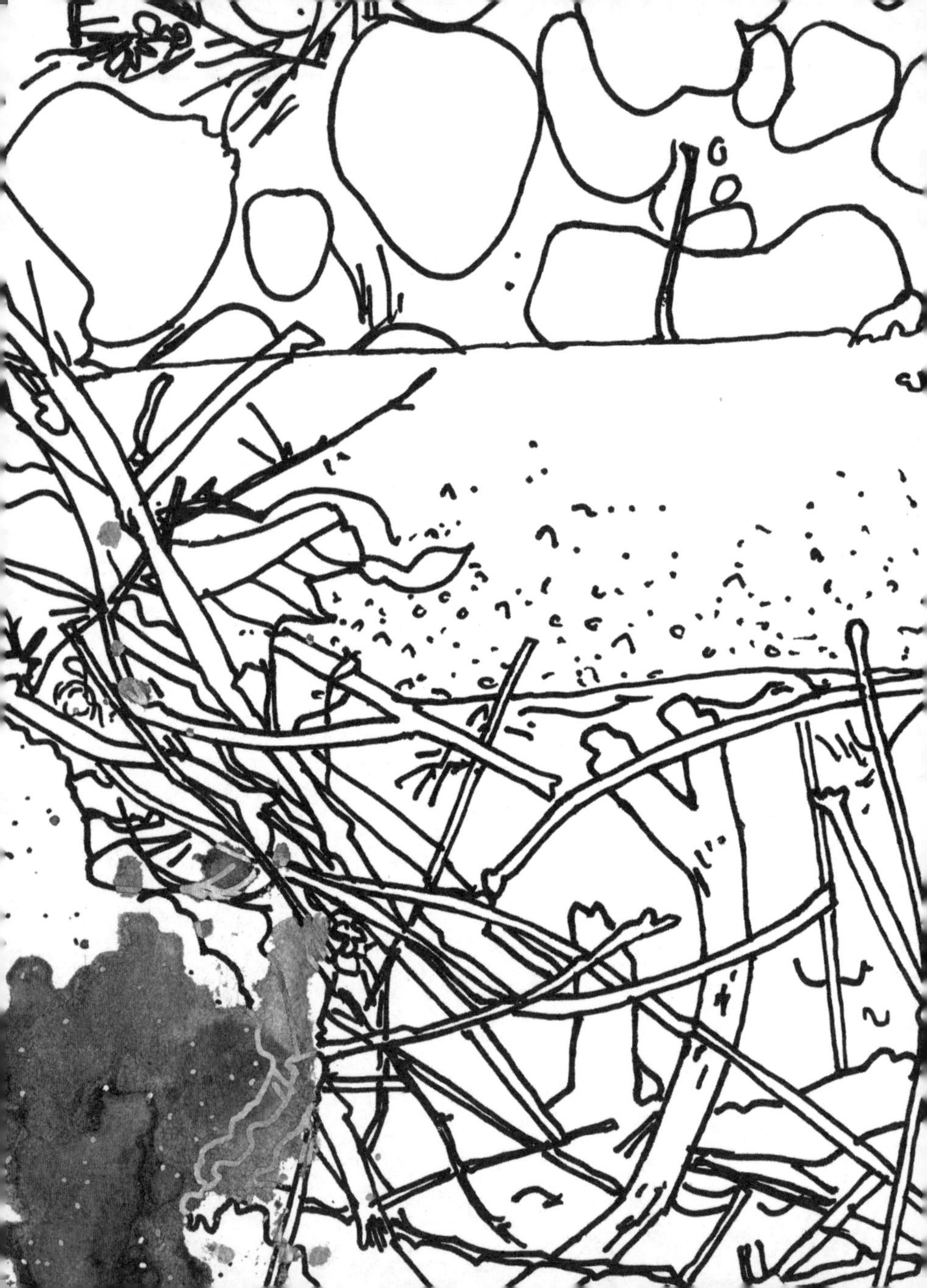

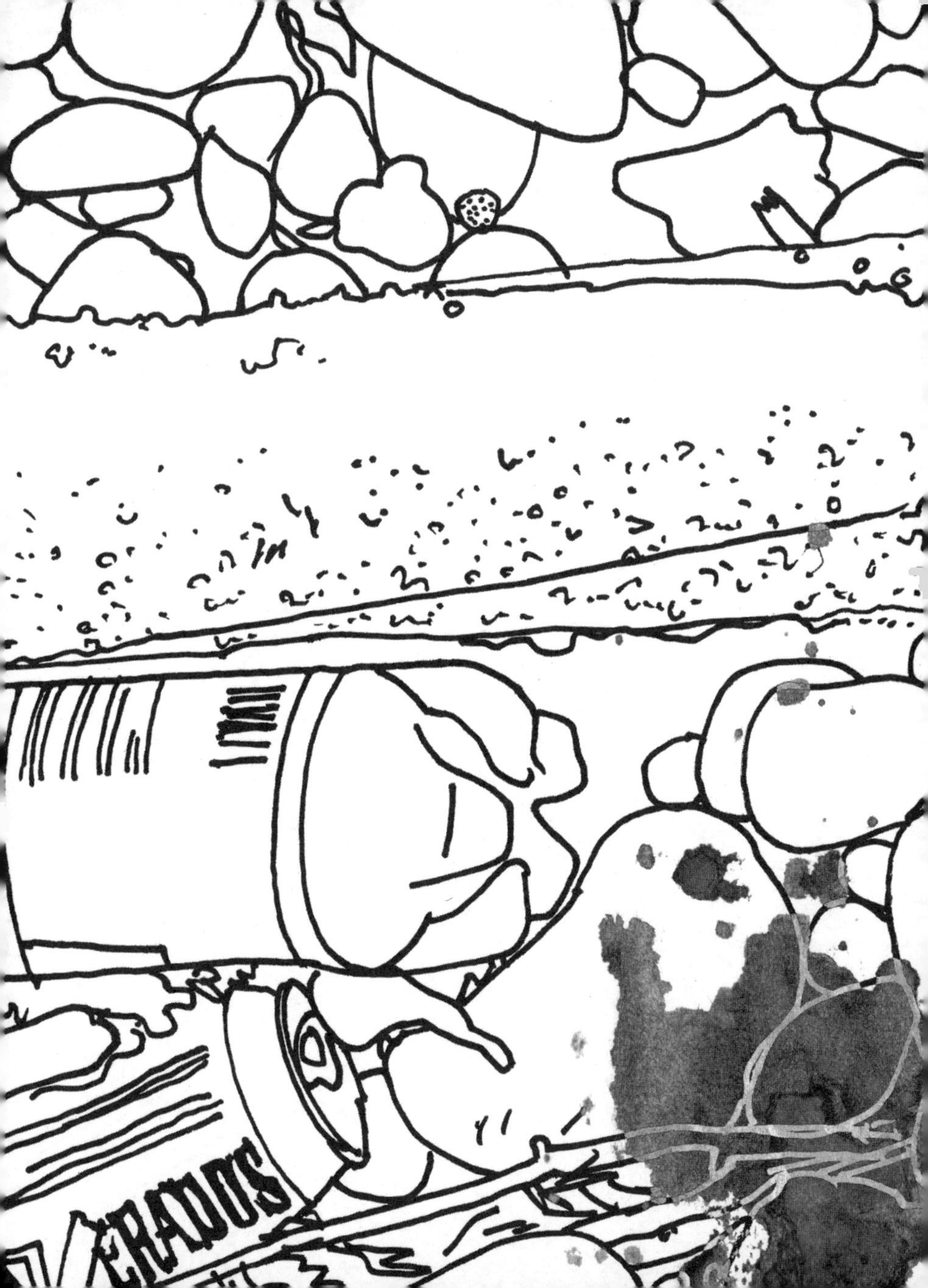

RADOS

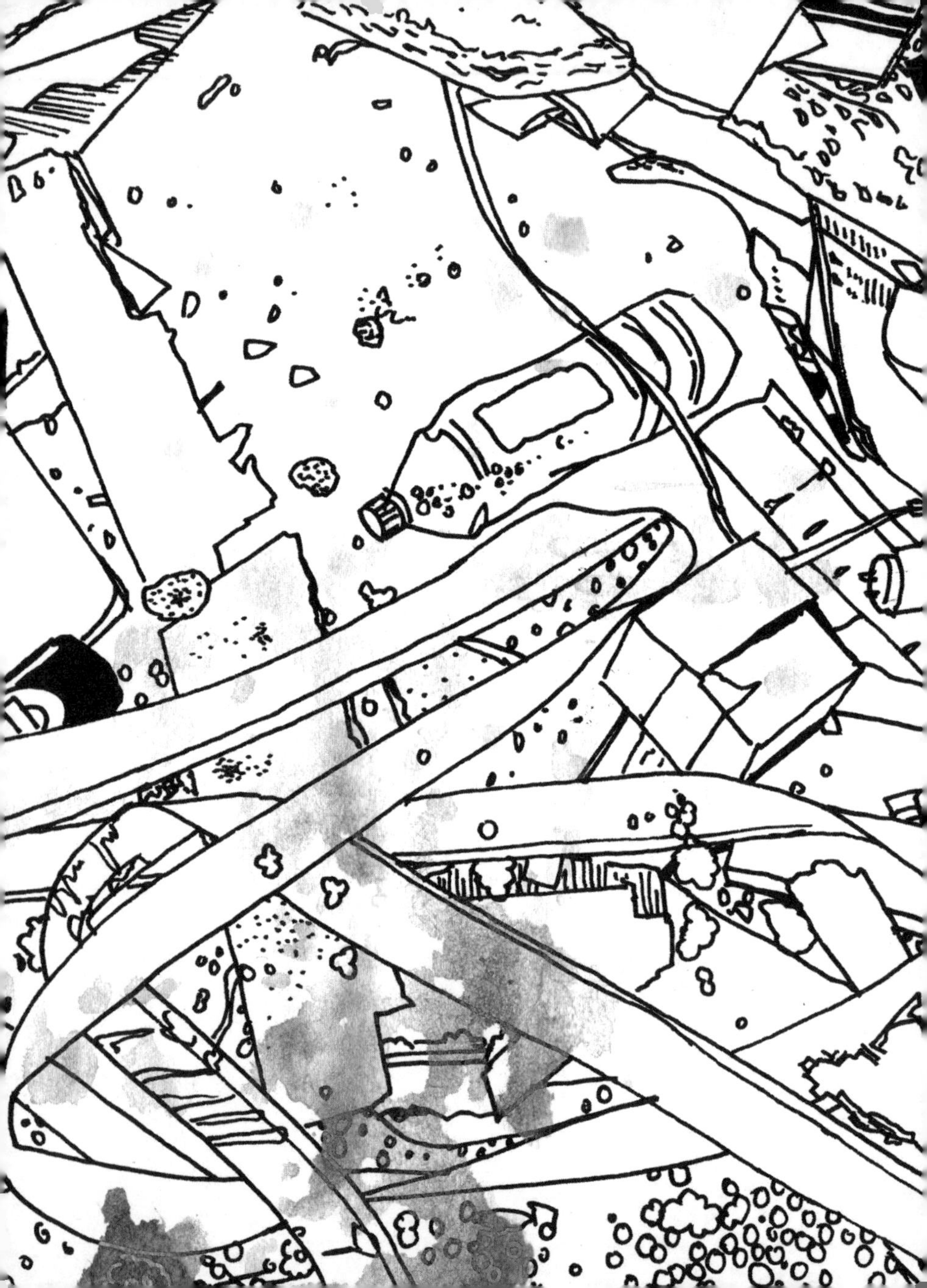

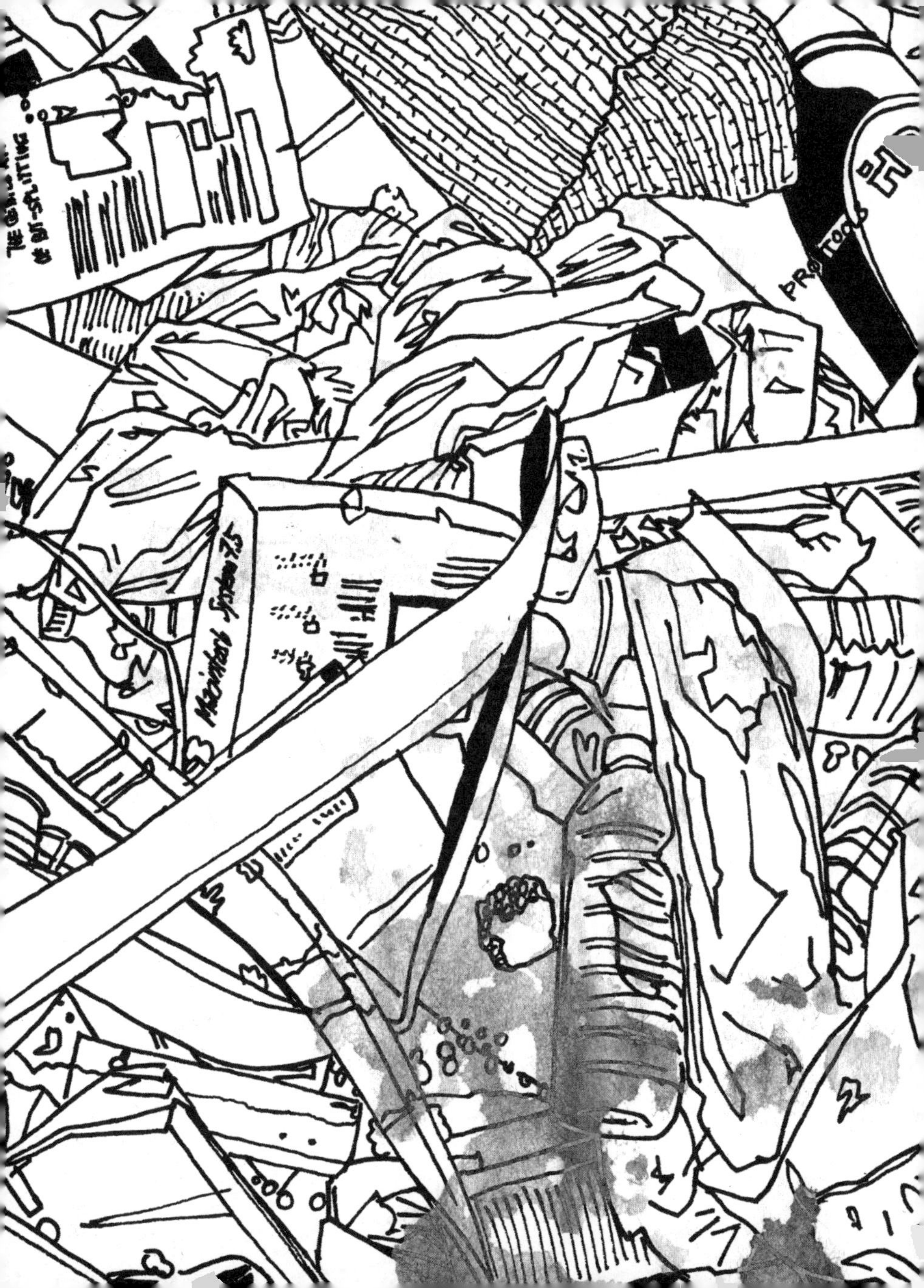

THE GENIUS
OF EAR-SPLITTING
Macintosh System 7.5
PRo TOOLS

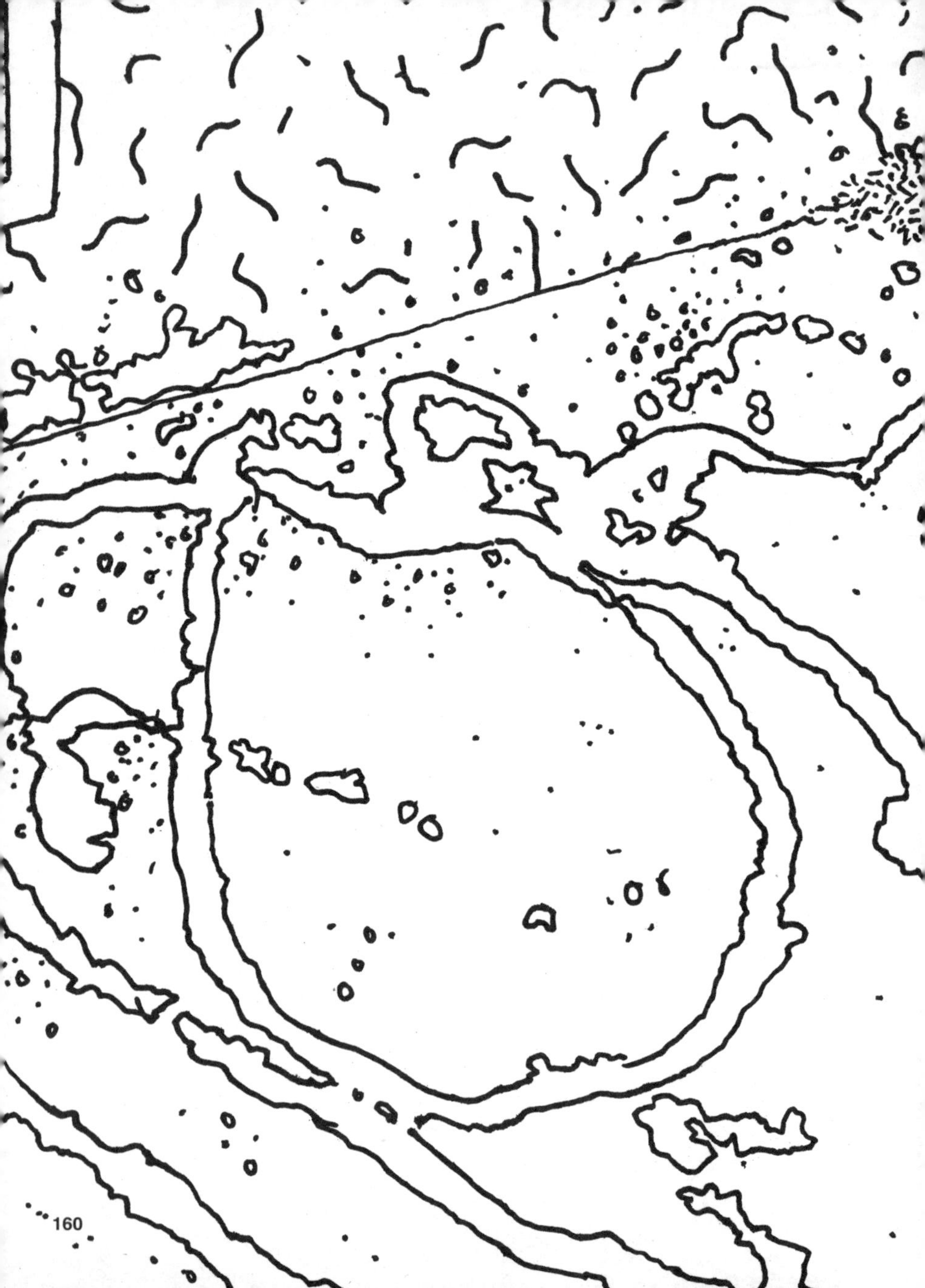

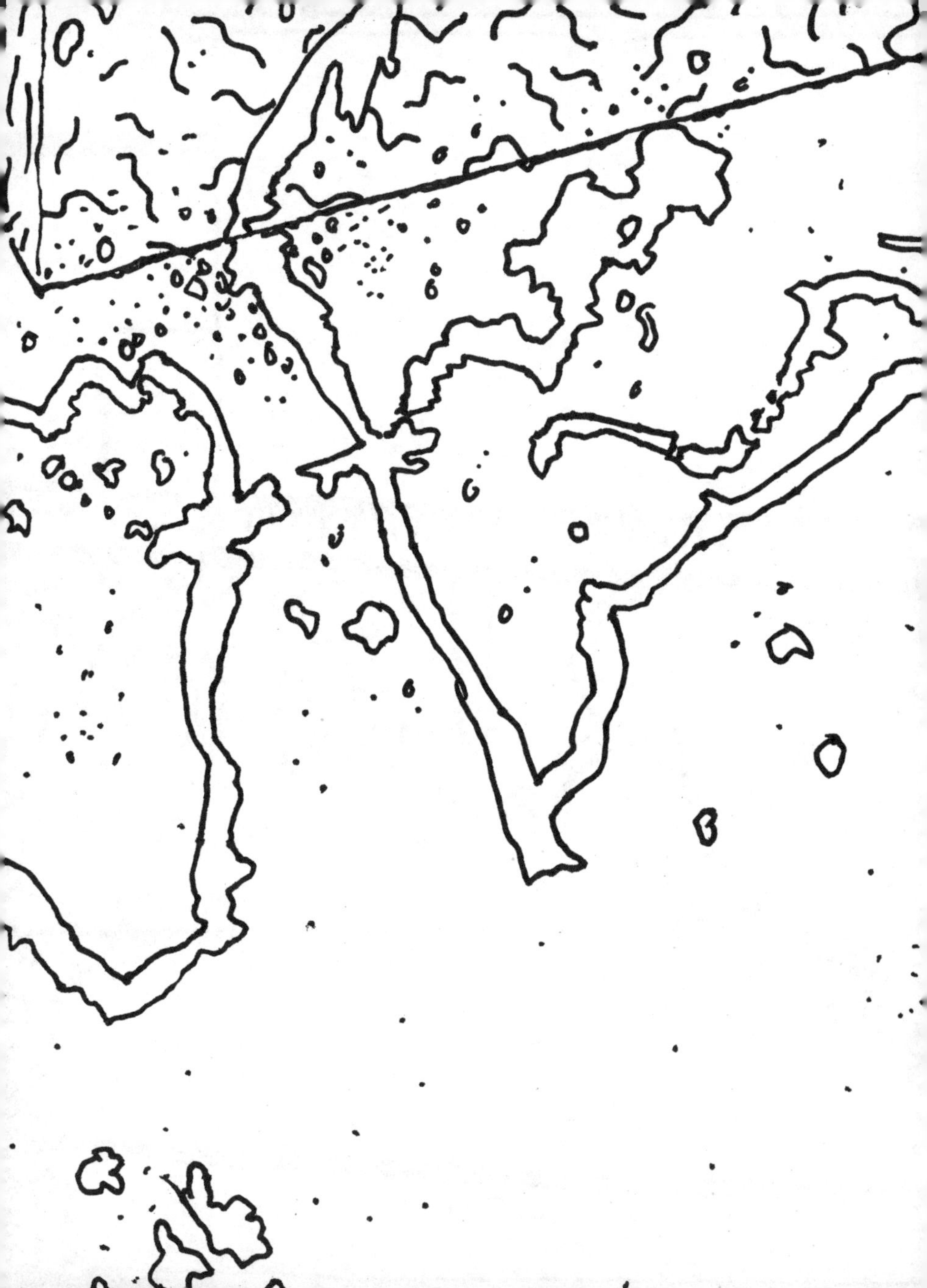

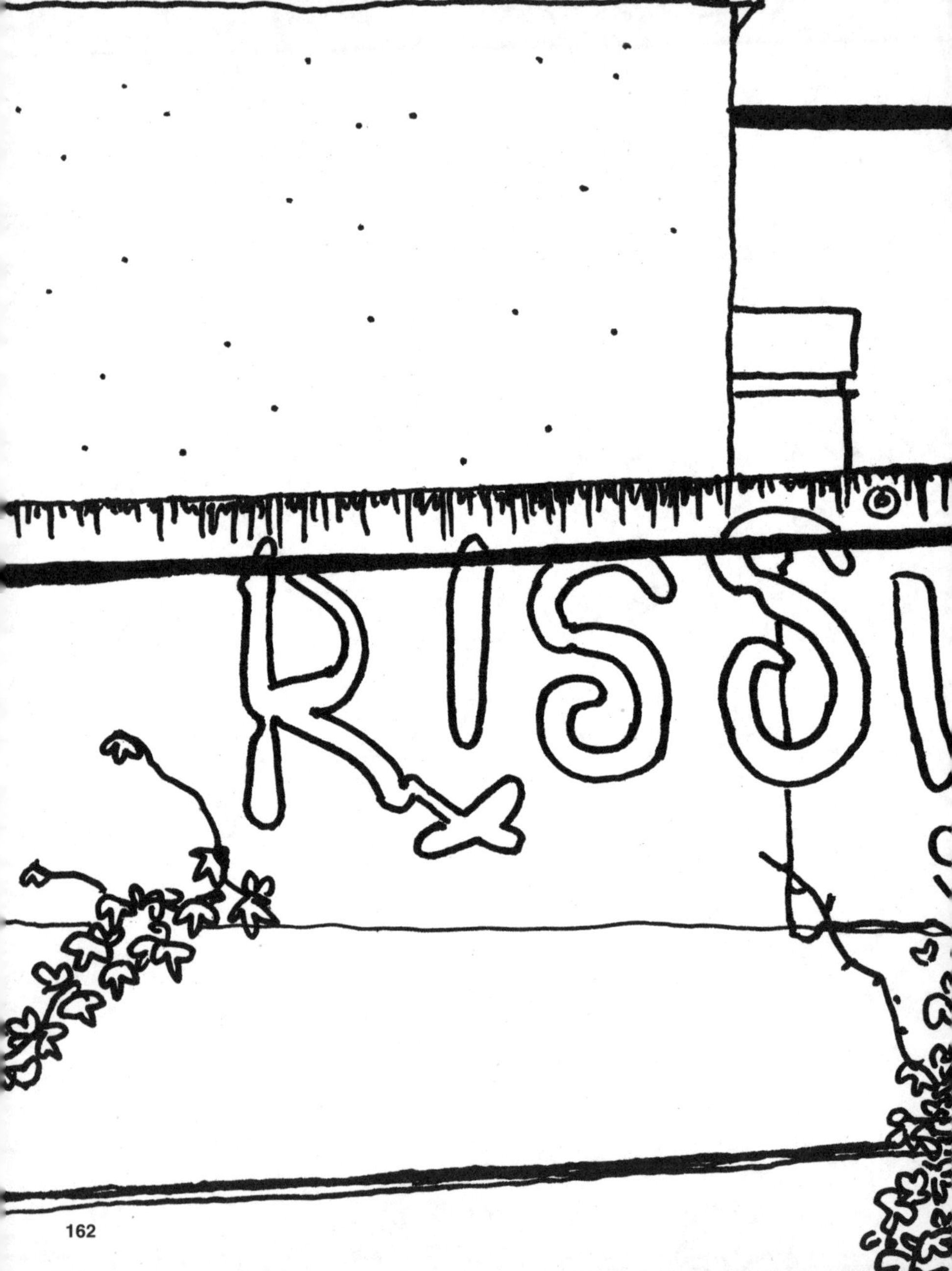

RISSI

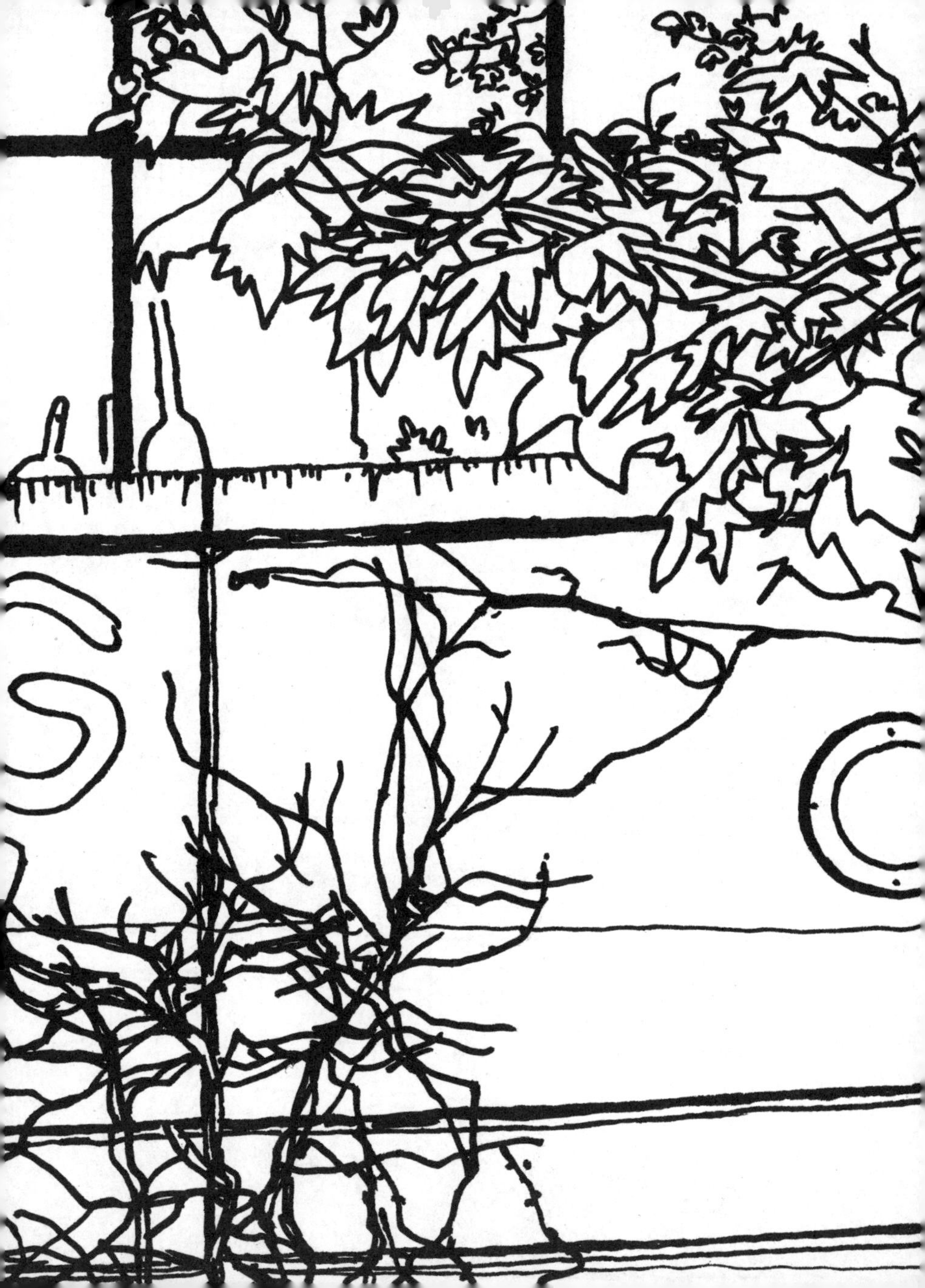

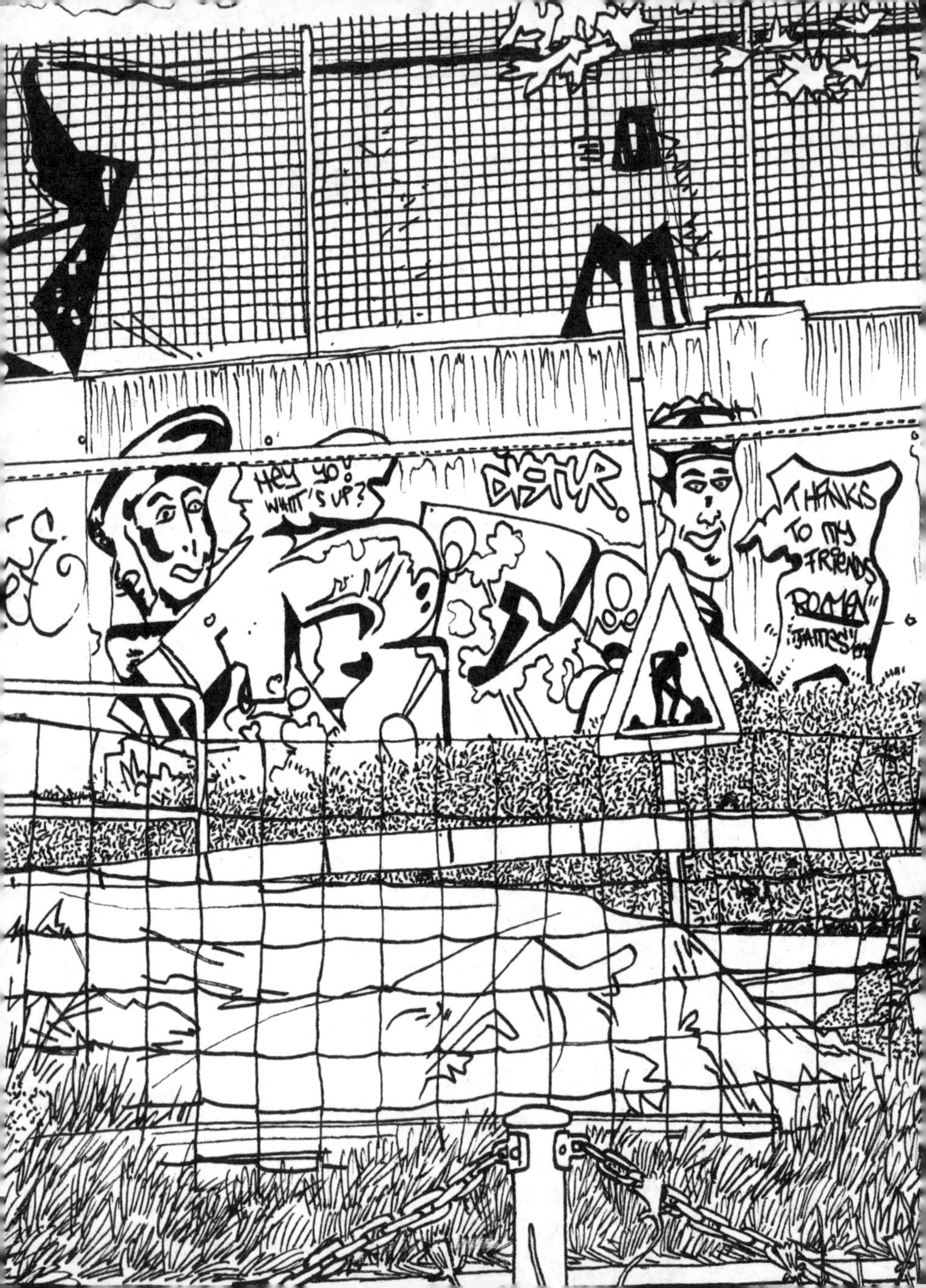

HEY YO! WHAT'S UP?
DISTUR
THANKS TO MY FRIENDS ROCMED JAMES

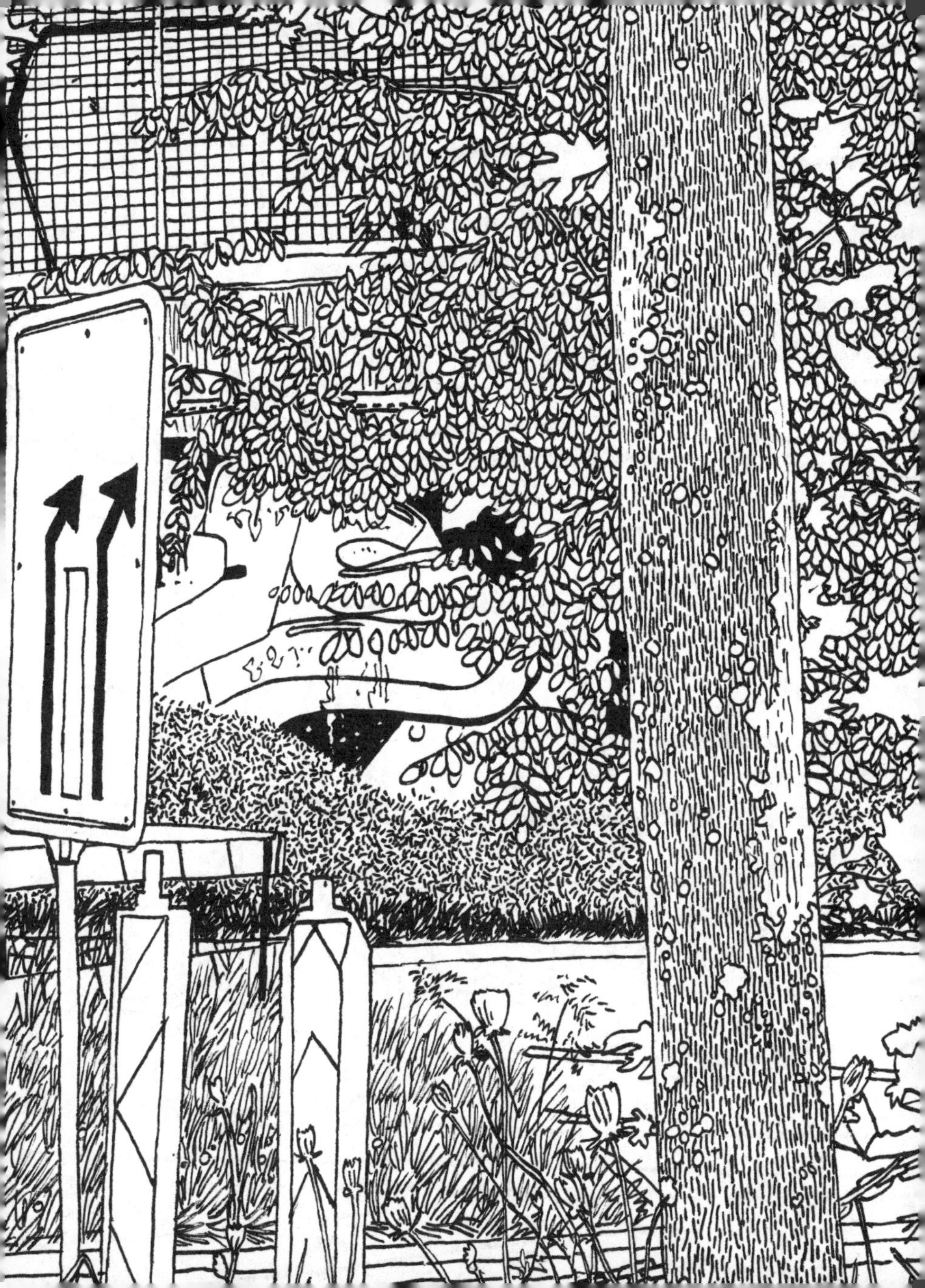

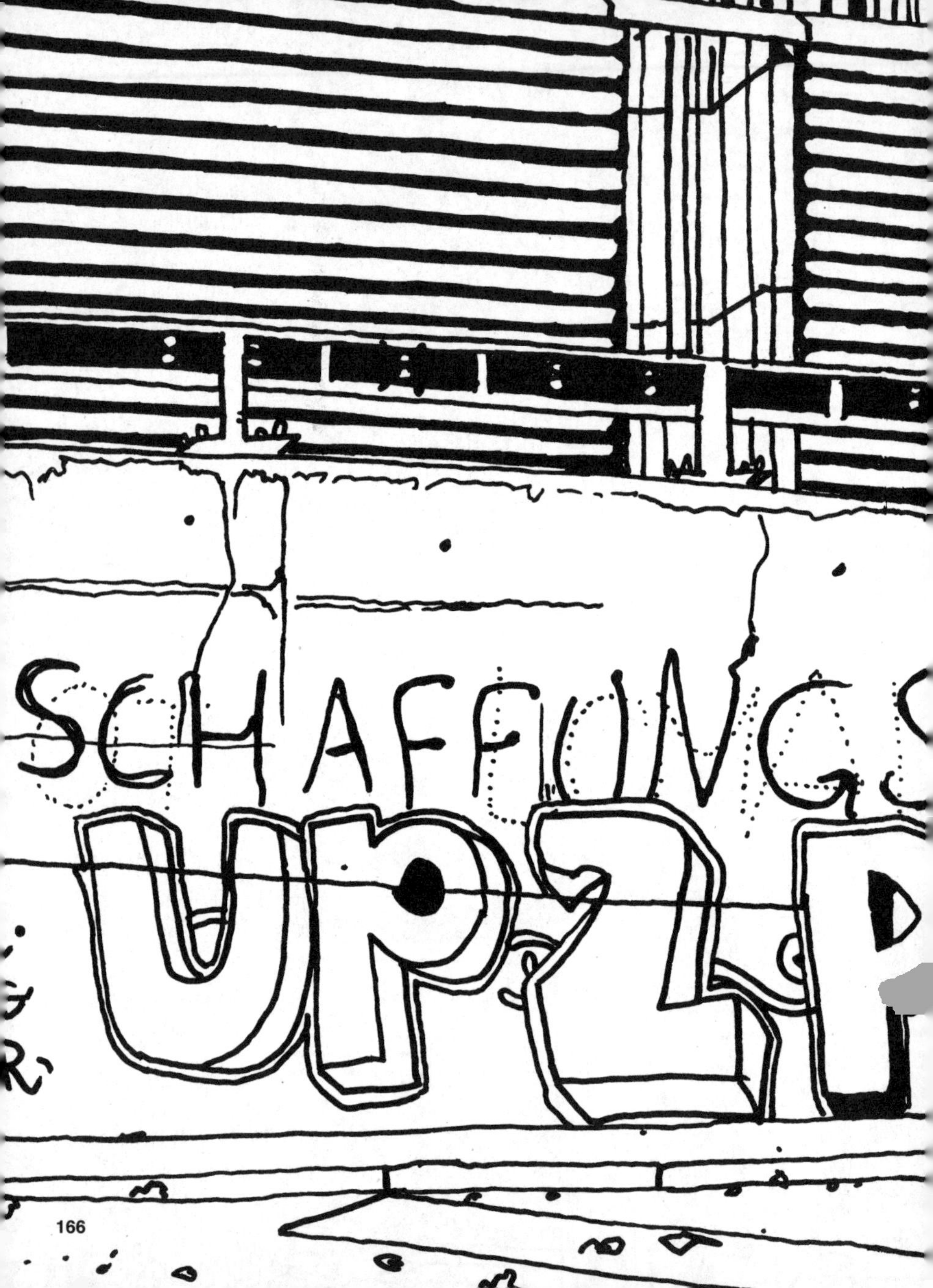
SCHAFFUNGS
UP2U P

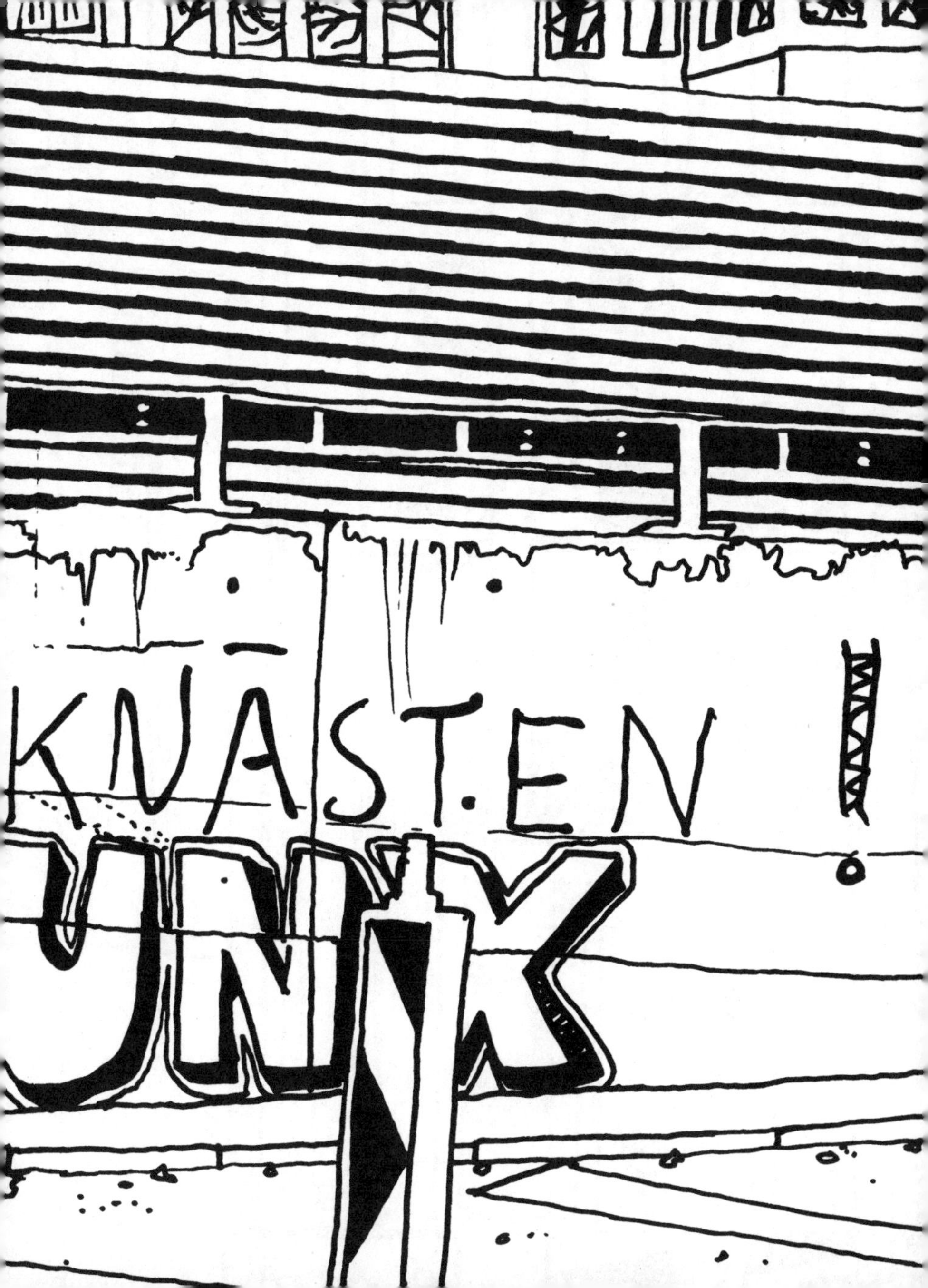

KNASTEN !
UNIX

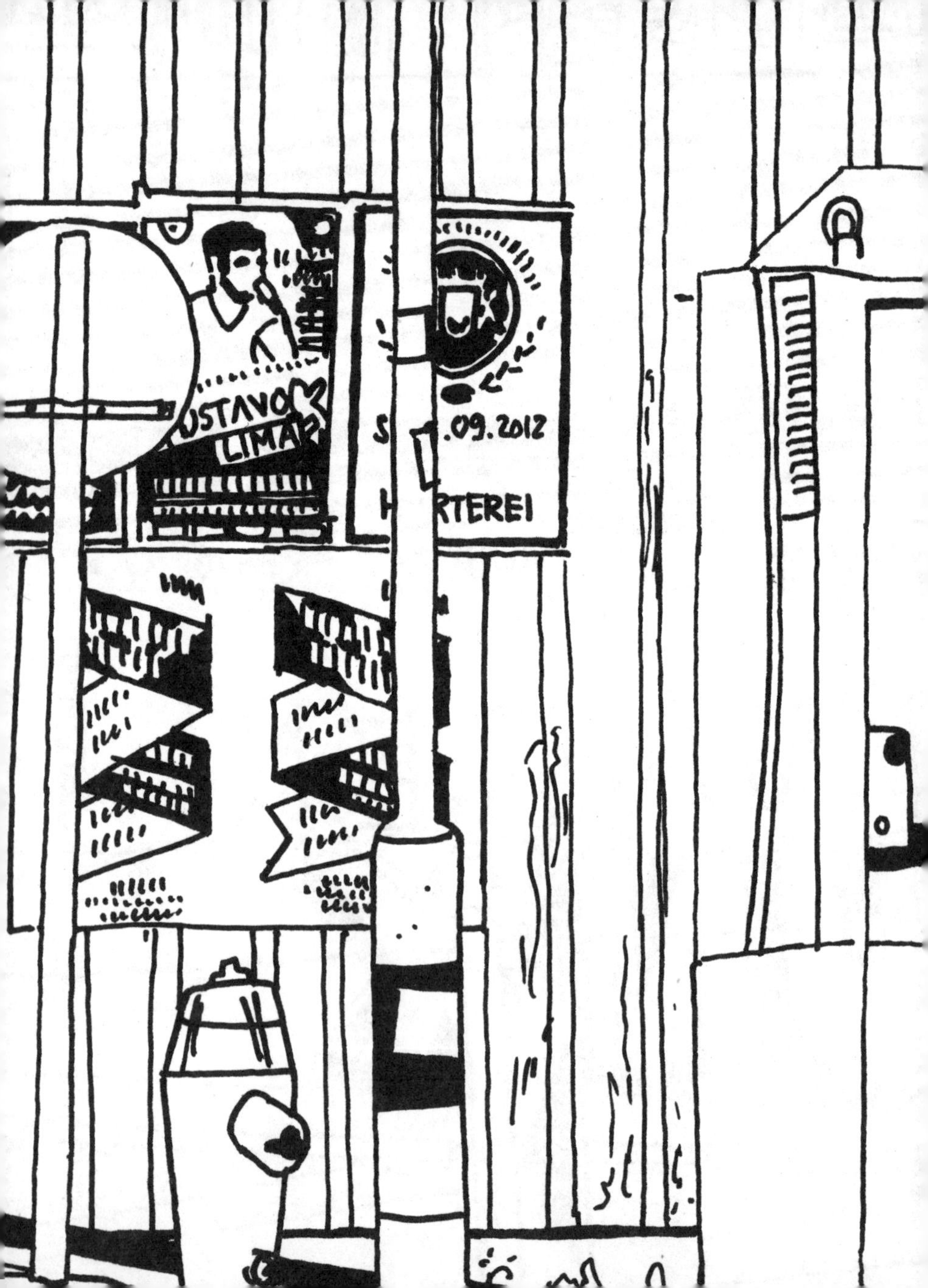

GUSTAVO
LIMA
.09.2012
RTEREI

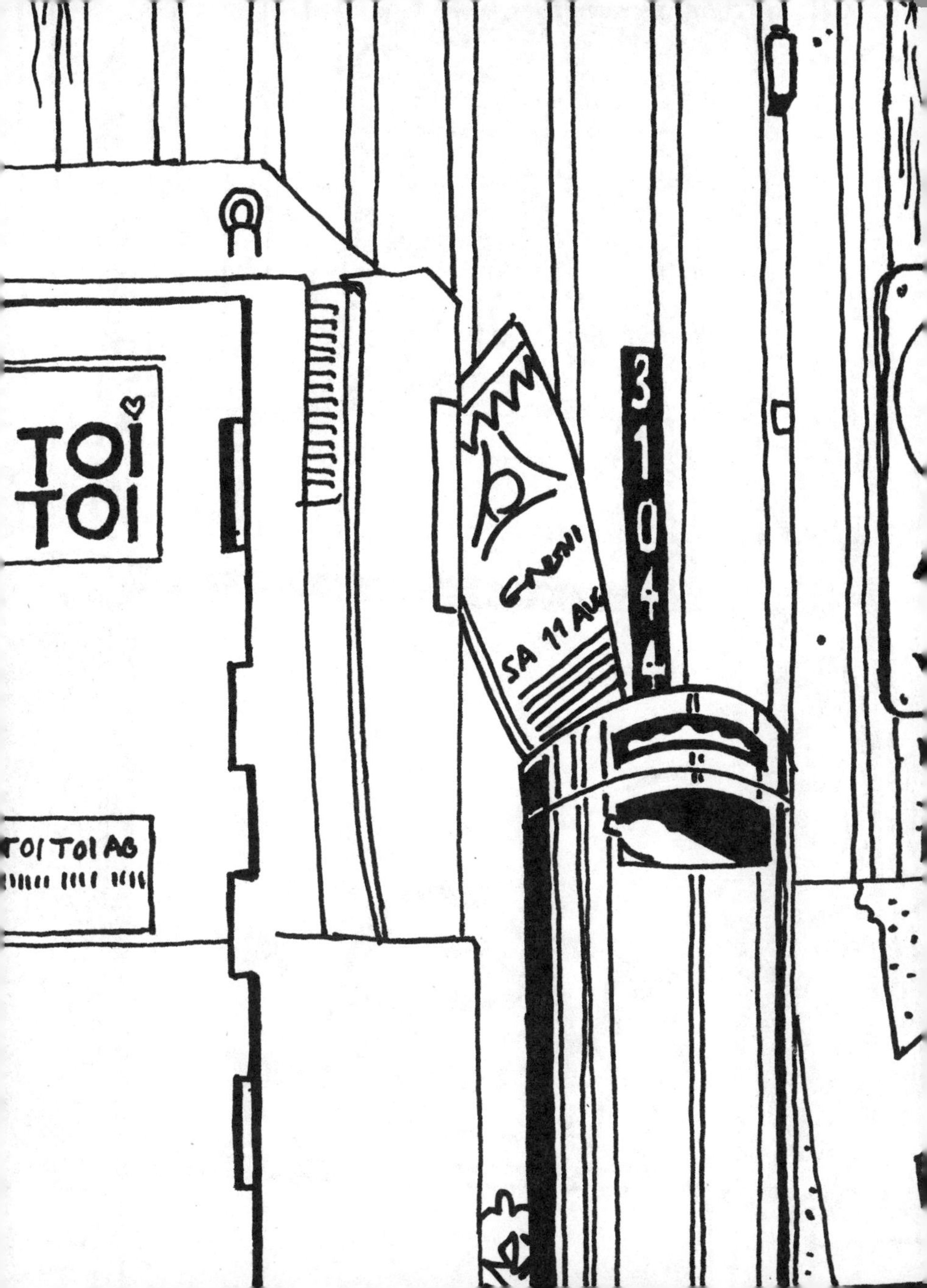

TOI
TOI
TOI TOI AG
3104
ENEHI
SA 11 AU

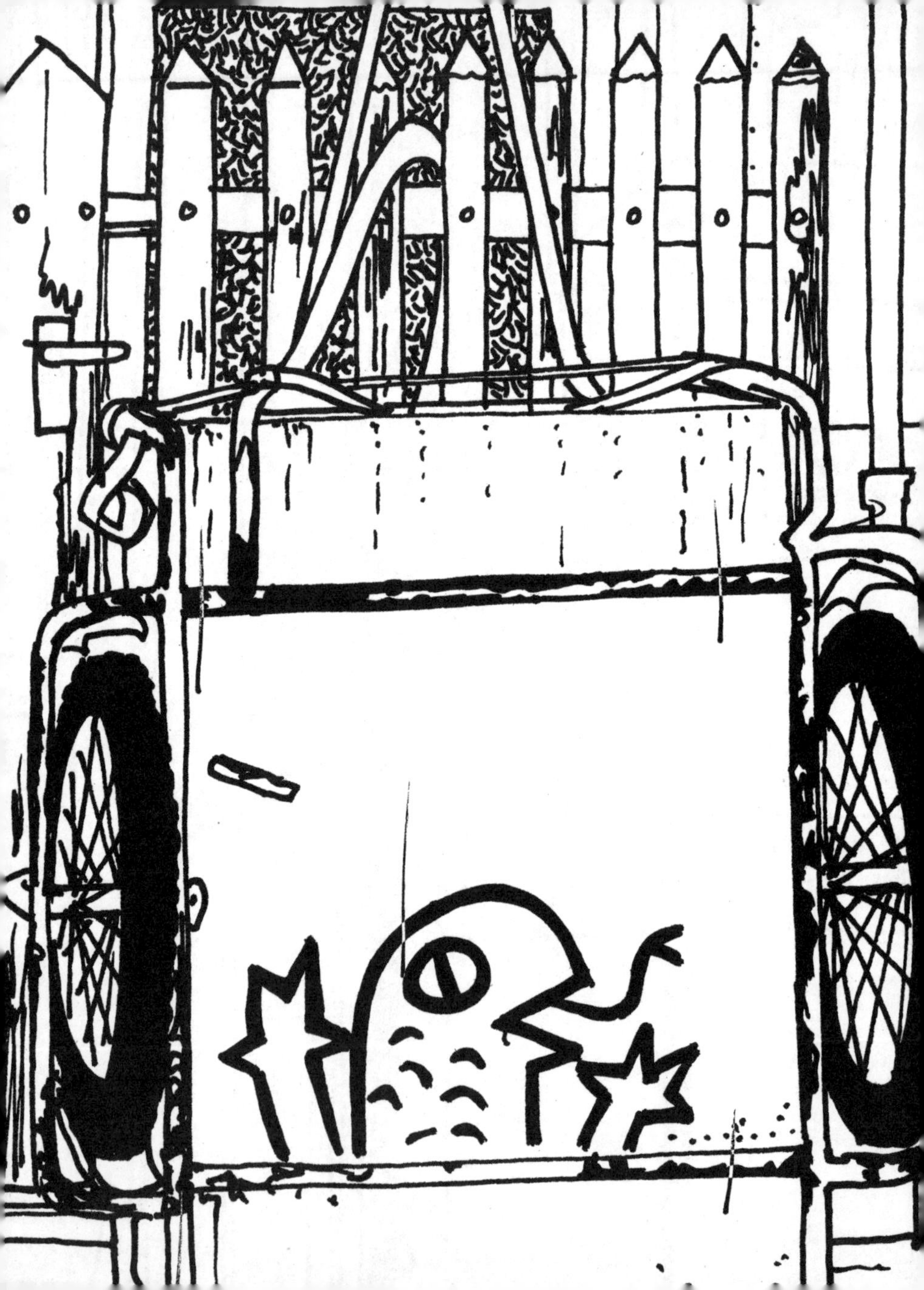

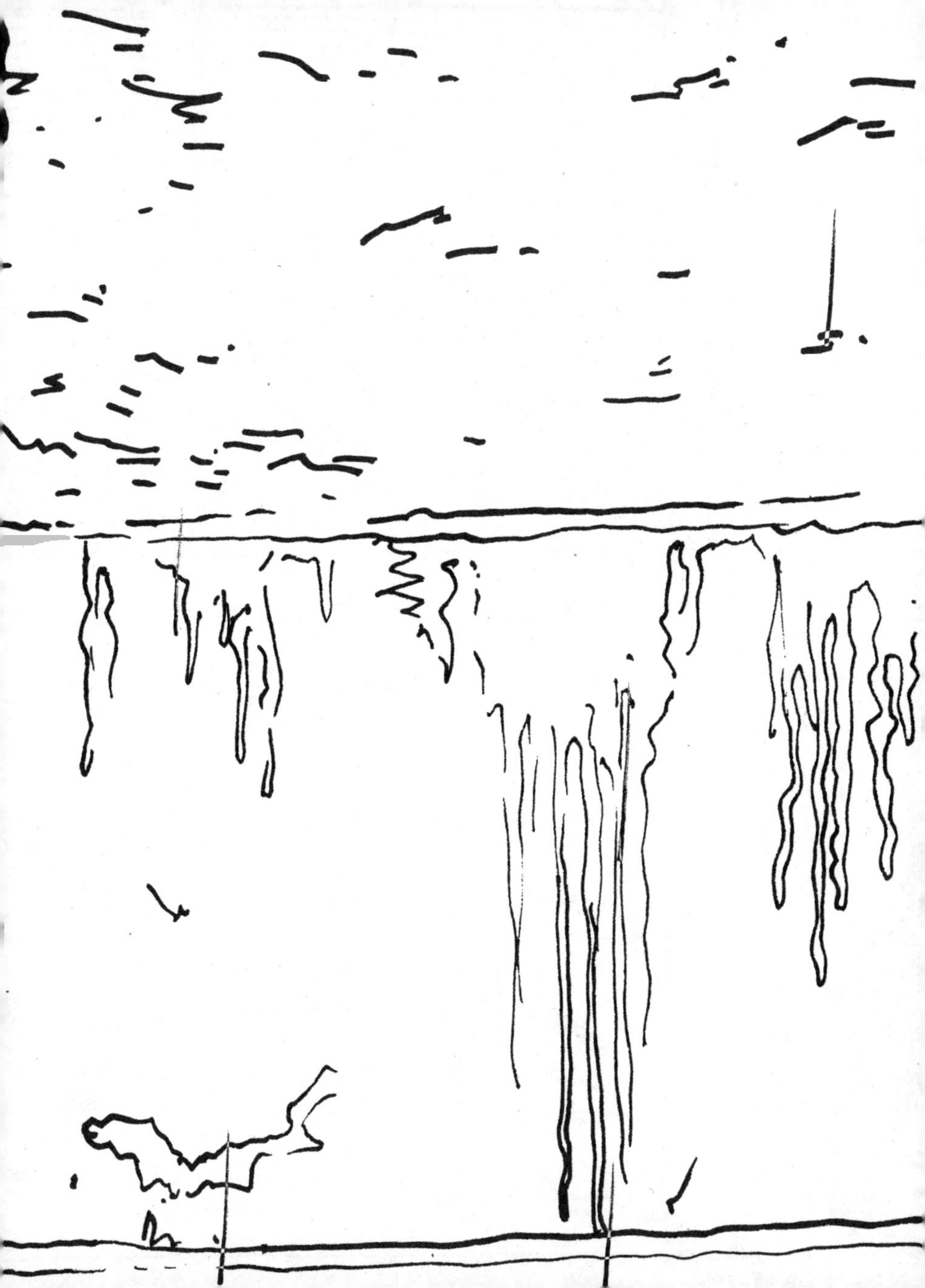

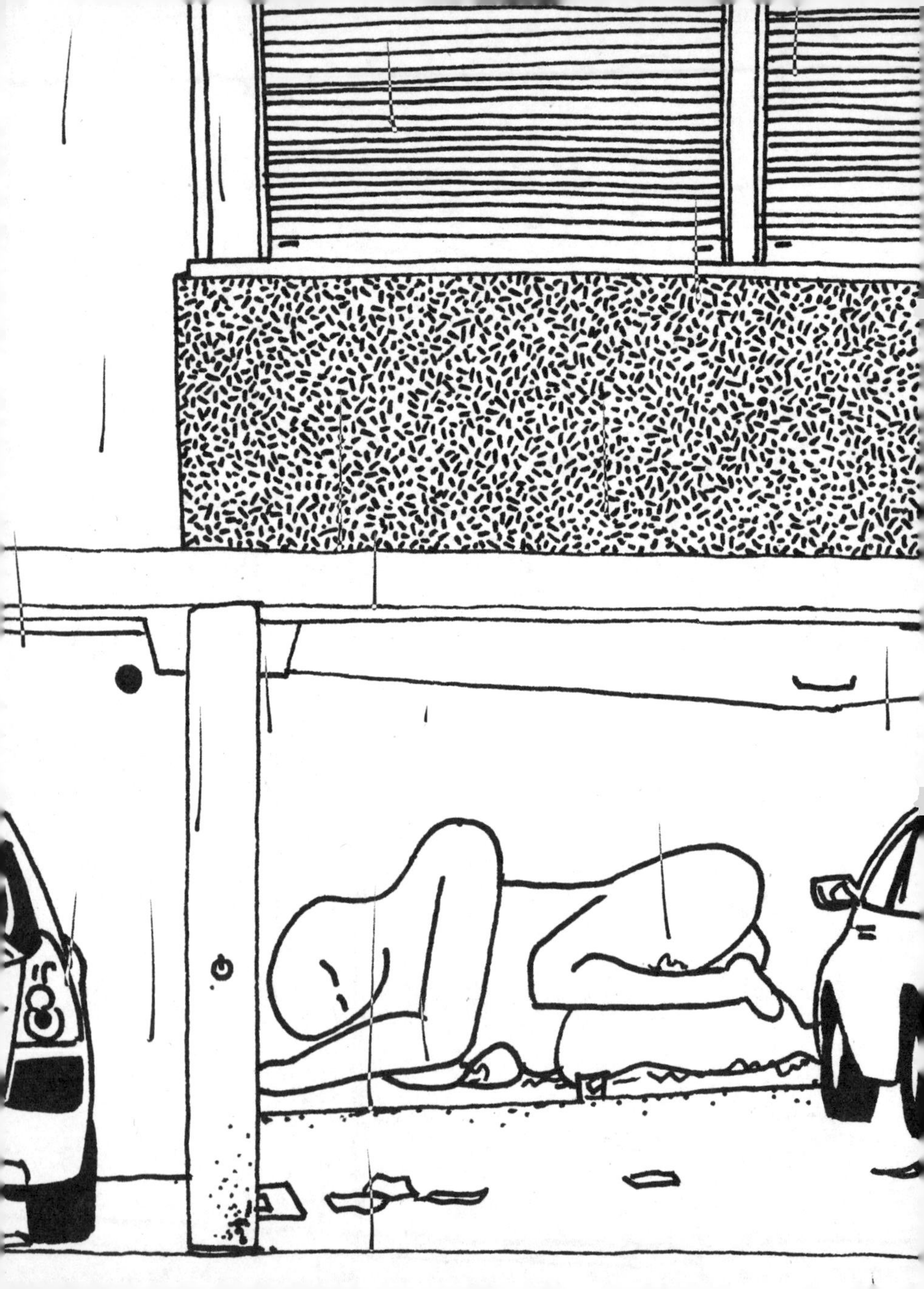

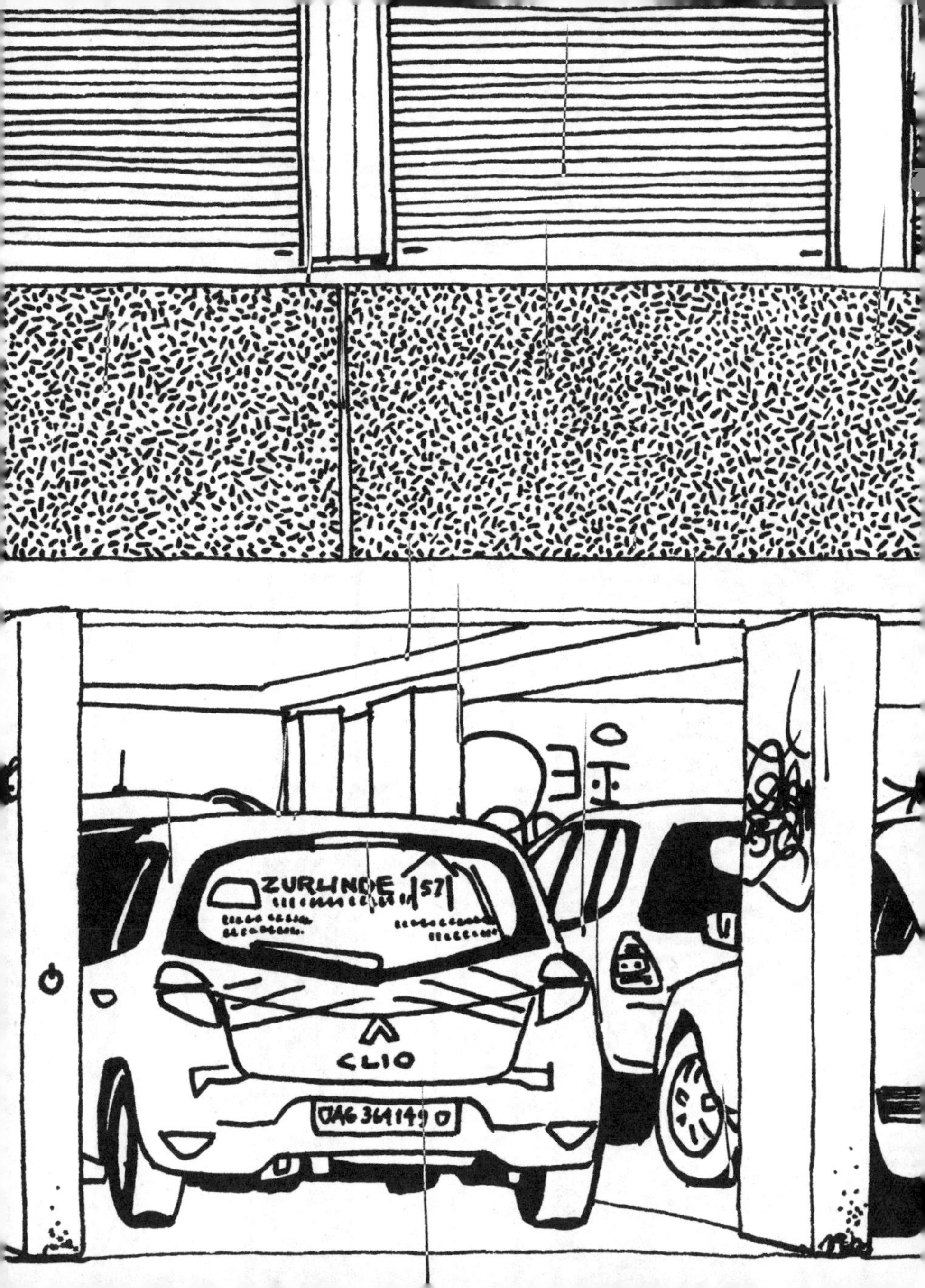

ZURLINDE 57
CLIO
AG 364149

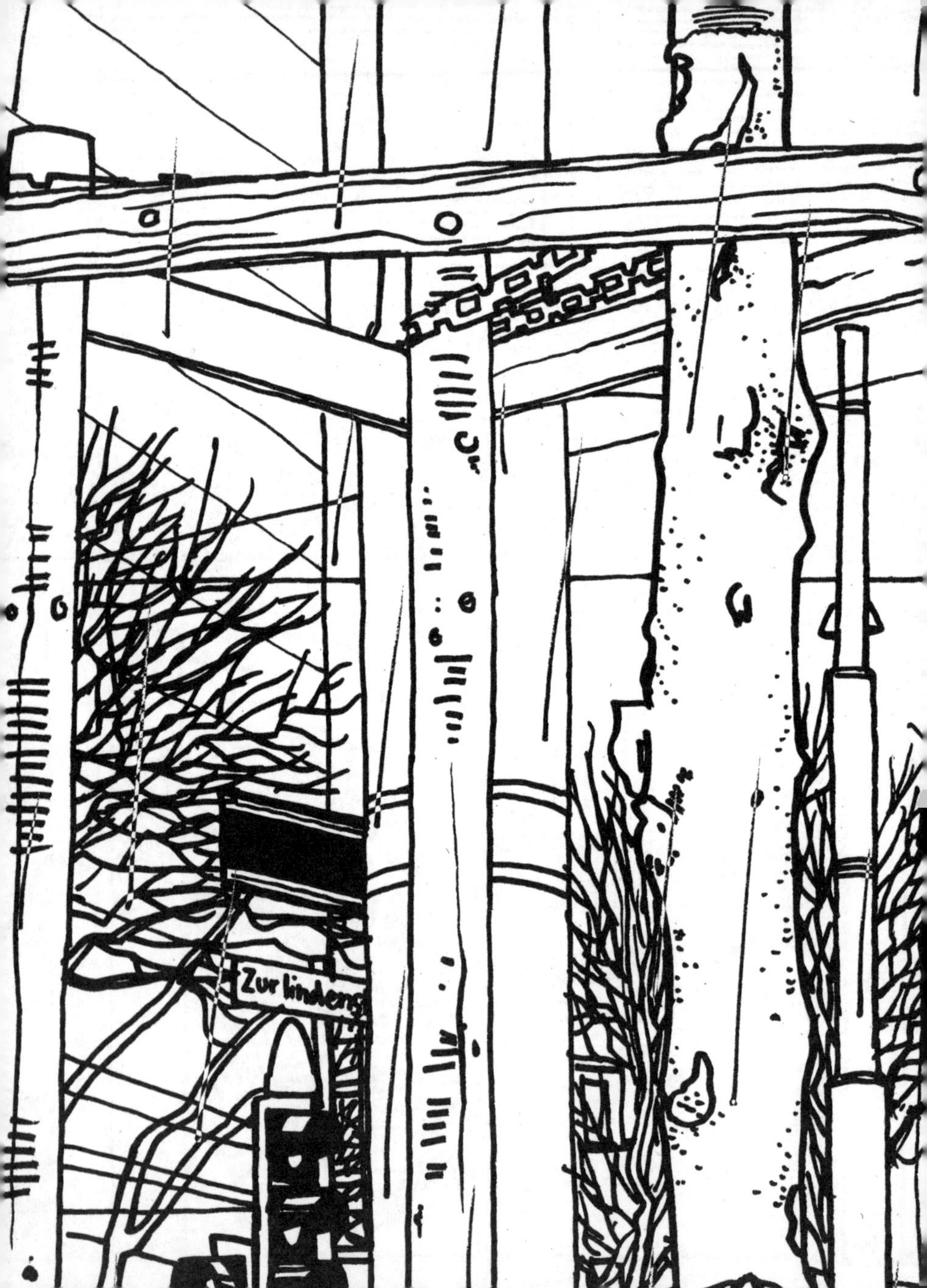
Zur Linden

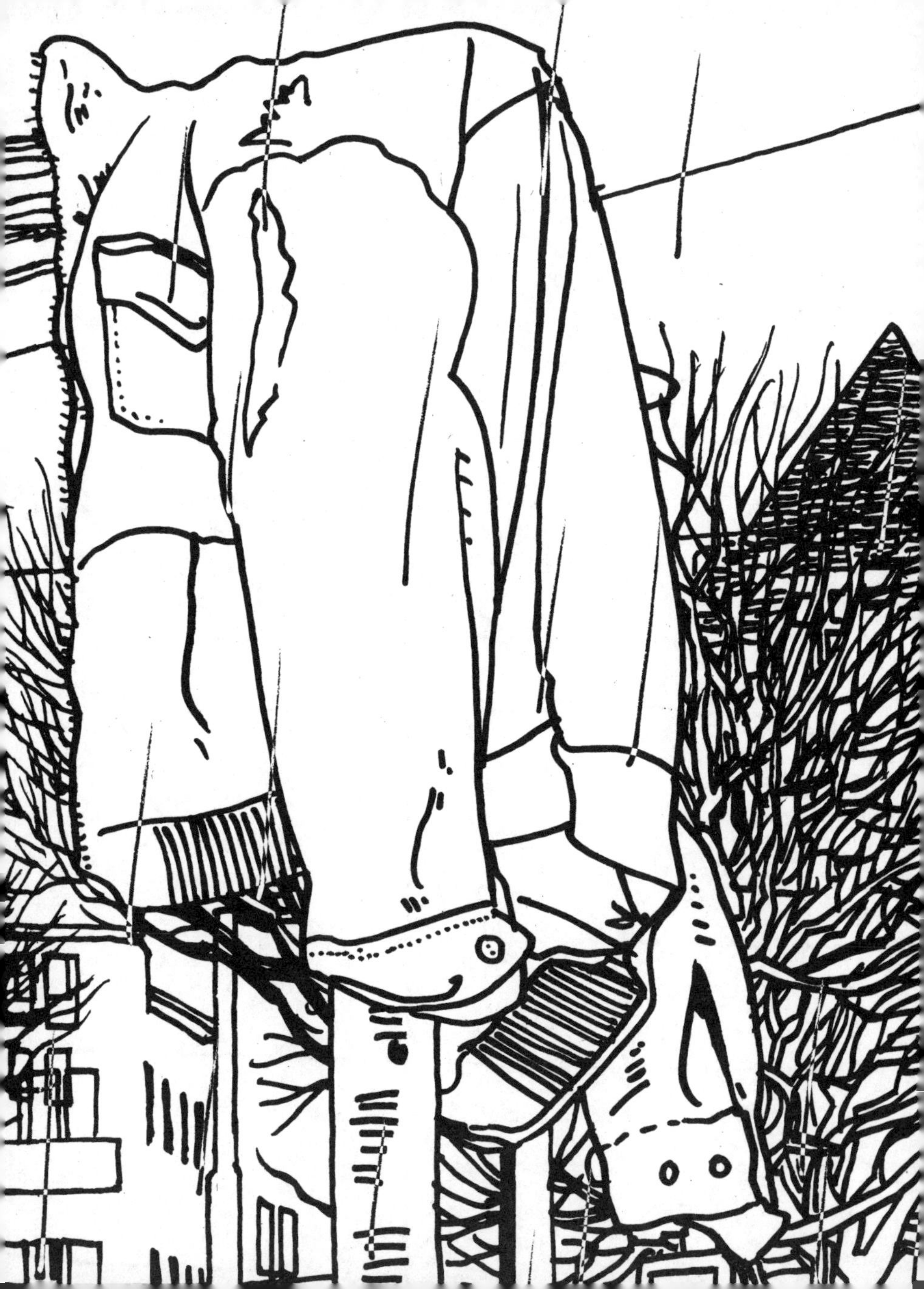

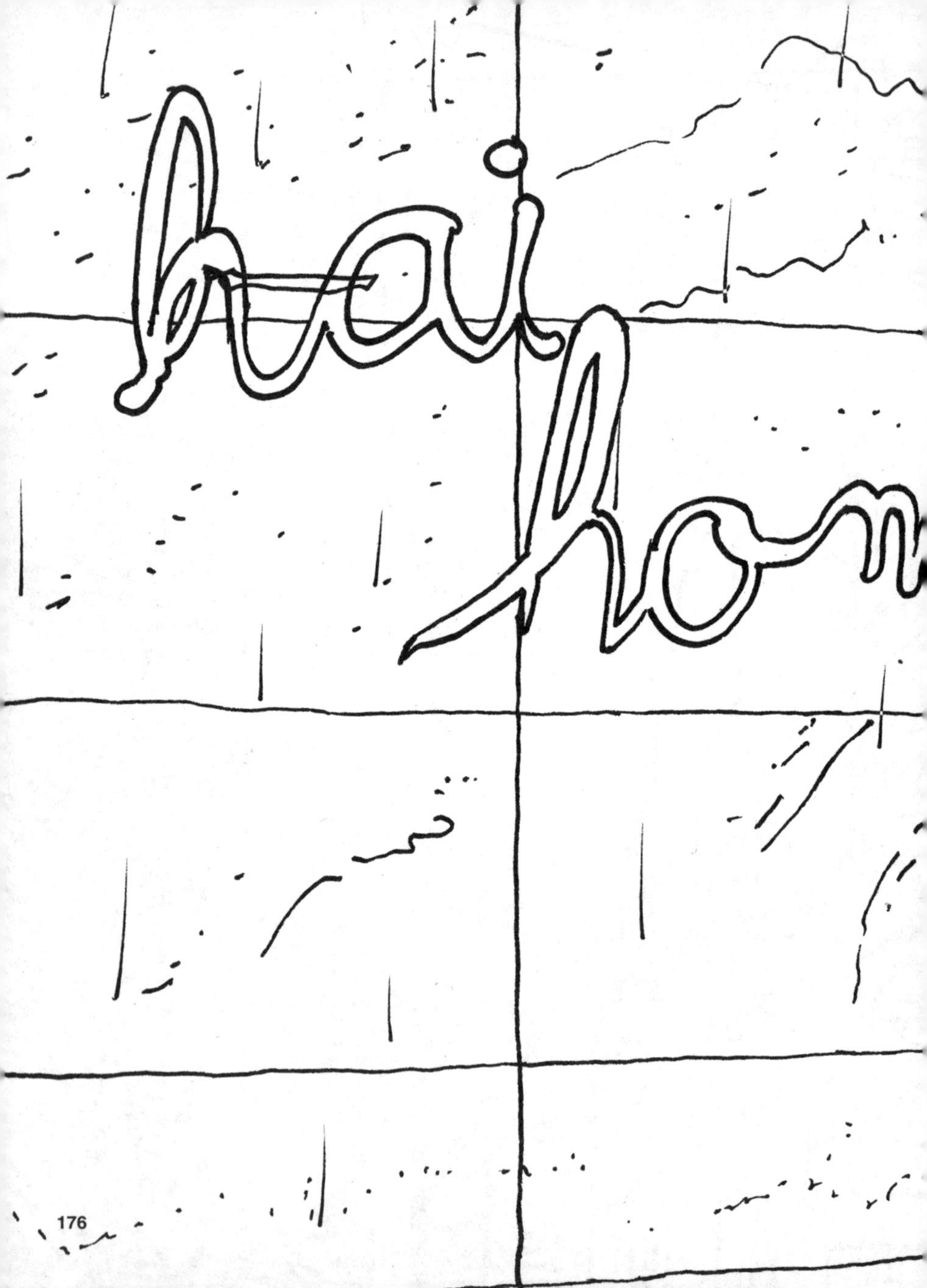

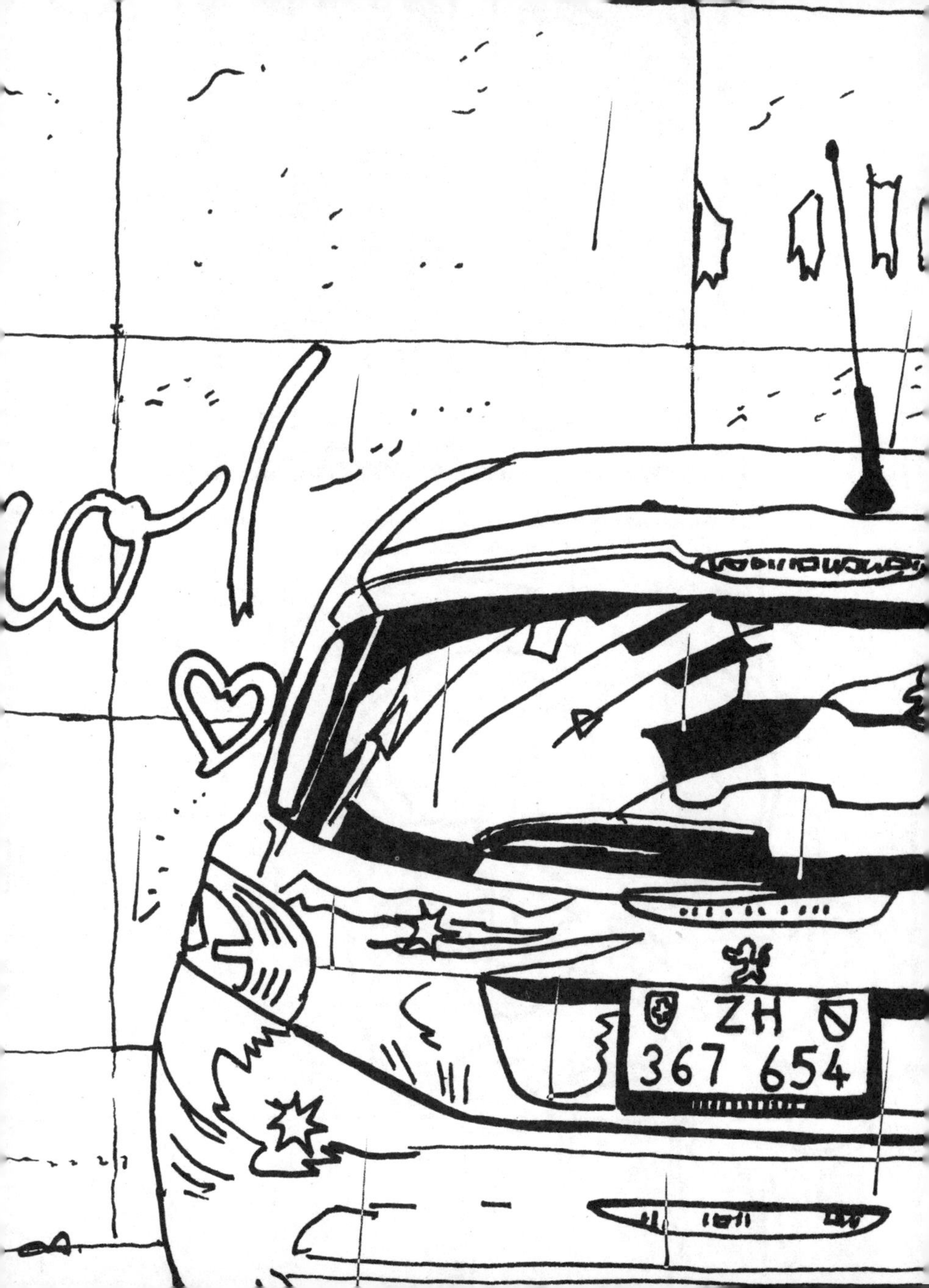

ZH
367 654

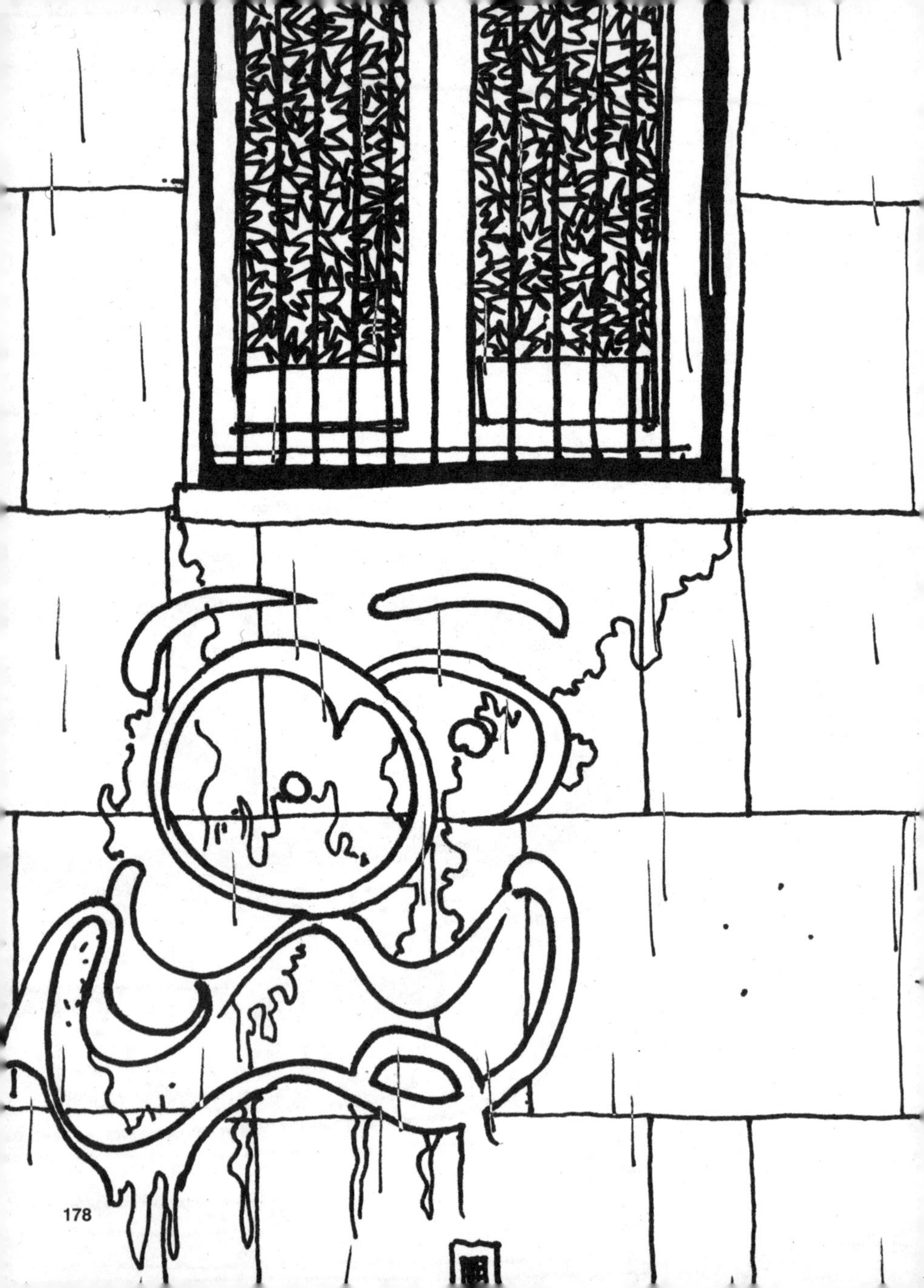

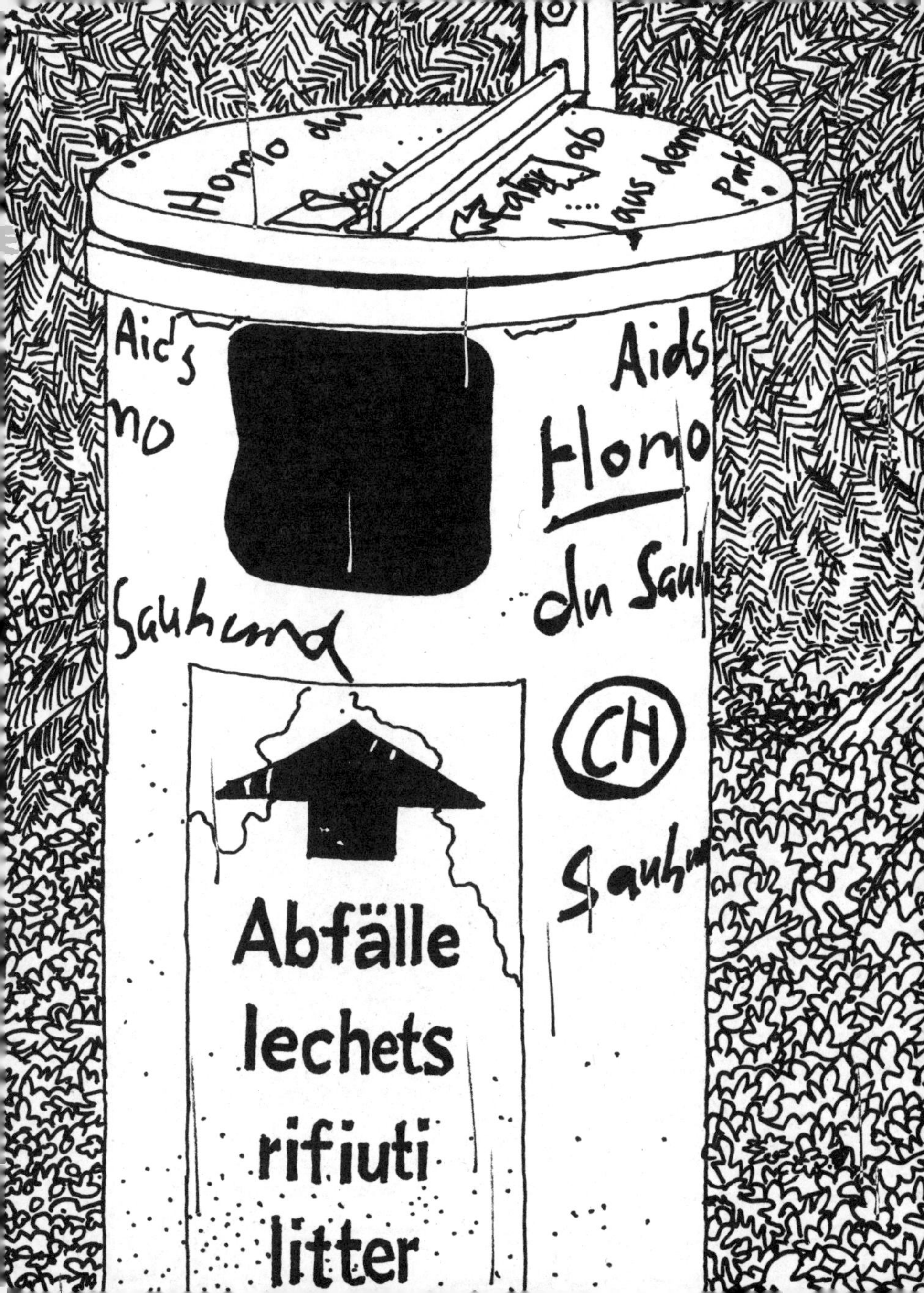

Homo du Sau
Fahr ab ..... aus dem Park
Aids no
Aids
Homo
du Sau
Sauhund
CH
Sauh
Abfälle
lechets
rifiuti
litter

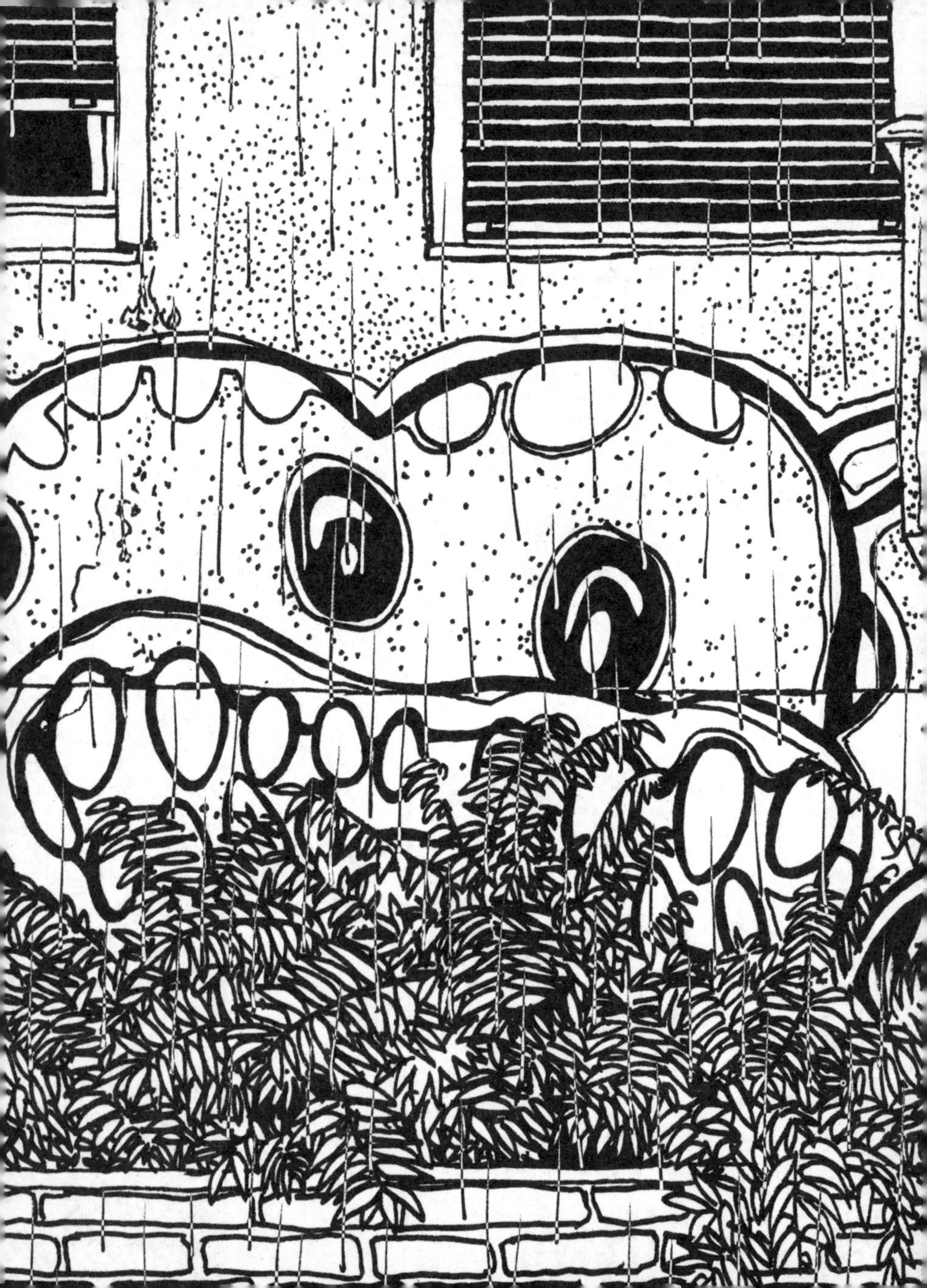

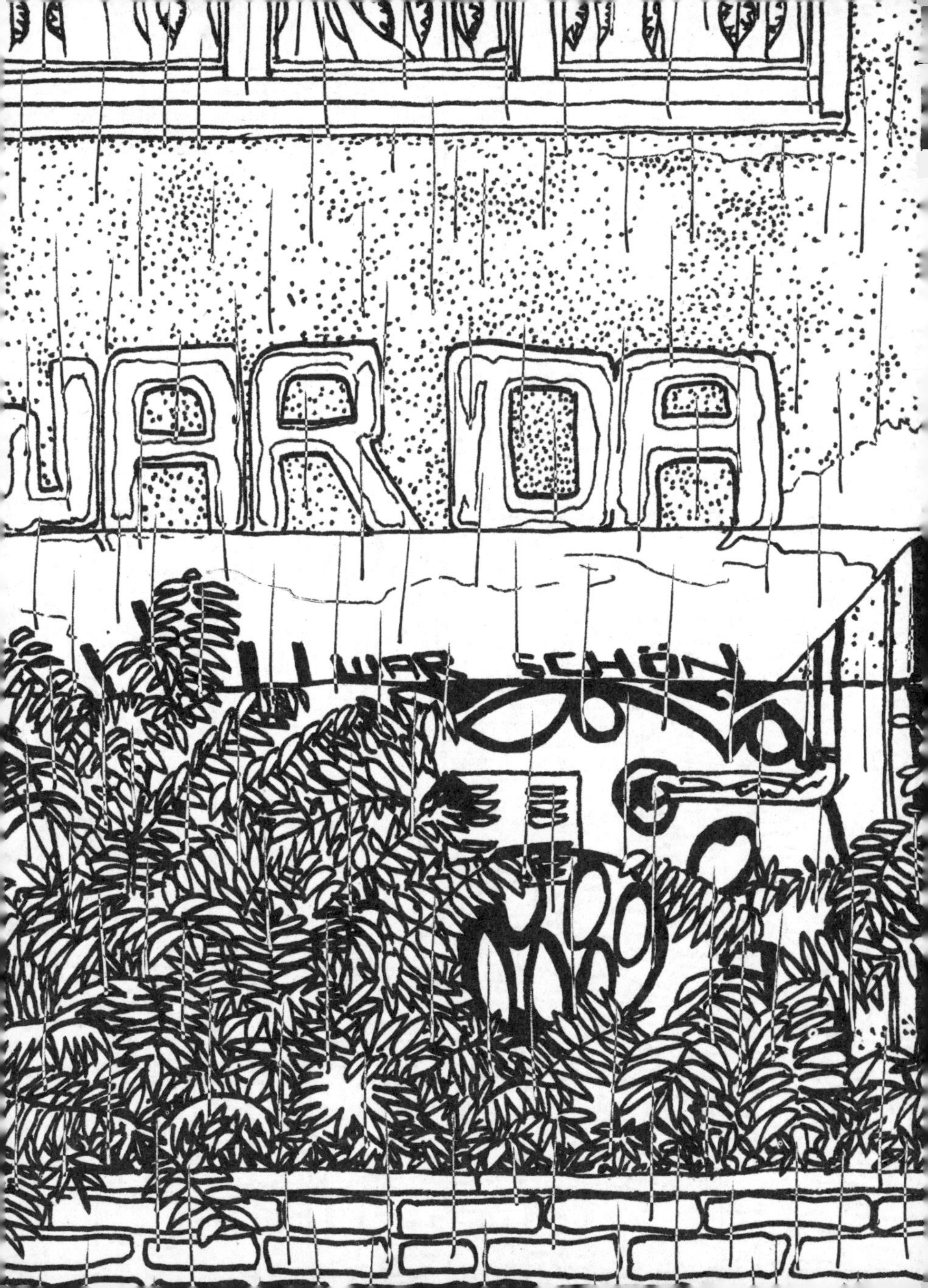
JAR DA
WAR SCHÖN

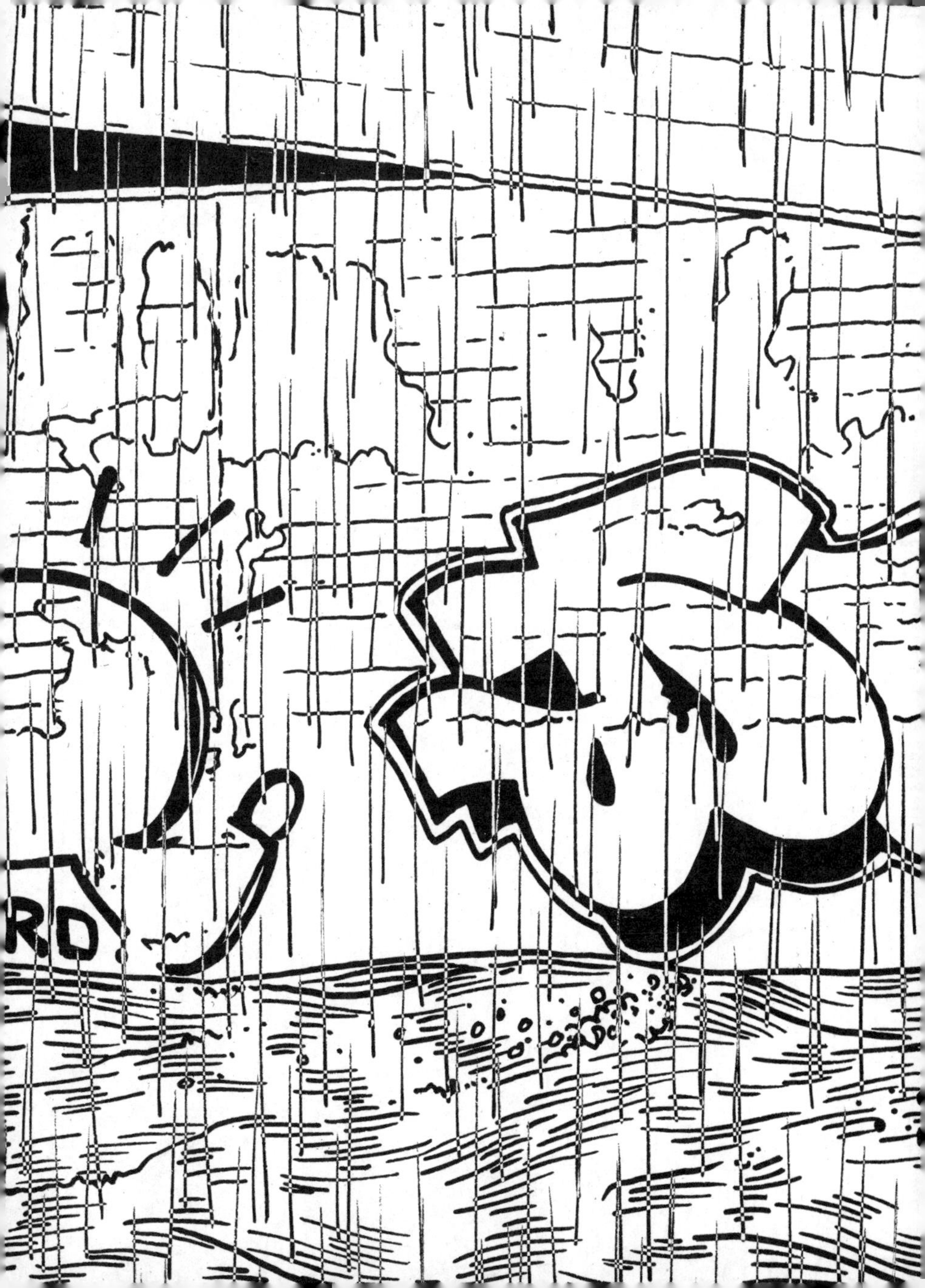

RD

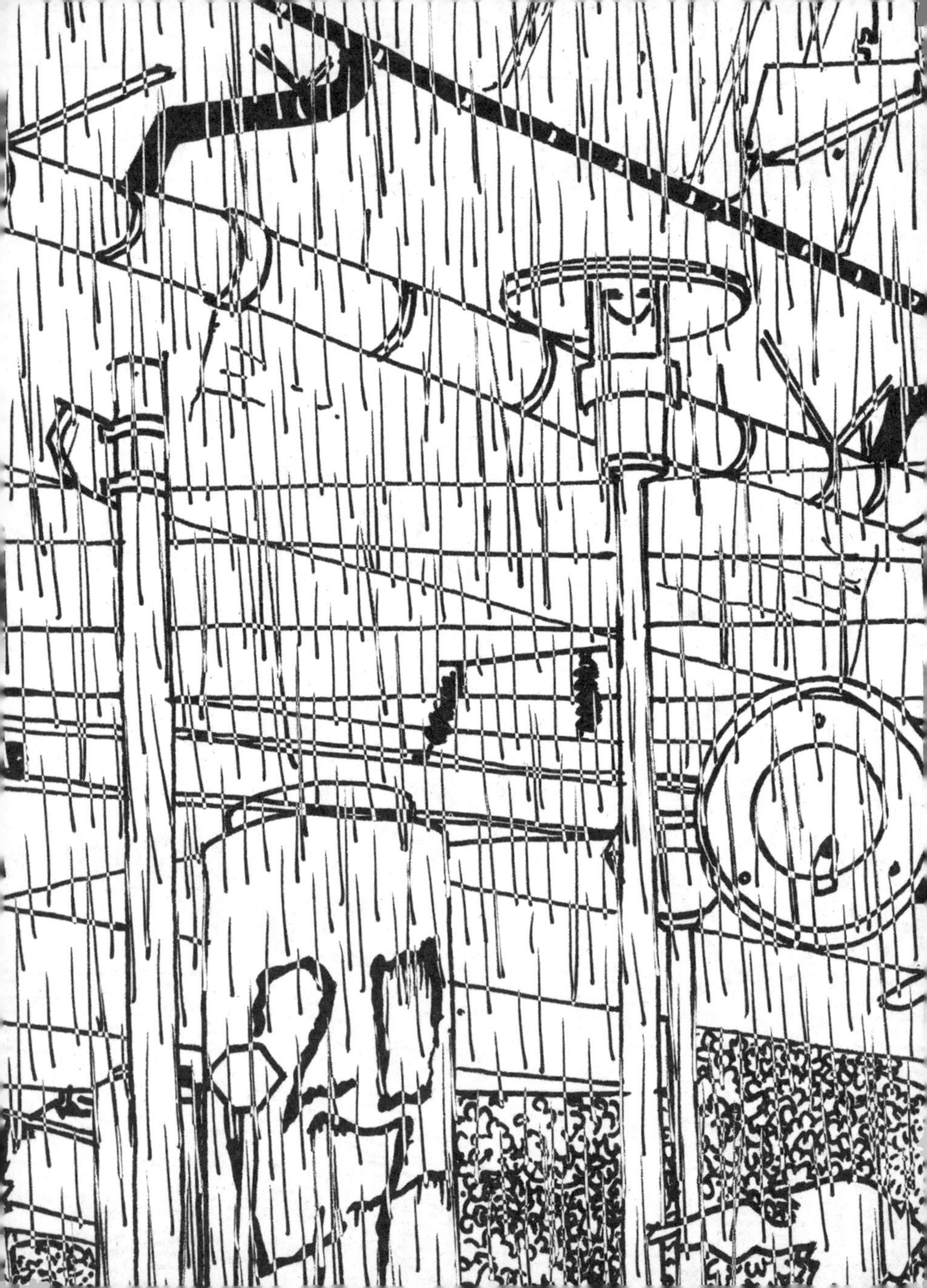

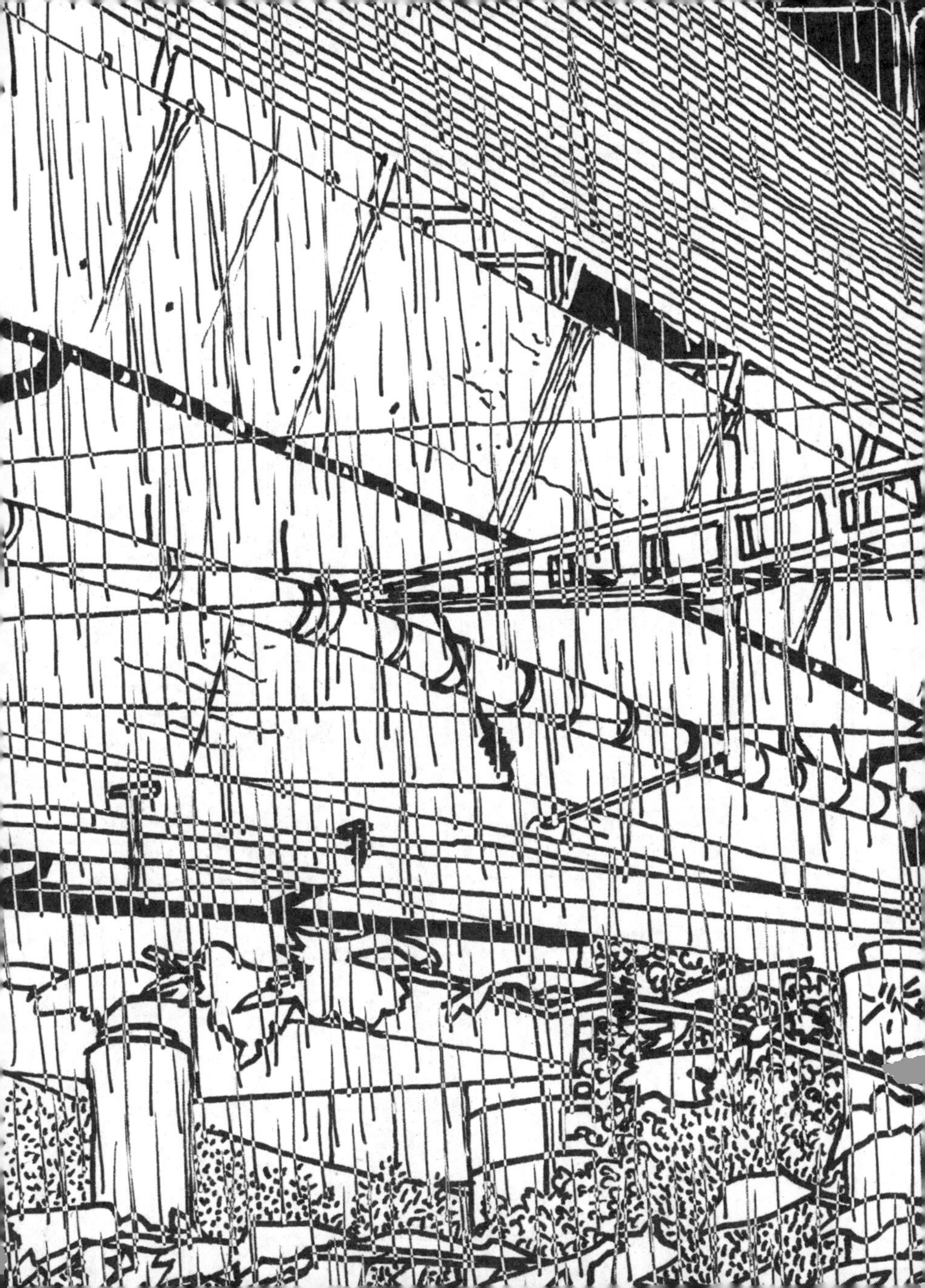

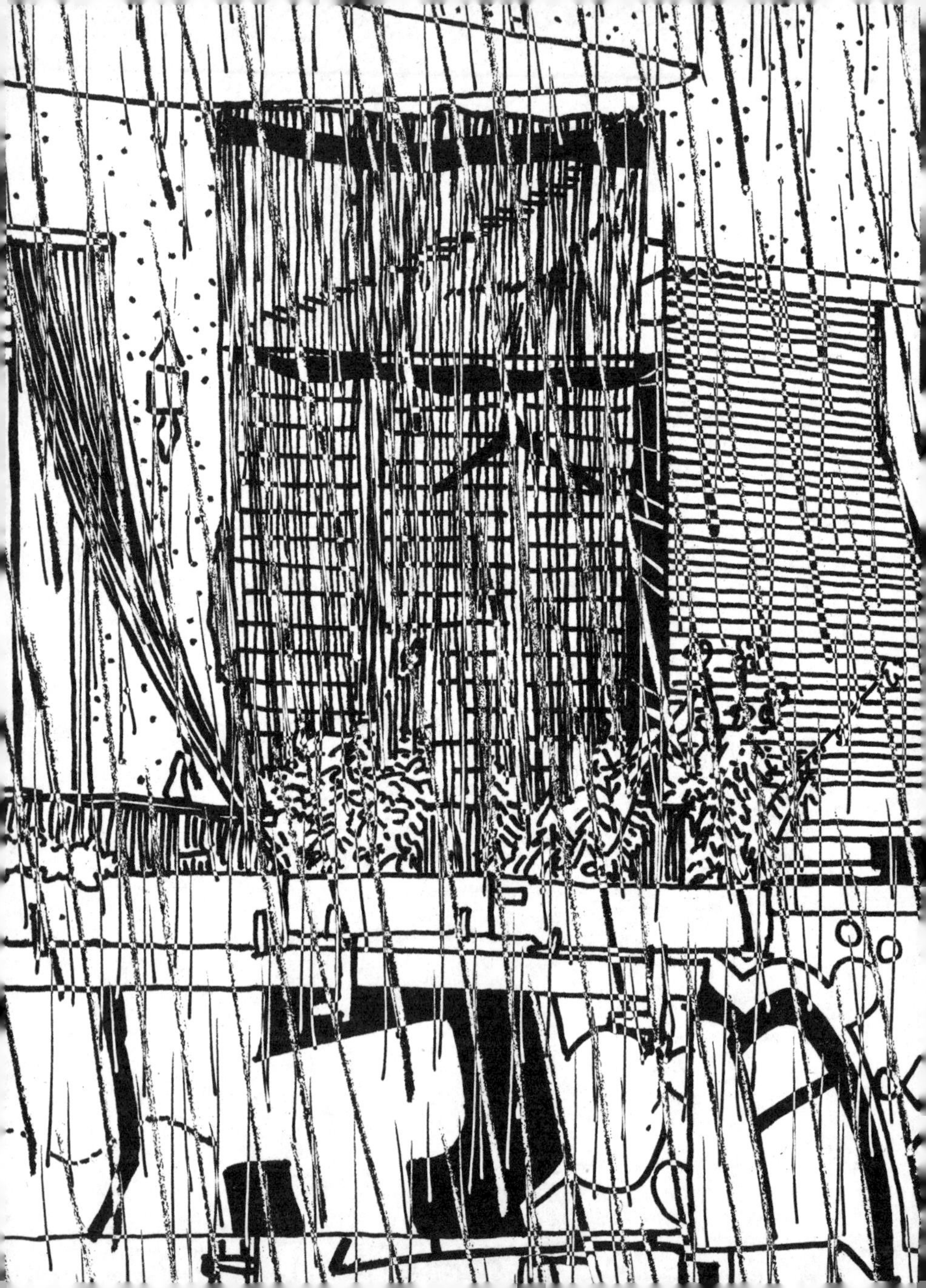

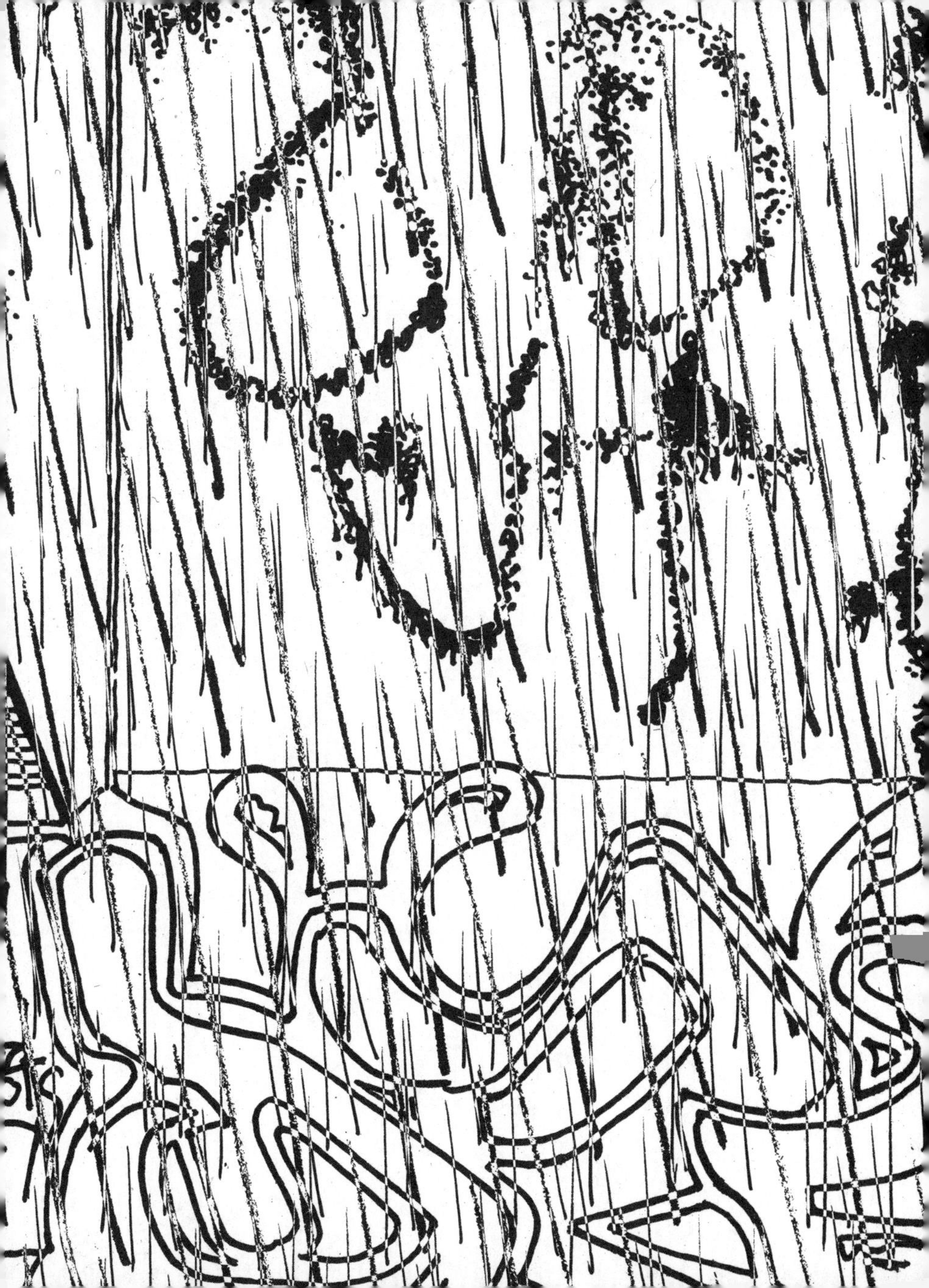

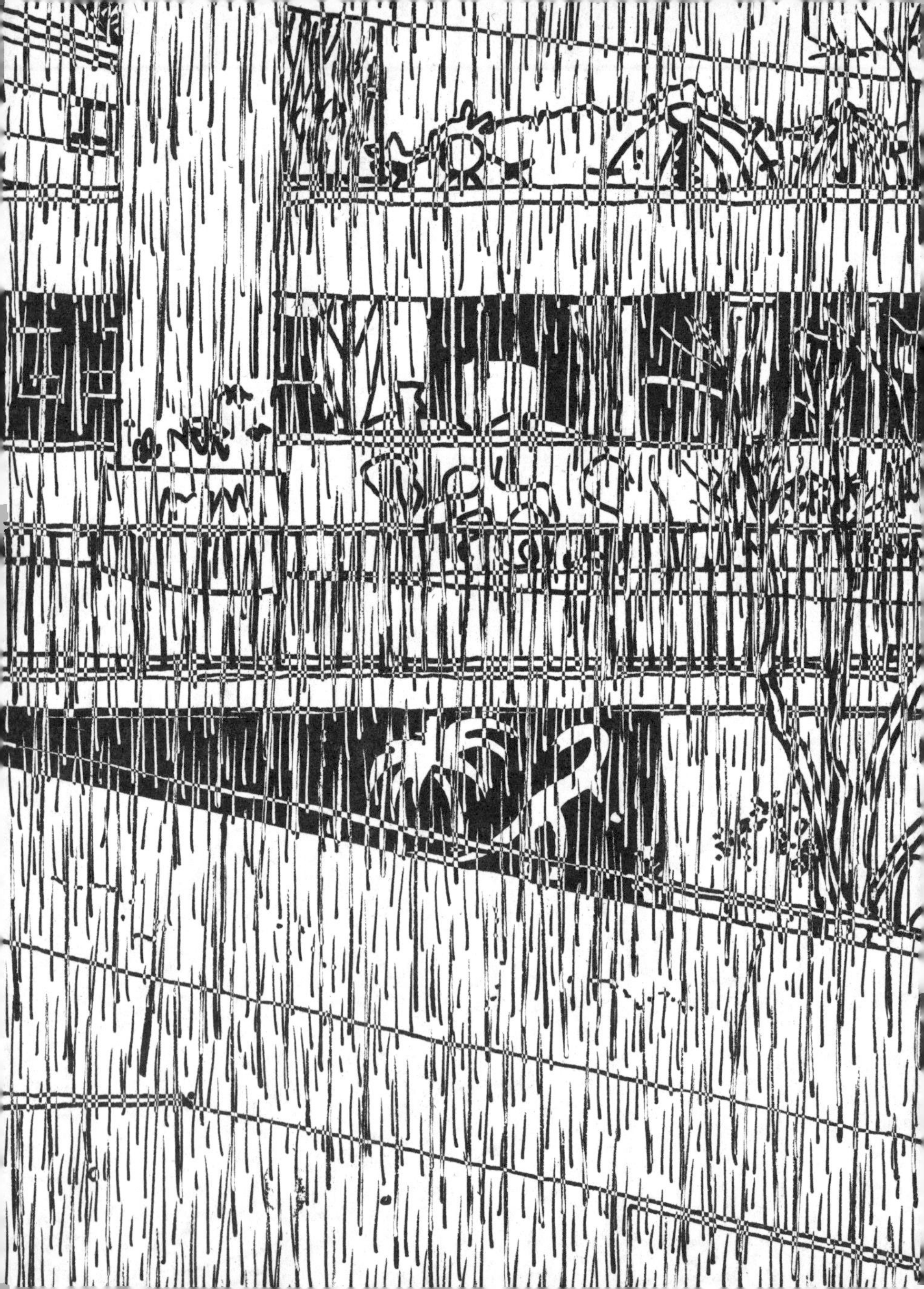

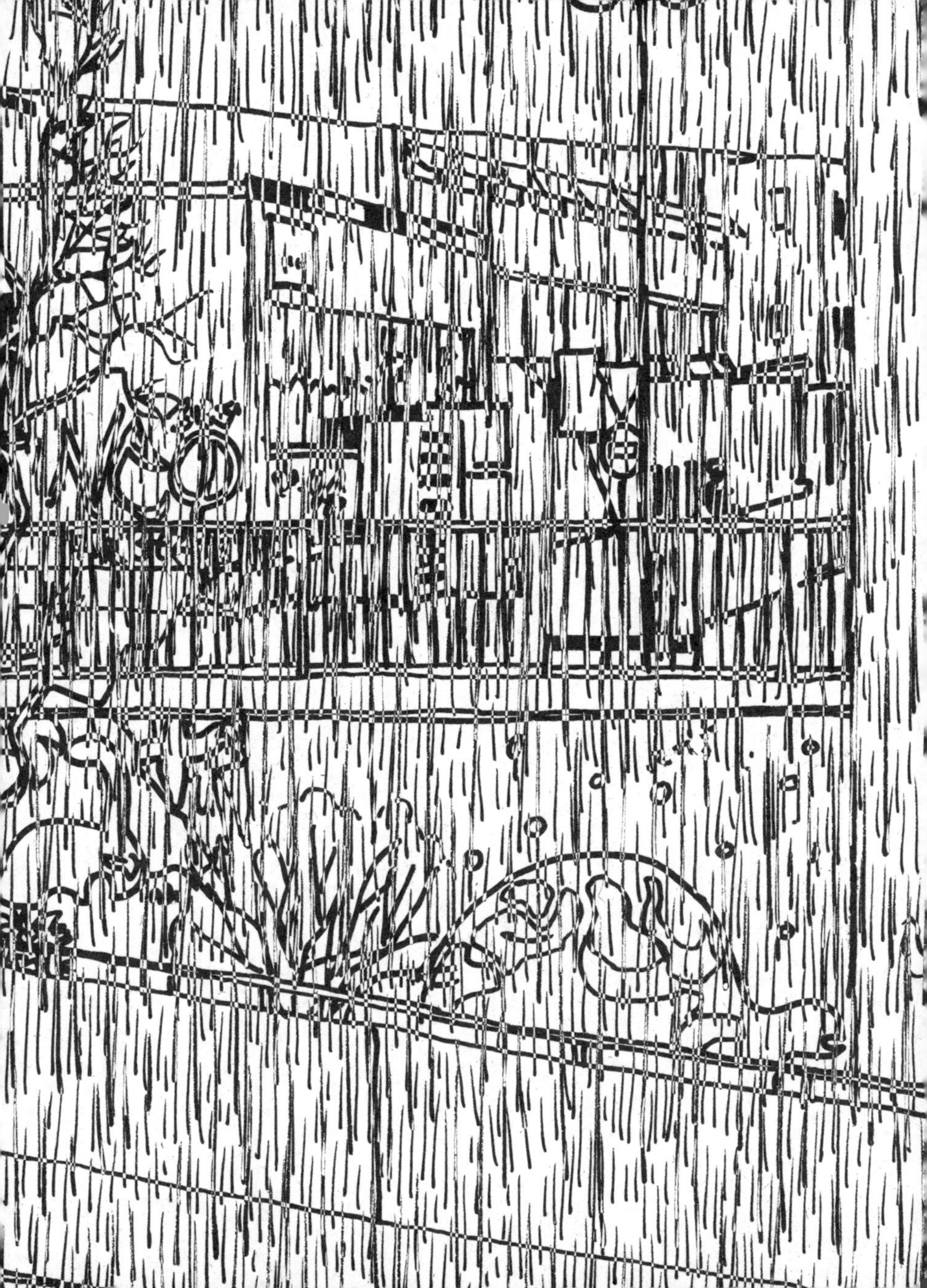

GRR51
Zzz Züri

Drawings, Scans, Layout & Production
Ingo Giezendanner, www.GRRRR.net

Kindly supported by
Präsidialdepartement der Stadt Zürich
Stiftung Kunstsammlung Albert & Melanie Rüegg
Stiftung Erna & Curt Burgauer

Special thanks to
Big Zis, Caro Cerbaro, Chris Jaeger Brown, Gimp, Habib Afsar, Jovana Hitz,
Kulturbüro Zürich, Mara Züst, Petra Schleemilch, Scribus, t.o.t.t.

First Edition

Published by Nieves
www.nievesbooks.com

ISBN 978-3-905999-42-6

Ingo Giezendanner
Zzz Züri

GRR51